THE CENTENNIAL CURE

Commemoration, Identity, and Cultural Capital
in Nova Scotia during Canada's 1967
Centennial Celebrations

In *The Centennial Cure*, the second volume in the Studies in Atlantic Canada History series, Meaghan Elizabeth Beaton critically examines the intersection of state policy, cultural development, and commemoration in Nova Scotia during Canada's centennial celebrations.

Beaton's engaging and insightful analysis of four case studies – the establishment of the Cape Breton Miners' Museum, the construction of Halifax's Centennial Swimming Pool, the Community Improvement Program, and the 1967 Nova Scotia Highland Games and Folk Festival – reveals the province's attempts to reimagine and renew public spaces. Through these case studies Beaton illuminates the myriad ways in which Nova Scotians saw themselves, in the context of modernity and ethnic identity, during the post-war years. The successes and failures of these infrastructure and cultural projects, intended to foster and develop cultural capital, reflected the socio-economic realities and dreams of local communities. *The Centennial Cure* shifts our focus away from the dominant studies on Expo 67 to provide a nuanced and tension-filled account of how Canada's 1967 centennial celebrations were experienced in other parts of Canada.

(Studies in Atlantic Canada History)

MEAGHAN ELIZABETH BEATON is a Visiting Assistant Professor of Canadian History in the Department of History, and a faculty member with the Canadian-American Studies Program, at Western Washington University.

STUDIES IN ATLANTIC CANADA HISTORY

Editors: John G. Reid and Peter L. Twohig

This monograph series focuses on the history of Atlantic Canada, interpreting the scope of this field in a way that is deliberately inclusive and accommodating. As well as studies that deal wholly with any aspect of the history of the Atlantic region (or part thereof), the series extends to neighbouring geographical areas that are considered in conjunction with or in parallel with a portion of Atlantic Canada. Atlantic Canada's oceanic or global relationships are also included, and studies from any thematic or historiographical perspective are welcome.

MEAGHAN ELIZABETH BEATON

The Centennial Cure

Commemoration, Identity, and Cultural Capital in Nova Scotia during Canada's 1967 Centennial Celebrations

UNIVERSITY OF TORONTO PRESS
Toronto Buffalo London

© University of Toronto Press 2017
Toronto Buffalo London
www.utppublishing.com

ISBN 978-1-4875-0151-8 (cloth)
ISBN 978-1-4875-2152-3 (paper)

___

Library and Archives Canada Cataloguing in Publication

Beaton, Meaghan Elizabeth, 1976–, author
The centennial cure : commemoration, identity, and cultural capital in Nova Scotia during Canada's 1967 centennial celebrations/Meaghan Elizabeth Beaton.

(Studies in Atlantic Canada history)
Includes bibliographical references and index.
ISBN 978-1-4875-0151-8 (cloth). – ISBN 978-1-4875-2152-3 (paper)

1. Nova Scotia – Cultural policy – History – 20th century.   2. Canada – Centennial celebrations, etc.   I. Title.   II. Series: Studies in Atlantic Canada history

FC2319.B42 2017   306.09716   C2016-907849-3

___

This book has been published with the help of a grant from the Federation for the Humanities and Social Sciences, through the Awards to Scholarly Publications Program, using funds provided by the Social Sciences and Humanities Research Council of Canada.

University of Toronto Press acknowledges the financial assistance to its publishing program of the Canada Council for the Arts and the Ontario Arts Council, an agency of the Government of Ontario.

Contents

Illustrations vii

Acknowledgments ix

Introduction: Canada's 1967 Centennial, Commemoration, and Region   3

1 "It was deliberate – a planned effort, not a natural development of history": Producing Nova Scotia's Celebrations for Canada's 1967 Centennial   23

2 "A true Scot would have sworn he was in Scotland": The 1967 Nova Scotia Highland Games and Folk Festival   50

3 "I sold it as an industry as much as anything else": The Cape Breton Miners' Museum   81

4 "Worthy of the great Nova Scotia traditions of the sea": Halifax's Aquarium and Centennial Swimming Pool   118

5 "The Centennial Cure": The Community Improvement Program   148

Conclusion: Canada's 1967 Centennial Commemorative Legacy   189

Notes   197

Bibliography   251

Index   273

Illustrations

Figure 3.1: Quarry Point with signs announcing the construction of the Cape Breton Miners' Museum as a 1967 centennial project, undated, Cape Breton Miners' Foundation   100

Figure 3.2: Nina Cohen unveiling Cape Breton Miners' Museum cornerstone, 31 July 1967, Cape Breton Miners' Foundation   106

Figure 3.3: Exterior of the Cape Breton Miners' Museum, undated, Cape Breton Miners' Foundation   107

Figure 4.1: Aquarium Project, Aza Avramovitch & Associates, architect, Maurice Crosby Photography Ltd, photographer; Nova Scotia Archives, Aza Avramovitch fonds, 2001–036/003 no. 3   127

Figure 4.2: "View of lecture area, Proposed Aquarium for the City of Halifax," Aza Avramovitch & Associates, architect, 28 December 1965; Nova Scotia Archives, Department of Attorney General, RG 10 Series E vol. 207   128

Figure 5.1: Brochure, *Action 2: Community Face Lift*, © Government of Canada; reproduced with the permission of Library and Archives Canada (2016); Library and Archives Canada/Centennial Commission Fonds/AMICUS No. 24752774/cover page   156

Figure 5.2: Brochure, *Action 6: Centennial Clean Up*, © Government of Canada; reproduced with the permission of Library and Archives Canada (2016); Library and Archives Canada/Centennial Commission Fonds/AMICUS No. 24752774/cover page   157

Figure 5.3: Brochure, *Action 2: Community Face Lift*. © Government of Canada; reproduced with the permission of Library and Archives Canada (2016); Library and Archives Canada/Centennial

Commission Fonds/AMICUS No. 24752774/"Miracle on Main Street" 162

Figure 5.4: Brochure, *Action 6: Centennial Clean Up*, © Government of Canada; reproduced with the permission of Library and Archives Canada (2016); Library and Archives Canada/Centennial Commission Fonds/AMICUS No. 24752774/"How Aware Are You" 172

Acknowledgments

This book would not have been possible without the generous support, guidance, and encouragement of many people. This study began at Trent University, where my doctoral supervisor Keith Walden shepherded this project along and was unfailing in his encouragement, patience, and good humour. All students should be so fortunate as to work with someone as inspirational and thoughtful as Keith. My other committee members provided invaluable support. Del Muise, whom I first met as an undergraduate at Carleton University, started me seriously thinking about post-war Nova Scotia history and gave me the confidence to pursue graduate studies. He has been a constant source of inspiration and is a trusted mentor and friend. Dimitry Anastakis, Susan Wurtele, and Edward MacDonald offered thoughtful comments that helped to shape this study. As a postdoctoral fellow at the Centre for Canadian Studies at Mount Allison University, where most of this book's revisions were completed, I found an engaging community that included Andrew Nurse, Hannah Lane, and Marie Hammond-Callaghan, whose encouragement kept me going at critical junctures. Thanks also goes to the History Department at Western Washington University, where my colleagues have offered a supportive environment. Len Husband with the University of Toronto Press helped guide me through the publication process and has been a valuable source of support. Three anonymous readers for the Press offered excellent feedback about how to improve this work. The final version of this book has benefited greatly from their thoughtful suggestions.

This project was generously supported by financial assistance from the Frost Centre for Canadian Studies and Indigenous Studies, Ontario

Graduate Scholarships, and the Symons Trust Fund for Canadian Studies. Research, travel, and publication grants from Trent University, Mount Allison University, and Western Washington University offered generous assistance that helped to complete this study. This book has been published with the help of a grant from the Federation for the Humanities and Social Sciences, through the Award to Scholarly Publications Program, using funds provided by the Social Sciences and Humanities Research Council of Canada.

Staff at Library and Archives Canada, Nova Scotia Archives and Records Management, Halifax Regional Municipality Archives, and the Beaton Institute expertly guided me through their collections. Alfonso Rojo and Peter Aykroyd generously shared their memories of the centennial celebrations. Calley Stapleton, Mike MacKenzie, Rowan MacKenzie, Casey MacKenzie, Stephanie Sernyk, Mateo Yorke, and Sarah Yorke graciously provided me places to stay while I conducted research in Halifax.

I consider myself very lucky to have had the opportunity to complete this project at Mount Allison University and Trent University, where I was surrounded by incredible colleagues, graduate students, and friends. At Mount Allison, Tasia Alexopoulos, Andrea Beverley, Shelly Colette, Jane Dryden, Lisa Dawn Hamilton, and Leslie Kern made my time in Sackville, New Brunswick, unforgettable, and they are proof that 5,000 kilometres never gets in the way of great friendships. The Frost Centre for Canadian Studies and Indigenous Studies at Trent University is an engaging scholarly community that provided me with an intellectually stimulating environment while I worked on this project. Faculty members Jim Struthers, Bryan Palmer, and Julia Harrison made the Frost Centre an inspiring place to study. Joan Sangster, in particular, has been a constant support of my work, and she has become a close friend and advisor. Fellow graduate students, including Donica Belisle, Sean Carleton, Caitlin Gordon-Walker, William Knight, John Marris, Christine McLaughlin, Sarah McDougall, James Onusko, Casey Ready, Julia Smith, and Amy Twomey, made the Frost Centre an inspiring place to work. Two fellow students deserve special mention. Kristi Allain and I travelled the long and winding road that is graduate school together and lived to tell the tale. She has been a close friend and indefatigable supporter of my work. I am also indebted to Ted McCoy, who asked important and challenging questions that made me think differently about this study. He propped me up when I felt that this project was an impossible task. Without his friendship I would not have survived my first year of the doctoral program, let alone the dissertation or its transformation into a book. I'm at a loss over how such a debt can ever be repaid.

I can't imagine what goes through one's mind when one's daughter, gainfully employed as a lawyer, announces that she wants to return to school to pursue a PhD. Nevertheless, my parents, Carol and Wayne Beaton, took the news in stride and never wavered in their love and encouragement of this project. My brother, Mike Beaton, and my sister-in-law, Rasa Augaitis, cheered me on throughout the years. During a particularly trying time when I was struggling to finish the dissertation that formed the basis for this book, Mike's intervention reminded me why it was important for me to continue with this study, and he urged me not to walk away from a project that was so close to completion. My partner, Tim Griese, has been an unfailing source of love, support, and good humour and kept my spirits up throughout this process. Finally, Clio, who has travelled me with from one coast to another, reminded me that sometimes the best way to finish a book project is to leave it in the office and go for a walk in the park.

THE CENTENNIAL CURE

Commemoration, Identity, and Cultural Capital
in Nova Scotia during Canada's 1967
Centennial Celebrations

Introduction

Canada's 1967 Centennial, Commemoration, and Region

It is now the task of historians to weave into the record of national life the experiences and achievements which formed part of our hundredth anniversary. It is to be hoped that those who chronicle these events will be able to recapture something of the brilliance and spontaneity of regional and local manifestations.
National Centennial Commission,
Sixth Annual and Final Report ... 1967–1968

In a rousing speech to the Canadian Centenary Council in 1965, Canada's Secretary of State Maurice Lamontagne pleaded with attendees to launch a campaign against the country's "cultural poverty." The minister argued that although Canada had made considerable "physical and material" progress since Confederation, not all sectors of society had kept pace. To the country's detriment, cultural development had "remained relatively anemic" during the last century, which had hindered Canada's prosperity, maturation, and growth. It was a serious problem that had to be solved. Infrastructure development was needed to provide citizens with increased and improved access to artistic, educational, and cultural activities: "Our universities cannot grow as fast as they should. Our research facilities are badly lacking, especially for the humanities and social sciences. Some of our best scientists and artists are leaving the country. We do not have a feature film industry. Our performing arts are facing a financial crisis. Our artistic groups cannot afford to tour their own country and when they survive, it is due mainly to the great sacrifices of a few individuals. These are just a few illustrations of our cultural poverty."[1]

Lamontagne remarked that Canadian culture required "protection against impoverishment and stimulus to improvement" in order to create optimal conditions for a thriving and engaged population.[2] Citizens had an important role to play through their patronage of, and participation in, cultural activities. Yet the state had a particular responsibility, he argued, to ensure not only that cultural institutions existed and were safeguarded, but that a supportive environment allowed them to flourish. As such, the federal government was prepared to intervene and take immediate steps to tackle the country's cultural poverty.

The solution was found in the federal government's plans for Canada's 1967 centennial celebrations that commemorated 100 years of Confederation. Cultural improvement was a cornerstone of Ottawa's 1967 mission. This was accomplished, in part, through the federal government's funnelling of millions of dollars to the National Centennial Commission (Centennial Commission), the Crown corporation given the task of coordinating and directing the year's events, to support programming for the centennial year. Two of the Centennial Commission's most important undertakings were the Programs and Projects of National Significance, and the Federal-Provincial Centennial Grants Program (Centennial Grants Program), both of which were seen by the federal government and the Centennial Commission as keys in the fight against the country's cultural poverty. The former program comprised cross-Canada programming that was deemed to be of national significance. The latter supported the construction of thousands of capital infrastructure projects that added "something of value" to the country that "might never be realized in the ordinary course of events."[3] These programs formed part of an ambitious cultural policy agenda dedicated to improving the country's national life by implementing infrastructure and supporting commemorative initiatives in communities across Canada.

This book examines the intersection of state policy, cultural development, and commemoration during Canada's 1967 centennial celebrations. It explores four initiatives that were undertaken in Nova Scotia to mark the 100th anniversary of Confederation, and investigates how the province responded to Lamontagne's appeal to stem Canada's cultural poverty. Centennial projects implemented across the province under the Programs and Projects of National Significance and the Centennial Grants Program were pillars in Nova Scotia's celebratory activities, much as they were in other provinces and territories across the country. They formed part of a significant post-war state development strategy to expand cultural activities and introduce infrastructure capital across Nova Scotia. These 1967 projects also reflected those larger social, cultural, economic, and political transformations that took place in post-war Nova Scotia. Further, they help us understand the province's experience within the broader context of the development of modern Canadian cultural and social history.

The four commemorative projects examined in this book cut a wide geographical swath across Nova Scotia and illustrate important themes in Canadian post-war history. The Cape Breton Miners' Museum and the Halifax Centennial Swimming Pool were local Centennial Grants Program undertakings. The Miners' Museum, constructed in Glace Bay, Cape Breton, illustrates how 1967 initiatives formed part of a comprehensive post-war economic and cultural development strategy to revitalize communities. Halifax's project, originally a public aquarium that was later replaced with a swimming pool, demonstrates urban renewal and modernization efforts, and the increasing importance of leisure as a right of Canadian citizenship during this era. Two other case studies – the Community Improvement Program and the Highland Games and Folk Festival – were developed as part of the Programs and Projects of National Significance. The Community Improvement Program drew attention to environmental concerns, citizens' ecological responsibilities, and the state of Canada's social welfare system. The Highland Games and Folk Festival, hosted in Halifax during the summer of 1967, points to Nova Scotia's shifting cultural identity during this era, and the emergence of more multicultural understandings of the country.

A focused investigation into one province's experiences during a national celebration reveals several insights. First, it offers a new way of understanding how 1967 projects and programming were important post-war development strategies that modernized the country. While a handful of studies focus on national undertakings such as the Voyageur Canoe Pageant and Expo 67, very few consider the impact of the centennial's community infrastructure developments and local activities as part of larger post-war state renewal, or study this process from a regional perspective. Nova Scotia, like all other provinces, took advantage of lucrative grant schemes that funded cultural capital projects and activities that revitalized communities. These undertakings became mechanisms for the federal government to support activities and infrastructure planning. In the process, these projects provided citizens with new institutions that dramatically transformed the province's cultural landscape. Nova Scotia supported thirty-six local projects under the Centennial Grants Program alone. They included the construction of community centres, swimming pools, museums, recreation areas, and libraries. In one way or another, each of these projects addressed Lamontagne's plea to alleviate Canada's cultural poverty.

Nova Scotia's centennial initiatives also offer insights into the province's fluctuating identity in the post-war era. Some 1967 projects reflected and reinforced long-standing anti-modern perceptions of Nova Scotia, and epitomized what Ian McKay calls the province's "tartanization" and the production of a "Folk" paradigm, both of which emerged as powerful social and cultural ideological constructions during the twentieth century. Yet other projects emphasized a progressive, modern, and urban province that challenged these dominant conceptualizations. They represented significant ruptures in anti-modern narratives, forcing a re-evaluation of these popular characterizations. As a result, local centennial projects both challenged and upheld popular understandings of Nova Scotia and its history. Often trapped between anti-modern and modern discourses, 1967 initiatives demonstrate a complex understanding of Nova Scotia during the 1960s, necessitating a reconsideration of the significance and the salience of the Folk culture and tartanism into the later parts of the century.

Further, incorporating the history of individual, community, and provincial experiences into the centennial's larger narrative offers a new way to assess the celebrations' impact. One of the Centennial Commission's key mandates was to ensure that all Canadians could participate in 1967 activities. Focusing on how Nova Scotians engaged with centennial programming reveals how successfully Ottawa involved the public in the anniversary. This book pays particular attention to how citizens, politicians, organizations, activists, bureaucrats, and communities orchestrated, moulded, and defined 1967 centennial programming. Further, these commemoration activities exposed regional conflict over infrastructure development and the memorialization process. Commemorations became contested terrain where social, cultural, and political issues clashed, pointing to competing notions of identity and community. This study, then, provides an intimate look at these local dynamics and shows how they shaped the province's celebrations to achieve social, cultural, and economic objectives.

Finally, centennial programming relied on collaborations between communities and all levels of government in order to implement commemorative initiatives. This study thus sheds light on the evolution of federalism and the operations of the state during the 1960s. Local actors responded to, negotiated with, navigated, and lobbied federal and provincial governments and their attendant agencies so as to capitalize on lucrative centennial funding for community projects. This had resonance for Nova Scotia in particular and for Atlantic Canada generally. The late 1950s and the 1960s saw a host of regional development initiatives implemented throughout Atlantic Canada to ensure that the region's four provinces were equal players within Canadian Confederation. Centennial projects comprised a part of Ottawa's regional development policies by other means. In addition, many communities saw these undertakings as unique and crucial growth opportunities that were unlikely to be offered again anytime soon.

Canada's Centennial Celebrations

Canada's centennial celebrations are revered in popular memory and many retrospectives as a time of overwhelming optimism about the country's future.[4] Pierre Berton famously describes 1967 as the "last good year," when the country "indulged in an orgy of sports events, folk dancing, historical pageants, parades, and youth exchanges."[5] Despite a politically and socially tumultuous decade, J.M. Bumsted notes that the country had "come of age," as Canadians "got the spirit" by participating in exuberant displays of national pride.[6] "Suddenly, Canada was fun," Jack Granatstein observes, stating that 1967 revealed "a swinging, with-it nation."[7] For Peter Aykroyd, the Centennial Commission's director of public relations and information, it was a "civilizing year" defined by "positive and benevolent" events that represented "the finest kind of impetus affirming and encouraging peaceful societal evolution."[8] While these accounts demonstrate a sense of idealism and excitement that is commonly associated with 1967, others have uncovered a much more complicated history.

Centennial programming constructed, perpetuated, and legitimized particular versions of Canadian history and a national identity. As Helen Davies argues, the Canadian government did not dictate how citizens should celebrate the year, but organizers nevertheless promoted a common vision of national identity rooted in the notion of unity over diversity.[9] Further, commemorative programming was often framed by Canada's colonial and settler legacy, as many 1967 activities effectively expunged Indigenous histories from the larger narrative of the year's events. The Centennial Voyageur Canoe Pageant, Misao Dean argues, was an "ideological project" that legitimated the power of the Canadian state and erased issues of class, race, gender, and Indigenous sovereignty from the historical record.[10] Similarly, the Yukon Alpine Centennial Expedition, PearlAnn Reichwein notes, promulgated a particular version of Canadian nationalism that contributed to long-standing mythologies of the north and created a narrative that ignored the history of Indigenous peoples and their land claims in the region.[11]

Very few studies have examined local or regional perspectives on Canada's 1967. Nevertheless, a handful of works have explored regional commemorations and their role in provincial state-formation across the country. Notably, Mia Reimers investigates three centennial celebrations in British Columbia during the post-war era. These commemorations – which marked both provincial centenaries and Canada's 1967 centennial – were central components of the Social Credit government's attempts to engage in "province building." British Columbia used these celebratory moments "as a means to both publicize and unify the province," that worked to "cultivate a *provincial* identity in BC's residents that would carry forward economic expansion."[12] Forrest Pass, who examines seven celebrations in British Columbia, including the province's 1858 centennial, argues that these events contributed to province-building and the rise of provincial consciousness. These celebrations created a "regionally specific meaning of Canadian nationalism," that also "defined British Columbia as a cohesive political and geographical unit."[13] Similar initiatives were undertaken in Alberta, whose 1955 golden jubilee was celebrated with infrastructure development projects, as well as a series of high-profile public events that commemorated particular identities.[14] Together, these celebrations reveal how British Columbia and Alberta undertook post-war province-building through anniversary celebrations.

Not surprisingly, much of the literature on Canada's centennial focuses on the 1967 International and Universal Exposition, commonly referred to as Expo 67, the year's most notable commemorative event. Between April and October 1967, host city Montreal welcomed over fifty million visitors who came to experience Expo's theme, Man and His World/Terre Des Hommes. Like the country's wider centennial celebrations, Expo 67 was memorialized through several popular retrospectives[15] and two National Film Board productions.[16] The event occupies a powerful place in the country's collective consciousness, standing out as a moment that heightened feelings of Canadian pride. Expo, Daniel Francis observes, "has come down to us through the filter of nostalgia as a unique moment of national achievement."[17] Geoff Pevere and Greig Dymond note that attendees reminisce about the event in a "dreamy, melancholy way" and that it became "a symbol of what memory insists was a simpler, brighter and possibly better time for Canada."[18] It was, as John Lownsbrough points out, one of the decade's cultural touchstones that emerged as "a metaphor for a myriad of hopes and aspirations that could dovetail into a collective pride."[19]

Yet recent work on Expo 67 uncovers a much more dynamic story, touching on topics as diverse as women's work on-site,[20] the event's environmental legacy,[21] its influence on the development of national cinema,[22] pavilion architecture,[23] and even how programming offered a "future gaze" for visitors to consume.[24] With thirty-eight pavilions housing exhibits from as many countries, it is not surprising that the expression and construction of national identities at Expo 67 figured prominently in Montreal. Even pavilion architecture reflected national, cultural, and political identities.[25] It was, however, difficult to ignore the inherent paradoxes of identity construction projects. Pavilions, Rhona Richman Kenneally and Johanne Sloan argue, were studies in contradiction where the "very concept of the nation [was] ... propped up, even while its ideological limits were being questioned."[26] As a result, Sonja Macdonald proposes, these competing narratives produced "new symbols of national identity."[27]

Expo 67, then, emerged as a site that embodied competing notions of identity. Gary Miedema reveals that the federal government and spiritual leaders used public religion pavilions to foster cultural and political stability, bolster national unity, and express a version of Canadian national identity rooted in the idea of unity through diversity. At times, however, the use of public religion resulted in considerable conflict.[28] Not surprisingly, expressions of Quebecois identity also emerged as sites of contested terrain. Pauline Curien observes that Quebec's *l'identité officielle* presented through the provincial government's pavilion contrasted remarkably with *l'identité populaire* that was expressed by Quebecois visitors. The latter reflected those massive social and political changes faced by the province in the 1960s, a dynamic that was virtually ignored by the former.[29] Young Quebecois artists articulated their visions of national identity through exhibits that conflicted with expressions of nationalism promulgated by the federal government.[30] Further, the Indians of Canada Pavilion emerged as a medium for the expression of Indigenous identities. That exhibit represented a transformative and highly politicized moment for Indigenous persons across the country. It offered a powerful story of Canada's ongoing legacy of colonization told from the perspective of Indigenous peoples, which contrasted greatly with government officials' visions for the pavilion.[31]

Intersections and Interpretations: The Transformative 1960s

Canada's 1967 centennial celebrations and Montreal's Expo 67 exemplified the excitement and exhilaration of the 1960s. The decade was a fundamentally transformational moment that raises questions about, and complicates our view of, the era's significance within the larger context of political, social, and cultural post-war developments. The emergence of diverse political and social movements, including civil rights, identity politics, the New Left, student activism, and the women's movement, point to a time of unparalleled dynamism. While the 1960s were a turning point during the twentieth century, differences arise over how "the Sixties" should be demarcated. Scholars have argued that the Sixties were a prolonged historical period that extends beyond the bookends of 1960 and 1969. The editors of *New World Coming* contend that the Sixties must be considered on a continuum that covers several decades in order to capture the epoch's significance and its full range of political, social, and intellectual movements.[32] As Sean Mills argues, this approach rejects suggestions that the period was a "profound rupture" in the post-war narrative, and instead underscores that the Sixties were "really just an accelerated period of change."[33] Those who have examined the post-war period in other Western countries concur. Andrew Marwick points out that this era can be properly understood only by taking into account those larger intellectual, political, and cultural trends that began in the late 1950s and ended in 1973–4, with what Eric Hobsbawm referred to as the close of the post-war's "Golden Age."[34] Van Gosse argues in his history of the American New Left that confining the Sixties to a ten-year period is too restrictive and "cannot carry the freight" of all those movements that are central to understanding this epoch. With few monumental events to bookend the decade – he suggests that "there is no self-evident beginning or ending, no Fort Sumter, Pearl Harbor, or Black Friday" – an expansive approach must be undertaken.[35]

Yet others challenge this narrative and argue that the Sixties must be seen as a significant rupture in the post-war era, one that was marked by clearly definable and logical beginnings and ends. Bryan Palmer argues that Canadian identity underwent such radical transformations from 1960 until 1969 – a time when the country "as it had been known ceased, for all practical purposes, to exist" – that this interval must be theorized in decadal terms.[36] By the time the Sixties came to a close, political and ideological forces had ripped asunder those traditional conceptualizations of a national identity rooted in notions of the country as a British colony. What was left in its wake was a severely fractured and ambiguous Canadian identity.[37] Generational and ideological developments that radically reshaped the Canadian and American labour movements further challenge the notion that the era should be conceived as stretching over several decades. Joan Sangster claims that the "long sixties" (generally defined as the era from 1965 to the mid-1970s) was a moment of "radical political rupture" that ushered in pivotal transformations vastly different from the pre-1965 post-war period. The establishment of new feminist organizations and the influence of a new generation of left activists during the long sixties marked a turning point in the labour movement.[38] This delineation of the Sixties as a critical break in the post-war years coincides with the work of American scholars who have shunned the temptation to define the epoch as an extended period. As Philip Jenkins points out, the Sixties are bracketed by political events that began with American President John F. Kennedy's 1963 assassination and ended with Richard Nixon's resignation from the American presidency in 1974.[39] Todd Gitlin argues that the era began in the early 1960s with the emergence of a powerful student movement and ended in 1969 with the Students for Democratic Society's "destruction and self-destruction."[40] Powerful ideological, political, and cultural forces such as these, then, signalled an era that cannot be conceived of as part of a more protracted post-war period.

Nova Scotia's centennial experience represents a moment when these two interpretive approaches – the Sixties as an extended epoch stretching over several decades and the Sixties as a critical rupture in the post-war period – intersect. The province's participation in commemorative 1967 events must be considered in light of the early 1950s Atlantic Revolution and regional economic development policies introduced later on that decade. Cultural capital infrastructure projects constructed to memorialize the centennial year were considered integral to the region's larger economic development. As such, it is imperative to employ an interpretive approach that considers the province's experiences from the early 1950s onwards. At the same time, the 1967 celebrations in Nova Scotia represented a radical turning point in the province's history with the emergence of a new cultural identity. Commemorations challenged the traditional conceptualizations of Nova Scotia as an antimodern and quaint destination, which were suddenly being pushed aside as more modern and multicultural portrayals of the province were taking hold.

Modernization

While this work on the Sixties is important for contextualizing Canada's centennial year, the roots of this event's significance for Nova Scotia extend deeper into the past. Two broader post-war developments – modernization and the evolution of the Canadian state – are essential to understanding the province's participation in the 1967 celebrations. Together, they provide a framework for contextualizing why cultural development was so critical for post-war Nova Scotia. Following the Second World War, Canada introduced a wide range of economic planning initiatives and modernization projects, and expanded social welfare programs.[41] Much like other Western countries, Canada adhered to Keynesian economic theory, which advocated for state intervention to help ease the transition from a wartime to a peacetime economy. In an effort to "prime the pump," the federal government spent millions of dollars on mega-structures that emerged as enduring symbols of post-war Canada. These included the St Lawrence Seaway[42] and the expansion of the Trans-Canada Highway,[43] projects that employed thousands, epitomized the government's new interventionist role in directing the economy, and became integral components of the state's modernization. Not all post-war projects were welcome, however. Toronto's proposed Spadina Expressway, for example, sparked backlash against high modernist planning agendas that threatened the prospects of environmentally responsible communities.[44] In addition to these infrastructure initiatives, the federal government took steps to ensure that the country's cultural life did not lag behind. In 1949 it appointed the Royal Commission on National Development in the Arts, Letters, and Sciences, commonly referred to as the Massey Commission. That commission recommended funding for a wide range of artistic, cultural, and educational activities that supported a distinct, vibrant, national life that was seen an integral component of modern Canadian society.[45] Taken together, these infrastructure and cultural undertakings exemplified the federal government's commitment to modernizing the country.

Atlantic Canada was not exempt from these modernization efforts. Margaret Conrad observes that there existed "two Atlantic Canadas" at the beginning of the 1950s: "one largely rural and isolated ... [and] the other essentially urban and fully integrated into mainstream North American culture." By the end of the decade, the former way of life gave way to major initiatives that left a dramatically altered region in their wake.[46] Edward MacDonald argues that post-war modernization in Prince Edward Island "was a process, both material and profoundly cultural," a transition that took place in all Atlantic Canadian provinces.[47] Perhaps the most dramatic change was the region's political and geographical transformation. With Newfoundland's entry into Canadian Confederation in 1949, the Atlantic Canada region was created, along with the possibilities of new political, cultural, and social constructs.[48] Taken together, these initiatives left virtually no aspect of life in the region untouched.

Atlantic Canada saw its share of major infrastructure projects, such as New Brunswick's Mactaquac hydroelectric dam, which became symbols of the region's post-war progress.[49] Labrador's Churchill Falls hydroelectric power station was a key component in Premier Joseph R. Smallwood's "develop or perish" strategy for Newfoundland that resulted in massive social and economic reforms.[50] Atlantic Canada's modernization efforts also included an expanded provincial civil service needed to keep pace with new post-war development and social welfare programs.[51] Governments ushered in legislative changes such as the liberalization of liquor laws that reflected a wider shift in societal and cultural values across the region.[52] However, changes undertaken in the name of progress had serious repercussions for some Atlantic Canadian communities. Halifax's horrific razing of Africville in the 1960s was initiated under the pretext of modernization and urban renewal.[53] Newfoundland's massive post-war resettlement program saw the state pressure thousands of residents to move to designated "growth centres" that were expected to develop into large industrialized centres that fuelled regional development.[54]

Modernization efforts also were tied closely to Atlantic Canada's burgeoning tourism industry. The expansion of the country's national park system in the region was undertaken expressly to attract visitors and cater to middle-class tourism demands.[55] Governments engaged in tactics such as land expropriation and community displacement to coerce local populations into participating in development schemes in the name of modernization.[56] Prince Edward Island's tourism industry "expanded and professionalized" and became closely managed under the watchful eye of the provincial government.[57] Other initiatives were introduced in the hopes of both buoying regional economies and expanding tourism activities. The Canso Causeway, which opened in 1955, was a new transportation link that connected mainland Nova Scotia to Cape Breton. The structure aimed to revitalize Cape Breton's struggling coal and steel sectors and was conceived as a key component of both the island's and the province's growing tourism industry.[58]

Further, Nova Scotia's tourism industry was connected intimately to the production of a distinct provincial identity. In stark contrast to its progressive reconstruction efforts through projects such as the Canso Causeway, Nova Scotia was cast as an anti-modern destination where life harkened back to an earlier, pre-industrialized era. The province was marketed as a welcome respite from the stresses of the modern world. As Ian McKay argues, the Nova Scotia government and the province's cultural producers were complicit in constructing a powerful "Folk" trope. These efforts were undertaken in order to achieve various social, cultural, and economic goals. The Folk were cast as innocent, quaint, romanticized, and unproblematic actors who embodied the province's cultural identity. These characters emerged as a visceral response to anxieties about modernity and capitalism, and became central figures in Nova Scotia's tourism industry.[59] Similar efforts were undertaken by tourism promoters in advertising travel to Grand Pré, the land of Henry Wadsworth Longfellow's fictional Evangeline. Railway advertisements underscored twentieth-century perceptions about Acadian identity that were based on ideas of the anti-modern and pastoral life. The result, as Monica MacDonald argues, is that "the legitimacy and significance of the Acadians' history and culture, as well as their past grievances and contemporary concerns were consistently misinterpreted or devalued … [and] were exploited for tourist dollars."[60]

These powerful tourism images obscured post-war efforts that characterized Atlantic Canada as modern and progressive. This paradox underscores the need for a more nuanced approach to examining the construction of Nova Scotia's cultural identity. Greg Marquis acknowledges that "Nova Scotia, like other provinces, had a countervailing discourse of modernity," with various actors who supported the region's modernization and contested its characterization as "an antimodern backwater."[61] Similarly, Herb Wyile notes, the danger and the irony of the powerful Folk paradigm is that it "masks the degree to which the region was and is industrialized and how thoroughly it is bound up in an increasingly global, modern, capitalist economy."[62] These popular anti-modern Folk images, then, contrasted sharply with the realities of life in the region.

The Evolution of the Canadian State

The evolution of the Canadian state during the post-war period provides another crucial framework for understanding Nova Scotia's participation in the centennial celebrations. The emergence of a cooperative federalism model following the 1963 election of Lester B. Pearson and his Liberal government ushered in a new era of federal-provincial relations.[63] Indeed, cooperative federalism was a fundamental ideological restructuring of the Canadian system of government.[64] It was defined by a close working relationship between the provincial and federal governments to develop and implement policy jointly, and a rapid expansion of bureaucracies to deal with this restructuring.[65] Under this system, the federal government played an increasingly important role in Canadian society, partly because Ottawa was assuming more responsibility in economic, social welfare, and development planning – areas that fell under the provinces' constitutional jurisdiction under sections 91 and 92 division of powers.[66] This expanded role in social welfare programming stemmed largely from the 1940 Royal Commission on Dominion-Provincial Relations, commonly referred to as the Rowell-Sirois Commission. That commission recommended National Adjustment Grants for the provinces, as well as a redistribution of monies to ensure that national standards were met so that citizens had equal access to programs.[67] The federal government's expansion of unemployment insurance, for example, was a direct result of the changing nature of Canadian federalism and was driven by the Rowell-Sirois Commission, Keynesian economic theory, and a desire to stabilize the economy.[68] Most provincial governments welcomed federal interventions into these arenas in order to ensure that the country's growing social welfare system was adequately funded. Further, the federal government's expansion into these areas, Penny Bryden argues, "served to enhance the role of the national government and strengthen Canadian unity."[69]

The federal government's increasing intervention into Canadian society had particular significance for Atlantic Canada. In the early 1950s, the Atlantic Revolution[70] emerged as a protest movement that was reminiscent of the 1920s Maritime Rights Movement.[71] It saw politicians, business leaders, and bureaucrats unite under the umbrella of common political and economic grievances. Supporters lobbied for improved federal government policies that created better conditions for the region, and they pressed for a reconsideration of Atlantic Canada's position within Canadian Confederation.[72] Leaders had just cause for concern. As Margaret Conrad and James Hiller emphasize, the region was faced with a series of harsh economic realities, including "low incomes, high unemployment rates, [and] mass out-migration."[73] The contrast with growth in other parts of the country was startling and highlighted the need to address regional inequalities. While the Atlantic Revolution ultimately failed to achieve its lofty objectives, it was nevertheless successful in other respects. Notably, as Conrad argues, "In defining a regional consensus based on the belief in a vigorous capitalist economy, an interventionist democratic state, and mass consumption, it ... brought Atlantic Canada into line with the dominant currents of North American culture."[74] As the years wore on, it became increasingly difficult for Ottawa to ignore the pleas to address regional economic disparities. Yet, as Donald Savoie points out, the issue was complicated, as Ottawa did not have an "explicit policy of regional development,"[75] nor did Canada's constitution contemplate a mechanism to address the issue.[76] Nevertheless, by the late 1950s the federal government made its first forays into developing policies geared specifically towards alleviating regional economic disparities. In 1957, Ottawa established a revenue equalization system that ensured equality among the provinces and created national standards for program delivery.[77] Equalization, Penny Bryden argues, became a hallmark of the post-war period and the development of modern Canadian federalism. It was lauded as "'the glue that holds the federation together' and 'one of the most tangible manifestations of Canadian solidarity.'"[78]

During the 1960s, the federal government rolled out a series of major policies aimed at alleviating regional disparities. These included the creation of the Agricultural and Rural Development Agency (ARDA) in 1961, the Atlantic Development Board (ADB) in 1962, the Area Development Agency (ADA) in 1963, the Fund for Rural Economic Development (FRED) in 1966, and the Department of Regional Economic Expansion (DREE) in 1969. These initiatives epitomized the new era of the federal government's intervention into economic planning and became some of Ottawa's most important attempts to address regional inequality. Yet, as James Bickerton argues, these agencies not only constituted band-aid approaches that failed to tackle the substantive causes of underdevelopment, they further perpetuated inequalities. Although the Atlantic Revolution placed regional development on the national agenda, subsequent policies were shaped by political, ideological, and organizational factors beyond the region's control.[79] Nevertheless, equalization programs became a powerful factor in Atlantic Canada's economic growth, and a cornerstone of the country's post-war development policies.[80]

Commemoration

One of the ways that the federal government chose to address regional economic disparity in Atlantic Canada was through the 1967 centennial celebrations wherein Nova Scotia's commemorative activities took on particular significance. Memorial projects were framed by governments, communities, and organizers as unique modernization and development initiatives that introduced cultural capital across the province. Yet programming emerged as something more than just a tool to alleviate the country's cultural poverty. Implemented under the guise of a national celebration, commemorative projects became highly politicized mechanisms that tackled regional economic disparities. It is not surprising that centennial programming was used for such purposes. History tells us that commemorations are employed frequently as vehicles to accomplish political agendas. In many cases, the state and elite groups direct the memorial process in order to achieve nationalistic mandates and maintain social control. These groups rely on images, symbols, rituals, and performances produced during commemorative activities to realize their goals. This process, Paul Connerton argues, creates a highly politicized "master narrative" that legitimizes power structures by conveying particular ideas about a country's history and its national identity.[81] These master narratives are produced through monuments, statues, and other public history sites constructed across a nation's landscape that, for example, propagate certain versions of a country's history.[82] These tactics, John Bodnar observes, are frequently undertaken by political elites in order to shore up feelings of "national unity and citizen loyalty" towards the state. They are employed as tools of containment that direct the population's attention towards sites and activities that maintain the social order. Nevertheless, as Bodnar argues, these state efforts clash with the public's attempts to control narratives. The result is a tension between vernacular and official attempts to shape public memory.[83] The work of Bodnar and others demonstrates, then, how citizens have contributed to the production of master narratives. Jonathan Vance points to First World War commemorations to reveal that the construction of the myth and the memory of the war were not simply the creation of social and political elites. Rather, they were moulded by Canadian society writ large, with ordinary citizens playing an active role in memorialization.[84]

Governments frequently use commemorations to promote national identity and unity, thus becoming nation-building tools. States rely on discursive language and images of what Benedict Anderson refers to as the "imagined community" in order to connect and unite otherwise disparate populations under a national banner. Community, he notes, "is *imagined* because the members of even the smallest nation will never know most of their fellow members, meet them, or even hear of them, yet in the minds of each lives the image of their communion."[85] Centennial celebrations have traditionally been used as platforms to disseminate governments' official versions of national identity. During Australian and American centennials, official federal government programming promoted a common national identity that was directed by "cultural centres" and disseminated to the "peripheries."[86] Canada was not immune to government and elite efforts to promote particular versions of national identity. Charlottetown's Founders' Hall, an extension of Prince Edward Island's nation-building tourism strategy that focused on the "grand narrative of Confederation," downplayed and silenced conflictual elements of the story of Confederation.[87] Matthew Hayday notes that Canada Day was historically used by Ottawa to promote ideas of "what Canadian identity *should* be, in the hopes that this vision would be accepted by Canadians."[88] Public events such as these function as key nation-building instruments that advance state agendas through what H.V. Nelles refers to as "politics by other means." During Quebec's tercentenary celebrations, political elites used public spectacles to produce a grand narrative of peaceful English and French coexistence throughout Canadian history in order to maintain social and political stability.[89] Commemorations, then, are used frequently by the state and elites as political and ideological tools in the nation-building project.

However, commemorative events and the production of a master narrative often are contested. Commemorations, John Gillis argues, emerge through "the coordination of individual and group memories, whose results may appear consensual when they are in fact the product of processes of intense contest, struggle, and, in some instances, annihilation."[90] This process uncovers sharp divisions among organizers over how historical events should be commemorated, as Ron Rudin acknowledges in his work on Quebec's memorialization of Laval and Champlain.[91] The construction of public history and popular responses to commemorative events, Rudin notes in a separate study on Acadian history in the Maritimes, underscores the often conflicting goals and outcomes of the memorialization process between the government, organizers, communities, and the public.[92] The result, Alan Gordon points out, frequently becomes "a contest that pits competing pasts against one another in a struggle to define the present."[93] As Ian Radforth argues, memorial activities are employed by elites to control access to public space, revealing how programming legitimizes "the political cultures and the power relations at work."[94] The commemorative process, therefore, provides insights into divisions among groups competing to define memorials in the public realm.

Opposing positions can culminate in activities that counter official narratives and produce alternative meanings. Keith Walden argues that commemorative events often emerge as contested grounds where official narratives are challenged by the public. His examination of Toronto's International Exhibition documents how this annual event "shaped understandings of modern, urban culture," where "deliberate messages" promoted by organizers through displays and exhibits "intersected and competed with other [messages] inside and outside the grounds, that were contradictory and subversive."[95] Exhibition organizers were not always successful in delivering their message to the public, which interpreted the event in different ways. Official state narratives of national events are frequently challenged by the public. The Canadian government promoted a shared pan-Canadian national identity during the 1927 Diamond Jubilee celebrations in order to achieve political and social stability. Communities, groups, and individuals across the country hosted celebrations that disrupted, challenged, and countered those larger national narratives that were promulgated by Ottawa and, in the process, constructed their own versions of what it meant to be Canadian.[96] Commemorative activities, then, emerge as highly contested terrains that point to competing interests and visions to define a country's history, national identity, and cultural and social norms.

Nova Scotia's 1967 centennial celebrations did not produce contestations between the state, communities, and individuals over whether the anniversary of Canadian Confederation should be commemorated. It was accepted that government involvement in the country's economic and cultural activities was a key marker of post-war life. Nevertheless, disputes emerged over *how* the province should mark the centennial. Debates between the federal and provincial governments, and organizers of Nova Scotia's Highland Games and Folk Festival demonstrate tensions over what cultures should be celebrated, and therefore privileged, during the event. Considerable disagreement among Cape Breton communities erupted with the selection of the Miners' Museum as the area's only local 1967 undertaking. The history of Halifax's local aquarium and swimming pool projects reveals competing visions and priorities over the city's urban renewal efforts. Community Improvement Program initiatives that promoted a progressive and modern Nova Scotia conflicted with popular anti-modern characterizations of the province. In these ways, Nova Scotia's centennial celebrations emerged as a contested terrain where governments, communities, and organizers clashed. Despite these quarrels, no one disputed the right of government to fund these cultural capital undertakings. Indeed, Ottawa's funnelling of monies into myriad projects points to the accepted importance of regional infrastructure developments in the post-war era. Yet as their histories reveal, each of these four projects demonstrates how commemorations assumed numerous, complex, myriad, and even contradictory meanings for Nova Scotians and their communities.

Outline of the Book

This book is divided into five chapters. Chapter 1 examines the federal and provincial government apparatuses established to oversee and direct the centennial celebrations. From its head offices in Ottawa, the Centennial Commission coordinated and executed 1967 programming and commemorations across the country. Nova Scotia's Confederation Centenary Celebration Committee (Centenary Committee) played a key role in local planning as the arbiter of local community projects that were undertaken across the province through the Centennial Grants Program. Nova Scotia's Highland Games and Folk Festival is explored in chapter 2. This public event was intended to showcase the province's ethnic diversity, yet, as its title suggests, there was little doubt about which group received top billing. This case study shows how this program reinforced stereotypes of Nova Scotia as a "Scottish haven," and the ways in which displays of ethnic song, dance, and traditions undermined this caricature. The Cape Breton Miners' Museum was constructed under the auspices of the Centennial Grants Program, and it is the subject of chapter 3. The museum stood as a symbol of Cape Breton's revitalization, and the island's economic and social transition during the post-war period. It examines the significant role played by Nina Cohen, a local community activist and volunteer, whose work with the museum propelled her into the national spotlight as an important player in heritage circles. Her work with the facility points to the profound influence that certain individuals wielded during the centennial celebrations.

Chapter 4 examines Halifax's Centennial Swimming Pool, another project initiated under the Centennial Grants Program. That undertaking focused on the importance of providing the city with accessible and affordable recreational services, an acute concern that arose in communities across North America during the 1960s. The pool, however, was not Halifax's first choice for a local centennial project. The city's original proposal to build a salt-water aquarium and research centre proved controversial and eventually became a political and financial quagmire. The history of Halifax's aquarium and swimming pool projects reveals post-war discourses about urban modernization and renewal. Chapter 5 examines the Community Improvement Program, one of the Centennial Commission's high-profile Programs and Projects of National Significance. This cross-Canada beautification initiative relied on discourses of citizenship, environmentalism, and community participation that encouraged citizens to participate in a wide range of activities to clean up the country and improve its aesthetics. The program was instituted to offset the effects of rapid post-war expansion, and as a vehicle to improve Canadians' living standards. Taken together, these chapters point to the myriad ways in which Nova Scotia commemorated the country's centennial celebrations. Lastly, the Conclusion draws together this book's findings and offers final thoughts about Nova Scotia's 1967 centennial celebration experiences, and the legacy of community projects that left an indelible mark on the province's cultural landscape.

Ultimately, this book argues that Nova Scotia's centennial projects illustrate those larger social, cultural, political, and economic changes that took place in the province during the 1960s. These case studies show the province's attempts to alleviate what Maurice Lamontagne referred to as Canada's cultural poverty through the introduction of capital infrastructure initiatives that dramatically altered Nova Scotia's cultural landscape and reimagined public spaces. They underscore the ways in which centennial projects emerged as significant modernization and regional development strategies. The history of these undertakings chronicles how the public became involved in the centennial celebrations and memorialization. Their histories also illustrate how local actors interacted and negotiated with the federal and provincial governments in order to achieve particular objectives for their communities. Further, Nova Scotia's fluctuating provincial identity was reflected in centennial initiatives. Some projects reinforced longstanding and popular conceptualizations of the region's anti-modern "Folk," while others underscored its modern, progressive, and multicultural composition. Together, the province's 1967 centennial projects reveal the ways in which commemoration, regional development, and cultural policy converged to reflect those larger transformations that took place in post-war Nova Scotia.

Chapter 1

"It was deliberate – a planned effort, not a natural development of history": Producing Nova Scotia's Celebrations for Canada's 1967 Centennial

Never before, perhaps not again for another 99 years, have Canadians organized for themselves such an outlay of money, coordination of exertions, progress toward goals deliberately chosen. And the fact that this was done in a year when...the nation was on the verge of permanent breakdown, was itself the most crushing rejoinder of the pessimists among us.
National Centennial Commission, *Canada 67*

On the night of 31 December 1966, hundreds of people descended on Halifax's Grand Parade Square, the popular downtown landmark, to usher in the new year. The boisterous crowd had gathered to celebrate a milestone in the country's history – the arrival of Canada's 1967 centennial year. To mark the occasion, the City of Halifax organized a ceremony hosted by Mayor Allan O'Brien. He welcomed the crowd, applauded the attendees for braving the night's "bitter cold," and stated that 1967 would be "a great year for both Halifax and Canada."[1] The province's lieutenant governor, Henry P. MacKeen, lit a ceremonial "flame of friendship," while bells from St Paul's Church rang out across the square. MacKeen spoke about the significance of 1967 and remarked that if it "helps to impress on us the necessity of understanding, tolerating, and appreciating the points of view and thinking of others, the centenary celebrations will have accomplished a great deal towards the ideals of unity, brotherhood, and peace."[2] Following the lighting, the mayor and Nova Scotia Premier Robert L. Stanfield raised Canada's centennial flag, the Salvation Army Halifax Citadel Band played, and a local choir sang. The ceremony concluded with addresses from church leaders who offered a thanksgiving litany and recited the Centennial

Prayer that had been composed by clergy from across Canada in honour of the year's celebrations.[3]

Similar scenes took place throughout Nova Scotia as the province's citizens gathered in cities, towns, and villages to welcome the centennial year. Dartmouth greeted 1967's arrival with fireworks, bell ringing, and a 100-gun salute. The mayor, Joseph Zatzman, presided over a gathering at Lake Banook, where he lit one of three ceremonial fires on the beach.[4] The south shore town of Bridgewater held a torchlight parade and rang church bells at midnight.[5] Digby's local Baptist church organized a special service to mark the start of the centennial,[6] while in North Sydney, Mayor J.S. Munro hosted a bonfire near the site of the community's new centennial park.[7] Levees were another popular way to ring in 1967. In Sydney, over 1,500 people attended a levee at Sydney Academy, a local high school, where citizens mingled with Mayor Russell Urquhart and members of the city's centennial celebration committee.[8] Thousands of revellers gathered at locations such as local Royal Canadian Legions, military bases, churches, and community centres. The lieutenant governor opened the doors of Government House in Halifax, where he welcomed the public to join him in the celebration.[9] These local gatherings throughout Nova Scotia did not garner as much press coverage as the New Year's Day ceremonies held in Ottawa on Parliament Hill and presided over by Liberal Prime Minister Lester B. Pearson.[10] However, local observances held across the country in all the provinces and territories exemplified centennial organizers' success in encouraging Canadians to participate in a wide range of commemorative activities.

Planning the Celebrations: The National Centennial Commission

These New Year's celebrations were just a handful of activities that represented the hard work of organizers across the country who had toiled to ensure that all Canadians could partake in centennial events. Federal and provincial bureaucratic apparatus, as well as organizers at the community level, coordinated Canada's 1967 activities such as these New Year's celebrations. Directing events at the federal level was the Centennial Commission, the Crown corporation that oversaw national celebrations. The Centennial Commission coordinated an astonishing number of events to ensure that all citizens had access to commemorative activities. Its efforts included everything from supporting local infrastructure projects to ensuring that Canadians had opportunities to experience national programming. In Nova Scotia, the Centenary Committee, a bureaucratic group established through provincial legislation, oversaw commemorative activities. Its work included coordinating local festivities and making decisions about funding the province's 1967 infrastructure projects. Together, the Centennial Commission and the Centenary Committee played key roles in organizing and administering centennial celebrations in Nova Scotia. They approved local centennial projects and controlled the attendant monies that supported cultural initiatives. In so doing, both groups enticed citizens to take part in commemorative activities by providing lucrative government support that funnelled grants into communities across the province.

The Centennial Commission's lofty ambition to involve all Canadians in 1967 festivities was a key component of its mandate. One of the organization's guiding principles was "to ensure, as far as possible, that every community in Canada would have some opportunity to share in the 1967 celebrations."[11] By its own account, the Centennial Commission was very successful in achieving this goal. In a popular photographic retrospective of the year's events, the organization applauded its efforts to immerse Canadians in a series of what it considered to be worthwhile endeavours. It lauded widespread citizen participation – described as "inspired amateurism" – that was "both typical and symbolic of Centennial Year." It even tied this involvement to larger goals of strengthening national identity and unity: "This was not merely a festival of hired performers and passive lookers-on. It was the response of a people to a new, perhaps belated realization of maturity. Centennial Year may have solved no Canadian problems, but it did give the nation a self-awareness and self-assurance that had not existed before, and a new faith that Canada's greatest centuries are still in the future."[12]

The Centennial Commission's promotion of commemorative New Year's activities across Canada was just one of the many ways that the agency fulfilled its mandate to bring citizens together to mark the nation's hundredth anniversary. The organization planned, coordinated, and financed copious programs, festivals, and ceremonies throughout the year. Many of these activities were intended to foster national unity, an emphasis that was integral to the year's events. The centennial arrived during a tumultuous time in Canadian history when the rise of the separatist movement in Quebec threatened to tear apart the country. Prime Minister Pearson and his successor, Pierre Elliott Trudeau, spent a great deal of their political energy trying to grapple with the political and cultural challenges posed by Quebec, and working to keep

Canadian Confederation intact. They promoted meaningful participation for French Canadians, both inside and outside of Quebec, in the social, cultural, economic, and political fabric of the country in an attempt to shore up allegiance to the federal government. The 1967 celebrations proved to be the perfect platform to promote the idea of a strong, united, bicultural French-English country, albeit to the detriment of other identities, cultures, and communities, including Indigenous populations. This emphasis on biculturalism, as many national centennial programs revealed, ultimately further entrenched a colonial and settler narrative of Canada's history.

Ottawa armed itself with an arsenal of millions of dollars to spend on a national celebration that carried a strong message of Canadian unity. Between 1963 and 1968, the Centennial Commission directed over $200 million into centennial programming.[13] This level of funding for social and cultural initiatives was unprecedented in the country's history. Monies were channelled into a staggering number of activities that included everything from the development of local community infrastructure projects and the creation of youth travel exchanges, to the publication of the *Dictionary of Canadian Biography*, and the administration of performing arts grants.[14] High-profile programs included the Voyageur Canoe Pageant, Festival Canada, Rural Beautification, Performing Arts, and the Community Improvement Program.[15] The wildly popular Confederation Caravans featured exhibits from across Canada, while the Confederation Train told the country's story from "time immemorial." Set to "deliver the stirring message of nationhood across the whole country," the train welcomed visitors with a whistle that sounded the opening bars of the national anthem, "O Canada."[16] Its cross-Canada adventures began on New Year's Day 1967, when it travelled westwards from Ottawa for its first series of scheduled stops. Pauline Vanier, wife of Governor General Georges Vanier, officially launched the train during a ceremony held at Ottawa's Union Station. Judy LaMarsh, Canada's Secretary of State, who oversaw the centennial celebrations, was also in attendance. She reminded attendees of the train's role in reaching out to all Canadians and facilitating participation in commemorative national programming. The train, and its launch, carried a strong federalist message of national unity. LaMarsh remarked that the project "reinforce[d] our conviction that our country does indeed stretch from sea to sea and that all of it, whether in the geographical centre or along the geographical perimeter, is an essential element of our unity."[17] Over 2.5 million Canadians visited the train during its sixty-three stops across the country, while 6.25 million people saw the Confederation Caravans, which travelled to communities inaccessible by rail.[18]

Moments like these, however, were years in the making. Programming such as the Confederation Caravans and Train were products of a highly structured government bureaucracy that directed the centennial celebrations. The Centennial Commission, the astonishingly intricate, complex, and massive organization that oversaw 1967 commemorations, was established in 1961. This signalled the beginning of the federal government's role in marking the anniversary. The Centennial Commission, and the provincial counterparts with which it worked, such as Nova Scotia's Centenary Committee, became centralized event organizers. Despite a mandate to implement activities that relied heavily on local, grass-roots initiatives, the histories of the Centennial Commission and the Centenary Committee demonstrate the extent to which these bodies controlled the year's celebrations. As one of the Centennial Commission's own publications observed, 1967 commemorations were very calculated and state-coordinated events. The year was a "unique achievement" because it was "deliberate – a planned effort, not a natural development of history ... Never before, perhaps not again for another 99 years, have Canadians organized for themselves such an outlay of money, coordination of exertions, [and] progress toward goals deliberately chosen."[19] Ultimately, very few spontaneous and uncoordinated events fell outside the management and direction of the Centennial Commission and, in the case of Nova Scotia, the Centenary Committee. The work of these two groups shows the central roles they played as arbiters and funders of centennial projects. Indeed, the Centenary Committee's mandate, in particular, reveals the exceptional control this organization had over programs, projects and, perhaps most important, centennial monies at the provincial level.

While the Centennial Commission became the authority on all things 1967, others had begun to think about how to celebrate the anniversary of Canadian Confederation much earlier. Helen Davies argues that preliminary discussions about commemorating the centennial dated as far back as 1956, when John Kidd, executive director of the Canadian Citizenship Council, recommended that his organization start deliberations about how to observe the occasion.[20] Working with the Canadian Association for Adult Education, the Canadian Citizenship Council held a series of conferences in 1959 and 1960 to discuss strategies. Delegates surveyed what other groups were planning and suggested ways to engage citizens in the celebrations. The year had to "provide opportunities for new Canadians, as well as native born, to learn about Canada's history," and projects had to "extend and strengthen good relationships between French-speaking and English-speaking Canada."[21] In 1960 these two voluntary associations merged to form the Canadian Centenary Council. The Centenary Council's objectives were to "stimulate interest in appropriate observances and celebrations of the anniversary of Confederation" and to work with the federal government to achieve these goals.[22] By 1967, this umbrella group boasted over 900 members that included citizens, government agencies, businesses, and voluntary organizations.[23] The Centenary Council played a major role in the celebrations' early planning stages and proved integral in organizing 1967 programming.

Despite the central role it eventually played, the federal government was "slow to get on side" with planning, and the Centenary Council often found itself working alone initially. Ottawa, it seemed, was happy to rely on those early efforts by voluntary associations that began planning in earnest.[24] Peter Aykroyd expressed concerns about the government's initial lacklustre approach and delayed involvement. In his candid history of the centennial, he describes the federal government's early involvement as evolving "at a snail's pace."[25] While the private sector mobilized its forces to foster Canadians' interest in the 1967 centennial celebrations, Ottawa dragged its feet. Voluntary organizations sympathetic to planning celebrations were forced to deal with a distracted Progressive Conservative Prime Minister John Diefenbaker, whose government was in turmoil. Initially, Diefenbaker was reluctant to spend public funds on commemorations for which his government would reap few, if any, political rewards. Just as frustrating, in Aykroyd's words, was the phenomenon of "procrastination." The centennial was seven years away, leaving Ottawa with what it believed to be plenty of time to prepare for the anniversary.[26] In the meantime, the federal government encouraged enthusiastic private agencies to assume responsibility for making headway on initial planning stages, as evidenced, for example, by a $25,000 grant to the Centenary Council in support of its activities.[27]

The federal government began to assume an increasingly proactive role by the early 1960s, likely realizing that it had to become more involved in planning as the Centenary Council's work promoting 1967 came to stand in increasingly stark contrast to its own minimal efforts.

The government established the beginnings of an administrative structure by striking the National Committee on the Centennial of Confederation (National Committee) in February 1960. This group was a consultative body composed of representatives from both the federal and provincial governments formed to work on centennial planning.[28] The National Committee first congregated in Ottawa in April 1961, where it spelled out its vision for the celebrations. At that meeting it drafted guiding principles that defined the federal government's role in centennial planning. Maurice Lamontagne, president of the Privy Council, summarized the National Committee's vision: "The Centennial should be a time of national stocktaking and rededication for the future." The celebrations had to embody the lofty ambitions of working to "maintain the Canadian identity and to strengthen Canadian unity." To support these goals, there needed to be a "programme [that had] a strong all-Canadian flavour" but one with "important provincial and local aspects." In particular, "special recognition" had to be granted to the 1864 Quebec City and Charlottetown Conferences, that youth be given an opportunity to "know the people and geography of Canada better," and that "undertaking lasting projects of a capital nature" be central to the year's celebrations.[29] These objectives framed an ambitious and extensive 1967 programming agenda.

However, a conflicting ideological tension emerged as planning unfolded. The celebrations were to be a reflection not only of the story since Confederation, but also of the "entire range of Canadian history, with full recognition of the contributions to the growth and development of this country by peoples of several races and many nationalities." Although this aim reflected the concern that all Canadians be included in the celebrations, it was tempered by what the National Committee saw as a need to pay particular attention to the country's "two founding races." Lamontagne noted that the centennial bureaucracy had to give consideration to "the principles of bilingualism and biculturalism."[30] This became more important to the state as the decade wore on and the idea and ideals of Canadian dualism took on greater meaning. This importance on Canadian dualism was reflected in the mandate of the Royal Commission on Bilingualism and Biculturalism, struck by Prime Minister Pearson in 1963. That commission made a series of recommendations on how to "develop the Canadian Confederation on the basis of an equal partnership between the two founding races."[31] Canadian dualism, then, became a touchstone for both the commission and the National Committee during a time when this idea was coming under increased scrutiny.

The National Committee sought to use the 1967 celebrations as a tool to accomplish national federal ambitions and shore up loyalty towards the Canadian state. Its mandate, the group hoped, would "foster ... Canada's unity based on the constituent cultural, historical and political parts of the Canadian Confederation."[32] These goals emphasized Canadian unity and identity, two themes that guided the centennial bureaucracy on how celebrations fit within these grandiose ambitions. To this end, Lamontagne and the centennial administration constructed programming that reflected these social, cultural, and political goals. This included allocating millions of dollars in federal funding for projects that emphasized Canadian history and supporting the country's cultural development. Ottawa proposed initiatives, some of which were already underway, such as the construction of the National Library, the partial restoration of the Fortress of Louisbourg, and Charlottetown's Fathers of Confederation Buildings. There was also discussion of a youth travel program and the beginnings of what would become the centennial publication program that included funding to produce hundreds of books about Canada.

In addition to reiterating these larger, national aims, the National Committee wanted to ensure that all Canadians had the opportunity to participate in the centennial celebrations. Its 1964 publication, *The Centennial Handbook*, noted that "a fitting and proper observance" of the centennial was "not a job for any one group or agency. It is a national undertaking, a project for all Canadians."[33] The importance of including as many Canadians as possible in national, provincial, and local celebrations permeated the literature about 1967 and was frequently invoked by National Committee (and later Centennial Commission) staff, politicians, media, and the public. Emphasis was placed on drawing young Canadians into the celebrations to ensure that they would come to know Canada's history, geography, and people.[34] These objectives all sought to encourage widespread participation and involvement in 1967 activities.

The National Committee's declaration of its guiding principles and recommendations for social and cultural programming were the beginnings of the federal government's celebration plans. Now all that was needed was a centralized bureaucracy to oversee this colossal agenda. By the fall of 1961, the federal government established a national agency to do just that. On 18 September, Diefenbaker tabled a resolution in the House of Commons to approve a national centennial agency. The prime minister remarked that 1967 would be "a dramatic year in Canadian history and an opportunity for Canadians to develop a fuller understanding of what it means and can mean to be a Canadian."[35] All agreed that the celebrations had to be a national priority. In what was likely a rare moment during their political rivalry, Pearson concurred with Diefenbaker's assertions about the importance of marking the centennial year. Pearson remarked that the "celebrations should encompass the whole range of Canada's history, not merely the achievements of Confederation itself." He reiterated the prime minister's assertion that 1967 provided an opportune time

> to re-examine the values of our national society, and to resolve that we will do perhaps more than we have been able to do in the past to strengthen those values, based as they are on the enduring concept of freedom, and based as they are also in a political sense on the foundation of two cultures, two languages and two traditions of the two founding peoples ... These two races, two cultures, and two nations in that sense ... have been enriched in the years that have followed by people of practically every strain, race and culture from all parts of the world.[36]

The Liberal leader also took this time to talk about the humility of Canadians – a line that was repeated frequently during the celebrations. As 1967 approached, Pearson stated that Canadians could "be proud of our growth, our progress and our achievements without being smug."[37]

Diefenbaker subsequently tabled Bill C-127, the *National Centennial Act* (*Centennial Act*), which quickly made its way through Parliament and received royal assent on 29 September 1961.[38] The act outlined the mandate for the 1967 celebrations and cultural policy programming. It established the National Centennial Administration (renamed the Centennial Commission in 1963), which was handed a broad range of objectives that required it to "promote interest in, and to plan and implement programs and projects relating to, the Centennial of Confederation in Canada in order that the Centennial may be observed throughout Canada in a manner keeping with its national and historical significance."[39] Monies were allocated to support the corporation's lofty and wide-ranging mandate, and it was declared a charitable organization.[40] In addition, the act established the necessary bureaucratic machinery. The positions of commissioner and deputy commissioner (whose title was changed to associate commissioner in 1963) were created, as were positions for eight directors to oversee administrative responsibilities.[41] The number of directors was later increased to twelve in 1963 to reflect heavier bureaucratic demands. Directors determined policies and made programming, administrative, and budgetary decisions.[42] In addition, a second body was legislated to steer the celebrations. The National Conference on Canada's Centennial (National Conference) was an advisory group that oversaw operations and deliberated about programming.[43] Members of the National Conference included the federal minister in charge of centennial celebrations, and up to sixty members appointed by the minister, with each province having a minimum of two representatives.[44]

The legislation, however, was not without its problems. Quebec Premier Jean Lesage charged that it was rife with ambiguity, making it unclear exactly *what* centennial was being celebrated. Starting in the fall of 1961, he engaged in a protracted series of exchanges with Diefenbaker and, after 1963, Pearson. The controversy began in October 1961 when Diefenbaker requested that Lesage name two members to the National Conference. Lesage replied swiftly, objecting that the act referred to 1967 as the "National Centennial." He wrote that the

> centenary could have been celebrated whether in 1634, one hundred years after Jacques Cartier, or at the beginning of the 18th century, one hundred years after Champlain whose glorious achievement it would be somewhat cavalier to suppress by a simple stroke of the pen. Your legislation is properly described by its title of "An Act respecting the Observance of the Centennial of Confederation in Canada," but this title is contradicted by Section 3 and by Section 17 which refer respectively to "The National Centennial" and "Canada's Centennial." I do not believe I can let this ambiguity of expression persist and I do not dare ask immediately of my colleagues, the Executive Council, to help me designate two persons to represent Quebec in the "National Centennial Conference" for fear of sanctioning by this action a situation which is unacceptable to the French Canadian sense of pride whilst furthermore their political representative would be forced from a position of dignity to adopt an attitude not in conformity with their real sentiments of friendship and their desire to cooperate. I rely upon your sense of justice my dear Prime Minister that you will admit that the history of Canada did not start in 1867, and that to think otherwise is to commit a very serious wrong to Canadians of French and of English expression whose ancestors founded this country much before Confederation.[45]

Diefenbaker refused to amend the legislation. By the time he was ousted from government in the spring of 1963, the matter remained unresolved. Pearson had no desire to prolong the issue, and he agreed to clarify the wording to address concerns from Quebec.[46] The legislation was renamed the *Centennial of Canadian Confederation Act* that December, and a series of nomenclature changes were introduced that clarified which "centennial" was being recognized. This included renaming the corporation the "Centennial Commission."[47]

Despite the establishment of this newly minted legislation, there remained serious concerns – voiced, in particular, by the Centenary Council – about the pace of the federal government's planning.[48] Nevertheless, key administrative pieces slowly began to fall into place when in January 1963 New Brunswick native John Fisher was appointed Centennial Commissioner. Fisher was a high-profile CBC broadcaster. His reports from across Canada had earned him a national reputation with the nickname "Mr Canada," and he was considered a popular ambassador who would promote the organization's goals.[49] Other senior Centennial Commission positions were filled by prominent Canadians. Robert Choquette, a well-known Quebecois writer and academic, was appointed Associate Commissioner. He was succeeded a year later by Georges Gauthier, a career bureaucrat who had made a name for himself in the federal civil service. Directors (not to be confused with the members of the Board of Directors) were soon appointed to oversee the myriad employees working in the organization's seven branches, each of whom was responsible for overseeing specific aspects of planning and administration. The seven directorates included Research, Federal-Provincial Grants, Administration and Financial Advisor, Planning, Public Relations and Information, Special Projects, and Regional Offices.[50] Through these directorates, the Centennial Commission carried out its multifaceted federalist agenda of strengthening Canadian identity and unity, and bringing citizens together for the celebrations. No branches expressed these goals as publicly or as forcefully as the Federal-Provincial Grants and Planning directorates, which were to execute projects across the country that would become reminders, some of them permanent, of Canada's centennial year. Although these branches focused on promoting a federalist agenda, their raison d'être was to pursue initiatives that encouraged citizens to celebrate 1967 at the local level.

The Federal-Provincial Grants directorate, headed by John Weldon, oversaw two major programs that left some of the most enduring reminders of 1967. The first was the Confederation Memorial Program, described as a "federal-provincial co-operative," that provided grants for the construction of a major memorial building in each provincial capital. Under this scheme, the federal government provided up to $2.5 million or half of the funding (whichever sum was less) to each province to construct "important memorials of cultural value."[51] The second program was the Federal-Provincial Centennial Grants Program (Centennial Grants Program), which provided monies for community projects across Canada.[52] This initiative fostered widespread citizen participation by encouraging communities to construct local memorial infrastructure projects. It worked on a shared $1 per capita funding basis between the federal and provincial governments, and a local sponsoring body, often a municipality or community group, referred to as the "initiating agency." Projects had to be "of a lasting nature." These included cultural institutions, museums, performance spaces, libraries, park and recreation areas, community centres, and swimming pools.[53] The Centennial Commission was adamant that the program not be used for municipal works such as sidewalk and street improvements, fire halls, cemeteries, or other developments deemed to be "contrary to the spirit" of the program. Undertakings had to be of "benefit to all the people" and "in keeping with the spirit of celebrating an anniversary." The federal government wanted to see projects that were of a "historical, educational, cultural or recreational nature."[54] The program was a cornerstone of the Centennial Commission's cultural policy. Billed as a cooperative undertaking between the federal and provincial governments, and communities across the country, it was touted as a "permanent benefit and reminder" of 1967.[55] It received widespread support when it was proposed to the federal Cabinet in 1961, and rolled out in August 1963.[56] To be eligible, communities had to secure one-third of the funding costs and ensure that the project was viable post-1967. The program ultimately funnelled $88 million across the country into 2,301 projects.[57] Nova Scotia received $756,000 in per capita federal monies, with a matching grant from the province that brought total government funding to $1,512,000.[58]

Aside from Expo 67, the Centennial Grants and Confederation Memorial programs were two of the most celebrated and successful undertakings of the year. They became long-lasting reminders of Ottawa's role in cultural capital planning. Completed projects were branded with a bronze or aluminium commemorative plaque adorned with the centennial symbol – eleven triangles, representing each province and territory, arranged in a stylized pattern that resembled a maple leaf. The plaque's purpose was to "memorialize works constructed to commemorate the centennial of Confederation in an appropriate and lasting form which ... ensure continuity of appearance from coast to coast, and ... place a strong visual emphasis on the forward looking spirit of the centennial itself."[59] Plaques noted that projects were joint efforts between the initiating agency, and the federal and provincial governments, and they visually reinforced and served as reminders of the state's role in infrastructure planning.

The Centennial Commission's Planning directorate also played a central role coordinating the year's events. Its director, Robbins Elliott, saw to it that his branch engaged Canadians and encouraged them to celebrate at the community level. His office was responsible for planning and implementing 1967 programming. Elliott and his team also oversaw national cultural undertakings deemed to be "Programs and Projects of National Significance." This was, without a doubt, an exceptionally broad job description, which saw Elliott's directorate accountable for a dizzying number of 1967 undertakings.[60] This included national initiatives such as the Confederation Caravans and Trains, Youth Travel, Performing Arts, Athletics, and the Voyageur Canoe Pageant, all of which aimed to put the Centennial Commission's broad mandate into practice. These programs emphasized the goals of "the maintenance of Canadian identity and strengthening Canadian unity."[61] With such grand federalist ambitions hinging on the branch's work, projects required significant financial backing to deliver the national unity message to Canadians. Ottawa was certainly ready and willing to ante up. By the end of 1967, the Planning directorate had spent over $158 million on bringing programming to communities across Canada. The most expensive projects were the Confederation Trains and Caravans at $48 million, followed by the Performing Arts in a distant second at $16 million, and Youth Travel not far behind at $13 million.[62]

Youth were expected to play a large role in the year's events, as the National Committee's guiding principles clearly had outlined. Targeting this demographic was one of the ways that the federal government sought to ensure widespread participation in 1967 activities. Youth, in particular, were being counted upon to carry out Ottawa's lofty aspirations of promoting, strengthening, and reinforcing the importance of national unity. The Planning branch's Youth Travel and Athletics programs were singled out as two of the best ways to accomplish these goals.[63] Youth Travel ran from 1964 to 1967 and was, by far, one of

Ottawa's most successful initiatives. During that time, over 40,000 high school students, aged fifteen to seventeen, journeyed across the country for week-long exchanges in communities to experience life in other provinces.[64] The program sought "to introduce young Canadians to the geography of their country, to its historic sites, to its political and educational institutions, to the various aspects of its cultural life, and to its artistic and industrial achievements, and ... give them a more intimate understanding of the social and economic conditions under which the nation is developing. The end result ... should be that participants would return to their homes broadened in outlook, enriched in mind and spirit, and with a vastly increased knowledge and understanding of Canada and its people."[65]

Youth Travel recruiters sought well-rounded students who were selected on the basis of their leadership skills, extra-curricular activities, and academic achievements, and who were deemed to be "worthy of his or her Province."[66] The program received critical acclaim for its federalist aims. One journalist noted that it "should open many windows and doors to invite the fresh air of national breeze," and quoted, Secretary of State Maurice Lamontagne, who remarked that exchanges were "one of the most effective ways to promote national solidarity."[67] Another journalist argued that Youth Travel's grand objectives helped to promote a cohesive national identity, writing that "Canadians complain that they do not know what being a Canadian means, they worry about their cultural identification, they criticize other countries for ignoring them." The writer proposed that "the best antidote to these complaints are programs for youngsters. They do not suffer from their elders' conceptual and emotional cramps and they might, given the right exercise, mature without them."[68] Pictures of happy students were splashed across the pages of Centennial Commission publications, and the program was hailed as a strategic weapon in the federal government's arsenal in its ongoing fight against Quebec separatists.

True to centennial organizers' aim of encouraging grass-roots participation, the Planning directorate additionally oversaw the Community Improvement Program. This scheme, headed by architect Roderick Clack, who worked as one of the directorate's project officers, focused primarily on local efforts to clean up the environment and improve the country's outdoor "living room."[69] The program drew on discourses of national unity to promote its activities. However, it was primarily framed as a way to engage citizens in collective community efforts as a meaningful way to participate in 1967 celebrations. Notions of citizenship and environmental stewardship permeated the program's literature. Fighting urban and rural blight was presented as crucial to promoting a "better Canadian way of life."[70] The scheme relied heavily on grass-roots community participation and touted "clean-up" schemes as productive centennial efforts.

The Centennial Commission invested a great deal of time, energy, and funding into cultural programming. The enormous amount of money spent, however, mattered little in comparison to what the Centennial Commission hoped its programming would achieve. In a speech at the opening of a local project in Levis, Quebec, in April 1967, Secretary of State Judy LaMarsh spoke about the celebrations' broader goals: "The important thing about all these centennial projects is that they are giving Canadians something they often lack – a common experience and a common participation in something that transcends our many differences of race and religion."[71] The Centennial Commission saw these initiatives as a means to strengthen national unity and promote Canadian identity. These projects were expected to encourage a shared experience that transcended the country's vast geographical, political, and social differences.

Nova Scotia's Confederation Centenary Celebration Committee

The large number of projects implemented across the country required the Centennial Commission to work cooperatively with the provinces. For their part, the provinces established extensive bureaucratic networks that assisted with the execution of 1967 cultural programming. They were key in directing the celebrations, especially at the local level. Prime Minister Diefenbaker recognized the significant role decentralized programming played in the celebrations. He stated at the National Committee's inaugural meeting in Ottawa in February 1960 that it was imperative that "special thought should be given to the place of regional interests in the national observances."[72]

Nova Scotia, like all other provinces, created a bureaucratic agency and a ministerial portfolio to help steer the 1967 celebrations and work cooperatively with the Centennial Commission. In 1961, Nova Scotia enacted the *Confederation Centenary Celebration Act* (*Centenary Celebration Act*), becoming Canada's first province to pass provincial centennial legislation.[73] The act established the Confederation Centenary Celebration Committee, whose mandate was to "encourage, promote, organize, produce, conduct or participate in fitting observance and celebration" across Nova Scotia.[74] Notably, the group was given the weighty responsibility of assessing the province's Centennial Grants Program applications and making the attendant funding recommendations to the provincial and federal governments, and the Centennial Commission. The Centenary Committee handed out over $1.5 million in government funding for projects built under this program across Nova Scotia between 1966 and 1968. As the gatekeeper that vetted proposals and acted as the arbiter of funds, the Centenary Committee played a powerful role in directing Nova Scotia's centennial cultural policy initiatives.

Assembling Centenary Committee members was a lesson in the minefield of Nova Scotia politics and geography. In March 1963, Conservative Premier Robert L. Stanfield appointed twelve individuals who represented a variety of constituencies to the Centenary Committee.[75] Stanfield was determined to ensure representation from all political stripes. The premier knew that a politically and geographically diverse group would help thwart accusations of patronage, always a likely scenario in Nova Scotia politics. The drive to ensure that the 1967 celebrations remained firmly outside the manoeuvrings of party politics also characterized the provincial and federal governments' working relationships when coordinating centennial programming. Throughout the 1960s, the Progressive Conservatives dominated Nova Scotia politics. Stanfield's first victory at the polls in 1956 signalled the beginning of a Tory reign that lasted until 1970. In Ottawa, the Liberals dominated federal politics for the better part of the 1960s. Lester B. Pearson's election in 1963 opened the door for that party presiding over the federal scene until the late 1970s. Opposing political parties at the federal and provincial helms did not present significant problems for a working relationship between these two levels of government – at least on centennial matters. Stanfield wanted to ensure that party politics did not enter the fray of centennial planning, and he took care to appoint a politically balanced Centenary Committee. His later defence of its decisions as fair and balanced reveals the premier's intention to ensure that provincial celebrations proceeded untethered to political affiliations.

Although Stanfield was conscious of establishing regional and political equilibrium on the Centenary Committee, a survey of its members shows that he was less concerned with striking a gender balance. The group was dominated by men. There were only three female members – Abigail ("Abbie") Lane, the prominent Dartmouth councillor who was appointed Centenary Committee chair; Isobel MacAulay;[76] and Ellen MacLean.[77] Lane was well-known for her distinguished journalism career. She was the editor for the women's section for the Halifax *Chronicle-Herald* from 1940 to 1948 and hosted *Around the Town*, a popular 1950s weekly CBC television segment. She was also an active Progressive Conservative party member. However, it was her municipal political career and extensive community work that made her a household name. She seized headlines in 1951 when she launched her "kitchen campaign" in her successful run for a vacant Halifax City Council seat.[78] Lane was appointed deputy mayor in 1955, becoming the first woman to hold that position. This appointment fuelled widespread speculation that she would run for mayor.[79] An active community volunteer, she served on the boards of the Halifax Mental Hospital and the Grace Maternity Hospital, and was a director of the Canadian Mental Health Association, president of the Halifax Welfare Bureau, and chair of the Halifax Board of School Commissioners.[80]

The Centenary Committee reflected representation from across the province. Many members were notable community leaders. Provincial archivist C. Bruce Fergusson, a native of Port Morien and a Rhodes Scholar, was named Centenary Committee secretary. A life-long Conservative party member, he had a distinguished career as a historian, was president of Nova Scotia's Historical Society and the Nova Scotia Branch of the Canadian Historical Association, and was chair of the National Historic Sites Committee.[81] Other members were appointed for their local achievements and prominence within their region. Wolfville's Ronald Stewart Longley, professor of history at Acadia University, had previously served as the town's mayor. He was an active community member, serving as president of the Rotary Club, director of the Apple Blossom Festival, and an executive member of the Union of Nova Scotia Municipalities.[82] Glace Bay's Dan A. MacDonald, one of two Cape Breton representatives, had served as the town's mayor since 1950 and was a past president of the Union of Nova Scotia Municipalities. Cape Breton's second member was J.H. Layton from Sydney Mines. Halifax members constituted a solid share of seats on the committee and included Isobel MacAulay, Keith C. Bishop, and D.G. Padmore, a retired member of the Royal Canadian Navy.[83] Members from elsewhere in the province included Julius Comeau from Meteghen, John M. Murphy from Truro, J. Austen Parker from Liverpool, A.J. Gorman and John R. Lynk from New Glasgow, and Ellen MacLean from Eureka. H.F. Pullen, manager of Expo 67's Atlantic Canada Pavilion, also served as a member.[84] Both Pullen and MacLean had significant experience as Canadian Centenary Council executive board members. Halifax councillor and committee member

H.R. Wyman was appointed as chair following Abbie Lane's sudden death in December 1965.[85]

Richard A. Donahoe, Nova Scotia's Attorney General, Minister of Public Health, and influential member in Stanfield's Cabinet, rounded out this administrative structure. A lawyer and Halifax mayor from 1952 to 1954, Donahoe was first elected to Nova Scotia's Legislative Assembly in 1954. He successfully ran in an unexpected by-election in the riding of Halifax South after the death in office of the much-revered Liberal Premier, Angus L. Macdonald. Donahoe held the seat for the next fourteen years, during which time he served in several prominent Cabinet positions. Perhaps his most public role, however, came with his appointment as Minister of Centennial Affairs. In that capacity he worked closely with the Centenary Committee and his federal counterparts in Ottawa to coordinate the province's 1967 activities.[86] Donahoe and Stanfield attended the Centenary Committee's inaugural meeting in Halifax on 28 May 1963. Addressing the group, the premier noted those larger centennial goals enunciated by the Centennial Commission. Stanfield emphasized that 1967 had to be defined by "widespread" citizen participation at the local level and that the Centenary Committee had to assume an active role in the celebrations.[87]

The Centenary Committee immediately set to work on what would become its most time-consuming role: arbitrating Centennial Grants Program applications. As the program's gatekeeper, the group made recommendations for the equitable disposition of Nova Scotia's $1.5 million in funding available under the per capita grants scheme. The Centenary Committee adopted a clear decision-making framework to facilitate disbursement of funds. In addition, it took steps to ensure that potential allegations of political interference, patronage, and preferential treatment would not interfere with either the group's work or the public's perception of its activities. Two-thirds of the group with a quorum of at least seven members was required to make recommendations on a community project. These recommendations were then forwarded to the provincial and federal governments, and the Centennial Commission, for approval. The group set a deadline of 1 January 1964 to receive project proposals.[88]

However, the question before the Centenary Committee was *how* to disperse funds. Stanfield and Donahoe advocated assessing proposals on a "regional basis," which, they argued, would encourage communities to work together on a few larger projects that maximized

Centennial Grants Program funding. The premier envisioned two to four undertakings only for the whole province, rather than spreading monies on many smaller projects across federal or provincial constituencies, or county by county. Although it is unclear why Stanfield and Donahoe favoured a regional system, or how regional boundaries would be decided, the Centenary Committee agreed that this was a practical and worthwhile approach.

Likely hoping to gain early public support for this regional approach, both politicians reiterated their position in the press. The premier argued that the Centennial Grants Program would be "hopeless" if initiatives were undertaken in every Nova Scotia community. Rather, the province had to pursue funding allocations that ensured "lasting results."[89] The public, it seemed, agreed. A *Chronicle-Herald* editorial noted that "scattering these funds [across all communities in the province] would be to waste them."[90] Donahoe advocated this regional approach to his federal counterparts at the National Committee meetings in October and December 1963 in Ottawa. He proposed that dividing monies into small pots prevented the construction of a "substantial project" that would make a significant difference in the lives of Nova Scotians.[91] Bruce Fergusson acknowledged the scheme's obvious limitations when he was asked about the practicalities of municipalities working together on a joint project, and whether cooperation was even possible. He argued that the Centenary Committee was "dropping heavy hints" that it preferred a regional approach. However, he conceded that this was as far as the group could go to avoid the spectre of heavy-handed interference in what was supposed to be a grass-roots initiative.

The realities of the application process, however, forced the Centenary Committee to re-evaluate its strategy. At its 31 January 1964 meeting, the group decided that proposals would be assessed on a per capita basis for each of Nova Scotia's eighteen counties. The reasons behind this abrupt policy change are unclear. However, some counties likely demanded that they each be given the opportunity to submit a proposal and vie for funds. Although there were no accusations of political favouritism about the mechanics or the optics of having only a handful of Centennial Grants Program projects dispersed throughout the province, perhaps this issue was brewing quietly in the background. Regardless, the tide had turned. The Centenary Committee and the premier were willing to bend to the public mood. Stanfield argued that in the interests of promoting wide participation in centennial programming local projects would be considered for each county on a $1 per capita basis. He remained adamant, however, that no funds beyond this amount would be made available.[92]

There were distinct advantages to this approach. It meshed well with centennial organizers' broader goals to afford as many communities as possible the opportunity to participate in programming. It also ensured that infrastructure opportunities were spread out across the province. Optics had to be considered. Stanfield agreed that a county-by-county disbursement ensured that the Centennial Grants Program was "fair and readily seen to be fully justified." To deal with "differences ... within each county," the premier suggested that each county reach an internal consensus prior to forwarding proposals to the Centenary Committee for consideration. When more than one proposal was received from a county, applications would be returned with a request that municipal authorities agreed on one initiative. The Centenary Committee retained the power to place its stamp of approval on a project.[93] The group approved this new assessment strategy. Yet when the 1 January 1964 deadline hit, the Centenary Committee discovered that only fifteen of the province's eighteen counties had submitted proposals. It therefore extended the deadline until 1 September 1964 in hopes of receiving viable applications from all jurisdictions.

The Centenary Committee worked hard to ensure that as many citizens as possible benefited from 1967 activities and from Centennial Grants Program funding. However, one Ottawa official doubted the group's effectiveness. In a confidential 1964 report, Peter Aykroyd, then the Centennial Commission's Director of Special Projects, critiqued the group's legislated mandate. Following a visit to Nova Scotia, the director wrote that although the *Centenary Celebration Act* conferred "broad powers," the Centenary Committee itself had "limited powers." The group successfully executed its duties in vetting projects, but he noted with derision that "as to their usefulness in carrying out other planning and preparations for Centennial generally in the Province, this remains to be seen." Aykroyd also expressed concern about the group's reluctance to assume more work, referencing a conversation with Chair Abbie Lane in which she expressed doubt about whether the Centenary Committee was willing to expand its responsibilities.[94] Some members, including Lane, felt that they were already undertaking significant roles and carrying a heavy load in centennial planning. The sheer volume of this demanding work was compounded by the fact that members were not financially compensated for their time. Lane noted, perhaps in hopes of changing her group's remuneration, that her colleagues in other provincial jurisdictions were paid to hold similar positions and perform the same tasks. There appears to have been little, if any, response to this report, either at the federal or provincial level. Nevertheless, in its 1965 "Plan of Action," in a likely attempt to justify their work, the Centenary Committee reaffirmed its mandate, and noted its responsibility to "awaken, stimulate and develop public interest and active participation in planning and preparing for Nova Scotia's observance of Canada's centenary."[95]

The Centenary Committee's workload increased significantly in the fall of 1964. Following the September deadline for Centennial Grants Program proposals, the group worked diligently to assess applications. At its November meeting held in Truro, the group announced that it had approved twenty-six projects, including grants for the Cape Breton Miners' Museum, Amherst's Centennial Building, a community centre in Wolfville, and several recreation parks across the province.[96] The number of approved projects exceeded the number of provincial counties, because some per capita grant allocations allowed for more than one undertaking to be funded. Successful applicants were advised of the results and told to start work on the final requirements for approval. Initiating agencies, often a community group or municipality, faced two major hurdles before they received the government's final stamp of approval. First, they had to raise the required minimum of one-third funding for their project. The remaining two-thirds were cost-shared equally between the federal and provincial governments, as outlined in the Federal-Provincial Grants Program Agreement that governed the program.[97] Second, they had to provide assurances that projects were sustainable in the long term, relieving governments from future maintenance and operations obligations. Successful initiating agencies were advised to start community fundraising as soon as possible in order to raise their share of funds and guarantee their undertaking's viability.

The Centenary Committee also informed forty-two applicants that their Centennial Grants Program proposals had been rejected. Projects were turned down for a variety of reasons, including those that were "ineligible generally, lacked sufficient evidence of required financing, were filed too late or were filed for an area where a project had been approved."[98] Not surprisingly, the selection of certain projects over others raised the ire of some communities. In June 1965, T.G. Adams, chair of Annapolis Royal's centennial committee, accused the Centenary Committee of playing politics. He charged that his town's proposal was rejected because Annapolis's member of the Legislative Assembly, Peter Nicholson, sat as a member of the opposition Liberals.[99] Stanfield's Tories had been in power since 1956 and were a mighty political force to be reckoned with in Nova Scotia. Given that they had ruled the province for almost a decade, it was easy to see how frustrations could be mounting. Adams's accusations caused a stir in Halifax, as everyone from the Centenary Committee to the Premier's Office reacted swiftly to refute the allegations. Stanfield wrote to Nicholson and argued that the charges were groundless. Serious consideration had been given to the Centenary Committee's composition, he noted, in order to ensure that it had "the confidence of Nova Scotians regardless of political affiliation." He staunchly defended Abbie Lane and acknowledged that although she was a Conservative, she was "a woman of independent thought."[100] Richard Donahoe wrote to Adams and asserted that charges of favouritism and political interference were "ridiculous." He pointed to three other counties represented by opposition government members whose projects had been approved.[101] Annapolis had failed to provide the necessary funding assurances, even when requested to do so by the Centenary Committee. The rejection of the project, he asserted, had nothing to do with politics.[102]

Quite apart from the Centennial Grants Program, communities undertook their own commemorative projects. One Nova Scotia town even attempted to curry favour and obtain political leverage from Ottawa's Centennial Commission. In February 1965, some Truro residents sought support for the municipal amalgamation of surrounding towns in a bid to become a city.[103] The Centennial Commission, not surprisingly, held a firm apolitical position – a policy it found itself reiterating time and time again. Nevertheless, J.M. Murphy, secretary of Colchester County's Centenary Celebration Committee, wrote to John Fisher, suggesting that his group needed an "outside agency to trigger" amalgamation discussions and asking whether the Centennial Commission would "be interested in lighting the fuse."[104] The commissioner, however, knew better than to wade into the debate. He told Murphy that despite having a "soft spot" for Truro, he could not become politically involved in the campaign.[105]

Centennial Grants Program funding was, without a doubt, an exceptional infrastructure opportunity. Yet not all Nova Scotia communities were ready to capitalize on the scheme. By the summer of 1965 several counties had yet to submit proposals. The twenty-six projects that were approved the previous fall did not maximize the per capita funding allocations set out in the Centennial Grants Program. This was not an ideal situation. Both provincial politicians and the Centenary Committee felt strongly that Nova Scotia had to ensure that all available government monies were exhausted. Many were convinced that an opportunity to construct cultural capital projects would not materialize again anytime soon. With $1,273,600 already dispersed, there remained $234,134 to be allocated.[106] The Centenary Committee moved quickly to do all it could to ensure funds were used. In June 1965, it announced that monies were still available for projects in nine counties – Annapolis, Antigonish, Colchester, Halifax, Lunenburg, Richmond, Shelburne, Victoria, and Yarmouth. Of these, three were entirely without any 1967 project. The remaining six had not exhausted all their available per capita funding for a variety of reasons.[107] Some, like Annapolis, were unable to guarantee that the requisite one-third in community funds would be raised. The most shocking appearance on the list was Halifax County. Its rumoured project, a state-of-the-art aquarium and scientific research centre, was bogged down in political and economic battles to such an extent that no funding proposal had been submitted to the Centenary Committee. The public and City Council were divided over the aquarium proposal, as political manoeuvring played out dramatically in the press. This high level of disagreement left the project in dire straits. Worse still was the possibility that Nova Scotia's largest centre would forego a Centennial Grants Program project, as well as the per capita monies available in government funds, because of political indecision and incompetence.

The Centenary Committee was adamant that Nova Scotia had to make use of all available funds. In July 1965, it invited proposals from the nine counties still eligible for grants and set a deadline of 1 September for applications, in the hopes that these areas would seize this second chance.[108] Many were shocked to discover that monies were still available. One *Chronicle-Herald* editorial expressed disbelief and pleaded for those nine counties to capitalize on this unique opportunity to build infrastructure. "It would be tragic indeed," the newspaper claimed, "if these community leaders who could now obtain funds practically sit back and do nothing here because a centennial grant would involve some time, effort and local expense." It stressed that it would be a "sad indication of the value Nova Scotians place upon this nation's heritage" if this development opportunity were to pass by.[109]

Applications from the nine counties poured in, and by November 1965, the Centenary Committee made additional funding recommendations to the provincial government. Unsuccessful in the first round, T.G. Adams and his committee re-submitted an application for Annapolis – this time with the required assurances – and were approved for a centennial grant of $13,200 to renovate the town's District Community Centre.[110] By this time, thirty-seven projects – many of which had already broken ground – had been approved across Nova Scotia. Other communities were actively engaged in community fundraising campaigns to meet their financial obligations, which had to be secured by 15 January 1966, and to provide assurances that their projects would be viable post-1967.[111] Many initiatives, such as the Cape Breton Miners' Museum, had already secured the requisite community funding and produced a business plan that provided resources for long-term sustainability. These terms were critical. Failure to meet them would result in government monies being rescinded, and a project would be considered abandoned.[112]

Despite best efforts to exhaust all available funds, it was clear by the summer of 1967 that not all proposed projects would proceed. The town of Canso, which had received approval for a community ice rink and recreation centre, failed to acquire property for the project or raise the required one-third community funding, and had not provided assurances that the initiative was viable after the centennial year. The Centenary Committee declared the centre abandoned and rescinded the town's $30,000 in Centennial Grants Program funding.[113] Others suffered similar fates but for different reasons. A public library to be housed at Sainte Anne's College at Church Point in Digby County was voluntarily – albeit reluctantly – abandoned in the spring of 1967. It had become collateral damage in the ongoing debate over whether the college should remain in Church Point or move to Yarmouth. Administrators were hesitant to construct a new facility in the face of institutional indecision. They abandoned the project and relinquished their $100,000 in Centennial Grants Program monies. However, these foregone grants meant that funds were available for other projects. Although the deadline for project proposals had long since passed, the Centenary Committee was willing, in this case, to accept proposals for other projects to ensure that all available funds were dispensed. Le Club Richelieu Church Point jumped on this opportunity and proposed the Clare Centennial Recreation Park as Digby County's project, which included a children's playground, tent site, skating area, boardwalk, tennis and badminton courts, and picnic area. While the group noted that "the population of Clare feels deeply sorry that [the library] could not go through," it hoped that the college's loss would be the county's gain. The group's request for $14,800 was quickly approved, and the Centenary Committee redistributed the excess funds between the Cape Breton Miners' Museum and Lunenburg's Fisheries Museum and Marine Aquarium.[114]

Nova Scotia's thirty-six projects approved and constructed under the Centennial Grants Program represented a wide array of undertakings. Of these, 40 per cent were considered "cultural," which included museums and libraries, while the remaining 60 per cent were categorized as "recreational," which encompassed community centres, swimming pools, arenas, and parks.[115] These percentages mirrored trends in other provinces. Across Canada, 55 per cent of Centennial Grants Program projects were considered recreational, reflecting the importance of expanding leisure infrastructure initiatives.[116] Opening ceremonies for these projects were major civic events that were usually marked with the raising of the centennial flag and hosted by prominent local, provincial, and even federal politicians. These ceremonies marked the culmination of hard work by communities to organize, fundraise, and support an initiative under the Centennial Grants Program banner. These projects "of a lasting nature" increased the visibility of 1967 across provinces, stimulated the economy, and, perhaps just as important, secured wide participation in centennial events.

A central component of both the Centennial Commission and the Centenary Committee's mandates was to ensure widespread grassroots participation in 1967 events. Popular discourses focused on the importance of community participation and locally run initiatives, which were both considered keys to making the year's celebrations a success. The Centennial Commission certainly emphasized the central role that "ordinary Canadians" were expected to play that year. "Public enthusiasm and participation," the Crown corporation noted in its 1965–6 annual report, were "essential ingredients in a national birthday celebration."[117] Notwithstanding these declarations, it was clear that, in the end, state apparatus largely directed how the 1967 commemorations were to be marked. Organizations such as the Centennial Commission and the Centenary Committee exercised great power over how the celebrations were devised and executed, and how the year was to be memorialized. Just as significant, these bodies retained considerable control over valuable resource distribution. In the case of Nova Scotia's

Centenary Committee, the group dictated how monies were to be spent throughout the province and vetted each county's proposals. The group's power over valuable resources that directed how celebrations took place was underscored by the fact that neither the provincial nor the federal government rejected any of the Centenary Committee's funding recommendations. This spoke to the crucial role the committee played as an arbiter of cultural projects. Despite Peter Aykroyd's assertion that the centennial was a "decentralized affair,"[118] this history shows that commemorations remained squarely under government control and direction through planned, coordinated, and centralized programming.

In its final report to the federal government, the Centennial Commission emphasized that Canada's year-long celebrations were unique and had achieved something on a grand scale that had not been previously contemplated, let alone accomplished. The report noted, "There was no precedent to follow or model on which to rely," and observed that "this is believed to be the first time that any nation set out in such a manner to celebrate a national anniversary throughout the course of an entire year."[119] Pierre Berton's *1967: The Last Good Year* claims that "no country in the world had ever before planned a year-long birthday party."[120] Centennial Commission planners had little precedent to work from, and the organization proceeded with planning on an ad hoc basis, an approach that was necessitated by the very limited direction it received from Ottawa. This ad hoc approach was underscored by "open-ended legislative guidelines" that left financial and programming decisions largely up to John Fisher and his team.[121] Canada's massive year-long celebrations, then, were something of an innovation in the Western world. Although the country's 1927 Diamond Jubilee of Confederation celebrations provided a template for commemorative activities, those festivities did not come close to matching the range of programming or the finances funnelled into the 1967 celebrations.[122]

Canada's emphasis on involving all citizens in every community in 1967 events was unique. The celebrations served as a template for other Western countries marking significant public occasions, including the United States, which looked to Canada's experiences as a model for its 1976 bicentennial celebrations.[123] The emphasis on mass citizen involvement in commemorations was unique in the post-war Western world. While many governments attempted to involve the public in celebrations, this did not necessarily translate into popular control over, or direction of, commemorative activities. The public participated in myriad ways, and its contributions to celebrations varied considerably.[124] Nevertheless, bicentennial celebrations in the United States and Australia, in 1976 and 1988, respectively, demonstrated a desire by governments to incorporate the wider population in festivities.[125] Lyn Spillman notes that bicentennial celebrations in these two countries were distinguished from previous commemorations in two important ways. First, the federal governments in both countries were considerably more involved in bicentennial event coordination and planning. Second, "by contrast with the centennials, the central promotion of the events at a vernacular, community level was more intense in the bicentennials. Central organizers cast their net as widely as possible. They saw their role as one of promotion rather than direction, but they did touch local community celebrations more than they had done a hundred years earlier." This impulse to include citizens in celebrations to shore up notions of national identity and unity served another purpose. It allowed governments to respond to conditions of modernity that challenged notions of national identity by framing an event that brought citizens together under a united front.[126] Canada's push for wide participation in 1967 events, then, was ground-breaking and shaped later celebrations throughout the Western world.

The Nova Scotia government and provincial centennial organizers certainly saw one of their roles as bringing citizens together under the umbrella of a large-scale public centennial event. As the next chapter – the first of four case studies – shows, the Highland Games and Folk Festival, one of the largest 1967 programs undertaken in the province, was a resounding success. It welcomed thousands of participants and visitors to participate in centennial programming. At the same time, this event both upheld and challenged popular understandings of the province. The result was a more nuanced understanding of Nova Scotia's history, but one that nevertheless privileged certain citizens' participation in particular ways at a critical juncture in the province's history.

Chapter 2

"A true Scot would have sworn he was in Scotland": The 1967 Nova Scotia Highland Games and Folk Festival

After all, Nova Scotia is New Scotland.
John Fisher, National Centennial Commissioner

On a sunny morning in August 1967, thousands of spectators packed Halifax sidewalks to catch a glimpse of an elaborate Scottish-themed parade as it wound its way through the city's downtown. The procession was an impressive display of pomp and pageantry. The parade was led by none other than Scotland's world-famous Muirhead Pipe Band, which played a selection of traditional songs from its homeland to the delight of cheering crowds. Piping and drumming bands from across Canada accompanied the group, as hundreds of kilted highland dancers followed behind and performed in time to the music. Throngs of highland games athletes marched along as twenty floats travelled the parade route. Even some audience members contributed to the Celtic atmosphere, donning kilts and dancing to the convoy's pipes and drums.[1] Spectators could be forgiven if they thought they suddenly had been transported to another time and place. "A true Scot would have sworn he was in Scotland," one local newspaper reported, describing that morning's scene where the "swirls of the kilt and scurries of the pipes reflected age-old Scottish traditions in the capital city of New Scotland."[2]

Tartanism Triumphs Again: A Highland Games and Gathering of the Clans

This ornate parade was part of the closing ceremonies for Nova Scotia's Highland Games and Folk Festival,[3] an extravagant four-day program that commemorated Canada's centennial. It was a popular provincial initiative that attracted thousands of competitors and spectators to Halifax that summer. In its nascent stages, the Highland Games and Folk Festival was imagined as a way to reinforce the idea that Nova Scotian identity was quintessentially and authentically Scottish. The celebration was envisioned as part of a larger social, cultural, and economic process that deliberately branded the region as innately Scottish. To be sure, the festival's inclusion of a multicultural folk festival disrupted the powerful Celtic discourses that largely framed the event. It pointed to a tension that was slowly emerging between the dominant and prevailing Scottish images and the fact that the province's cultural identity was much more complex. Indeed the folk festival served as a powerful reminder that there was much more to Nova Scotia's history that went beyond popular folk and tartanized characterizations.

The Highland Games and Folk Festival was a provincially organized event, but the initiative originated, oddly enough, with Ottawa bureaucrats. In 1965, concerns were raised that not all of the country's regions had plans to mark the first 100 years of Confederation in a grand style befitting the occasion. "In looking at the celebration side of the centennial in Canada," Centennial Commissioner John Fisher remarked, "we are conscious of some geographical gaps." With two years to go before the country was thrown into 1967 festivities, he was worried that no large-scale undertakings were planned for the Maritimes or Ontario,[4] in stark contrast to sizeable commemorative programs already being organized in other parts of the country. This included British Columbia's Trade Fair and Naval Review, Calgary's international rodeo, Winnipeg's hosting of the 1967 Pan Am Games, and the possibility that Regina would sponsor what was sure to be a spectacular centennial event, an International Meat Show. Looking eastwards, Quebec City was planning for Canada's 1967 Winter Games, while Montreal was busy constructing Île Notre-Dame in preparation for Expo 67.

Fisher had just cause for concern. Part of the Centennial Commission's mandate was to ensure that Canada's birthday was observed in every region of the country.[5] Canadians were busy preparing local community celebrations. However, Ottawa wanted to make sure that 1967 was commemorated with a series of larger events. The Centennial Commission therefore encouraged all provinces to introduce strategically located programming and noted that it would provide significant financial grants as incentives to ensure that regional attractions took place that appealed to locals and tourists alike. When it came to Nova Scotia, Fisher, who had attended Dalhousie Law School and launched his broadcasting career in Halifax, knew exactly what he wanted to see implemented. "Although it is unofficial, without commitment, and purely exploratory," the commissioner wrote to Richard Donahoe, Nova Scotia's minister in charge of centennial affairs, "I have been wondering how you might react to the suggestion that Nova Scotia be host to a world-wide gathering of the clans and Highland Games." Fisher believed that such an event would pay tribute to Nova Scotia's historical connections to Scotland and draw participants and spectators from the "Old Country" into Canada for 1967. The commissioner was convinced that a highland event was the perfect way to celebrate the province's cultural heritage. "After all," he wrote, "Nova Scotia is New Scotland."[6]

The Centennial Commissioner's comments spoke to popular understandings about the historical relationship between Nova Scotia and Scotland, and the supposed natural and logical connections between these two regions. Ian McKay reveals that during the twentieth century state and cultural producers promoted and firmly entrenched the concept that Nova Scotia was, in essence, a "Scottish haven." This was accomplished through tactics that included the Nova Scotia government's adoption of an official provincial tartan,[7] promotional literature that touted the area's apparently inherent Celtic nature, and the formal designation of historical sites deemed significant to the history of Scottish settlers.[8] The idea of Nova Scotia as a quaint, Celtic refuge was further promulgated by Angus L. Macdonald, the legendary Liberal premier. Macdonald, who dominated provincial politics from the 1930s until his death in office in 1954, was heavily invested in these cultural pursuits, and his name was synonymous with these endeavours.[9] T. Stephen Henderson argues that the tourism industry "flourished" under the premier's watchful eye, and that his "efforts to shape Nova Scotia into a veritable 'New Scotland' for the tourists' gaze were inspired partly by a desire to cash in on public demand for nostalgia and 'otherness,' and partly by his own romantic conviction that the best Scottish culture could be found in the province."[10] These ideas were captured most fittingly one year after Macdonald's death during the 1955 opening ceremonies of the Canso Causeway, the permanent link connecting mainland Nova Scotia to Cape Breton Island. That celebration epitomized the notion that the province, and Cape Breton in particular, was Scotland's North American counterpart.[11]

These efforts collectively became known as "tartanism," a powerful social and cultural process that branded Nova Scotia as a sacred land deeply rooted in Celtic traditions, where Scottish identity retained a prominent and privileged position. McKay defines tartanism as "the system of signs testifying to the supposed Scottish essence of Nova Scotia."[12] Tartanism had – and continues to have – serious repercussions for the region, especially for Indigenous, African-Canadian, Acadian, English, and Irish communities, among other cultural groups, whose histories were, at best, marginalized.[13] This was unquestionably a process central to colonial and settler narratives in the province. Ian McKay and Robin Bates problematize tartanism's inherent racism and the "politics of whiteness," arguing that this phenomenon "implied ... a ranking of white races with Scots on top." This resulted in a "form of racialized heritage that obscured the facts of that history and ruled out alternative interpretations of its meaning."[14] This translated into a racialized and politicized mythical portrayal of the province whereby the Scots "deserved social and cultural leadership positions." As McKay and Bates argue, "Constantly hailing the white races of Nova Scotia in tourism literature, for example, does not overtly call for the subordination of people of colour. Nevertheless, such a practice applied the concept of race to a host of phenomena, from heather to folksongs, which it then assorted into a hierarchy of significance. As the Scots became the more celebrated of the white races in the fast-expanding tourism industry, that industry privileged things that were Scottish over things that were not."[15]

Tartanism was also used as a regional economic development tool to shore up Nova Scotia's burgeoning tourism industry.[16] Marjory Harper and Michael Vance contend that these efforts were driven by the "commercial dictates of 'heritage,'" where the quest for economic stability and cultural identity gave "a particular potency to the heritage hunters' search for an imagined past in which the myth is so much more attractive than the truth." The result was nothing short of a "tartan travesty," where "Scottish identity has become little more than a series of unconnected marketable goods."[17] Tartanism, then, produced a commercialized Nova Scotian identity based on distorted, colonial, and settler historical interpretations of the province.

Planning for the Provincial Celebration

John Fisher's Scottish highland games and gathering of the clans proposal relied on and fuelled notions of tartanism, a concept that held currency both within Nova Scotia and outside the province's borders. The commissioner undertook nothing less than a personal crusade to see his vision become a reality. He became the driving force behind this event that bolstered the common perception that Nova Scotian identity was defined primarily by the province's historical connections to Scotland. This was undoubtedly propelled by his personal ties to Nova Scotia, which likely shaped his understandings of the province's cultural heritage. He engaged in a protracted campaign with senior Nova Scotia government and centennial officials about his proposal, but Ottawa bureaucrats did not need to be convinced of its merits. Centennial Commission officers took up the cause with gusto and pressured their Nova Scotia counterparts to move forward with plans for a Scottish celebration. The province responded slowly, albeit positively, to the proposal. In May 1965, the province's Centenary Committee started consultations in earnest about the feasibility of holding a highland games and gathering of the clans.[18] This was not enough, though, for Robbins Elliott, the Centennial Commission's Planning branch director. Merely a week after the Centenary Committee decided to assess the event's viability, he contacted C. Bruce Fergusson, the group's secretary, to express concern that he had not yet received a final decision from the province about Fisher's proposal.[19]

The Centennial Commission was not prepared to let a small matter like Nova Scotia's slow response get in its way of planning an event on the province's behalf. Ottawa officials, likely spurred on by Fisher, embarked on an aggressive lobbying campaign to gather high-profile political support that could be used as leverage to induce Nova Scotia into a speedy and positive decision. Although Elliott conceded that Ottawa had no choice but to wait on the province's decision, his staff was instructed to keep a close eye on any developments and not to be afraid to use what leverage they had to help the program come to fruition.[20] For his part, Elliott enlisted the help of Alasdair Graham, the future Canadian senator who was then special assistant to the powerful Liberal Minister of Labour, Allan J. MacEachen. A successful appeal to this regional Cabinet minister's office for support, Elliott knew, would undoubtedly put significant pressure on the province and strong-arm it into moving forward with the event. Graham not only responded favourably to the proposal, but even suggested numerous Scottish-themed activities for a week-long celebration. National and international participants could be invited to compete in highland dancing, athletic, and band piping contests. He suggested that a concert by Don Messer, the famous New Brunswick fiddler whose popular *Don Messer's Jubilee* was a CBC television mainstay throughout the 1960s, could be held. In addition, a Highland Ball might be staged with attendees in Scottish costume.[21] Despite Graham's enthusiasm, his response did not speed up a decision from Nova Scotia's Centenary Committee. By the fall of 1965, with no decision from Nova Scotia on the horizon about holding an event, Fisher's patience waned and he reminded Donahoe that Ottawa remained "very interested" in seeing a Scottish program take place.[22] The province was determined, however, that it would not be pressured, and it firmly reminded Ottawa that the decision to host an event was Nova Scotia's and Nova Scotia's alone.[23] Donahoe informed the National Centennial Conference's November 1965 meeting in Halifax that the province still had Fisher's suggestion under advisement. It was a not-so-subtle reminder that, even in the face of mounting pressure from Ottawa, Halifax intended to retain jurisdiction over any provincially organized 1967 projects.

Behind the scenes, Nova Scotia centennial officials knew that a major celebration could prove lucrative, and that a decision had to be made sooner rather than later if they wanted to capitalize on the opportunity and receive funding from Ottawa. Consultations revealed that there was interest in holding a highland games, a provincial talent competition,[24] and even a regatta.[25] Of those options, senior bureaucrats believed that a Scottish festival would be a particularly worthwhile and popular 1967 tourist attraction.[26] In January 1966 the Centenary Committee requested that Frank Wallace, Atlantic Canada's Halifax-based regional centennial officer, propose a provincial program.[27] Wallace, an engineer from Nova Scotia, worked at his father's advertising firm, Wallace Advertising Agency. As regional officer, he implemented Centennial Commission initiatives across Atlantic Canada.[28] To assist Wallace with drafting the proposal, the Centenary Committee struck a subcommittee whose members included Bruce Fergusson, Provincial Centennial Planning Coordinator Lorne V. Hutt, Provincial Chair of the Centennial Committee on the Arts Lester Page, and Centenary Committee members Isobel MacAulay and James Bond.[29] Ottawa was pleased, even relieved, that Nova Scotia finally had taken action and hoped that plans for a highland games and gathering of the clans festival would soon be underway.[30]

However, when Wallace submitted his program proposal in February 1966, it was clear that his vision for a provincial celebration differed significantly from John Fisher's. Instead of a Scottish highland games and gathering of the clans, Wallace proposed an "ethnic festival" that showcased all of Nova Scotia's "major racial origins." Titled "Spectacular Celebration," the event would take place during a designated

"Centennial Week" in August 1967.[31] The showcase event would present a narrative of the province's history since Confederation that relied on participation from Nova Scotia's cultural communities that Wallace wanted included, namely the "English, Irish, Scottish, Welsh, French, German, Netherlands, Negroes, Italian, Jewish, Polish, Scandinavian (Danish, Icelandic, Swiss, Norwegian), native Indians, [and] Asiatics." These groups, Wallace proposed, would help present an all-inclusive and harmonious history of the province. Other events Wallace suggested included Scottish highland games, and performances by Acadian, African-Canadian, and Mi'kmaw groups. The result would be "a fabric picture of all Nova Scotians woven of the various threads." Programming would include athletic competitions, aquatics in the Northwest Arm, a parade, pipe band competition, visual arts exhibition, centennial ball, interfaith service, and performances by the Halifax Symphony. Most events would take place at the Garrison Grounds, the only Halifax site that could accommodate large-scale performances and the thousands of spectators and participants expected to attend. A cooperative publicity campaign undertaken between the federal government and Nova Scotia's Travel Bureau and its Bureau of Information would ensure that the province took full advantage of this unique tourism opportunity.[32] It was an ambitious and wide-ranging proposal that, Wallace believed, would be a major summer tourist attraction.

Although the Centenary Committee's subcommittee was "appreciative" of Wallace's efforts, it rejected his proposal in March 1966. It instead recommended holding a Scottish highland games and a folk festival, a program that was more closely aligned with Fisher's vision. The committee proposed that the highland games would be the main event, with a folk festival, undoubtedly inspired by Wallace's proposal, slated as a secondary and complementary component.[33] Several factors likely influenced the committee's decision. Wallace's ambitious week-long program required considerable funding and much planning on relatively short notice. Although Nova Scotia did not know how much the Centennial Commission was prepared to ante up, organizers were convinced that Ottawa's intense lobbying and its desire to see Fisher's program implemented meant that it could expect a significant sum. The province likely did not want to jeopardize 1967 funding by proposing an event that was not aligned with the Centennial Commissioner's vision. The group also certainly knew that a Scottish program could be marketed easily in a province where tartanism held significant sway. The government was already heavily invested in promoting Scottishness as an integral component of the tourism industry. As such, this kind of program meshed well with Nova Scotia's broader tourism industry goals. Further, organizers may have dismissed the idea that other cultural groups had much of a tradition and history that could be celebrated. Some no doubt saw a multi-ethnic show as a risky proposition that would be an insufficient draw to entice participants and spectators to Halifax. With so many centennial events taking place in 1967, organizers likely wanted to capitalize on a clearly branded program that played to the province's strengths. Whatever the reasoning, the Centenary Committee approved a highland games and folk festival as the province's 1967 program.[34]

Isobel MacAulay and Wallace drafted a new program, which they tabled with the Centenary Committee in June 1966. Titled the Nova Scotia Centennial Highland Games & Folk Festival (Canadian Championships), the event would take place in Halifax from 24 to 27 August at the Garrison and Wanderers Grounds. That site was in close proximity to Citadel Hill and adjacent to the Halifax Commons, the city's popular downtown outdoor recreation area. It was the only site, the authors noted, that could accommodate the 1,000–1,500 participants and the thousands of spectators expected to attend. Although the proposal offered two distinct elements – a highland games and a folk festival – it unambiguously emphasized the central role that Scottish events and traditions were expected to play in the program. Wallace and MacAulay wrote that the event would mark 1967 "in a colourful and dramatic way," allow visitors to experience first-hand the "many facets of the exciting Scottish heritage," and "honor and perpetuate the memory of N.S.'s (New Scotland) highland Scottish pioneers." Highland games had occupied a central position in Celtic heritage throughout the centuries, and Halifax's event was expected to carry on this tradition. Scotland's earliest games, Wallace and MacAulay noted, comprised athletic competitions intended to prepare men for battle and "lend dexterity and skill at the arts of war." Scottish history was passed on through music and dance, two central components of highland games. Stories were told by "the bards and historians of the people" during these events that were then passed down through the generations. "The dance was the prerogative of the male, the warriors," the authors wrote, "as was the music of the great pipes. The plaintive loreing of a lullaby or love song was the prerogative of the woman – the homemaker."[35] Highland games, they noted, preserved Scottish history and served as tools of cultural transmission.

Nova Scotia's Highland Games and Folk Festival was set to follow in these sacred footsteps. Hoping to replicate those cultural markers that were central to Scottish highland games, Wallace and MacAulay proposed a series of music, dance, and athletic competitions and demonstrations. Three of the four days were dedicated exclusively to Scottish highland games, with participants from Canada and Scotland invited to take part. Activities included amateur and professional highland dancing, as well as individual and group piping and drumming performances. Highland athletic events such as the hammer throw, shot put, and javelin would take place, in addition to high jump, discus, relay, and running contests. Special invitations would be extended to certified judges who would preside over competitions and "lend a professional air to the festivities." Highland societies from across Canada would be consulted about formal procedures that guaranteed the program's integrity and legitimacy.[36] All necessary protocols had to be respected and carefully incorporated into the event to ensure that this was an authentic Scottish highland gathering. Programming had to emphasize an "atmosphere of sociability," a crucial component of any highland games. A Scottish parade through Halifax's downtown would foster a "highland atmosphere," and a formal de rigueur Gaelic "Ciad Mile Failte" opening ceremony should be included. Participants could enter a golf tournament where competitors were required to wear kilts. Exhibits that showcased "Gaelic language and literature, clan lore, Gaelic music and song and other examples dedicated to the preservation of the Celtic culture" had to be displayed. Together, these elements would legitimize the event as a Scottish celebration and recreated those components necessary to bring a celebratory highland spirit to Halifax in 1967. "The Highland Games are as Scottish as the heather or the tartan itself," Wallace and MacAulay wrote, noting that "there is nothing to match a great highland gathering for pageantry and spectacle."[37]

The final day of the provincial celebration would be devoted to a provincial folk festival to showcase handcrafts, displays, and performances. It was clear, however, that the folk festival was conceived as a complementary attraction that was secondary to the highland games. In spite of this supporting role, the folk festival was overseen by a group of well-respected and active members of Nova Scotia's arts community who had agreed, Wallace and MacAulay noted in their proposal, to work with provincial celebration organizers to bring that part of the program to fruition. The group that oversaw the folk festival was chaired by Lester Page, the chairman of the Committee on the Arts, and included Evelyn Garbory, artistic director for the Committee on the Arts, and Donald Wetmore, arts supervisor for the provincial Department of Education. They worked closely with the Nova Scotia Folk Arts Council, a voluntary organization whose mandate was to support folk arts in the province. Although the Folk Arts Council had been established only in April 1966, it had already hosted a very successful international cultural gathering and was expanding its activities.[38] On the basis of this work, it was asked to oversee the provincial folk festival. It enthusiastically agreed and produced a comprehensive strategy to maximize involvement from Nova Scotia's cultural communities. Participants would be selected from nine regional folk festival competitions to be held across the province in the spring of 1967. Groups and individuals would perform before an expert panel of judges who would select finalists for the Halifax program. Performance categories included "ethnic" and "non-ethnic" vocals, instrument, dance, and best original, authentic, and modern folk-song. In addition, awards would be given for the best "displays of ethnic crafts, designs, cooking recipes, [and] history albums."[39] The council hoped that this wide range of competitive divisions would pique the interest of individuals and cultural groups from across Nova Scotia.

Concerns were raised, though, about whether a folk festival would generate enough interest to justify holding the event. Organizers therefore decided to award fifty-six cash prizes for the best performances in order to encourage entries, guarantee high attendance numbers, and foster a hearty dose of competition. It was a surprising move. Only several months previously, Frank Wallace had predicted that a multi-ethnic event would be a major attraction for both locals and tourists. Now he questioned whether a similarly themed folk festival would even entice spectators to the grounds, and he advised that cash prizes should be awarded as incentives. Offering inducements was likely a contentious decision. Monetary incentives were not part of provincial arts organizations' policies, nor were they hallmarks of the folk arts sector generally. However, some believed that this mechanism was necessary to ensure participation, as centennial year would see cultural groups involved in many other celebratory activities taking place across Nova Scotia.[40] While such tactics served material purposes, Stuart Henderson observes, they commercialized "visible exhibitions of difference ... as tangible commodities to be judged and evaluated."[41] Organizers wanted the folk festival to be just as successful as the highland games, and proffering prizes would likely attract participants and spectators. They were well attuned to the predicament of awarding prize money, but pressures to ensure a successful program necessitated this tactic. Wallace and MacAulay undoubtedly faced pressure from the Centenary Committee to ensure high attendance numbers at the folk festival. While highland games were sure to attract visitors, they were likely instructed by the provincial committee to implement inducements to shore up attendance numbers.

While Nova Scotia faced considerable pressure to implement an entirely Scottish program, the inclusion of a folk festival, however secondary, meshed well with broader 1967 goals. Part of the Centennial Commission's mandate was to recognize Canada's rich and diverse cultural tapestry, and to help citizens "gain a better knowledge of the true face of their country and to love it more."[42] Ottawa encouraged programming that showcased "the contributions to the growth and development of [the] country by peoples of several races and many nationalities."[43] A folk festival, then, was an entirely fitting commemorative event. Yet, while the Centennial Commission saw considerable value in these spectacles, questions have been raised about how ethnic communities are represented in the public sphere. Folk festivals are used often as tools that showcase "other" groups, where participants are frequently portrayed as "quaint and exotic," "primordial and ancient," and not "members of modern, urban twentieth-century society."[44] Philip Bohlman suggests that such festivals are sites where ethnic communities are presented as and reduced to mere displays of music, costume, and food.[45]

Canada was not immune to such spectacles. The Canadian Pacific Railway (CPR) sponsored folk festivals in the 1920s and 1930s to showcase immigrants' cultural heritage. J. Murray Gibbon, the railway's publicity manager who spearheaded many of these festivals, believed that folk arts and music activities could "serve as unifying elements and a means of communicating cross cultures" in the name of nation-building.[46] Yet these spectacles further allowed the dominant white majority to display tolerance towards other cultural groups while simultaneously maintaining their own power. Stuart Henderson's work on the CPR's folk festivals argues that these performances entrenched the idea of a core national identity where "there is only 'us,' the hegemonic class of white, Anglo-Celtic Canadians, and 'they,' the Other Europeans."[47] Eva Mackey posits that during such events, ethnic communities are "mobilized as picturesque and colourful helpmates and allies in the nation-building project." The result, she argues, is an entrenchment of a Canadian mythology of tolerance that simultaneously maintains a dominant Anglo-Canadian core culture identity.[48] There are also serious concerns about portrayals of Indigenous groups in folk festivals. Daniel Francis argues that images of Indigenous peoples are frequently manipulated to freeze groups "in an historical stereotype," that also contain perceived threats to Anglo-Canadians.[49] As a result, such gatherings, Anthony Shay notes, serve as a means for "the majority Anglo community to feel good about its ability to be tolerant and culturally inclusive," and provide communities with "validation of their cultural worth." Folk festivals, then, morph into "a commodity with market value" where performances are reduced to consumptive displays, rather than authentic expressions of culture and identity.[50] Performances are often limited to non-threatening displays of handcrafts, dance, and food. Nova Scotia's centennial folk festival was premised on similar principles, with participants showcasing their heritage for spectators to consume.

The Centenary Committee was pleased with Wallace and MacAulay's highland games and folk festival proposal and gave its stamp of approval in June 1966. The group quickly turned its attention to the practical issue of bringing the program's concept to life.[51] This task proved to be difficult, as organizers were plagued with funding, administrative, and media problems. Troubles began that month when the Antigonish Highland Society's E.R. Gourley complained that the public had not been consulted about the program. He argued that his group had organized highland games since 1861, and that these collective years of professional experience had been overlooked by the celebration's planners, which would be to Nova Scotia's detriment. To add insult to injury, his group had not been given the opportunity to host, and he asserted that it presided over the only area in the province that could successfully hold such a program. "We all feel that if Highland Games were to be staged anywhere in Nova Scotia," Gourley wrote, "that they should have been staged in Eastern Nova Scotia the heart of Highland traditions and Scottish heritage."[52] The society's objections had little impact. Richard Donahoe, no doubt hoping to do damage control, assured Gourley that his group would be called upon for its expertise. However, the realities of the program's size required practical consideration, and Halifax was the only location that could cater to the thousands expected to attend.[53] The province also likely started to see the potentially lucrative possibilities of hosting a large-scale festival in Halifax and was no doubt anxious to test the city's capacity to handle a sizeable event.

Tourism was becoming an increasingly significant industry for the province. Government officials presumably wanted to see whether the 1967 program could create an appetite among locals and visitors for large festivals.

Nova Scotia forwarded its Highland Games and Folk Festival proposal to Ottawa with a request for a $75,000 grant, an amount that would be matched by the province.[54] Despite its initial enthusiasm for a Scottish-themed program, the Centennial Commission's response was surprisingly slow.[55] While this frustrated Halifax organizers, they remained keenly aware of John Fisher's commitment to provincial programming, and Ottawa's dedication to an equitable distribution of 1967 resources that would ensure regional parity so that all Canadians could participate in the celebrations.[56] Finally, in February 1967, the event was given the green light when Ottawa confirmed funding.[57] While Halifax organizers breathed a sigh of relief, they now faced serious time pressures. The celebration was scheduled to kick off in only six months, and planning had been delayed while Halifax awaited Ottawa's funding decision. It wasn't until late 1966 that the Centenary Committee had even turned its attention to hiring an event director. The committee, likely feeling the sting from the Antigonish Highland Society's earlier indictments about consultations, carefully solicited stakeholder input about a director from that group, and from the Association of Scottish Societies of Nova Scotia, the Festival of the Tartans, Festival of the Strait, and the province's nine highland societies.[58] Centenary Committee member A.J. Gorman cautioned Donahoe that some deference had to be paid to the Antigonish Highland Society: "You know as well as I do how seriously some of them take anything in connection with Highland Games. And I certainly don't want Antigonish on my neck."[59] The search for a director proved to be challenging. Two favoured candidates from Antigonish, C.I.C. MacLeod and E.R. Gourley, declined the position, citing travel conflicts[60] and poor health,[61] respectively. Likely wanting to keep some control over the event, MacLeod and Gourley encouraged Patrick Heron to tender his name for consideration. Heron was a sales manager and announcer at New Glasgow's CKEC radio and television stations, and had some highland games organizing experience. Desperate to fill the vacancy, the Centenary Committee offered Heron the job, which he enthusiastically accepted in February 1967.[62] An advisory board, including Gourley, MacLeod, and Isobel MacAulay, was appointed to assist the new director.[63] The Centenary

Committee was relieved that it had filled the position, but became aware of potential issues that foreshadowed later problems. Lester Page noted that his folk festival team "had no illusions about Heron." The group was clearly uncomfortable with the selection but was in no position to press for an alternative.[64] The Highland Games and Folk Festival was just six months away and there was no time to waste.

Heron quickly proceeded with planning, taking direction from the 1966 Wallace and MacAulay proposal and frantically pulling together a schedule. Adding to this pressure was the fact that Heron was acutely aware of the mixed feelings about his appointment. He tried to put his detractors at ease. The director conceded that he faced serious time pressures, and that while he did not want to appear "overconfident, arrogant, or bold," he informed the Centenary Committee that he hoped to "outstrip every Highland Games Activity which has ever been staged" in both "North America and the Old Country of Scotland."[65] Nova Scotia's celebration, he predicted confidently, would be "the second best thing to Expo" that year.[66]

Yet, as the Highland Games and Folk Festival quickly approached, it was clear that not all of its components had been well-managed. Just days before the opening ceremonies, serious concerns arose when several high-ranking federal and provincial centennial officials sounded the alarm that the event had received scant media coverage. Heron faced accusations that he had not undertaken an extensive or an effective promotional campaign. This allegation was shocking, given Heron's background in media and sales. To be sure, Nova Scotia's Bureau of Information had promoted the program,[67] and several newspapers had carried a handful of articles about the event. Yet there were worries that these efforts were so minimal that the celebration would fail to attract spectators. National Centennial Director Hugh O. Mills raised the alert when he discovered that Ottawa officials had difficulties obtaining event information and that few local people knew about the program. He was concerned about the province's reputation, should the event prove disastrous. Mills contacted local media guru Bruce Cochran, whose public relations firm Bruce Cochran Associates Ltd was contracted with the Centennial Commission to promote national programming throughout Nova Scotia, and asked for help promoting the event.[68]

Bureaucrats and the local press flew into action. An emergency meeting was convened on 21 August, a mere forty-eight hours before the opening ceremonies. Attendees included Patrick Heron, Lester Page, Bruce Fergusson, Hugh Mills, Bruce Cochran, Lorne Hutt, regional Centennial Commission Officer Bruce Myers, as well as representatives from the *Chronicle-Herald*. Tensions ran high at the meeting. Heron conceded that the celebration's magnitude had left him unable to devote much time to local and provincial publicity efforts, but he was confident that the national and international media campaign was successful and would translate into huge crowds. Scottish societies from across Canada had been contacted about the program, and Heron had travelled to Scotland to promote the event, encouraging Scots to cross the Atlantic that summer to visit their North American counterparts.[69] These efforts, though, were not enough for federal officials. Cochran was appalled and cautioned that Ottawa should prepare itself for a disaster. He predicted that although it was "too late to do a complete salvage job," eleventh-hour publicity could save "everyone getting a black eye." While Cochran wholeheartedly assisted with these last-minute efforts, he distanced himself from any association with provincial organizers and emphasized his limited role in the episode.[70] Publicity was boosted in what little time remained, with funding that Cochran expeditiously obtained from the Centennial Commission. Ottawa was unambiguous, though, that this assistance was not to be misinterpreted as federal meddling in or dictating an event they considered to be outside their jurisdiction.[71] It was an unusual response. Ottawa happily masterminded the program's theme and heavily lobbied to promote a particular vision, but when it came to execution, the province was left to handle matters on its own.

The next day, Halifax was flooded with a deluge of publicity for the provincial celebration. Mills secured last-minute advertising with Simpson's, Eaton's, and several local merchants, and he shored up publicity at his own store, Mills Brothers, located in downtown Halifax along bustling Spring Garden Road.[72] Cochran pushed out a flurry of media releases, as Nova Scotia Information Services held a widely publicized press conference with Scotland's Muirhead Pipe Band where the public was invited to meet the group. The *Chronicle-Herald* carried full-page advertisements that trumpeted the program's schedule and encouraged the public to attend "the Greatest Scottish Highland Event Ever to Happen in North America!" Photographs featured the Muirhead Pipe Band, kilted dancers, and highland games athletes preparing for competition.[73] Organizers pulled out all the stops and hoped that their efforts would produce results.

The New World Welcomes the Old World: The Clans Converge in Halifax

Any lingering concerns about publicity and attendance numbers were quashed when Nova Scotia's Highland Games and Folk Festival opened to great fanfare on 23 August 1967. The opening ceremonies officially launched both the folk festival and the highland games segments of the celebration. Yet spectators and participants were left with little doubt that programming focused primarily on commemorating Scottish culture, identity, and traditions. Performances, demonstrations, speeches, and media reports all underscored the notion that the event was, first and foremost, a celebration of all things Scottish. Activities got underway that morning with an ornate parade through downtown Halifax. The internationally renowned Muirhead Pipe Band led the program's 1,250 competitors through the city's streets in a colourful display of sights and sounds. Pipers, highland dancers, and athletes marched along as the masses of musicians performed traditional Scottish songs.[74] The Muirhead Pipe Band recently had captured the World's Pipe Band Championship in Oban, Scotland, and their attendance in Halifax was the crown jewel of the celebration. The band's addition to the roster was a coup for Heron and his team, who knew that its star-power alone would attract many to the festivities. It came as no surprise, then, that the group was entrusted to lead the opening ceremony's hour-long parade.

At noon, the parade reached the Wanderers Grounds, which had been transformed for the event. Two large platforms – a main stage for formal ceremonies and dancing competitions and a second stage for band and individual piping performances – had been constructed. The open-air grounds were outfitted to accommodate up to 10,000 spectators with seating for 7,000.[75] Organizers had planned well, as the event welcomed between 8,000 and 10,000 visitors each day. The official opening ceremony was no exception, as thousands made their way to the grounds for the event. Nova Scotia's Lieutenant Governor H.P. MacKeen kicked off the festivities when he fired a ceremonial cannon.[76] Acting Premier G.I. Smith invoked the Gaelic salutation "Ciad Mile Failte," a greeting that graced the event's official program. He welcomed attendees to Nova Scotia's capital city and extended a special salutation to those from Scotland.[77]

While the main stage was packed with dignitaries (whose official invitations noted that the event would "be in keeping with the Scottish tradition of Nova Scotia"[78]), none received more attention than Scottish parliamentarian Hugh Fitzroy MacLean. His presence was carefully orchestrated by organizers who believed that a successful festival required a prominent Scottish presence. He symbolically validated the event, ensured continuity with "Old World" traditions, and helped brand the festivity as an authentic Scottish celebration. The Muirhead Pipe Band certainly added to the celebration's lustre. However, Heron and his advisory board knew that having a Scottish dignitary on hand confirmed the program as a legitimate Celtic festival. They looked no further than Sir Fitzroy. A prominent writer, historian, and Scotland's Conservative Member of Parliament for the constituency of Bute and Northern Ayrshire, Sir Fitzroy was already fortuitously scheduled to visit Canada that summer. Heron drew upon historical and social connections between new and old Scotland to entice him to extend his travels and attend the Halifax event. "As you know, Nova Scotia has a strong Scottish heritage," Heron wrote, noting that the "MacLeans, Camerons, and other Scottish names are as common as days of the week, and they fill the pages of our phone books."[79] Sir Fitzroy accepted the invitation, and the press trumpeted his arrival that summer, noting that he was "coming to make sure we do things in the proper highland manner."[80]

Sir Fitzroy was front and centre at the opening ceremonies. His address to the crowd that day provided a sense of Scottish authenticity that Heron and his team craved. The parliamentarian remarked that he "never felt more truly at home than here in Nova Scotia at these games."[81] Local coverage described the kilted Sir Fitzroy as giving "a perfect demonstration ... of how the ideal guest behaves in another country." This was a stark comparison, the newspaper noted, "in the wake of General de Gaulle's mischievous visit" to Quebec where he had declared "Vive le Québec libre!"[82] Sir Fitzroy underscored the historical connections between the province and his homeland. "I had known for many years," he reflected, "that Nova Scotia had a strong Scottish element."[83] Organizers and dignitaries were delighted. Lieutenant Governor MacKeen thanked the Muirhead Pipe Band and Sir Fitzroy for "lending distinction and atmosphere to the celebrations."[84] More speeches followed from politicians and centennial officials, as did demonstrations from highland dancers and Scotland's highland games athletes. The Muirhead Pipe Band, accompanied by several musical ensembles from across Canada, then took to the stage. They performed a rousing rendition of the iconic "Scotland the Brave," a composition considered one of Scotland's unofficial national anthems, to close out the opening ceremony.

The program that unfolded over the next several days was carefully orchestrated to ensure the legitimacy and authenticity of the highland games. Heron secured sanctioning from several professional organizations in Scotland and Canada. The Athletic Association of Canada and the Nova Scotia branch of the Amateur Athletic Union of Canada had approved the track and field events. The Official Board of Dancing and the College of Piping, both located in Glasgow, Scotland, gave Halifax their blessings for their respective fields. Heron even clinched the attendance of several high-profile and certified Scottish judges who presided over the highland games competitions. Seamus MacNeill,[85] Scotland's chief pipe judge and principal of Glasgow's School of Piping and Dancing, oversaw the competitions in his field. Scotland's chief highland dancing judge, James L. MacKenzie, who was already in Nova Scotia that summer to attend the Gaelic Mod and teach lessons at the Gaelic College in St Ann's, Cape Breton, also adjudicated.[86] In addition, Daisy MacKenzie, co-chair of the Scottish Sanctioning Board, attended to judge highland dancing competitions.[87] The Scottish Sanctioning Board had approved the highland dancing events which meant that winners were crowned dominion champions. In addition, St Ann's Gaelic College awarded two scholarships of $250 each to the winners in the dancing and piping competitions. These prizes and the presence of esteemed adjudicators lent an air of professionalism and prestige to the event.

The first of three days devoted to highland games activities got underway that afternoon at the Wanderers Grounds. The local press coverage vividly captured the events and bolstered the perception that the celebration was predominantly a Scottish gathering. The site was transformed into a "mass of sound, colour and movement in the traditional Highland games fashion," as pipers, dancers, and athletes took to the fields for the start of competition.[88] Participants recruited from across Canada and Scotland did not disappoint. Over 250 athletes competed. Provincial records were broken in numerous track and field events, including the men's mile run, men's relay, the women's discus, and the men's triple jump.[89] Amateur athletes showcased their skills in the shot put, javelin, discus, as well as the high, long, and broad jumps. To be sure, not all athletic competitions were considered traditional Scottish highland events. However, organizers branded them as part of Old World traditions by including them alongside highland games events. Some of Scotland's most accomplished professional highland games sportspersons were on hand to give special demonstrations. Bill Anderson, Arthur Rowe, and Henry Grey, all of whom held world records in highland games events, were billed as the best of that country's "heavy athletes."[90] The media captured many colourful moments as these athletes, decked out in their kilted highland regalia, participated in the hammer throw, throwing the stone, and the caber toss.[91] Demonstrating "true Scottish vigour," they gave spectators the invaluable opportunity to "witness the prowess of outstanding Highland athletes."[92]

Scottish bands and pipers gave acclaimed demonstrations and competed during the event. The Muirhead Pipe Band's daily performances were cast as some of the centennial celebration's most exciting attractions.[93] Band members were kept busy during the entire event as they provided music for highland dance competitions and interacted with spectators.[94] As professionals, the band did not compete. That task was left to the other assembled masses of musicians. This included pipe bands from every Canadian province (except Newfoundland, which had no formally organized band), with thirteen groups from the Maritimes alone,[95] who showcased their skills in several categories, including marches, reels, piobaireachd,[96] and strathspeys.[97] They provided the public and the media ample photo opportunities. One particularly powerful image captured in the press featured three pipers' shadows on Halifax's streets. "Dark legends of the Highlands are quickly evoked," one newspaper observed, as these musicians marched in the opening ceremonies.[98] Images of young pipers underscored that Scottish traditions were alive and well, and continued to be nurtured across the country.[99]

Highland dancers also converged in droves and staged lively performances that showcased several styles including the highland fling, sword dance, seann triubhas,[100] and Irish jigs. Dancers from Vancouver, Victoria, and Toronto captured most of the top prizes. Chief highland dancing adjudicator James L. MacKenzie remarked that while Nova Scotia's competitors were becoming stronger, he was concerned that the region's youngest were "pushed out to dance before they were ready."[101] These youth were colourful subjects for the media, and their images were plastered across newspapers.[102] Young highland dancer Cindy McQuay from Calgary was described as a "wee lassie" and was photographed performing the highland fling in her kilt. In an attempt to bridge the distance between Old and New Scotland, the *Chronicle-Herald* posited that "the fling and the kilt are the same, no matter how far Scotsfolk stray from Scotland."[103] The presence of the youth underscored the notion that the highland spirit continued to hold a powerful place in the province's cultural identity.

The Folk Festival: A Brilliant Mosaic of Sights and Sounds

The program's organizers and the media did their part to reinforce ideas about those long-standing cultural and social connections between Scotland and Nova Scotia. However, the 24 August folk festival was, for many, a central component of the centennial celebration. The event was billed as a gathering that "encourage[d] the preservation of ... ethnic culture and ... instill[ed] pride in the younger generation in their heritage." It featured handicraft displays and performances from many cultural groups.[104] Although some performers came from across Canada, most participants were from Nova Scotia who had been chosen from nine regional festivals held across the province that spring. The Nova Scotia Folk Arts Council had organized competitions in Antigonish-Guysborough, Halifax, Yarmouth-Clare, Richmond-Inverness, Dartmouth, the South Shore, Annapolis Valley, Cumberland, and Sydney. These local festivals were popular, as many came out in droves to cheer on participants. Antigonish's gathering attracted 1,800 spectators, while Halifax hosted an audience of 6,000. Sydney's four-day festival was by far the most popular, with over 400 participants and 10,000 audience members. Over these nine regional festivals, 2,000 participants competed before crowds of 23,000. From these competitions, over 400 participants were invited to take part in the provincial finals in Halifax.[105] Regional folk festival coordinator Claude Bede downplayed the festivals' evaluative components and curiously remarked that these events had taken place in a "friendly non-competitive atmosphere."[106] Bede was delighted that these local gatherings had been so popular and felt that they signalled a significant moment in the province's cultural development.

Bede was convinced that the festivals' success signalled a larger desire to expand folk activities across the region. Their popularity underscored support for Nova Scotia's arts sector and demonstrated that these activities held a "valid place" in the province's cultural and social development.[107] Nova Scotia's arts community had to capitalize on this unique opportunity. To this end, Bede suggested a series of initiatives to move forward. He singled out some of the province's ethnic groups whose own burgeoning folk arts scene could serve as valuable templates for others looking to expand their activities. Acadian groups were particularly active in this field, the coordinator observed, and should be encouraged to draw on "the beauty of their cultural background" and share their experiences. Bede suggested that organizers be sent to Acadian festivals to recruit performers who could foster cooperative undertakings with other groups. In an apparently benevolent offer, he noted that more work was required to "aid the native Indians ... to re-discover their rich heritage," and he hoped that African-Canadians and the Dutch would be encouraged to "continue the good work [they had] accomplished" that year. These festivals were so successful that some planned to make the gatherings an annual event,[108] although there is little evidence that they continued in this format post-1967. Bede was emphatic, however, that any future folk festivals must not coincide with another major program such as the highland games, which had overshadowed the provincial folk festival.[109]

In spite of its secondary role in the program and worries that it would not have a broad appeal, the provincial folk festival was a resounding success. Spectators may have been intrigued by the idea that there were provincial groups other than the Scots whose history, traditions, and culture were worth celebrating. The festival likely challenged many peoples' beliefs about what they knew about non-Scots communities. Earlier concerns about the program's ability to draw spectators were for naught as the day-long event attracted a crowd of over 8,000. Lester Page and the Folk Arts Council were delighted. The attendance numbers were all the more impressive, considering that the event had received scant press coverage. Indeed, most advertisements for the folk festival that boasted a "brilliant mosaic" of "gay ethnic performances" had not appeared until 23 August, a mere day before the event.[110] It is difficult to discern whether adjudicated performances, prizes, and free admission (contrasted with the highland games daily admission fee of fifty cents for adults and twenty-five cents for children[111]) enticed many to the site. It is unlikely, however, that these inducements were significant enough to bring out this large crowd, as the public was likely unaware of these incentives. Newspaper advertisements made no mention of prizes or competition. Reporters, likely carefully coached by festival organizers, made few references to the adjudicated events. Performers were "not judged competitively," but were selected on the "quality of performance."[112] Organizers walked a fine line in making these distinctions. They were cognizant to underscore that performers were not competing against one another, nor were cultures being judged in relation to one another, despite being selected from regional competitions to perform in Halifax.

The day featured a wide range of music, costumed performances, and handicraft displays. Eighty groups and individuals presented, and adjudicators chose thirty-six to appear in the evening's special gala pageant.[113] Spectators and the media alike were captivated. A Dutch folk group from Antigonish and a Polish troupe from Sydney – that revealed "a bit of Polish flavour with all its gaiety and colour" – danced for the crowds and were praised for their lively and colourful performances.[114] Other presentations included a Lebanese group from Sydney, a Bulgarian ensemble from Pubnico, and a company of Swedes and Finns from Cape Breton. Although the other three days of the provincial event were dedicated to highland games, the Scots were not to be left out of the folk festival. The Scottish Country Dancers from Port Hawkesbury, a Highland choir from Amherst, and fiddlers from Sydney took to the main stage that day.[115] One of the most popular performances was by the Nyanza Micmac Children's Choir, a Cape Breton group composed of Mi'kmaw children from a local reserve who, led by a group of nuns, sang in Mi'kmaw.[116] The *Chronicle-Herald* featured a picture of the choir as it sang in front of a "wigwam" and was described as "a truly Canadian entry"[117] in the festival. While most participants were from Nova Scotia, a handful of performers from across Canada took part in the celebration. Ukrainian and Slovakian dancers from Toronto were showcased, a Polish choir from Montreal sang, and "The Minority," an English-speaking group from Quebec, performed songs in both English and French. Two large choirs from Quebec also sang for the crowds.

The festival featured a mosaic of cultural performances, although participants were expected to come together as one in a display of symbolic unity. At the end of the day, participants joined on the main stage and sang the national anthem in what many thought was the festival's most poignant moment.[118] The display thrilled organizers and observers. Further, it embodied the Centennial Commission's mandate that despite their diverse origins, all Canadians were ultimately united in their diversity. Some federal ministers agreed that such displays had to be the focal point of 1967 celebrations. In her 1969 memoir, Judy LaMarsh noted that that the purpose of the centennial was "to deepen the sense of unity among the Canadian people."[119] She asked rhetorically, "When will we ever stop making the July 1 special program a paean to our diverse ethnic roots, and begin to make it a tribute to our Canadianess?"[120] There clearly was support for folk arts displays and ethnic performances, but many believed that they should assume a secondary position during 1967 celebrations. While ethnic demonstrations were encouraged by organizers, these displays were to be contained and considered ancillary to the wider goals of showcasing a cohesive Canadian identity.

Accolades poured in for the provincial folk festival. Organizer Evelyn Garbory (albeit a biased observer) proclaimed that it was "a real triumph!" Folk Arts Council President Donald Wetmore remarked that the performances made "New Canadians proud of their heritage" and "encourage[d] them to preserve that heritage for future generations."[121] It was even proposed that the festival should become an annual event.[122] One writer suggested that the festival had to be considered very successful, given that it stood out remarkably from, and had not been overshadowed by, the Scottish program. While "one could expect Highland Games [would] be part of New Scotland's celebration," organizers deserved praise because they celebrated many cultural communities integral to the province's history.[123] Pageants, music, and handcraft displays had showcased how different groups contributed to both the region's development and Canada's rich cultural mosaic.[124] Larger issues were also at play. Some commented that the program stood as a reminder that from such spectacles of cultural diversity there emerged a stronger sense of national unity and identity. Such overt displays of nationalism apparently had the ability to contain and control the "separatist spirit" – a not so subtle reference to the political and social transformations taking place in Quebec:

> Participants ... presented a variegated exhibition of the cultural heritage which national and ethnic groups have brought to this country. Micmacs, French, Italian, Ukrainian, Chinese – the list was long of those who demonstrated the artistry which, in their homelands, has prevailed for generations. Beyond the entertainment and the pageantry, however, lay the most moving experience of all. For it was obvious to some observers, at least, that this was a mosaic of Canada, a land whose own developing tradition is, in part, the sum total of all that her people have brought to her ... The folk art festival demonstrated that out of a diversity of backgrounds there can come a national unity. It is not necessary for one group to swallow another, nor is it needful to exploit a separatist spirit.[125]

For many, then, the program not only highlighted the contributions and histories of Nova Scotia's cultural groups, it embodied the centennial spirit of national unity and identity.

The folk festival had captured the imagination of many. However, the program's closing ceremonies on 27 August left little doubt that this event was, above all else, a celebration that demarcated the privileged position that Scottish heritage and culture enjoyed in the province. The event concluded in much the same way as it had begun – with another Scottish-themed procession through the streets of Halifax, again dominated by pipers, highland dancers, and bands. "Nova Scotia's Highland Heart swelled with pride and hereditary nostalgia," the *Mail-Star* noted, as the "gala, skirling" procession with its powerful Celtic symbols wound its way through the streets.[126] The parade made its way to the Wanderers Grounds where, like the opening, the formal closing ceremonies were filled with speeches from centennial bureaucrats and politicians. Centennial Commissioner John Fisher remarked, "It has been said, that without Scots to run things, there would have been no Britain, no Commonwealth," and that "Nova Scotians, of course, claim the same thing about their native sons vis-à-vis Canada." He stated that he hoped Sir Fitzroy's upcoming visit to Cape Breton afforded him the opportunity to "hear the pipes from the cliffs above the water and know that we've kept the faith." Federal minister Allan J. MacEachen showed off his linguistic abilities when he made his remarks to the crowd in Gaelic and noted that Nova Scotia was, of course, the ideal setting for a Scottish celebration.[127]

The evening's two-hour "Concert of Champions" featured highland games and folk festival presentations. Although the evening was "a wee bit chilly," thousands converged on the site to "celebrate with the Scots and those Scottish at heart." Scotland's Johnny Forest, the kilted master of ceremonies, presided over the closing with the "necessary flavour of the Scottish dialect." Some in the crowd were apparently quite taken with the moment, as one woman rushed the stage to greet the host.[128] Reports are unclear whether she was Scottish or just Scottish at heart. Although folk festival performers were featured, it was clear that the evening was largely a Scottish event. One report noted that the spectacle "still maintained the flavour of Scotland – even though the Armdale Chorus sang a Jamaican folk song." Crowds were entertained with gospel songs from the Preston Spiritualaires, Edmonton's sailor uniform–clad Dell Hill Dancers, and the comedic stylings of Cape Breton's Hughie and Allen. A newspaper photograph of a group of Shriners who participated in the closing parade were described as, and excused for, not being Celtic, with the caption "Not Highland but still popular."[129] Performers who fell outside of these Scottish traditions were held up as anomalies and secondary actors. Not surprisingly, the media focused on the ceremony's Scottish elements. Vancouver's Kiwanis Boys

Pipe Band played "Road to the Isles," and Scotland's chief piping judge Seamus MacNeill entertained the masses with "a slow haunting selection on the bagpipes."[130] The evening featured performances by winners of the highland dance competitions, including presentations by "four wee lassies," a girls miniature pipe band from Glace Bay, and highland dancers from Antigonish. The finale was, of course, reserved for none other than the (surely exhausted) Muirhead Pipe Band, which played "Scottish Soldier." The press painted a vivid picture of this performance. The *Chronicle-Herald* observed, "The skirl from scores of Scottish pipes cut the misty night air of New Scotland" with the band's "red kilts swirling and drums rolling."[131] Such colourful descriptions no doubt thrilled organizers who had worked diligently to replicate an authentic Scottish atmosphere.

Even the audience could not escape being cast in a very particular Celtic light. The *Mail-Star* described the crowd as belonging to either Scottish or non-Scottish groups. "They were all there – the Frasers and the Lindsays, the MacDonalds and the Rosses, the MacLeans and Munros, Wallaces and Forsythes and MacIntyres," it observed, noting that "even the Sassenachs followed the swinging tartans with their eyes and their hearts and tapping toes."[132] *Sassenach*, a Gaelic word referring to a Lowland Scot that is customarily used in jest, was invoked for those who did not appreciate the Scottish music. While the sounds of mass bands and piping were described as "a magic, haunting, romantic sound, a few Sassenachs cover their ears and profess lack of understanding."[133] One photograph that featured a young piper in competition noted, "On such a hot day, when a laddie is in a piping contest, only a Sassenach would suck on a lemon in front of such an earnest competitor."[134] Such media portrayals attempted to paint the audience as a group that was clearly taken in with the event's many Scottish sights and sounds.

Although most commentators praised the Highland Games and Folk Festival, several critiques materialized in the event's wake. One searing review came from four individuals in New Glasgow who wrote to Centenary Committee Secretary Bruce Fergusson and expressed their profound disappointment with the program, which they referred to as a "Spectacular Flop." The highland games, they argued, failed to live up to their billing as "the greatest ever to be staged in North America," and described it as a "sad affair." They condemned everything from the event's management, to the composition of the bands, to the prize money awarded to competitors. They levelled accusations that the Muirhead

Pipe Band had been relegated to the role of accompanists rather than high-profile guests who deserved more solo performances.[135] While the New Glaswegians were displeased with the event's last-minute preparations and many of the program's elements, the group seemed to hold personal animosity against Director Patrick Heron. The authors noted that they were "dumbfounded" by his selection as director, an indication that despite their earlier nomination of Heron as director there was a much more complicated background and relationship at work than appeared on the surface. Others pointed to concerns about organization and public relations. A *Chronicle-Herald* editorial denounced the event as "far from being the outstanding show that it might have been." In spite of "top-notch performers, an excellent presentation of folk art, and exceptionally fine weather," the newspaper pointedly noted that "something was obviously lacking." It criticized the weak public relations and media campaign and argued that there were significant scheduling problems, noise issues, and concerns about the site. With no program information available a week before the event's opening, organizers had managed to make it "one of the best kept secrets of the year." It even speculated that serious questions would now be raised about Halifax's ability to host the upcoming 1969 Canada Summer Games.[136] These censures revealed issues that stemmed from last-minute preparations and decisions by senior bureaucrats, such as the hiring of a director just six months prior to the event, more than anything else.

After the pomp and ceremony had died away, serious personnel and financial issues came to light. Seamus MacNeill criticized the field design for being too large, which detrimentally encouraged spectators to wander the grounds and created crowd control issues.[137] However, these matters were relatively minor compared to the later deluge of complaints. Heron's tenure as director was terminated on 31 August, but unresolved matters challenged both the Centenary Committee and the provincial government.[138] The directorship had taken a significant toll on Heron, who was hospitalized for two weeks after the closing ceremonies and was unable to resolve several issues.[139] Eileen Cameron Henry claimed she was paid only $250 of the $500 promised to her by the director for production of the program's brochure. She alleged that her political stripes were to blame.[140] "If I were of the same political persuasion as Mr Heron," Henry wrote, "I have no doubt the debt would be paid very quickly. I happen to be a Liberal, by inheritance and by choice ... I will not be brushed off by a lot of words, from you, or from anyone. I, too, have quite a bit of Irish in my ancestry, and there's no race on earth that hates an injustice more."[141] She made it abundantly clear that she would never have agreed to undertake this work unless she believed she was contracted with the province.[142] Henry was eventually paid the outstanding balance but only after a protracted series of letters was exchanged between her lawyer and the provincial government. Similar complaints about non-payment of fees followed from Scotland's highland dancing judge Daisy Mac-Kenzie, and Cape Breton comedy group Hughie and Allen, who performed at the closing ceremonies. The province's lawyers were left to clean up these outstanding accounts, which were not resolved until June 1968.[143] To Heron's credit, he had been asked to assume responsibility for a major provincial centennial event where "one year's work ha[d] to be crowded into six months." Taking stock of his experience in a final report to the Centenary Committee, the director addressed the major publicity crisis that loomed just days before the opening ceremonies, and admitted that he and his team had lost opportunities to work with provincial organizations to promote the celebration. There were lessons here. Halifax's hosting of the 1969 Canadian Summer Games, Heron warned, would be a good indication of how the province dealt with these major events in the future, the handling of which was important should Nova Scotia decide to invest in future large-scale initiatives.[144]

Looking back in February 1968, the Centenary Committee provided a tepid assessment of the provincial centennial celebration. Serious organizational issues threatened to derail the event at every turn. Eleventh-hour hiring decisions, a disastrous publicity campaign, and funding difficulties jeopardized the plans of centennial bureaucrats who were determined to see Halifax host a Scottish celebration. Despite its deficiencies, the group concluded that, overall, the 1967 Highland Games and Folk Festival had been relatively successful.[145] Although the program strayed somewhat from Centennial Commissioner John Fisher's original proposal, it stayed true to his vision that Nova Scotia host a large-scale event that emphasized the province's Scottish identity. Organizers' promotion of the highland games as the most important aspect of the centennial summer event positioned the Scots as a group that deserved special recognition. The Scots were presented as the group that had made the most historical contributions to the province and that most accurately defined Nova Scotia's core cultural identity. Centennial officials, the media, and participants were complicit as they engaged in performances and discourses that privileged a Scottish identity.

This event marked a significant moment in the ongoing public construction of Nova Scotia's Scottish identity. But it did not operate in a vacuum. The celebration reinforced a particular characterization of the region that emerged during the twentieth century that saw it branded, for all intents and purposes, as a displaced Scottish region. Yet the privileging of this identity created a paradox that is difficult to overlook. Although the Highland Games and Folk Festival commemorated 100 years of Canadian Confederation, there were few reminders at the site that it was this anniversary that was being celebrated. Rather, the event became a vehicle to honour the pre-Confederation "Old World" traditions of Nova Scotia's Scottish settlers. Everything from the celebration's proposal, to the music, dancing and athletic events, to the speeches, underscored that what was being memorialized was not Canada's 1867 Confederation. This discrepancy becomes even starker when compared to the cosmopolitan and modern imaginings of Canada's future that were on display in Montreal at Expo 67.

This history reveals that during the 1960s the idea that Nova Scotia *was* New Scotland was widely accepted. Tartanism was enthusiastically promoted both within the province and outside its borders. While Ian McKay has explored how cultural producers and state actors within the region promoted a close association with Scottish identity, this event demonstrates that those outside of Nova Scotia also played a role in the construction of and adherence to this ideal. Scottish dignitaries promulgated this perception in their appraisal of the program and invoked language that perpetuated the idea of natural connections between the province and their native country. Chief piping judge Seamus MacNeill praised organizers' efforts and remarked that the event's atmosphere was "just like that at any Scottish highland games."[146] Sir Fitzroy commented that Halifax's highland games had been superior to those that took place in his homeland.[147] As Paul Basu argues, there persists a common notion that the world's diasporic Scottish population is "more Scottish than the Scots."[148] This idea unquestionably framed the celebration. Commentary by MacNeill and Sir Fitzroy shored up the notion that Nova Scotia was keeping Celtic traditions alive and well. They noted that the province not only replicated Scottish cultural events, it also was able to execute them on a scale that exceeded traditional activities in the "homeland." This 1967 event effectively, and very publicly, maintained the Scots position as the province's dominant Anglo-cultural core, a central component in Nova Scotia's complex characterization.

In spite of the odds, the Highland Games and Folk Festival proved to be quite successful. Although tartanism reigned supreme, there were moments that challenged those dominant Scottish discourses. The program's popular folk festival became a significant site of resistance that disrupted those commonly accepted assumptions about the region's core identity. It was a potent reminder of Nova Scotia's diverse composition and signified the emergence of a broader, more nuanced, and multicultural understanding of the province's history. Ultimately, the folk festival demonstrated that cracks were beginning to show in a province where Scottish culture and identity had traditionally played a defining role in the post-war era. The very inclusion of this cultural mosaic program points to serious challenges to the region's characterization as a predominantly Scottish area. It further indicates that, despite their trepidation about attendance numbers, organizers were invested in showcasing the province's various cultural groups.

Although the folk festival did not usurp those dominant Celtic constructions, it exposed serious fissures in the powerful characterization of Nova Scotia as a Scottish sanctuary. The event was popular with Nova Scotians and visitors who flocked to the grounds to experience the program. Its success indicates that the Centenary Committee, to their detriment, questioned the festival's popularity by treating it as a secondary event. Rather, attendees were interested in the spectacle and wanted to experience, however superficially, this multi-ethnic program and the opportunity to appreciate genuine artistic expressions by the province's many groups. Organizers' dismissal of the event's importance contrasts with what the general public regarded as an inviting and intriguing program component. To be sure, the festival marginalized groups and reduced their performances to consumptive public displays. Nevertheless, its inclusion points to a significant challenge to the prominent and entitled position of Nova Scotia's Scottish identity, and that there was room for a more inclusive understanding of the province's history. In a region where tartanism was a stronghold, the festival's success suggested that a more nuanced and diversified understanding of citizenship and identity was materializing. Certainly Scottish identity retained its privileged position in Nova Scotia that summer. Yet this provincial centennial event was a transitional moment that pointed to a broader and deeper understanding of Nova Scotia's pluralistic composition.

The 1967 Highland Games and Folk Festival left many in the province to contemplate possible future large-scale provincial festivals. As

Patrick Heron had noted in his final report to the Centenary Committee, there were lessons to be learned from this centennial event, should Nova Scotia decide to pursue other similar initiatives. The celebration had opened the Nova Scotia government's eyes to the impact that such undertakings could have on the province's rapidly expanding tourism industry. It was a new world of possibilities. Prior to 1967, the government had not been particularly concerned with, nor was it interested in, delivering large-scale events. The biggest cultural undertakings in the province had been annual highland games in Antigonish and St Ann's. Local festivals, such as the Annapolis Valley's Apple Blossom Festival, which began in 1933,[149] and the Nova Scotia Provincial Exhibition, which began in 1946, existed in earnest in the first half of the twentieth century. The fomer, a provincial government-sponsored event, was a means to promote the local apple industry, lure tourists to the area, and showcase local talent.

The scale of those events, however, paled in comparison to the 1967 celebration. While Halifax was attuned to the revenue potential generated by a vibrant and attractive tourism industry, its forays into large-scale festivals was new. As one of Nova Scotia's first major cultural events, the provincial centennial celebration arguably created an appetite for festivals, as the provincial government considered expanding its activities in this area. The provincial government had been heavily invested in its tourism industry since the 1930s. However, this centennial event was the first time that Nova Scotia realized the full potential of festivals on a larger scale. With a scarcity of large-scale festival traditions in the province, this was new territory for Nova Scotia. Arguably, the 1967 Highland Games and Folk Festival was the first step of the commercialization of the province's cultural groups on a grand scale that signalled the beginning of more coordinated festival tourism activities. The province's "festivalization" became more dramatic post-1967. The Nova Scotia government poured monies into larger festival attractions and made a much more deliberate and aggressive attempt to develop similar cultural undertakings. Now armed with attendant funding, many local, community, and provincial festivals proliferated in the decades that followed and made expansion into this area all the more feasible.

The result was that the province started to throw public monies behind and heavily promote large summer festivals. One of the largest in this area was the Royal Nova Scotia International Tattoo, developed after the popular and successful 1967 Canadian Armed Forces Tattoo that had toured extensively across the country.[150] Nova Scotia's Tattoo launched in 1979 and marked the province's hosting of the International Gathering of the Clans, the first time that event had ever been held outside of Scotland. The 1979 Tattoo was a resounding success. It held such lucrative tourism possibilities that the event's organizers and the provincial government decided to make it an annual summer event.[151] Other major cultural festivals such as Cape Breton's Celtic Colours International Festival, held each fall in venues across the island since 1997, have since emerged as a vital part of the province's tourism strategy. Along with the Lunenburg Folk Festival and Canso's Stan Rogers Festival, such initiatives point to the increased festivalization of Nova Scotia in the latter half of the twentieth century. Although it is clear that events such as the Tattoo and Celtic Colours are not direct results of the Highland Games and Folk Festival, the 1967 event undoubtedly laid the foundation for, and drew attention to, the impact of larger festivals. The event's legacy included showing how tartanism and large-scale programs could be commercially successful on a grand scale. It revealed lucrative tourism opportunities and paved the way for increased government involvement in cultural events that took programming to unprecedented levels. In this sense, 1967 marked a transition for the province as it contemplated the expansion of its tourism industry and how to best capitalize on this burgeoning sector of the economy.

Chapter 3

"I sold it as an industry as much as anything else": The Cape Breton Miners' Museum

The proposal is not for a mines museum but specifically for a *miners'* museum – an institution honouring in perpetuity the men who work in the deeps – in bringing the coal up into the light of day.

Cape Breton Post editorial, 5 January 1963

On 31 July 1967, Judy LaMarsh, Canada's Secretary of State, stood in front of a large crowd gathered at Quarry Point in Glace Bay to mark the official opening of the Cape Breton Miners' Museum. The heavy rains earlier that morning did not deter the thousands who assembled later that afternoon to celebrate one of Canada's most exciting and original local centennial initiatives. "The Cape Breton Miners' Museum ... is alone in its class," LaMarsh remarked during her public address, stating that there was "no other like it in Canada."[1] The project was a spectacular achievement. Constructed under the auspices of the Federal-Provincial Centennial Grants Program, the museum memorialized the Cape Breton coal industry and featured exhibits about miners' lives, their communities, and their work underground. It displayed artefacts and presented historical information about trade unions, technical equipment, geology, and coal companies. The museum also offered tourists the opportunity to descend into the Ocean Deeps Colliery, a coal mine that was purpose-built for the museum. Colliery tours were led by retired Cape Breton miners and gave visitors a fleeting glimpse of life underground. "This must be a hazardous way to make a living," LaMarsh proclaimed after visiting the colliery during the opening day's events, stating, "I wouldn't want to work in a coal mine."[2] Not surprisingly, this tour became one of the site's most renowned attractions. The museum's commanding architecture was captivating, and the Atlantic Ocean provided a dramatic backdrop. The project's unique and interactive presentation of the history of coal mining, coupled with its half-million-dollar price tag, made the Cape Breton Miners' Museum one of the country's pre-eminent and most expensive memorials erected in celebration of 100 years of Confederation.

The Legacy of Cape Breton Coal Mining

The Miners' Museum opened during an intense public debate about the faltering and highly unstable coal and steel industries, which had been Cape Breton's economic engine for over eighty years. The site's emergence during this upheaval signalled a crucial moment for the island. From 1963 when it was first proposed as a centennial project until its official opening in 1967, the Miners' Museum was shrewdly positioned by organizers as an integral component of the island's revitalization and the province's increasingly coordinated tourism strategy. It became a potent symbol of Cape Breton's post-war social and cultural transition. The museum also represented the island's shifting economy and identity that, in many ways, embodied a larger development strategy that redefined the region.

Coal mining in Cape Breton dates back to the development of mineable seams by the French in 1720. However, it wasn't until 1893 when Boston financier Henry Melville Whitney secured a lucrative ninety-nine-year lease from the Nova Scotia government for exclusive access rights to the province's coal reserves that the industry experienced phenomenal growth.[3] Whitney spared no expense. He poured $18 million into his Dominion Coal Company, which quickly became a very profitable and powerful force. By 1900, it "controlled some 300 square miles of coal lands, containing an estimated 1.4 billion tons of coal, 12 working collieries, 100 miles of railway track, 10,000 employees, and an average annual output of 4 million tons."[4] The company's growth epitomized larger developments taking place across the region. By the turn of the century, the Maritimes' age of "wood, wind, and water" waned and was replaced by the era of "coal, steam, and iron."[5] Coal was at the centre of this revolution. During the twentieth century's first decade, the number of workers employed in the Maritime coal industry climbed from 9,184 to 14,977, as production rose by an astounding 93 per cent, stimulated by rapidly expanding foreign and domestic markets.[6] Nova Scotia's coalfields were integral to the provincial economy and powerful symbols of the region's industrial transformation. Production was fuelled primarily by reserves in Cape Breton, New Glasgow, Stellarton, Springhill, and Amherst. Cape Breton's vast coalfields cemented the island's reputation as one of Canada's most important industrial centres. While industrial capitalists who controlled the mines turned impressive profits, so too did the Nova Scotia government. Royalties generated from coal production alone comprised an estimated one-third of government revenues and firmly established the industry's importance to the province.[7]

Cape Breton's coalfields were some of Canada's richest with an estimated one billion tons in reserves. They included mines in Inverness and the industrial area of Sydney, Glace Bay, New Waterford, Sydney Mines, and Reserve Mines. Workers – mainly from Newfoundland, Europe, and the United States – soon arrived, seeking work in this rapidly expanding industry. Coal companies required thousands of workers to keep pace with production demands, and many flooded into the region, triggering dramatic demographic changes as communities expanded at phenomenal rates. Industrial Cape Breton's population soared from 18,005 in 1891, to 57,263 in 1911.[8] Glace Bay was by far the island's largest coal town. Workers arrived in droves seeking employment in the Dominion Coal Company's collieries, and the town's population climbed from 6,945 in 1901, to 16,562 by 1911.[9] Glace Bay's workforce depended almost entirely on the company. The 1908 edition of the *Canadian Mining Journal* reported that "everybody in Glace Bay is either the servant of the Coal Company, or the servant of the servant of the Coal Company."[10] This state of affairs came at considerable social and economic costs. Dominion Coal exerted exceptional power as Glace Bay's primary employer and wielded tremendous control over the community through company houses and stores. The company invested little in the town's growth, outside of its capital, which was funnelled into mineral production. As David Frank remarks, "Glace Bay embodied the physical bleakness and social dependency of the early-twentieth-century company town."[11]

The industry experienced remarkable growth during its early years. In 1898, over 1.5 million tons of coal was extracted from Cape Breton's reserves, and by 1903, that number jumped to 3.2 million tons.[12] There was no shortage of buyers, as domestic and foreign markets boomed and kept demand high. Sales were fuelled additionally by Sydney's steel plant, one of the largest consumers of island coal, which had opened in 1901. That year, Whitney founded the Dominion Iron and

Steel Company on the basis that the seemingly endless coal reserves easily could provide the energy required to run the plant's operations. The coal and steel sectors flourished during these early years and secured Cape Breton's reputation as "one of Canada's most promising industrial frontiers."[13]

But industrial expansion came at considerable cost. Intense labour conflicts erupted in the coal and steel sectors amid rapid changes in the workplace and the market, creating an exceptionally volatile environment. Between 1901 and 1914, Maritime workers participated in 411 strikes totalling 1,936,146 striker days. Protests in the region's coalfields were "exceptional," Ian McKay argues, because of their duration and the sheer numbers of those participating.[14] Strikes often turned violent as companies called on the police and the government's armed forces to crush protests, enforce discipline, and protect company property. The Cape Breton coal miners' bitter and divisive 1909–10 strike illustrates the brutality employees faced. Workers had walked off the job to fight for union recognition and secure wages commensurate with the cost of living, which had increased by 21.7 per cent over the previous five years.[15] In response to the walkout, the state deployed the militia, and the company called on its own police force to bring protesters into line.[16] Between 1920 and 1925, over 58 strikes erupted in Sydney's coalfields, and police were called in frequently to deal with work stoppages. David Frank notes that most protests erupted over "work assignments, fines and suspensions, and the role of the communities and the union within the workplace."[17] Company police were used during the 1923 Sydney Steel strike, and state troops were called in during the 1922 and 1925 coal strikes.[18] Frank describes the 1925 strike as "the saddest, most difficult struggle in the history of the Cape Breton coal miners." On 11 June, during a violent confrontation in New Waterford, British Empire Steel Company police shot and killed coal miner William Davis.[19] It was a defining moment of Cape Breton's class struggles that left an indelible mark on the island's industrial culture.[20]

Shifting markets, labour conflict, sporadic government intervention, and other tumultuous economic forces kept the island's coal industry in constant flux and uncertainty. While domestic production flourished under Canada's 1879 National Policy, tariff protections eroded by the early twentieth century and island coal was undermined by competition from the United States.[21] As the decades wore on, the demand for coal and steel plummeted. Coal companies pointed to weak markets to justify substandard wages, and they implemented cost-cutting measures that were imposed on the backs of workers.[22] A limited consumer base exacerbated Cape Breton's coal industry vulnerability. Half of all sales were to Sydney Steel, which, in 1913, consumed 1,362,000 tons of coal. Although the outbreak of the First World War dramatically increased Nova Scotia coal and steel production – the former generated 44 per cent of the country's total output, and the latter supplied one-third of Canada's pig iron – this recovery proved temporary. By 1918, demand fell sharply across both industries. Cheaper American coal once again flooded the market, throwing the Cape Breton coal industry into a crisis.[23]

Hard times continued throughout the interwar years. Despite remedial solutions offered by the 1926 Royal Commission on the Coal Mining Industry in Nova Scotia[24] and the 1934 Jones Commission, fluctuating markets and labour unrest continued to hinder production. In 1939, Nova Scotia experienced thirty-nine strikes in its coalfields, and another fifty-five the following year.[25] Chaos continued throughout the 1940s as "indiscriminate suspensions and dismissals ... produce[d] work stoppages and impede[d] production."[26] During the Second World War, the federal government adopted industrial strategies that resulted in significant domestic competition. Steel production contracts were consistently awarded to companies outside the Maritimes, and Sydney's plant became underutilized.[27] Troubles worsened during the post-war years, when oil and gas replaced coal as a preferred energy choice. Further, the 1946 Royal Commission on Coal issued a dire warning about the industry's future. "At least 100,000 people are dependent, directly or indirectly, on Nova Scotia coal production," it noted, predicting that "without aid additional to the present tariff the industry will be unable to support that number, with resulting social and economic dislocation." However, the commission recognized the central role that the industry played in Nova Scotia and recommended wage increases and a pension plan for workers. In response to the report, the federal government created the Dominion Coal Board, to assist with operations.[28]

Problems nevertheless persisted. Despite coal's continued decline as a marketable and profitable resource, the federal government continued to buoy the industry, even though it increasingly believed that escalating reliance on state funds made coal a questionable investment. The 1958 Royal Commission on Canada's Economic Prospects noted that Nova Scotia's coal industry was unsustainable in the long term, citing high production costs and competition from more efficient alternative energy sources. Chair Walter Gordon also was concerned that Cape Breton's dearth of alternative employment options necessitated coal mining's continued operations. He thus recommended subsidies to keep the industry afloat.[29] Although the number of those employed in mining had declined by a dramatic 22.2 per cent during the 1950s,[30] coal continued to play a central role in the provincial economy. The Atlantic Provinces Economic Council estimated that in 1958 approximately 25 per cent of Nova Scotia's economy was in one way or another tied to coal. These statistics warned of the potential economic crisis should coal production suddenly cease. The result was that Ottawa capitulated to Gordon's recommendations for increased subsidies. In 1959, it poured $15 million into the sector, which resulted in the production of 3 million tons of coal. This was in addition to the $74 million the federal government had sunk into operations since 1945, which had extracted just over 23 million tons.[31]

Two more investigations into Cape Breton's coal industry followed. The 1960 Royal Commission on Coal, headed by Supreme Court of Canada Justice Ivan Rand, was struck to find a solution to the sector's ongoing troubles. It was no easy task. Rand recognized that major changes had to be made, but that this would be a challenge, considering coal's profound economic, cultural, and social ties to the Cape Breton community. "Generations have succeeded to the home, the traditions, and the mining occupations of their fathers," he wrote, noting that the industry's "roots in the soil of the Island are very deep."[32] He could not, though, ultimately envision a prosperous future for Cape Breton that was in any way based on coal. A region's primary reliance on an extractive industry was an inherently dangerous state of affairs. Nova Scotia's Department of Labour statistics revealed that the number of men working in mining and quarrying had dropped steadily, from 11.3 per cent in 1911, to 4 per cent in 1961.[33] Rand recommended introducing alternative employment opportunities in order to provide a more balanced and stable environment. Creating jobs in other sectors would offset the impending crisis that would be wrought by the inevitable mine closures. He encouraged expansion of the tourism industry and referred to positive developments taking place at the Cape Breton Highlands National Park and the Fortress of Louisbourg. Rand further advised that the island market its Scottish heritage to attract visitors and pump money into the area.[34]

The coal industry limped along, aided by continued massive subsidies that sustained production and kept the workforce afloat. By the mid-1960s, the Dominion Coal Company was poised to shut down operations. Federal funding that increased substantially with each passing year had become problematic. In light of these ongoing issues, Ottawa appointed J.R. Donald to head yet another royal commission on Cape Breton coal.[35] Donald's report confirmed that the industry was unviable and he endorsed closing the mines. He knew that this was a difficult proposition and tempered his recommendation by acknowledging the industry's vital historical position in the region. Coal mining, he wrote, was a "way of life" for many, and there were "traditions and emotions" that were likely to "befog and obscure the issues and the remedies."[36] Mounting extraction costs, declining employment, competition from alternative energy sources, and increasing reliance on subsidies to ensure continued (albeit severely reduced) operations placed the sector in a precarious position. In 1964–5, coal production amounted to 4.3 million tons, achieved through $22 million in assistance. This subvention cycle "conditioned" companies, workers, and even communities to government support, despite the industry's indisputable "unprofitable nature."[37]

The federal government, Donald argued, shouldered a hefty responsibility to recognize the significant "social problem" it had created through ongoing subsidies. As such, Ottawa was morally obligated to assist with economic diversification on the island.[38] The statistics were startling. Coal mining provided work for an estimated 7,500 Cape Bretoners, while the steel plant employed 3,500. Together, these operations employed 26 per cent of the island's workforce and one-third of wage earners in Sydney and Glace Bay.[39] Yet the coal mining industry had no choice but to reduce operations in anticipation of eventual cessation. It was imperative that Cape Breton's economy spawn alternative employment opportunities to diversify and stabilize the workforce. Neither Rand nor Donald proposed that expanding the tourism sector would offset the thousands of anticipated job losses in the coal and steel sectors, but both were hopeful that the tourism industry would spawn broader employment opportunities that would provide some diversification and stability to the area.

Although sympathetic to the area's plight, Donald concluded that "no constructive solution to unemployment and the social needs of Cape Breton" could "be based on coal mining."[40] The industry had, at most, another fifteen operational years, during which time 2,500 young miners would be in search of work. It was irresponsible and unethical, he noted, to continue supporting workers in a trade that neither imparted "practical skills" nor prepared them for other occupations. Continued coal operations would ultimately be "a disservice to the individual and to the economy as a whole." Donald proposed a series of steps to shut down the industry that included early retirement programs and establishing the Cape Breton Development Corporation, a federal Crown agency, to facilitate this transition.[41]

These myriad warnings about the economic, social, and cultural repercussions of a single-industry town were underscored in a 1966 urban renewal study of Glace Bay. Funded by the Canada Mortgage and Housing Corporation, planner Norman Pearson's investigation harshly condemned the town's lack of municipal planning. He criticized Glace Bay's volatile economy as a result of coal operations and drew a stark picture of "the human consequences of ruthless and thoughtless industrialization." The area had been ravaged by decades of boom and bust cycles, where rapid industrialization had resulted in "incalculable" human costs:

> Mining companies do what they must to produce and sell coal and keep a good financial position and beyond that they may do something indicating acceptance of social responsibility, but usually little more than society expects or requires. And the sad truth of Canadian industrialization is that our society has expected little and required little. We are still a largely undirected society, and pay scant attention to the human consequences of the industrial process. Canada has a fair proportion of the ghost towns and disasters of single-enterprise communities; and their redeeming feature is only that they are small in size, and that development is generally intensive. They became low density slums ... [T]he present state of places like Glace Bay is a standing rebuke to Canadian society ... [T]o the planner, there can be no doubt that all parts of our urban and industrial society are entitled to a national minimum of civilized life.[42]

Pearson observed that Glace Bay looked like a "waste-lands" with "the typical devastated appearance of a mining community" that had a "peculiar and distinct visual character." The town was defined by its dismal living conditions and offered little infrastructure to foster cultural pursuits. One of the more serious systemic issues facing Glace Bay was the prevalence of company houses.[43] For decades, housing was seen as "a condition of employment, and maintenance as a company operation." Problems emerged during the post-war era when these homes were sold off to coal-mining families. Home ownership was a new concept for many in the community who had little experience in maintenance and upkeep. Urban renewal, Pearson argued, confronted numerous economic, social, and psychological issues. Ultimately, a coordinated urban renewal plan, implemented with the assistance of government leadership and funding opportunities, was vital for Glace Bay's future.[44]

Nina Cohen and the Memorialization of the Cape Breton Coal Miner

By the time Pearson's report was released, plans were already underway to diversify the island's economy. While it was clear that coal production had a limited role to play in Cape Breton's future, mining was nevertheless envisioned as the basis for a unique renewal strategy. Tourism played a major role in Nova Scotia's post-war economic plans, and Glace Bay residents foresaw an opportunity to become part of this expanding sector. Locals were no doubt influenced by studies that recommended developing cultural attractions as a way to diversify the regional economy. They looked, not surprisingly, towards what they knew best – coal – as a source of inspiration. A museum memorializing the coal industry, then, was a logical decision for a community whose history was defined by its connection to the resource.

The idea of memorializing the coal sector started to receive serious support in 1959. That year, two prominent Cape Bretoners, Layton Fergusson, Glace Bay's Progressive Conservative Member of the Legislative Assembly, and his brother, C. Bruce Fergusson, provincial archivist and Historic Sites and Monuments Board of Canada (HSMBC) member,[45] proposed a museum to honour the coal industry and its workers. They approached Alvin Hamilton, federal Minister of Northern Affairs and National Resources, and J.D. Hebert, chief of the National Historic Sites Division, about the idea. Glace Bay, they argued, was a logical choice for a national museum because of the industry's historical importance to the area.[46]

Despite vigorous lobbying, the HSMBC did not support the project. The proposal, Hebert noted, commemorated "a national industry ... at a location chosen with circumspection yet remaining essentially arbitrary."[47] Fergusson pleaded Glace Bay's case but was unable to convince the ministry otherwise.[48] Notwithstanding HSMBC's recognition of the Canadian lumber trade at sites in New Brunswick and British Columbia, the board now had little interest in recognizing industries in general. Hebert also challenged the contention that Glace Bay had a specific geographical claim as the only logical site that could memorialize Canada's coal-mining industry. Although the ministry's mandate included identifying "places" of historical significance, this was interpreted as "commemorating people, societies, industries, and only vaguely trying to camouflage the fact that place is not considered of great importance." Locations such as Estevan, Saskatchewan, he noted, could assert similar entitlements. Other factors worked against the proposal. By 1961, Nova Scotia would be home to six national sites, including the Halifax Citadel scheduled to open that year. The province was responsible for 48 per cent of the HSMBC's 1960–1 construction budget, with an even larger amount allocated for operations, pointing to an over-concentration of resources. It was time, Hebert explained, to explore historic sites in Canada's previously neglected regions.[49]

Without HSMBC's support, Glace Bay shelved its plans. However, the town's prospects for a coal mining museum altered dramatically in 1963 when Ottawa officially announced the Centennial Grants Program (although program details were well-known across the country by 1962). With federal and provincial funding available for up to two-thirds of the cost of local projects constructed in celebration of 1967, many believed that this was an ideal opportunity to revive plans for a museum. Leading the charge was Nina Cohen, a respected community volunteer, philanthropist, and social activist from Glace Bay. She was a founding member of Cape Breton County's United Appeal, the Council for Cancer Units, and the local Red Cross Society's Women's Auxiliary. Cohen's work extended beyond social welfare causes. She was a business leader, holding executive positions with the Cape Breton Tourist Association and Sydney's Business and Professional Women's Club. She served as national president of Canada's Hadassah-Wizo from 1960 to 1964 and worked with the Canadian Jewish Congress's War Orphan Placement Service that found homes for children displaced by the Holocaust. Through this program, Cohen and her husband, Harry, adopted two young Holocaust survivors, Joseph and Sigmund, who arrived at Halifax's Pier 21. Recognized locally and nationally for her work, Cohen was honoured as Cape Breton's Woman of the Year, in 1961 and 1965. The National Council of Jewish Women named her Nova Scotia's "Woman of the Century" in 1967 for her exceptional "service to her country, service to her community, service to her people."⁵⁰ One journalist described her as "a vivacious woman with an electric personality that drives her to almost impossible community accomplishments."⁵¹

Cohen, however, is best known for her work with the Cape Breton Miners' Museum. At first glance, it seems that Cohen, an upper-class Jewish woman, was an unlikely candidate to become the project's most vocal and effective advocate. Yet, growing up in Glace Bay, she had a long-standing connection to the island's miners and was deeply affected by their difficult lives. Her deep ties to the community helped to legitimize her work representing miners. Nina Cohen was born in Glace Bay in 1907. Her parents, Max and Rose Fried, had moved from New York to Glace Bay in 1904, lured by business prospects in Cape Breton's booming coal and steel towns. Cohen's parents devoted considerable time to local charitable causes and instilled in Nina the importance of social activism. Notably, her mother's work as a labour activist organizing coal miners during the violent strikes of the 1920s left an indelible impression on Cohen, who frequently spoke about her roots in the mining community.⁵² There was no better way to honour these workers, she believed, than through a Glace Bay museum devoted to telling their stories.

But why was a museum such an obvious project for the area? Until the late 1950s, there was little museological experience in Cape Breton. Baddeck's Alexander Graham Bell Museum opened its doors in 1956, and major reconstruction of the Fortress of Louisbourg began in 1961.⁵³ Yet with virtually no other museum familiarity on the island, a community museum was a new venture. There were likely several reasons why Cohen saw it as an ideal project. She undoubtedly was aware of the Fergussons' earlier attempts to found a museum, and Ivan Rand's statements that Cape Breton should expand its tourism industry were fresh in the community's mind. In many ways, then, the groundwork had been laid. Yet Cohen had another compelling reason why a mining museum was a logical undertaking. It was an ideal project that filled a gap in Canadian history. She remarked that during the 1960s "the miners were never mentioned in ... any of the [country's] social history," and that a museum dedicated to their work addressed this glaring omission. Miners lived a "life of sacrifice," Cohen noted, and she could think of no better way to honour them than through a public memorial that told their stories.⁵⁴

Yet it was only in 1963 when the federal government announced the Centennial Grants Program that the museum proposal gained the traction, monies, and leadership needed to move forward. Cohen started organizing in early 1963, even before the program was officially launched. One of her first stops was to consult with her close friend Katharine McLennan, honorary curator at the Fortress of Louisbourg, about basic museological matters.[55] She also met with Harold Gordon, Dominion Steel and Coal Company's vice-president of mining operations. Although enthusiastic about plans for a museum, he warned that, regrettably, the corporation's huge debt load meant that it was in no position to make a financial contribution. Undeterred, Cohen forged ahead. She called a 3 January 1963 meeting at Sydney Academy, a local high school, to discuss the proposal. Attendees included members of the public, politicians, media, and representatives from the coal, tourism, and business sectors, all of whom wholeheartedly backed the initiative.

Cohen's vision was that the museum would be a cultural site that told the social and cultural history of coal miners and their communities. Further, the project would serve as an archive to preserve artefacts and safeguard workers' stories.[56] In bringing these narratives to the public fore through a museum, Cohen and other supporters were very much ahead of their time. In the early 1960s, few professional historians, let alone members of the public, were turning their attention to telling stories of the quotidian life of the working class. Donald Wright notes that at the dawn of that decade Canadian historians were working primarily in intellectual, economic, and political history, fields that were expanding quickly.[57] This, however, was beginning to change by the mid-1960s. Canada's National Museum in Ottawa began to adopt a "broader Canadian history mandate," partly as a result of the Massey Commission's recommendations. This was accompanied by a push by the National Museum to acquire objects and produce exhibits that "show how people lived: not only in opulence and beauty, but also in mediocrity and occasionally in ugliness." Apart from these efforts, the proliferation of local, community-based museums across Canada in the late 1960s contributed to broader representations of history in the public realm.[58] Diversity at this level resulted in expanded understandings of citizens' experiences whereby the new social history – including labour history – was slowly emerging.[59] The collective result was greater attention to those stories and narratives of everyday life that had been largely absent from the country's public history sphere. This mandate was also what drove Cohen and museum supporters whose commitment to tell the story of miners, their work, and their communities unquestionably made this project a pioneer in museological circles. "The proposal is not for a mines museum," a *Cape Breton Post* editorial noted, "but specifically for a *miners'* museum – an institution honouring in perpetuity the men who work in the deeps – in bringing the coal up into the light of day."[60]

Although the museum was to be located in Glace Bay, its success depended on the cooperation of all local mining communities. It was imperative, MLA Michael MacDonald remarked at the January 1963 meeting, that the whole region come together to support the initiative. Establishing an attraction in the heart of industrial Cape Breton was a strategic decision, Bert MacLeod, chair of Cape Breton's Tourist Association, noted. He speculated that the museum would increase traffic and counterbalance tourist sites located outside the industrial communities. It had the enormous potential to be a compelling point of interest that would lure visitors and broaden the region's economic base.[61] In addition, museum practicalities were considered at the meeting. Inquiries were made into various sites for the building's location, suggestions were made for possible revenue sources, and architectural plans were contemplated. A model shaft mine, geological maps, historical photographs, and technical equipment were cited as possible displays. While enthusiastic about the proposed exhibits, Lou Frost, Dominion Steel and Coal Company's chief engineer, remarked that they would be costly, especially if tours of a mining shaft were included. Expenses were also at the forefront of the minds of organizers who recognized that funding had to be secured from the public, unions, local businesses, and all levels of government. Other potential revenue sources included proceeds from a museum coffee shop and a gift shop. The latter, Cohen proposed, could sell wood carvings, products made from local sea shells, drawings of "the typical Cape Breton miner," and an "authentic Cape Breton doll" (though it was unclear what distinguished this from an authentic Nova Scotia mainland doll). The group gathered at Sydney Academy that day was ambitious. Organizers planned to approach the Canadian Broadcasting Corporation to produce a film about the museum's construction and to ask the federal government to issue a commemorative stamp honouring the coal miner.[62]

Cohen struck while the iron was hot. Buoyed by the enthusiastic response to the proposal, she initiated an ambitious campaign to see the museum named one of Nova Scotia's Centennial Grants Program projects. Success, she believed, hinged on assembling high-level support from influential individuals sympathetic to the cause. Her first stop was obvious. She petitioned Bruce Fergusson in March 1963, knowing that the provincial archivist would be a strong ally. She chose well. As the newly appointed secretary to Nova Scotia's Centenary Committee – the group that recommended projects for Centennial Grants Program funding – Fergusson was poised to become a key player in the province's 1967 celebrations. Cohen implored Fergusson to "speak up" for the proposal when it went before his group for consideration.[63] To help write the proposal, Cohen enlisted Lauchlin "Lauchie" D. Currie, a Nova Scotia Supreme Court justice, and a powerful former Liberal MLA for Glace Bay whose had served as Minister of Mines under Premier Angus L. Macdonald.[64] Currie and Macdonald were close friends of Cohen's family who were very politically active and had long been associated with the Liberals.

The Centenary Committee did not have long to wait to hear about Glace Bay's plans. When the group met for its inaugural meeting in May 1963, it had two proposals to consider: the first for the Cape Breton Miners' Museum, and the second for provincial adult residential education centres.[65] Centenary Committee member and Glace Bay Mayor Dan A. MacDonald remarked that the museum proposal enjoyed widespread community support. He underscored the initiative's importance because coal mining had shaped the area's history.[66] However, Cohen and her group had to wait for a decision about their proposal until after the Centenary Committee's 1 January 1964 submission deadline when all local 1967 proposals for Centennial Grants Program projects would be considered. Successful applications then would be forwarded to the provincial and federal governments, and the Centennial Commission. An undertaking was christened a 1967 Centennial Grants Program project only when it was endorsed by all three bodies.

In the meantime, Cohen and her team formalized their association when the Cape Breton Miners' Foundation was established under provincial legislation in March 1964. Its objectives included promoting the culture and history of Cape Breton coal mining and providing work for unemployed miners, their families, and pensioners.[67] Attesting to the vital role she played in all aspects of the museum, Cohen was named the foundation's chair. Other executive members included the Fortress of Louisbourg's Katharine McLennan, local mine developer David Burchell, and Justice Lauchie Currie. The foundation also became a voting member of the Canadian Centenary Council, an organization that brought together citizens, businesses, and voluntary associations to encourage development of meaningful centennial projects.

Although they were a year and a half away from receiving grant approval, this did not deter museum organizers from forging ahead with plans. In the summer of 1963, Douglas Shadbolt was hired as the Miners' Museum's technical advisor. Shadbolt was a professor of architecture at the Nova Scotia Technical College who had designed the Atlantic Canada Pavilion at Expo 67. In his capacity as advisor, he assessed the project's viability, technical requirements, architecture, exhibits, and costs. He positioned the museum as a central component of industrial Cape Breton's economic development and renewal strategy. In addition to generating much-needed employment, the project had the potential to draw tourists to the region. Shadbolt was clearly enthusiastic about the museum. However, he flagged one issue that organizers had to address. It would be difficult to secure the necessary financial guarantees, he warned, as the foundation had been "discouraged" from starting its fundraising campaign prior to the Centenary Committee's sanctioning of the museum as an official local 1967 project. Cohen's team was in an unusual predicament. It wanted to assure centennial organizers of the museum's viability. However, locals had pledged support "as far as people can commit themselves" without the museum's official endorsement as a 1967 project.[68] Although confident enough capital could be raised, Shadbolt knew that this dilemma stymied organizers' efforts.

Securing funding proved to be one of the group's biggest challenges. Under the terms of the Centennial Grants Program, Cohen and her team had to raise $142,000, a sum equivalent to their one-third share of the project's total $426,000 construction costs. Another $46,000 had to be guaranteed annually for post-1967 maintenance and operations to ensure the museum's long-term viability without reliance on government monies.[69] Securing this capital and these guarantees were critical because initiating agencies unable to do so had their Centennial Grants Program grants rescinded. Local organizers therefore were encouraged to launch fundraising initiatives as soon as 1967 projects were approved by the Centennial Commission. Nina Cohen took this advice to heart. As early as June 1964, well before the Miners' Museum's approval as an official local 1967 project, she started lobbying the Nova Scotia government for monies over and above those available through the Centennial Grants Program. However, while Premier Robert L. Stanfield supported the museum, he flatly refused to commit additional funds. He also declined Cohen's request that he appoint two provincial representatives to the museum's Board of Trustees to help "guide" the project's "destiny."[70] Stanfield wanted to ensure that the province remained at arm's length to preclude the appearance of favouritism.

Cohen was undeterred. In August 1964, she approached Stanfield again, employing a new tactic. The project, she argued, rightfully deserved a place within Nova Scotia's burgeoning museums network. A government-funded cultural institution in industrial Cape Breton ensured that the system was truly provincial, with representation from across the region. Cohen characterized her project as equally important and as "legitimate as the Army or Maritime Museum," two Halifax-based institutions that received provincial government monies.[71] To this end, she boldly informed the premier that her project's operational budget estimates included an annual sum of $7,000 from the Nova Scotia government. "Entirely apart from any special consideration having to do with the difficult problems of transition in the mining areas," she wrote, it was only fair that the museum receive "even treatment" with institutions already within the provincial museums system. Further, the museum's unique pedagogical value made it a prime candidate for government monies beyond what was available through the Centennial Grants Program. The request, she noted, was "commensurate with the sacrifices and noble efforts of those men and women ... ennobled in the museum." She wrote, "We of our generation are charged with a dual responsibility – that of an appropriate and meaningful monument to the Centenary of Confederation and the sacred obligation to prepare the second century for the future citizens of our land – our youth. Museums are necessary for both the present generation and the generations yet to come ... this is our legacy and their inheritance. We ask only for the privilege of providing a lasting anniversary gift for the biggest birthday party our nation has ever known."[72]

Stanfield again refused the request, noting that committing additional funds was "wholly contrary" to the terms of the Federal-Provincial Grants Program Agreements that governed the Centennial Grants Program. The province could not make an exception for the Miners' Museum without providing similar assistance to all 1967 projects. While the government contributed annually to some cultural institutions, these monies were never guaranteed, nor were they ever granted in perpetuity. The premier noted that although he wanted "to be helpful" and did not want to "say or do anything that might dampen ... enthusiasm," the government's hands were tied.[73]

While Cohen attempted to extract monies from the provincial government, Glace Bay officials stepped forward to do their part. Town council made a one-time $15,000 donation, provided another $5,000 annually for 1965, 1966, and 1967 for maintenance,[74] and granted the museum tax exemption status for its first five years of operation.[75] The pressure to secure funding mounted quickly. In November 1964, the Centenary Committee recommended to the Nova Scotia government that the Miners' Museum receive Centennial Grants Program monies.[76] Cohen and her team were ecstatic that the museum was on its way to becoming Cape Breton County's official 1967 project. The Centenary Committee's blessing was a crucial step, yet several hurdles remained. Notably, organizers still had to satisfy the province that they could raise their one-third share of costs and that the museum was sustainable post-1967. Cohen and her team knew they had their work cut out for them. They officially launched their fundraising campaign in December 1964, setting their sights high at $250,000, a goal that would cover capital costs and guarantee the museum its first two years of operations.[77]

Raising a quarter of a million dollars in 1960s industrial Cape Breton was no small task. Asking citizens who lived in an economically unstable region to contribute capital towards a museum was a difficult proposition. Organizers nevertheless proved adept at procuring community monies, thanks to a well-executed public relations and donation campaign. Brochures were produced, appeals were splashed across newspapers, corporate sponsorships were solicited, and supporters worked tirelessly to ensure that the museum was never far from the spotlight. Fundraising campaign headquarters opened at 373 George Street in downtown Sydney, and an aggressive media campaign soon followed.[78] In February 1965, the *Cape Breton Post* published an open letter from Nina Cohen and Norman Lynk, the general building campaign manager, soliciting donations from the public. The eye-catching one-page spread featured a hand-drawn picture of a coal miner. It noted that the museum was a "labour of love in a community spirit," and a "long over-due memorial" to miners that would stand as a "monument to the past and a bright beacon illuminating the years ahead."[79] A corporate fundraising drive soliciting donations from local businesses emphasized the museum's historical and educational value. Reminding potential donors of the tenth anniversary of the 1956 Springhill mine disaster that killed thirty-nine miners and injured many more, the campaign underscored the country's debt to the industry's workers and the importance of memorializing the "bravery of thousands of coal miners."[80] These appeals were framed by discourses of masculinity and sacrifice that drew attention to miners who paid the ultimate price for their labour in the industry. Commemorating those who died in Canada was certainly not new. Jonathan Vance argues that memorials to those who died in the First World War, not surprisingly, focused on discourses of sacrifice. The idea of men giving their lives in order to protect Canada's future and Western civilization, generally, framed war memorials and gave particular potency to these acts of remembrance.[81] The impetus of Miners' Museum organizers to commemorate the lives of coal miners was framed in similar ways. Men who died working in the mines had to be recognized for the sacrifices they made.

However, the foundation's funding drive ran into a serious obstacle in February 1965. Rumours circulated in the local press and throughout Cape Breton that organizers had to raise $250,000 by 31 March 1965 or the project would be cancelled. Some even believed that the museum had become the "target of deliberate obstruction."[82] Cohen and her team feared that these rumours would stifle contributions and irreparably harm the campaign. The issue was considered so serious that Norman Lynk implored the government to take immediate action and quash the stories.[83] The province responded quickly. Richard Donahoe, the minister in charge of centennial affairs, issued a terse press release that noted that the museum's fundraising efforts were "being handicapped by unfounded rumours." He confirmed that there was no deadline for initiating agencies to prove that necessary monies and guarantees were secured.[84]

In the end the rumours had little effect. Donations rolled in from the public and local business, including $10,000 from the United Mine Workers on behalf of all Canadian coal miners.[85] By August 1965, $152,000 had been raised.[86] This was enough to satisfy the Nova Scotia government that the Miners' Museum was viable, and it forwarded the project's application to Ottawa for approval by the federal government and the Centennial Commission.[87] While the foundation was still far from its $250,000 goal, the Nova Scotia government publicly stated that it was satisfied that the remaining funds would be procured. Privately, however, it harboured serious reservations. Donahoe told Cohen that he hoped that the approval would "stimulate renewed interest" and hasten her group's efforts to secure the remaining funds. Although "reluctant" to accept the museum's maintenance and operational estimates, the province believed that the project was a worthwhile undertaking.

All the same, the minister cautioned that "no effort should be spared" to continue fundraising.[88]

Cohen and her team soon received the news they were waiting for. In December 1965, Ottawa endorsed the project, and the Cape Breton Miners' Museum was officially anointed as a Centennial Grants Program initiative.[89] Cohen and her team were ecstatic, and they quickly forged ahead with construction plans. That month, the Dominion Coal Company deeded its Quarry Point property to the foundation for the museum's construction.[90] The conveyance included the rights to remove coal from the property and sell it as part of the fundraising efforts. An estimated 4,000 tons were subsequently extracted and sold at $10 per ton.[91] Museum construction began at Quarry Point in May 1966, but not before a ground-breaking ceremony was held to mark the moment. Leopold LeRoux, a ninety-nine-year-old retired miner on hand to represent coal miners, turned the first sod while dignitaries and the press stood by.[92] Pieces of earth taken from Nova Scotia's coal-mining communities were deposited in the soil during this ceremony to symbolically "make the museum a truly representative Centennial project."[93] The ceremony received extensive coverage, and the foundation was inundated with inquiries about the project. Media reports, including a high-profile cover story for the journal *Mining in Canada*, propelled Glace Bay into the spotlight as the town prepared for what became one of the country's most talked about centennial projects.

While the ground-breaking ceremony signalled the beginning of the museum's construction, the journey towards this moment was not without its problems. In November 1964, a firestorm of controversy was ignited when the Centenary Committee announced that the Miners' Museum was Cape Breton County's *only* official Centennial Grants Program project. Several communities protested that the museum dominated valuable 1967 resources by funnelling all per capita funding into one area. Sydney's Mayor Russell Urquhart "blasted" the Centenary Committee's decision and vowed to take the matter up with the premier. Councillor A.X. MacDonald remarked that while the municipality had endorsed the Miners' Museum in principle, it should not be the county's only 1967 project.[94] Others questioned whether the enterprise was even an appropriate initiative. The *Cape Breton Post* initially characterized its selection as a "surprising development" that was met with a "lukewarm response." It questioned whether it would even be an appealing tourist attraction and proposed, in its stead, a war monument or some other "practical" undertaking that better served the

Figure 3.1: Quarry Point with signs announcing the construction of the Cape Breton Miners' Museum as a 1967 centennial project, undated, Cape Breton Miners' Foundation

community.[95] Criticism, however, was scaled back in the following days, as the newspaper reminded readers that

> most of us are too close to the coal industry to see its changing facets in farsighted perspectives. To some it's the old, sad story of familiarity breeding contempt. People of the future will see it in another light – the light in which discarded implements and objects become rare and rate as antiques. In the view of this writer the committee's choice was a decision of destiny. The Sydney lady, who grew up in Glace Bay, who has been the champion of the Miners' Museum, worked for its realization so dynamically, fluently and convincingly that she won influential advocates to her cause.[96]

Others withheld endorsements and badly needed monetary gifts. The town of Sydney Mines initially refused to support the project, arguing that the foundation had engaged in a "highly organized and high pressure campaign" to win Centenary Committee approval.[97] Strangely, criticism was not confined to Cape Breton. The *Antigonish Casket* suggested that it was "hardly reasonable" to fund a museum in a county that was "practically destitute of ... cultural and recreational facilities."[98] For the newspaper, a museum, apparently, did not constitute a "cultural" undertaking.

The backlash was swift. One *Cape Breton Post* editorial noted that the museum would serve as "a constant reminder of the men and women whose toil was the very basis of the lively nature of [the island's] communities." It was only appropriate that a 1967 project reflect the coal industry's role in shaping the region.[99] Cape Bretoners also jumped to the museum's defence. In a letter to the *Cape Breton Post*, Sydney resident Claude Richardson alluded to divisions within the industrial community, and he noted, "We may have difference of racial origin, religious denomination, political affiliation, but generally the things that divide us are of much less importance than the many, many things that unite us and give us a common interest and concern."[100] Local businessman Harvey Webber, who succeeded Cohen as the foundation's chair, wrote that the museum was an important and "lasting link" to coal miners' histories. It was an "imaginative educational tourist attraction" that would "draw tourists further into Cape Breton and lengthen their stay on our Island."[101] The *Cape Breton Highlander* denounced those municipalities that refused to back the project and insisted that this was the "latest evidence" of the island's "blindness and backwardness." Residents were colourfully instructed to tell their local politicians to "cut out the stupid claptrap and get solidly behind the Miners' Museum."[102] In the spring of 1967, United Mine Workers District President Bill Marsh remarked that the political storm surrounding the museum's selection had heightened feelings of disunity between Cape Bretoners, and he bluntly noted that the "tendency to fight among ourselves is crucifying our chances of prosperity."[103]

Objections to the museum faded over time. By March 1965, the area's municipal governments endorsed the museum, as did local organizations including Sydney's Business and Professional Women's Club, the Cape Breton Tourist Association, and the Boards of Trade for Sydney, Sydney Mines, and New Waterford. Donald MacDonald, secretary of the Canadian Labour Congress and a Sydney native, stated that it was "a matter of keen regret" that Canadian coal miners had yet to be commemorated. His group was pleased that their contributions to the national economy and the labour movement were finally being recognized. In particular, he noted that there was "universal respect and admiration accorded the very term 'Cape Breton Miner,'" and the project was a fitting tribute to their work.[104]

The Miners' Museum was vigorously protected under Nina Cohen's watchful eye. She contended with political and media attacks and even dealt with a perceived threat from another local 1967 project. Located on Nova Scotia's northern mainland, the town of Stellarton, home to one of the province's most valuable coalfields, had received Centennial Grants Program funding to build its own miners' museum.[105] Controversy erupted in 1966 when the *Chronicle-Herald* featured a picture of Stellarton's project under construction and described it as a "miners' museum" that included a "model mine."[106] Cohen was incensed. She complained that the article conflated the Glace Bay and Stellarton projects and argued that the former was the only 1967 initiative entitled to use those descriptions.[107] Cohen wrote to A.P. Hanson, Nova Scotia's centennial liaison officer, who coordinated the province's Centennial Grants Program, and criticized the Centenary Committee's endorsement of two museums that had "the same name and purpose." She claimed that her group had been the first to incorporate as the "Miners' Museum" and demanded redress, arguing that what amounted to Glace Bay's intellectual property rights had been infringed. Two similarly named attractions were sure to create confusion and mislead the public, she noted, and that visitors to Stellarton would believe that they had visited "THE Miners' Museum" and miss out entirely on Glace Bay's attraction.[108] Donahoe intervened and conceded that while Glace Bay's project was "larger and perhaps more imaginative" than Stellarton's, the Centenary Committee could not deny a project to a town that had such a long association with coal mining. He recommended that the Glace Bay project step up its efforts to publicize the museum's unique opportunity to tour a coal mine.[109]

Cohen heeded Donahoe's advice. As part of her ongoing efforts to distinguish the Glace Bay museum, she set her sights on an initiative to safeguard workers' stories. In 1966, after hearing about a coal miners choir in Wales, Cohen and St Francis Xavier University's Jack O'Donnell, along with New Waterford miner and church choir singer Myles MacDonald, founded the Men of the Deeps, a choir composed of retired coal miners whose songs recounted stories of workers' lives and labour struggles.[110] The choir was established under the umbrella of the Miners' Folk Society and its mandate was "collecting material for a permanent record of the life and traditions of the Cape Breton coal miner."[111] Cohen approached renowned Nova Scotia folklorist Helen Creighton for help compiling traditional coal-mining songs for the choir's repertoire. However, they uncovered only a handful of pieces. To counter this dearth, the foundation launched a juried contest to solicit "original and traditional songs" from the public for inclusion in the choir's catalogue.[112] "Don't confine yourself to major events for subject material,"

Creighton advised budding composers, adding that "folk music and song is a record of happenings and everyday people."[113] Such an initiative points to the complexities of "constructed" versus "authentic" culture, drawing attention to Ian McKay's discussions of Nova Scotia's Folk construction. The competition generated a bevy of submissions that were judged by a panel of prominent Nova Scotians that included Creighton, Lieutenant Governor Harry MacKeen and his wife, Alice, and Justice Lauchie Currie. Submissions were incorporated into the choir's songbook, singers were assembled, rehearsals held, and the group was quickly on its way.[114] The choir was an instant hit. Following its sold-out debut at Sydney's Vogue Theatre in November 1966, the group went on to give six highly acclaimed performances at Expo 67.[115]

However, the foundation continued to grapple with financial challenges in the lead-up to the museum's opening. By early 1967, additional monies were needed as construction costs and unforeseen expenses inflated the project's original budget. The foundation pulled out all the stops. Cohen pleaded for consideration from Member of Parliament Allan J. MacEachen, Minister of National Health and Welfare and a stalwart in Lester B. Pearson's Liberal government, despite earlier insistence that no additional funds would be available. Cohen described the situation as an "emergency" and wrote that Ottawa surely would not want to "see the museum short of adequate and proper completion on opening day before such a distinguished and large attendance."[116] The project, she noted, was so important to Cape Breton's revitalization that it should not come to a standstill over final construction costs. Serendipity was on Cohen's side. By that spring, it was clear that Canso's community recreation centre, the town's Centennial Grants Program project, would not proceed. The town had not secured a site, nor had it raised any of the requisite community funds. Its $30,000 grant was rescinded, $23,613 of which was reallocated to the Miners' Museum for construction costs.[117]

With finances secured, Cohen turned her attention towards the museum's opening ceremonies. The event had to match the museum's status as one of Canada's most anticipated 1967 initiatives, and she resolved that it would be a grand event befitting the project. The foundation wanted Bruce Cochran Associates, a Halifax-based public relations firm, to handle the opening ceremonies. That firm had coordinated the project's successful and well-publicized 1966 ground-breaking ceremonies, and it was clear to Cohen following that event that Glace Bay required the company's ongoing services. The foundation lacked the resources to hire media experts, and Cohen asked Ottawa to assist with Cochran's costs. "Our inability to cope with many of the facets of publicity and public relations," she wrote, "and the pressures that build up for follow-through ... is due to the fact that we have no public relations firm east of Halifax to engage for needed services."[118] Cohen's determination to have these expenses covered by the Centennial Commission reflected the tenacity with which she championed the museum. She proposed to Centennial Commissioner John Fisher that Ottawa hire Cochran to coordinate publicity for the opening ceremonies. It was nothing short of a "miracle," Cohen noted, that her group had raised its share of funds in an economically depressed region. The least Ottawa could do was assume additional public relations costs to ensure the event's success.[119]

However, Ottawa bureaucrats were concerned about Cochran assuming this work in addition to his demanding task of promoting the Centennial Commission's national programs throughout Nova Scotia. Peter Aykroyd, Director of Public Relations and Information, advised that it could become an all-consuming job for the firm. "You know what would happen if Mrs Cohen felt that [Bruce Cochran] was at her beck and call," Aykroyd warned.[120] Nevertheless, Fisher supported the foundation's request and noted that he was "quite keen" on the museum and wanted to "help this endeavour to the utmost."[121] Cochran proposed a $4,800 budget for the additional work. "Mrs Cohen, as you know, is a very talented and persuasive person," the media guru remarked.[122] Ottawa authorized a $3,000 limit, "or less (if you can be as forceful as the lady in question in your negotiations!)," Marcel Dubuc, the Centennial Commission's Associate Director of Public Relations and Information, proposed, warning Cochran that his new assignment was not to monopolize his time.[123] This episode is revealing. It speaks to the ways in which Cohen translated her social standing in Nova Scotia into tangible benefits for the museum. The deference to her request was, in effect, undoubtedly recognition of the powerful and influential role she played in local and provincial political and community circles.

Post-war Industrial Cape Breton in Transition

When the Cape Breton Miners' Museum opened on 31 July 1967, celebrations were held throughout Glace Bay to mark the occasion. The day began when 10,000 people congregated along the town's streets for a parade that featured a girls' pipe band and fifty floats competing for prizes in categories that included the most historic, dramatic, and humorous entries.[124] The festivities then moved to Quarry Point, the museum's site, for the official opening ceremony. Speeches were given by a veritable who's who of dignitaries, including Centennial Commissioner John Fisher, Nova Scotia's Lieutenant Governor and Glace Bay native H.P. MacKeen, Judy LaMarsh, Premier Stanfield, and Richard Donahoe. Their speeches paid tribute to the history of Cape Breton coal mining, the industry's workers, and Nina Cohen's extraordinary efforts to see the museum become a reality. As one of Canada's unique and most expensive Centennial Grants Program projects, it is not surprising that the ceremony attracted such a bevy of dignitaries and that Nova Scotia's centennial officials deemed the opening a high priority. Officials singled out the central role that Cohen played in the museum's success and noted that the project had only become "a reality through [her] untiring efforts." Other factors came into play. The opening provided an unparalleled publicity opportunity for the government to garner good press.[125] In the wake of devastating royal commissions that wrestled with the coal industry's problems, government officials likely were keen to be seen as a positive presence and supporting the region's economic initiatives.

Following speeches, the crowd was entertained by the Men of the Deeps. The flags of Nova Scotia, Canada, and the centennial were unfurled, and Donahoe uncovered the commemorative centennial plaque that adorned all local 1967 projects. Nina Cohen unveiled the museum's cornerstone and she was presented with the building's keys. Lieutenant Governor MacKeen cut the museum's ribbon and declared that the project was "emblematic of the great contribution the country has made to Canada's development and industrial efficiency in war and peace. It pays honour to coal miners and will forever perpetuate the Cape Breton mining industry."[126] The ceremonies then moved indoors, where United Mine Workers' International President W.A. Boyle presented the memorial dedicated to workers who had lost their lives in service to the industry. He remarked that the plaque "symbolize[d] the never-ending fight which we must all carry on to assure that the men who work in our industry will be adequately protected in the future."[127] Dignitaries were offered VIP tours that included a visit to the Ocean Deeps Colliery. The doors were then thrown open to the public who flocked to catch a glimpse of the new facility that was heralded as a spectacular achievement for the town.[128]

The building itself was impressive. Halifax architectural firm C.A. Fowler & Co. had been selected to design the facility following a juried

Figure 3.2: Nina Cohen unveiling Cape Breton Miners' Museum cornerstone, 31 July 1967, Cape Breton Miners' Foundation

competition in the summer of 1965 that was chaired by Douglas Shadbolt. It was an imposing brick structure nestled at the edge of Quarry Point that featured a tall shaft that protruded from the complex. Inside, the museum had amassed an impressive collection. Cohen's team had reached out to Cape Breton's mining towns to record stories and collect donations to ensure that exhibits reflected coal communities' diverse experiences. Photographs of workers and the mines filled the museum's walls. A rainforest display showed coal's geological origins, and a large map pinpointed North America's reserve sites. Displays and exhibits offered a social history of mining that included tools used by workers and depicted technical aspects of operations. One display included mining equipment worn by Lieutenant Governor MacKeen's father, who had worked in the Caledonia Colliery.[129] A prominent United Mine Workers sign greeted visitors as they made their way to a display devoted to the role that unions played in the industry and workers' lives. The museum even housed a revolver used during the 1925 strike. The building also featured a theatre for Men of the Deeps' performances, and the lobby housed a gift shop that sold

Figure 3.3: Exterior of the Cape Breton Miners' Museum, undated, Cape Breton Miners' Foundation

handcrafts made by local paraplegic miners who had sustained injuries working in the pit. Former miners hired by the museum stood at the ready to take visitors on the tour of the Ocean Deeps Colliery, the purpose built coal mine that became one of the site's most popular attractions. Together, the exhibits, performance space, and guided tours embodied shifts that were slowly taking place in Canadian museums in the late 1960s. The representations of quotidian and working-class life placed the Cape Breton Miners' Museum at the forefront of the emergence of this new social history with a focus on community and labour history.

The opening ceremonies were a resounding success. They attracted a flurry of national media coverage that praised the project as one of Canada's most inventive local centennial initiatives. Yet the museum also emerged as a powerful symbol of Cape Breton's post-war economic, social, and cultural transformation. The slow and painful phasing out of the island's coal industry had forced citizens and the government to look towards viable alternative employment opportunities. Tourism was targeted by the federal and provincial governments and royal commissions as a growth area. The sector was heralded as a promising new economic frontier that could temper job losses in the coal and steel sectors. This is not surprising, given the provincial government's efforts to foster a diversified economic base and develop attractions to entice visitors to the region. The Miners' Museum embodied this shift. Supporters predicted it would piggyback on developments such as the

Alexander Graham Bell Museum and the Fortress of Louisbourg that signalled the beginnings of a lucrative tourism industry that expanded rapidly throughout the latter half of the twentieth century.

Nina Cohen and her foundation were poised to take advantage of this burgeoning tourism industry. They carefully positioned the Miners' Museum as an integral component of the island's growing tourism sector and characterized the facility as a symbol of the region's revitalization. Not only did the project bridge the gap between the island's historical reliance on the coal and steel sectors and its future as a cultural destination, it fit within the province's economic strategy. Since the 1930s, Halifax had invested millions in the tourism sector in order to attract visitors to the region. This history is vividly illustrated through Ian McKay's work on Nova Scotia's Folk culture and the provincial Historical Sites Advisory Council.[130] By the 1960s, tourism was undeniably a key component of the provincial economy. Between 1962 and 1967, Nova Scotia's spending on promotional campaigns had increased by an astounding 200 per cent. In 1966 alone, Nova Scotia welcomed 750,000 visitors, who spent $54 million during their stays. The province anticipated a massive influx during Canada's centennial and wanted to ensure that it was poised to reap the economic benefits that would accompany that much-anticipated summer boom. In 1967, it spent $1.2 million on provincial information services and travel bureaus to welcome visitors.[131]

Museum organizers shrewdly played on the province's dedication to developing tourism attractions as a central element of the project. The site was first and foremost a memorial to coal miners. But it was also a vehicle to draw visitors into industrial Cape Breton and a key infrastructure piece in the region's revitalization strategy. Douglas Shadbolt's 1964 report emphasized that the facility would expand the island's tourist base and be a huge draw for tourists after the 1967 pandemonium faded away. He predicted that the province would develop a new "Cape Breton circuit" or "East Shore Scenic highway" that linked Louisbourg, Baddeck, and Glace Bay to facilitate the travel of those tourists expected to make their way to the island to visit the region's cultural attractions. The Fortress of Louisbourg alone was expected to attract upwards of 250,000 visitors annually, and Glace Bay anticipated welcoming 100,000 of these tourists to its museum. Travellers on North Sydney ferries bound for Newfoundland would further boost those numbers. The Fleur de Lis Trail development and Mira's new camping site would encourage visitors to extend their stays. Shadbolt predicted that, taken together, the "potential tourist draw" was "enormous."[132] Further, visitor numbers would be increased as a result of those postwar developments that saw travel became an increasingly accessible leisure activity for an expanding middle class.[133] In addition, the Centenary Committee recognized that the museum created a potential tourist boom and development opportunities for industrial Cape Breton. Chair Abbie Lane noted that the project would be "a tremendous tourist attraction, and industry in itself."[134] The foundation's vice-president, Norman Lynk, predicted that all of industrial Cape Breton would reap the benefits. During a 1965 presentation to Sydney City Council, he provided a snapshot of anticipated visitor activity. He estimated that tourists who stayed an extra day in the area to visit the museum would pump an additional $2 million into the local economy.[135]

Despite the museum's obvious tourism and economic development advantages, a cultural site about the social history of the coal-mining industry was a difficult proposition in 1960s Cape Breton. It presented an intriguing paradox. Coal mining was an active, albeit dramatically diminished and struggling enterprise. The project's goal to "preserve" stories of workers and their communities in a tourist attraction was, for many, tantamount to acknowledging the industry's inevitable demise. This was a troubled and unsettling memory for many. The site commemorated an industry that had seen its share of disasters, labour unrest, and the painful process of deindustrialization. It captured these memories and narratives within its walls and became a site that straddled several museological categories. The project celebrated and preserved the history of coal miners as individuals, their collective struggles, and their representation through unions and as part of a larger working-class community.

The museum further challenged the popular images of the Nova Scotia Folk. Herb Wyile argues that coal miners disrupted traditional characterizations of the innocent and uncomplicated Folk characters as discussed by Ian McKay. Those workers and their industry did not fit seamlessly into the "Folk paradigm" as those labouring in other resource sectors such as lumbering, fishing, and farming did. Mining, with "its history of labour turbulence, its much more palpable capitalist relations, and its much more obvious physical rigours present greater obstacles to the celebration of the figure of the independent petty producer of Folk mythology." In contrast, the Folk "efface both the industrial capitalist contexts of labour in Nova Scotia, instead creating idealized images of independent, pre-modern toil close to the elements." Coal miners and the industry's inherent dangers, then, disrupted those popular provincial personas.[136] Further challenging those Folk ideals was the fact that the museum was a site of dark tourism, also known as thanatourism, a space defined by death and tragedy.[137] The industry's dangers were a central component of the museum's larger narrative. Exhibits included stories of mining explosions, violent strikes, and difficulties faced by extractive communities. Death, injury, and struggle, it seemed, were always front and centre. Such a display was intentional. Cohen noted during the museum's early planning stages that exhibits had to acknowledge the realities such as "the bravery of draeggermen who descended into the mine after an explosion, with death lurking in every footstep, unmindful of personal safety in the desire to save the life of a buddy."[138] From the sale of crafts made by paraplegic miners to stories of mining accidents, there was no escape from or glossing over the hazards faced by workers each time they descended into the pit.

The rush to memorialize coal mining through a museological project, for many, was tantamount to conceding that the industry had no future on the island. Although J.R. Donald's *The Cape Breton Coal Problem* decisively concluded that operations could not and should not continue, this was a hard pill for the community. Coal mining was an active, albeit contracted and struggling sector. Nevertheless, this push to commemorate the industry signalled its death knell. The situation was exacerbated by the language used by museum supporters who frequently spoke about the goal to "preserve," "safeguard," and "save" miners' stories before it was too late. Judy LaMarsh underscored this paradox during her speech at the museum's opening ceremonies when she paid tribute to the vital role that the mining industry continued to play in Cape Breton. "It is something which continues to breathe," she told the crowd, "and which still contributes to the economic life of this area, this province and this country."[139] Her remarks reinforced the industry's precarious and turbulent state. While LaMarsh praised the project for preserving coal miners' stories, her address also reflected the government's reluctance to insert the proverbial final nail in the industry's coffin. This revealed the fine line the federal government walked when it came to Cape Breton coal.

Not surprisingly, Nina Cohen frequently spoke about the urgency to salvage accounts of the industry before all traces disappeared. "The Cape Breton miner is no ordinary man," she remarked in 1965. "His story has a heartbeat. It should not be allowed to die and it *could* die in our own time." The museum provided workers with "the position and stature they have earned and deserved" and ensured that their histories were protected. Further, the quest to preserve these accounts left a legacy for future generations. Cohen hoped that the project developed "a pride of inheritance among the youth of the area" and guaranteed that this history was well-documented and lived on in the public realm long after the mines closed.[140] Many lauded Cohen's efforts. Journalist Richard Guimond described her work as "an absolute necessity in helping preserve memories of a way of life that is fast disappearing."[141] The public and the media latched onto similar descriptors. Local businessman Harvey Webber praised the project as a "lasting link" to the history of those who "made Cape Breton famous." He underscored the project's urgency and remarked that workers' legacies would "soon be forgotten if not preserved in some permanent form."[142] The media also drew stark images of a dying industry and a regional way of life. "One by one our mines may be closed, and so end an era," Elizabeth Hiscott wrote for the *Atlantic Advocate*, noting, "To men who died in the coal mines the Miners' Museum is a monument. To loved ones surviving them it may be an association with sad memories. But to Cape Bretoners generally it is a source of pride."[143]

The Miners' Museum was a potent symbol of industrial Cape Breton's economic and cultural transition in the 1960s. It embodied the dual purpose of preserving stories of coal mining's past and representing the possibility of future economic prosperity of a thriving tourist industry. For locals, it was a powerful emblem of the island's industrial past and its current state of economic instability. For tourists, it was an exciting attraction with captivating exhibits and the chance to tour a coal mine that lured them into industrial Cape Breton for a unique museological experience. The museum was a resounding success. Tourists, locals, and schoolchildren flocked to the facility in droves, making it one of Nova Scotia's most popular centennial attractions. By October 1967, over 25,000 visitors had toured the facility since opening its doors to the public in July.[144]

While the Miners' Museum placed Glace Bay on the map as a cultural destination, it also made a lasting impact on the life of its most ardent and passionate supporter. Nina Cohen's name had become synonymous with the site. Her role was so crucial to the project's success that the *Cape Breton Post* headlined July's opening ceremonies as "Nina's Big Day." It noted that the event represented the culmination of "three years of planning, prodding, pushing and pleading, mostly by Nina

Cohen" to see the project to fruition. It was a moment, the newspaper noted, that rightfully belonged to her.[145] Cohen was, ultimately, one of the project's most valuable assets. She personified Glace Bay's perseverance and embodied the sense of community that Norman Pearson had identified in his urban planning report. Her determination to see the museum become a reality points to her phenomenal ability to garner both symbolic and pecuniary support for a project that reimagined industrial Cape Breton. Cohen herself underwent a radical transformation. Her multifaceted work as the project's chief architect and advocate of Cape Breton culture secured her a higher community profile that propelled her from a local to a national figure in museological circles. In 1968, Judy LaMarsh appointed Cohen to the Executive Board of Trustees of the National Museum. She was the first woman appointed to this board and the only woman to serve during her three-year term. Cohen's role as the Miners' Museum's most influential advocate further points to the significant role that individuals played in shaping local community projects and engineering the ways in which Canada's 1967 celebrations were marked. Her position as a powerful community activist and her ability to rally supporters and their monies ensured the museum's success from the moment she took up the cause in 1963. Right up to the opening ceremonies, she deftly manoeuvred the politics of centennial bureaucracy and attracted much-needed financial support.

Much changed for Cohen after the din of the centennial summer's excitement died down. In May 1968, Cohen and her husband sold their Sydney home and moved to Montreal. Harry Cohen's rapidly declining health and their desire to be closer to family forced the move. Nina Cohen was unhappy with her new life. She confessed to Helen Creighton that it was "very difficult to adjust" to Montreal. She noted that she found herself "spending so much time in 'small talk' among people who are purely social minded," which was not her "cup of tea."[146] Her sudden move to Quebec forced her to shelve the miners' folklore collection she had planned to undertake with Creighton. Life away from Cape Breton would, it seem, never be the same.

Cohen returned to Glace Bay in 1968 for the museum's first anniversary celebrations that were attended by Canada's governor-general, Roland Michener, and his wife, Norah. In her address, Cohen remarked that the project was a testament to "the hopes and aspirations of so many Cape Breton families for the future." She stated, "Economically, Cape Breton is one of the poorer sections of Canada ... and the future of coal mining in this area is not at the moment too promising. Still, our museum represents a people of neither poverty nor pessimism – but rather a people of great wealth ... a wealth of the spirit, for Cape Breton's greatest attribute is her human resources – and it is with both courage and faith that we of Cape Breton face the future."[147] Her words echoed across the region as coal mining's future was more precarious than ever. That year, the federal government's Cape Breton Development Corporation assumed Dominion Coal's assets in order to phase out coal production. In a similar move, the provincial government created the Sydney Steel Corporation, which took over the assets of the struggling steel plant.

In 1982 Nina Cohen reflected on her work with the Cape Breton Miners' Museum. She remarked that the Centennial Grants Program had provided the area with a unique opportunity to undertake an important community infrastructure project. It was an offer that was simply too good to pass up. She noted with dismay that Cape Breton was "always referred to as a depressed area," stating, "We never got a ... decent break and you know there are certain circumstances [over] which you have no control, and it was conditions, general conditions and we were at the end of the line and ... we were the last to be considered and half the time we didn't get what we needed and therefore you can't prosper under those conditions."[148] The Centennial Grants Program was an opportunity to set a different course. Cohen further remarked that although she felt "very guilty" that the Miners' Museum had secured all of Cape Breton County's centennial funding, she nevertheless knew that the project provided long-term benefits for the entire island:

> I did not feel badly about it in the sense that I knew everybody in Cape Breton would ... feel the increase in revenue because this was a real industry you know we took miners on staff from other mining areas and the tourists were going through Cape Breton and stopping everywhere, their lodging, their gas ... picking up souvenirs you know the overnight the meals ... but I just felt sorry for the other communities that felt left out but I don't think that lasted long because they were very proud of the publicity that went with it and ... they knew that once and for all they were put on the map.[149]

Further, while Cohen later acknowledged accusations that she considered the project as her "own," she hoped that Cape Breton miners felt it was their project.[150] In the end, the initiative proved worthwhile. Early objections faded into the background as the reality of the decision of the Centenary Committee, Halifax, and Ottawa was accepted across the island. These protests, in many ways, were tempered by the museum's efforts to ensure that exhibits represented mining communities across the island and captured a way of life for Cape Bretoners that many saw coming to an abrupt and painful end. What emerged was an urgent need to preserve an aspect of the island's identity and culture for future generations and tourists alike.

On 19 August 1980 tragedy struck the Miners' Museum when a fire razed the facilities and resulted in extensive massive damage to exhibits, collections, and archival records.[151] The cause of the fire was never conclusively determined. Two million dollars and a massive reconstruction later, the museum reopened its doors on 3 July 1982.[152] Monies for the rebuilding effort came from insurance, corporate gifts, public donations, and government funds.[153] Announcing the federal government's contribution towards the reconstruction, Cape Breton–East Richmond Member of Parliament David Dingwall stated that the museum was "a vital Canadian cultural institution, a vital link to our history and heritage, and a source of pride to the people of industrial Cape Breton."[154] The Cape Breton Development Corporation's Terry MacLellan noted its central role representing miners' quotidian life. She stated that the museum "shows us where we have been and where we are going," and that it "gives us a reflection of the coal miner and teaches us that history isn't made only [by] kings and queens but by ordinary people."[155] The museum's reconstruction was important for the community. It was a significant source of tourism revenues and it brought visitors to the area. At the time of the fire, it welcomed an average of 30,000 visitors annually, 75 per cent of whom were from outside the province.[156] Although these figures fell short of the 100,000 that Douglas Shadbolt anticipated would visit the site each year, the museum was considered a success. The rush to rebuild the Miners' Museum and the monetary support received from both public and private sources reflected the institution's importance for both the town of Glace Bay and Cape Breton's tourism industry.

Ultimately, the Cape Breton Miners' Museum played a key role in the redevelopment of industrial Cape Breton. It helped to rebrand the region as a cultural destination and diversify its economic base. The project extended the possibilities of the Centennial Grants Program and demonstrated how government funds could be diverted successfully into social capital initiatives that became more than a simple commemorative exercise. Centennial programs, then, not only presented infrastructure development opportunities for many areas but, in some cases, allowed communities the opportunity for reinvention. What is striking in this case is that a museum received federal and provincial monies to support a project that openly celebrated the central role played by workers and their unions in shaping the industry's history. During a time when the Canadian state and businesses were engaged in aggressive and sometimes violent actions against strikers, it is likely that a museum celebrating labour's tumultuous history in Cape Breton would have been possible only under the auspices of the Centennial Grants Program. The project's construction could be read as an attempt by the state to appear pro-labour during a time when it was actually engaged in fighting the post-war labour accord.[157] What is also remarkable about the museum was that, unlike other 1967 initiatives such as the Community Improvement Program discussed in chapter 5, there was not a focus on tackling those environmental consequences that resulted from decades of mining. Despite Norman Pearson's 1966 report that noted the harsh effects of deindustrialization and the need to engage in more thoughtful urban planning, there was little attention paid to coal mining's environmental legacy. While museum supporters concentrated their efforts on commemorating coal mining's history and shoring up a burgeoning tourism industry, few drew attention to the broader effects that industrialization had on the natural world.

Cohen saw the museum as key to revitalizing Cape Breton's struggling economy. Her phenomenal ability to persuade supporters to open their pocketbooks and manoeuvre the political landscape made her one of the undertaking's most valuable assets. Cohen's political connections opened many doors and, arguably, helped her gain access to levels of political power not necessarily open to the public. In this regard, her social capital translated into significant clout, the importance of which cannot be underestimated. She came to the table with an ability to involve influential individuals whom she was able to rally towards her cause. Whether it was soliciting Lauchie Currie's help in drafting the museum's proposal for the Centenary Committee, assembling a high-profile panel to vet folk song submissions for the Men of the Deeps repertoire, or drawing out additional funding from John Fisher and the Centennial Commission, Cohen's ability to garner support for her cause can be attributed as much to her position as an important Cape Breton community volunteer as it was to her political connections. Even faced with a long-standing Tory provincial government, Cohen was able to access the halls of privilege and ensure support for the project in ways that few others would have been able to accomplish. As a result, she attracted significant political, community, and media support for the project.

As a woman taking the lead in preserving an aspect of Nova Scotia's cultural, social, and labour history, Cohen was in a unique position. She acknowledged her unusual situation representing miners and working to preserve their history: "You don't think of a woman doing this for miners which is such a masculine and you know rugged occupation and I had never been down a mine and I have long fingernails and [Abbie Lane] says they don't go together."[158] Further, Cohen recognized those initial widely held "suspicions" of miners, who questioned whether she should lead the project. These objections faded as Cohen's ability to organize and attract much-needed funding overshadowed lingering doubts. Her work with Helen Creighton on the Men of the Deeps repertoire to solicit songs that reflected working-class experiences also placed her in a unique position – an upper-class Jewish woman advocating and representing coal miners.

Cohen championed the museum as a key component that eased the transition of an area traditionally dependent on the extractive coal industry, to one that was increasingly reliant on a burgeoning cultural industry. Over the course of several decades, Cape Breton's tourism sector would purportedly be worth a billion dollars annually. The Cape Breton Miners' Museum unquestionably played – and continues to play – a central role in this sector. Within the public history context, the museum is one of several industrial heritage sites in Nova Scotia that commemorate the central role that mining, steel, and forestry played in the province's economic, social, and cultural history. Important questions have arisen about the process of representing and interpreting these sites. As Robert Summerby-Murray argues, there are concerns over what kinds of histories are being presented in museums, alongside those pressures to develop a "landscape of consumption and spectacle" in the name of tourism development.[159] Nina Cohen was acutely aware of such concerns. As the Cape Breton Miner's Museum was being developed, Cohen knew the site had to present a history of miners and their communities, all while developing a public history site that would attract visitors to the region. In this process, she worked to attract support for a project that became, in her eyes, a social justice initiative. Despite the facade that the Centennial Grants Program was structured as an apolitical project, backroom politics played a role in the process, and Cohen drew on her connections to attract much-needed support at critical junctures. The broader issue of Cape Breton's economic position was of great personal concern to Cohen. Commenting on the project fifteen years after its opening, she stated, "I sold it as an industry as much as anything else."[160] Tying the project to larger themes of memory, commemoration, regional economic development, and tourism, Cohen's work with the Cape Breton Miners' Museum garnered both her and the museum national profiles. Ultimately, the museum became a symbol of hope and revitalization for industrial Cape Breton in the 1960s.

Chapter 4

"Worthy of the great Nova Scotia traditions of the sea": Halifax's Aquarium and Centennial Swimming Pool

> Perhaps we made a mistake in undertaking such an ambitious project ... Had we elected to erect an insignificant Centennial project we would have accomplished our purpose. It now appears that in choosing a monumental building we have perhaps exercised bad judgement.
>
> Halifax Mayor Charles Vaughan

In January 1966, Halifax resident Leo McKay wrote a scathing letter to the *Mail-Star* denouncing the city's local centennial project. A large saltwater public aquarium, funded through the Federal-Provincial Centennial Grants Program, was slated for construction in downtown Halifax. It was a controversial proposal that deeply divided the public, politicians, and the press, and it became a flashpoint for debates about the city's development and urban revitalization. Leo McKay knew where he stood on the issue. "An aquarium is, in my opinion, nothing better than a glorified swimming pool for a bunch of fish," he wrote, charging that "the time, care and pampering of these fish will mean more dollars being set aside for this purpose. The fact that a city council should see fit to provide such a pool for a bunch of fish instead of making money available for a swimming pool for children of the city is indeed regrettable." In a poignant and prophetic statement he concluded, "Imagine, a $600,000 grant for a swimming pool for a bunch of fish when our children lack such facilities."[1] McKay's letter struck at the heart of the debate over the aquarium. Although the project captured the city's imagination and offered a modern and exciting vision for urban renewal, the aquarium was not meant to be. Municipal political machinations, building costs that soared to a million dollars, and pressures to provide badly needed recreation facilities signalled the aquarium's death knell. When the project was cancelled in late 1966, eleventh-hour politicking successfully diverted its earmarked funds towards the new municipal swimming pool already under construction for the 1969 Canada Summer Games. In a remarkable move, Halifax City Council quickly christened the pool as a replacement project in order to ensure that funding allocated for a local centennial project would not be foregone. By 1967, all that remained of the aquarium was a hefty bill for design costs and completed architectural plans for a project that never broke ground.

The spectacular rise and fall of Halifax's aquarium and its replacement with a municipal swimming pool raises questions about the Centennial Commission's commemorative process. The Centennial Grants Program was framed as an initiative that emphasized the state's role in nation-building through its funding of local infrastructure projects. However, the program proved to be far less about celebrating 1967 than it was about meeting local needs. Money spent under the guise of this national program was, in reality, used for more practical aims. Projects chosen by communities had little, if any impact on building a sense of Canadian national unity or identity. Ultimately *why, where,* and *how* centennial funds were spent was not as important as ensuring that local needs were satisfied. Communities prioritized their wants and shifted undertakings as they saw fit, demonstrating the Centennial Grants Program's fluidity and flexibility.

Modernization and Urban Renewal in Post-war Halifax

The aquarium was an ambitious and exciting undertaking whose construction was envisioned as an integral part of Halifax's modernization efforts. Moreover, the project reflected urban renewal trends taking place in many North American cities in the 1950s and 1960s. Although Halifax's post-war transformations materialized slowly, changes were well underway by the mid-1950s as the city started to experience massive social, economic, and political changes that affected virtually all facets of life.[2] A population boom and a demographic shift from rural areas to urban centres altered the city as boundaries expanded and outlying communities were annexed.[3] From 1941 to 1971, Halifax's population grew by 126 per cent,[4] and the city boasted 23.7 per cent of the province's population.[5] New residential and transportation infrastructure was introduced to accommodate this growth. The Angus L.

Macdonald Bridge and the Halifax International Airport opened in 1955 and 1960, respectively. Improved highway systems facilitated rapid urban growth as suburb expansion increased demands for better municipal transit and utility services.[6] Downtown residential initiatives, which included public housing expansion, promised a modern city and lifestyle.[7] In 1964, the Central Mortgage and Housing Corporation started work on Uniacke Square in Halifax's north end that included the construction of residences, schools, a recreation centre, and a library.[8]

Commercial developments drastically altered both consumer and business patterns. Shopping shifted from the downtown to outlying areas as the Bayers Road district grew and the Halifax Shopping Centre opened. The Halifax Port Commission oversaw major harbour initiatives such as a new container port that transformed the city into a central link in marine transportation along the eastern seaboard. Burnside Industrial Park opened and provided businesses with the opportunity for expansion.[9] Government agencies such as the Atlantic Development Board (later renamed the Department of Regional Economic Expansion) brought investment into Atlantic Canada, including Halifax.[10] The provincial government also fostered commercial expansion. Conservative Premier Robert L. Stanfield's Crown corporation Industrial Estates Limited (IEL), created in 1957, promoted regional economic initiatives throughout the province. Although IEL suffered political and economic missteps and was responsible for many failed ventures, it attracted businesses to the region. This included Clairtone Sound Corporation's move from Ontario to set up shop in Stellarton, and the establishment of Volvo's manufacturing facility in Dartmouth.[11] These myriad developments signalled the area's growth as a cutting-edge destination for business, research, and investment.

Legal reforms also ushered in major changes for Halifax. Revisions to municipal electoral laws dramatically altered voting patterns in the mid-1960s. Eligible voter numbers skyrocketed by almost 50 per cent during the 1966 municipal election following the 1964 abolishment of the law that held that only direct taxpayers could vote. As a result, women flooded voter lists and turned out in droves to exercise their right. That year saw the mayor and all council seats up for election at the same time – a first in the city's history. Halifax's long-standing rule that prohibited a mayor from serving consecutive terms was struck off the books.[12] Liberalized liquor laws altered the city's nightlife and shed some of Halifax's perceived image of stodginess, a reflection of the region's modernization. These changes transformed the city into a lively metropolis with bustling restaurants and bars.[13] In addition, residents took up numerous social justice causes. Citizens "joined the war against poverty, participated in a vital and lively citizens' movement, and prospered as a result of massive amounts of federal funding designed to ease regional disparity and expand the defence, medical, educational and research establishments."[14]

Urban planning discussions dominated municipal politics from the mid-1940s until the 1970s as Halifax was inundated with reports from professionals hired to guide urban growth.[15] This included the city's infamous 1957 strategic urban renewal report from University of Toronto professor of town and regional planning, Gordon Stephenson. His report recommended extensive property clearances, beautification projects, and commercial and residential development all in the name of improving Haligonians' lives. "Because of its age and economic history there are substantial parts of Halifax which should be transformed," Stephenson wrote. "Healthy new growth should be promoted for the immediate benefit of the people of the City and Province and to the ultimate benefit of Canada."[16] His recommendations, however, had grave consequences for one community. Stephenson proposed the demolition and redevelopment of Africville, the 150-year-old African-Canadian community in the city's north end. He notoriously described the area as an "encampment, or shack town" whose residents lived "a life apart."[17] This dovetailed with city council's 1954 recommendation to expropriate the community. Beginning in 1964, Halifax systematically razed the area. It bulldozed the community and targeted the so-called slum as prime for redevelopment. Africville was discursively constructed by experts and municipal politicians as a problem that had to be eradicated. Its destruction was construed as necessary for the city's renewal. As Jennifer J. Nelson argues, Africville is a story of white domination through the social construction of a slum neighbourhood. It exposed the powerful discourse of Halifax's planning efforts that masked racist anxieties that were manifested through the needs of social and political elites. This was done to "better control deviant populations, whose values and behaviours would tarnish white urban space."[18] City council believed that clearing the land was its only option to deal with a community whose existence flew in the face of Halifax's urban revitalization efforts.[19]

A City Divided: The Politics of Planning

A new and state-of-the-art oceanographic facility fit nicely into Halifax's modernization objectives. Critics had long called for major urban initiatives, and an aquarium – branded as "sorely-needed downtown development" – fit the bill.[20] The project's advantages, though, were more than that. A contemporary research and education facility that served the Atlantic coast would bolster the city's reputation as a leader in cutting-edge marine study and expand on local universities' well-established expertise in this field. However, major financial backing was required to make the project a reality. In 1961, when news of the impending announcement of the Centennial Grants Program spread like wildfire, Halifax saw an opportunity to move forward with the project. Halifax, like other communities across Canada, wanted to capitalize on this unprecedented and potentially lucrative deluge of government funding. That spring, the city's Conservative Member of Parliament, Robert J. McCleave, suggested to Nova Scotia's Attorney General and minister in charge of centennial celebrations, Richard A. Donahoe, that a public aquarium or marine museum was an ideal way to commemorate the centennial year. Halifax, Charlottetown, and Quebec City were Canada's cradles of Confederation and should be earmarked for special recognition, McCleave argued, through the construction of unique infrastructure projects in each city.[21] There had been talk of building an aquarium in Halifax since 1940, and the Centennial Grants Program seemed the perfect opportunity to forge ahead with plans.

However, McCleave's proposal initially garnered little attention.[22] Indeed, an aquarium proposal was not seriously considered until an April 1963 meeting of interested stakeholders from the scientific community was held at Dalhousie University, hosted by the Nova Scotia Institute of Science. Researchers, educators, and influential stakeholders from post-secondary schools, government departments, and science institutions who attended the meeting noted that there was an urgent need for such a facility. Together, they touted an aquarium's numerous advantages and threw their support behind the proposal. The Nova Scotia Research Foundation, Dalhousie University's Institute of Oceanography, the National Research Council, and the Fisheries Research Board argued that they could make "immediate use" of an aquarium, which had the potential to attract research grants and carve a niche in marine exploration.[23] The group lobbied Halifax City Hall, but the necessary political support for an aquarium was slow to materialize. Halifax City Council started to consider potential Centennial Grants Program projects only in early 1964.[24] Nevertheless, the lure of a modern oceanographic facility was so compelling that city council quickly recommended that it, in conjunction with Halifax County, build an aquarium as the local centennial project.[25]

The aquarium was also envisioned as a major tourist attraction for Halifax. Canada's two other public aquariums in Vancouver and Quebec City were built in the 1950s. Both were popular and respectively welcomed an average of 400,000 and 250,000 visitors annually.[26] Halifax did not have any statistical forecasting to predict attendance numbers, but the city was confident it could replicate their success. Supporters believed that the facility could attract locals and tourists alike and boost tourism throughout the Maritimes in general. Hundreds of thousands of visitors from Canada and abroad were expected to travel across the country for centennial festivities and to Montreal for Expo 67. The city predicted significant profits and economic spinoffs from tourists extending their stays and travelling to destinations outside of Quebec.[27] An aquarium, many believed, was just the project that the city needed to attract these visitors to the region.

While many entertained lofty expectations for the aquarium, municipal political debates over practicalities and price tags quickly overwhelmed the project. Problems soon emerged after city council submitted its Centennial Grants Program application to Nova Scotia's Centenary Committee in the summer of 1964. Although the provincial group approved the aquarium in principle that fall, its endorsement came with strict conditions. Project costs were estimated at $386,000, which included federal and provincial government contributions of $92,000 each for a combined total centennial grant of $184,000. However, the city had to provide ironclad assurances that it could cover the remaining $202,000 and guarantee that the facility could operate post-1967 without reliance on government funds. Architectural plans also had to be submitted.[28] Once these conditions were met, the application would move forward to the provincial and federal governments, and the Centennial Commission for final approval. Although city council was prepared to shoulder its $202,000 share, it hoped to secure an external sponsor to lessen this monetary burden. This task was left to the city's centennial subcommittee, which was chaired by L.A. Kitz, a prominent Halifax lawyer who had served as mayor from 1955 to 1957. Kitz's group set to work in the summer of 1964 to procure additional funding, keenly aware of the project's high costs. It was soon clear, however, that the aquarium's $386,000 price tag was underestimated, as the project's budget increased dramatically over the course of several months.

Kitz's first stop was to solicit support from Hédard Robichaud, the federal Minister of Fisheries and Member of Parliament for Gloucester, New Brunswick. This was a strategic decision. As a research institution, the aquarium would be an attractive initiative for Robichaud's department. Further, the minister was likely to back an undertaking that attracted visitors to his region. By October 1964 the project's costs had increased to $400,000, and funding from the fisheries department, Kitz argued, would go a long way to secure the aquarium's future.[29] Robichaud was sympathetic to the appeal and indicated that additional federal government monies would be forthcoming. However, the minister was unaware of, or was perhaps ignoring, the Federal-Provincial Centennial Grants Program Agreements funding protocols. Those agreements capped federal and provincial governments' Centennial Grants Program contributions at predetermined sums based on per capita provincial and territorial populations, and they strictly precluded additional government monies for local 1967 projects. Ottawa swiftly intervened. Centennial Commissioner John Fisher decisively rejected both Kitz's request and Robichaud's intended departmental support.[30] This response should not have come as a surprise. The Centennial Commission was responsible for upholding agreements that restricted Ottawa's financial obligations and kept 1967 spending under control. In addition, these agreements curtailed potential political interference and ensured that the Centennial Grants Program operated in a non-partisan fashion outside the reach of backdoor lobbying. The intention was to keep 1967 programming and the Centennial Commission free from heavy-handed patronage interventions.

Despite this failure to secure additional government support, Halifax forged ahead, making slow but steady headway with its aquarium plans. Recognizing the enormity of its task in bringing the project to fruition, city council established a board of directors in June 1965 to oversee this process. Appointees were selected from Atlantic Canada's scientific community and included representatives from the Bedford Institute of Oceanography, Dalhousie University, Saint Mary's University, the National Research Council, the federal Department of Fisheries and Oceans, and the Nova Scotia Research Foundation.[31] It was a powerful and influential group that city councillors hoped would help ensure Halifax's success when its application went before Nova Scotia's

Centenary Committee for approval. Board members played an active public relations role touting the aquarium's many advantages. Alfonso Rojo, a biology professor at Saint Mary's University, championed the project, arguing that an oceanographic facility was key to the city's urban renewal efforts, and it would attract other infrastructure into the region. The aquarium would also become a vital research and educational asset to engage the public and, in particular, students at all levels. Rojo cautioned that exhibits had to be comprehensible to all who came through the facility's doors, and that the project should not become "a mere showcase of aquatic forms."[32] As a public site, the aquarium was expected to reach beyond its scientific research purposes and make a meaningful contribution to the city's cultural life. City council agreed. Councillor and future mayor Allan O'Brien praised the positive impact the project would have on Halifax's growth. The attraction was framed as a cornerstone of Nova Scotia's tourist industry that, in addition, would be of "great civic interest" to all citizens.[33] It further underscored the point that the province's social, cultural, and economic history was defined by its connection to the ocean. The *Chronicle-Herald* boasted that the aquarium was "worthy of the great Nova Scotia traditions of the sea."[34]

The aquarium's architectural plans reinforced the notion that Halifax looked to redefine itself as a modern city. Following city council's inquiries with nine architectural firms, Halifax architect Aza Avramovitch was asked to produce preliminary designs.[35] Avramovitch had made a name for himself with his work on local projects that included Dartmouth Academy, the Nova Scotia Home for Coloured Children, and Northwood Manor. He had also placed third in the Cape Breton Miners' Museum design competition. Born in Belgrade in 1921, he had worked as an architect in Paris, Geneva, and Montreal before moving to Halifax in 1959. He taught design at the Nova Scotia Technical College and maintained an architectural practice with his firm, Aza Avramovitch Associates Ltd.[36] In addition, he was a regular commentator on Halifax's urban planning and was a champion of city hall's revitalization efforts during the 1960s, such as the construction of the Halifax North Memorial Public Library in 1964, landscaping at the Halifax Commons, and building the Scotia Square complex. The city was "abandoning the traditional strictly utilitarian approach," he argued, and predicted that it was "heading in an enlightened and highly cultural direction," while "leading in the creation of a proper environment and thus awakening a somewhat dormant civic pride."[37]

Avramovitch's aquarium plans reflected these principles. Blueprints were drawn up in consultation with a New York firm that specialized in oceanographic facilities. The building itself was designed to be an attraction, featuring a sleek architectural concept that reflected Halifax's grandiose vision to present itself as a progressive and modern city. Landscaping featured walking paths around the building that was surrounded by open green space, shrubbery, and trees. The building was conceived as a large hexadodecagonal concrete and stone multi-use facility that allocated spaces for both research and cultural projects.[38] A large 42-foot, 83,000-gallon aquarium in the centre of the building was designed to house beluga whales, with a feeding platform and a seating area for the public. Smaller aquariums and exhibits surrounded the larger pool along the outside walls. Cold, warm, and saltwater tanks were included to showcase a wide variety of aquatic life, including seals, sharks, and reefs. There were offices for research, laboratories, staff, and a library. In addition, the basement housed a living and dining space with two bedrooms, presumably for researchers working in residence. There were even working and living quarters provided for artists-in-residence.[39] Avramovitch's design was widely praised and the project was heralded as one of the city's upcoming flagship destinations.[40]

Despite these positive developments, there remained significant financial concerns. The city failed to meet Nova Scotia's Centenary Committee's 1 September 1965 deadline to guarantee that its share of project costs were secured. City council blamed the delay on several factors. A suitable property for the aquarium had not been found, without which it was impossible to finalize architectural costs. Budget details also remained incomplete. The Centenary Committee recognized the project's enormity and extended the city's deadline until 15 January 1966 to finalize its plans. Yet questions loomed whether the aquarium's $400,000 budget was sufficient to construct the enormous multi-use facility. In light of these concerns, two experts, federal Department of Fisheries engineer Terry Foley, and Vancouver Aquarium Curator Murray Newman, were hired by the aquarium's board of directors to advise on the project. Foley and Newman reported that the $400,000 budget was wholly inadequate, and they questioned the aquarium's long-term viability should it not be well funded. With a larger budget, the facility could prove lucrative for the city, netting anywhere between $40,000 and $50,000 annually.[41] However, until additional funds were secured to make the aquarium viable, Foley and Newman argued that Halifax would have to reconsider its project.

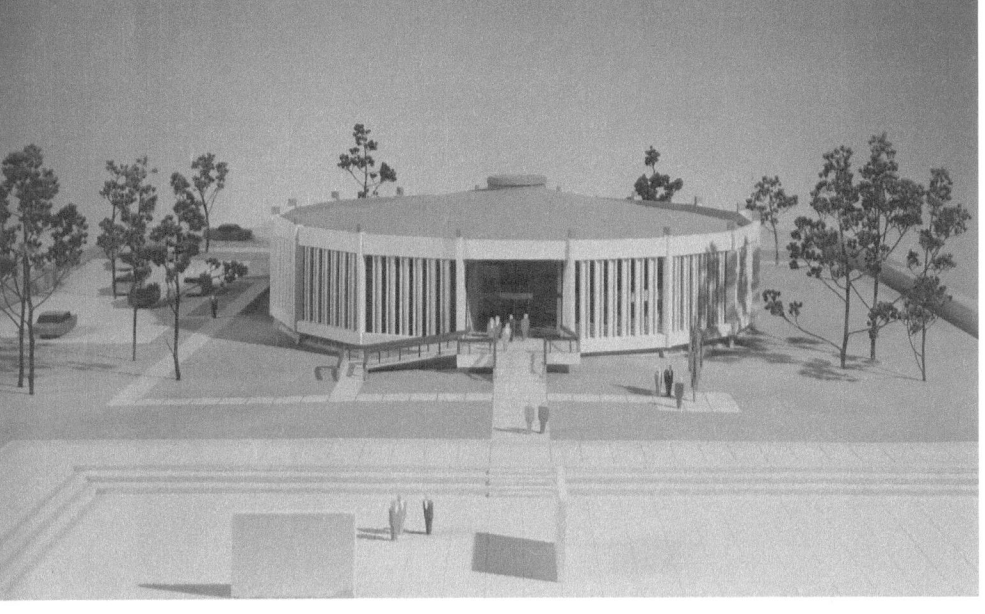

Figure 4.1: Aquarium Project, Aza Avramovitch & Associates, architect, Maurice Crosby Photography Ltd, photographer; Nova Scotia Archives, Aza Avramovitch fonds, 2001-036/003 no. 3

In the fall of 1965, public and political scrutiny mounted. While the project held great potential for modernizing the city, doubts lingered over whether it was practical for the city to continue its unequivocal support of the facility. Centennial year was bearing down quickly, and concerns were raised about Halifax completing such an enormous project in a short time. The city's delay in finalizing its Centennial Grants Program application became a lightning rod for criticism. Many Nova Scotia communities had already broken ground on their local 1967 projects, and Halifax appeared lax and disorganized by comparison. This was an acute concern for Centennial Commission staff, federal and provincial politicians, and the media. The city's every move became increasingly scrutinized as the weeks wore on and little progress was made. Richard Donahoe took the unusual step of criticizing Halifax City Council and implored it to quickly finalize details. During a press conference at the Centennial Commission's national meetings held in

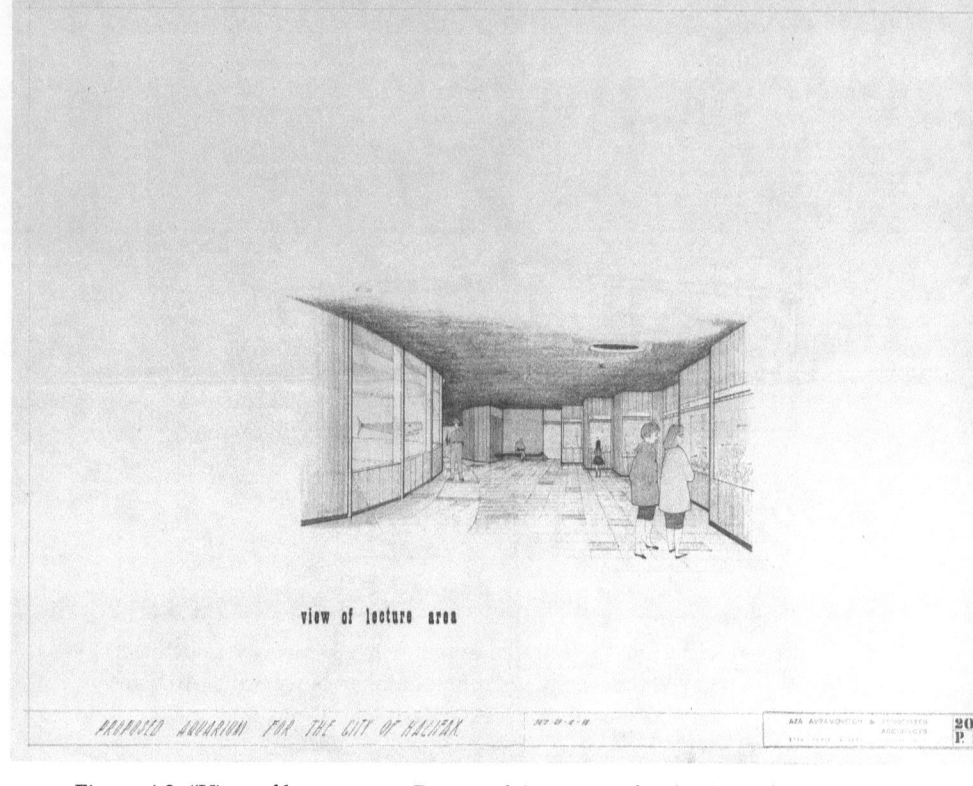

Figure 4.2: "View of lecture area, Proposed Aquarium for the City of Halifax," Aza Avramovitch & Associates, architect, 28 December 1965; Nova Scotia Archives, Department of Attorney General, RG 10 Series E vol. 207

Halifax that fall, Donahoe went so far as to question whether the city would even be able to pull the project together and remarked that the provincial government was "a little unhappy" with the city's delay. If Halifax did not take immediate steps to move forward, it risked losing out on its 1967 funding altogether.[42] The city also came under heavy fire from the local press corps. A scathing December 1965 *Mail-Star* editorial accused municipal politicians of procrastination, condemned its leadership, and denounced the ongoing delays. It speculated that these issues were so serious that they would ultimately lead to the aquarium's demise. Despite these censures and dire predictions, the newspaper noted that the project still enjoyed wide public support and lamented that it would be a shame if the aquarium collapsed because of administrative disorganization.[43] Ottawa was also worried. In an interview with Dartmouth radio station CFRD, Frank L. Wallace, the Centennial Commission's Atlantic Provinces regional officer, remarked that centennial organizers would "bend over backwards" and do everything possible to ensure the aquarium's success, even granting another time extension if needed.[44]

Not surprisingly, these public reprimands did not sit well with city council. Halifax Mayor Charles Vaughan blamed the delay not on finances but on troubles finding a suitable site for the facility. An ideal location had been identified on Halifax's popular waterfront that was owned by the federal Department of National Defence. However, the city had failed to secure rights to the land after negotiations with Ottawa had stalled.[45] It wasn't until December 1965 that city administrators found a promising site at the corner of Bell Road and Ahern Avenue that was owned by the Province of Nova Scotia. The property was part of the Halifax Commons, a protected public space established in 1763 located in the heart of the city's downtown.[46] Its proximity to the future site of the provincial Museum of Science made it ideal for working partnerships between the two institutions.[47] The city and the Nova Scotia government quickly finalized an agreement for Halifax to acquire the property.[48]

Despite this progress, other issues brewed in the background. At city council's 13 January 1966 meeting, Councillor L.E. Moir argued that acquiring the Halifax Commons property should not proceed without further consultations, and he worried about intrusions onto the green space. He proposed that an alternate site in the south end's Point Pleasant Park provided a location better suited for the aquarium. If no decision on the property was reached, he suggested cancelling the project and constructing an Olympic-size swimming pool in its place. His proposal died on the floor, and city council voted narrowly in favour of acquiring the Halifax Commons property.[49] While many breathed a sigh of relief as the aquarium inched closer to securing its new quarters, the close vote to procure the land indicated that city council was very divided on the project. City council also faced time pressures with a looming Centennial Grants Program application deadline, and budget decisions had to be made. With aquarium costs now pegged at $600,000, Halifax had to act quickly and decisively if it wanted to keep the project alive. City council approved borrowing an additional $200,000, which brought the city's total commitment to $416,000, but resolved that it would not entertain any further funding.[50] Many councillors were concerned that assuming obligations over $416,000 spelled serious trouble that would stretch the city too thin and likely force a municipal tax increase, a prospect that many dreaded. With finances secured, the city finalized its Centennial Grants Program application. Provincial and federal funding was pegged at $184,000 and the city guaranteed the remaining $416,000.[51] To assess what kind of facility could be accomplished with this new budget, Halifax councillor Hedley Ivany, Aza Avramovitch, and member of the aquarium's board of directors Carl Boyd spent nine days visiting aquariums in San Francisco, Los Angeles, Coney Island, Vancouver, Quebec City, and Niagara Falls.[52]

Many worried that Halifax had assumed a huge and perhaps ill-advised financial burden, and that the project's new home on the Commons compounded these difficulties. Halifax's Downtown Business Association argued that the facility required a continuous fresh supply of saltwater, and its location at the Commons, over a kilometre from the harbour, required major infrastructure – at considerable taxpayer cost – to pump ocean water to the site. Although the organization voted unanimously in favour of relocating the aquarium to a more appropriate waterfront site, its concerns went unacknowledged by the city, and the project moved forward.[53] In May 1966, the aquarium's board of directors gave its stamp of approval to Avramovitch's architectural plans that were designed to ensure costs did not exceed the $600,000 earmarked for the project.[54] The aquarium passed its final Centennial Grants Program hurdle on 5 May 1966, when the federal government and the Centennial Commission approved the project and authorized funding. That June, Ottawa and Halifax officially announced the aquarium as the city's official Centennial Grants Program project.[55]

Although the project seemed to be well in hand, the province raised concerns in the spring of 1966. Donahoe publicly admonished Halifax, stating that it had to move forward quickly to break ground on the project or risk forfeiting its $184,000 in Centennial Grants Program funding if the aquarium was not completed by the end of 1967.[56] Nova Scotia's Provincial Centennial Coordinator Lorne Hutt accused the city of being so disorganized that it failed even to start basic planning for community celebrations.[57] These comments were vociferously refuted by city hall. Mayor Vaughan countered that the minister's statements were "most disturbing" and that the project was moving forward. Political tensions reached a crescendo that May when Vaughan complained to

A.P. Hanson, Nova Scotia's centennial liaison officer, that the local press had carried numerous stories about the city possibly losing its funding. He blamed Hanson for spreading misinformation about the project.[58] Donahoe abruptly replied that he was "amazed" that the mayor had levelled such accusations, admonished Vaughan for not taking the matter up directly with him as the minister responsible, and reiterated that construction on the aquarium had to start immediately to ensure completion by the end of 1967.[59]

While the province worried about the aquarium's completion date, city council was more concerned about steadily rising project costs. Tensions boiled over at its meeting of 26 May when it was reported that Aza Avramovitch's professional fees for architectural designs had jumped from \$35,000 to \$49,000. Compounding these difficulties was the aquarium's board of directors report that project costs could easily surpass \$600,000, and a statement from Avramovitch that he had "grave doubts" that the project could be constructed for anything less.[60] In light of these reports, Councillor Hedley Ivany stated that he would file a motion at the 16 June council meeting to abandon the project. He characterized this move as "shock treatment" to force city council out of its quagmire, debate the project, and take a decisive position on the aquarium. The public, he argued, needed leadership and clarification about how far councillors were willing to extend the city financially, especially as taxpayers were "rather divided" about the project.[61] Ivany remarked that spending less than \$600,000 was "cutting the birthday party too slim," and he encouraged fellow councillors not to be short-sighted and reminded them of the project's numerous advantages. The aquarium, Ivany argued, was not to be seen as a "luxury or a birthday cake" but rather as an investment in the city's modernization and urban renewal. There were added pressures. The city had to ensure that the project was as sophisticated as similar aquatic facilities that were housed in or planned for Vancouver, Calgary, Quebec City, and Montreal.[62] The *Chronicle-Herald* urged city council to press forward with its plans, and in what seemed to be a show of support, featured an extensive article on Vancouver's aquarium.[63] Describing it as the "University of the Sea," the article underscored the aquarium's importance as a research facility, noting that "though it holds no final examinations and grants no degrees, [it] is still considered a top educational institution." The aquarium, described as "blessed – and to a degree plagued – by success," was touted as Vancouver's most popular attraction other than Stanley Park, and had welcomed 3.5 million visitors since its opening in 1956. The facilities were used extensively by the University of British Columbia, the Fisheries Research Board of Canada, and the federal Department of Fisheries.[64] Its success was held up as an example of what could be accomplished in Halifax.

These positive media reports helped Ivany achieve his desired results. At the council meeting of 16 June, the councillor, convinced by wide public support, declined to file his motion to rescind the project and stated that he supported the aquarium so long as it could be completed on budget. Avramovitch's "grave doubts" about the budget, however, lingered, as did practical considerations. Centennial year was only six months away and the city had little to show for its efforts. Ground had yet to be broken. Financial resources were strained at best. Faced with this reality, councillors were encouraged to aggressively pursue funding partnerships with private industry, and the federal and provincial governments. Mayor Vaughan reported that the wheels were in motion to approach Ottawa again for more funding.[65] Yet faced with a previous rejection for additional monies, the mayor knew his options were limited.

Nevertheless, in June 1966, Vaughan approached Hédard Robichaud in a desperate bid to procure additional monies.[66] Surprisingly, Robichaud reported that Ottawa was prepared to entertain Halifax's appeal.[67] With this dangling carrot that buoyed hopes, many believed that the federal government would bend to the request, despite restrictive Centennial Grants Program Agreements. The local Halifax press pointed to Ottawa's cost-sharing assistance in the 1950s between Ottawa, the University of British Columbia, and the City of Vancouver for Vancouver's aquarium – a precedent that placed Halifax in good stead for similar consideration.[68] That July, Vaughan felt "optimistic" that a federal grant would be forthcoming following a meeting with Robichaud and federal health and welfare minister, and member of Parliament for Inverness-Richmond, Allan J. MacEachen, to lobby for further funds based on Vancouver's cost-sharing scheme.[69] Support continued to pour in for the project, with the *Chronicle-Herald* noting that it would "be an undoubted civic amenity" and a "national asset":

> We are still in the process of nation building, and the thousands of Canadians, native born and new, who come to the Atlantic coast on summer vacation should be made aware of this basic part of our national heritage. What better way to make them aware than through the medium of a well planned aquarium? Moreover, Halifax is one of the great educational

centres of this country, and the primary centre for oceanographic studies ... Mayor Vaughan and the Halifax Centennial Aquarium Board are to be congratulated upon the alacrity and zest with which they are tackling this project.[70]

The mayor also lobbied Prime Minister Lester B. Pearson and highlighted the potential wealth of research, education, tourism, and economic development opportunities that would accompany an aquarium.[71]

When no federal funding materialized by September, Vaughan brought his case once more to Robichaud. He pleaded that the minister's predecessor, James Sinclair, had promised to support an aquarium in Atlantic Canada through a cost-sharing arrangement similar to that of Vancouver. Without this assistance, the aquarium was in jeopardy. The mayor was determined to keep the project alive. He conceded, however, that the aquarium may have been ill-conceived and poorly executed. "Perhaps we made a mistake in undertaking such an ambitious project," Vaughan wrote, noting that "had we elected to erect an insignificant Centennial project we would have accomplished our purpose. It now appears that in choosing a monumental building we have perhaps exercised bad judgement."[72] Despite these lobbying efforts and Robichaud's sympathetic stance, the appeal fell on deaf ears. In the end the federal government was unwilling to support the aquarium beyond its allotted centennial funds.

The city's problems escalated rapidly from there. By September 1966, it was clear that costs had soared beyond Halifax's grasp. Construction tenders were staggering, with the lowest bid coming in at $984,666.[73] A 29 September 1966 motion at city council to pledge an additional $300,000 towards the aquarium not surprisingly was soundly defeated as councillors were unprepared to dip once more into Halifax's coffers.[74] The project, according to the *Chronicle-Herald*, was now a full-fledged disaster, "mired in a financial bog" from which the city seemed unlikely to emerge unscathed.[75] Councillor Don LeBlanc agreed. He argued that the city could not realistically afford the project, and that Halifax should pursue a "small but meaningful centennial project" in its place.[76] The media, however, pressured the city to move forward. A *Mail-Star* editorial noted that although it was "regrettable" that costs had soared so high, Halifax could not "afford to allow this project to go down the drain." City council, it argued, had a "duty" to proceed with the project.[77] Astonishingly, not all had lost hope. That October, Mayor Vaughan, Councillors Ivany and Matheson, and the aquarium's board chair, E.G.

Young, met with the provincial Centenary Committee seeking a time extension to secure additional funds. Vaughan asked whether Halifax, if forced to cancel the aquarium, could roll its allotted $184,000 into an alternative project. The Centenary Committee did not take a definitive position on these issues that day and reiterated that it was not able to procure more monies for the project.[78] In addition, the city's request to secure $300,000 from the Nova Scotia government was rejected.[79]

While the project foundered, the October 1966 municipal elections resulted in major changes for Halifax City Council. Long-serving councillor and New Democrat Allan O'Brien was elected mayor in a dramatic race against incumbent Charles Vaughan. O'Brien cast himself as the "action candidate" and focused his campaign on bringing "business-like efficiency" to the city, as well as a clear direction for urban renewal and strategic planning. His political advertisements stressed cooperative leadership, with one noting that "the city's too big for a one man show," an obvious swipe at Vaughan's time as mayor.[80] Vaughan, who had won the 1957 and 1963 mayoralty races, ran on his political record and underscored his urban revitalization efforts.[81] His campaign emphasized a burgeoning "New Halifax," where under his leadership the city saw improved park areas, modernized transportation systems, new industrial and residential initiatives, and the new Scotia Square complex.[82] Vaughan even attempted to capitalize on a 1 October *Financial Post* photo story titled "Halifax's Changing Skyline," that showcased the city's recent commercial developments. His campaign reprinted that montage in a local newspaper and referred to it as "evidence of success."[83] The irony was remarkable. Vaughan focused his campaign on a record of urban development success, yet he was unable to lead his council towards completion of the aquarium, which was cast as a cornerstone of civic progress.[84] O'Brien handily won the election and was sworn in as mayor on 1 November 1966 – a very public and political affirmation of Vaughan's unpopularity.[85] His election signalled a desire among Haligonians for more decisive leadership on urban planning.

With the municipal election over and time pressures mounting, city council turned its attention to reassessing the aquarium. Neither councillors nor the board of directors had been able to secure additional financial assistance. Ground had yet to be broken at the site. Centennial year loomed but a month away and the city had made no real progress. The project was now too far gone. Many worried that Halifax had jeopardized its $184,000 in centennial funding altogether. Others voiced concern about the significant political and public embarrassment if the city could not pursue an alternative 1967 project. Faced with this reality, municipal councillors rescinded the project on 1 December 1966.[86] In its place, they approved a swimming pool as Halifax's new local centennial project. They hoped to siphon the city's Centennial Grants Program monies into the new municipal swimming pool that was already under construction for the 1969 Canada Summer Games.[87] The pool was being built on land close to the Commons at the intersection of Cogswell and Gottingen streets. This eleventh-hour decision to support a pool as Halifax's new local centennial project was not an easy one, but councillors were left with little choice. Luckily, city council quickly received approval from the Centenary Committee to transfer its centennial funds to the new pool project. The provincial and federal governments and the Centennial Commission understood the urgency of the situation and also gave their stamps of approval.[88] The addition of $184,000 in centennial funding to the new swimming pool's budget resulted in significant upgrades to the facility. The design was altered to increase the pool's size from twenty-five to fifty metres, which enhanced the facility's ability to provide improved recreational services and programs, instruction, and public swims.[89] Meeting these new specifications was both logical and practical. The influx of centennial monies meant that architectural alterations were accomplished easily. That no last-minute centennial project would have to be negotiated or constructed was the key to Halifax's success. It was through heavy political lobbying (and a certain amount of humility and regret) by the new mayor that the city successfully made this switch. The *Chronicle-Herald* called the aquarium the "first casualty in a new austerity at city hall" and observed that Halifax would have to "make do with a centennial splash in a $460,000 swimming pool."[90]

Despite the media's tepid response to the aquarium's cancellation, the recent mayoral election indicated that the public was ready for a municipal council that would not overextend itself with a costly centennial project. Most importantly, the announcement that the city's new swimming pool would be the recipient of Halifax's original centennial funding effectively calmed any dissenting voices that had rallied against the aquarium. Although this change was sudden, the expeditious decision to fund a pool was a logical decision that many politicians and citizens were able to support. The fact that extended debate was not required at city hall or within the community was due to two significant factors. First, Halifax recognized that a new community pool was a high priority for residents. The city's Recreation Commission had long acknowledged a need for more public swimming facilities and had been working hard to pinpoint a location and secure funding for expanded services. Haligonians had also been vocal about the need to improve facilities in order to bring services up to the level expected of such a populous city. Second, recreational facilities, particularly for youth, had become significant in the post-war era. This was illustrated through those projects constructed under the Centennial Grants Program across the province that were designed to cater to communities' recreational demands and the needs of Nova Scotia's youth.

Leisure and Public Recreation in Post-war Halifax

In Nova Scotia, 60 per cent of projects funded through the Centennial Grants Program were defined as recreational initiatives. They included parks, skating rinks, swimming pools, and community centres that became some of the province's most popular and enduring reminders of 1967.[91] Many of these recreational projects stressed the importance of healthy lifestyles and the need to provide activities for the country's youngest citizens. In the process they revealed the central role that discourses of "youth" played during the centennial. When recreational project organizers lobbied for centennial grants and campaigned for community support, they frequently spoke about the importance of providing activities for youth and leaving a legacy for future generations. These projects were branded as facilities that provided youth with "safe," "secure," "supervised," and "proper" spaces where they could spend their free time participating in programs under the watchful eye of adult supervisors. Such initiatives proved to be popular solutions to a host of post-war concerns about the proper development of children and teens. The experts agreed. Youth required outlets for physical activities where they could be instructed on "proper" and "normal" maturation processes that ultimately ensured their development into democratic, responsible, and ideal adults.

Leisure emerged as a fundamental component of Canadian citizenship rights during the Great Depression. Those rights expanded significantly throughout the post-war era as provincial governments increasingly acknowledged leisure as "a universal citizen right."[92] Public recreation programs expanded alongside Canada's social welfare state and reflected larger notions of democratic ideas. They also responded to concerns that citizens were entitled to minimum living standards that made for a productive and balanced workforce.[93] Post-war studies reflected these larger worries. A 1946 Canada Youth Commission report concluded that rapid urban growth, industrial labour pressures, and increased leisure time and standards of living had made organized recreation a necessity in modern life. Further, recreation was branded as a cure-all for easing "mental disorder" and stemming juvenile delinquency.[94] In addition, disposable income, urbanization, social mobility, and more leisure time had resulted in an increased demand for recreation infrastructure and services.[95]

Pressures to provide adequate leisure pursuits for the public were especially acute during the post-war era. During this time, the community recreation movement designed and implemented policies, programs, and services that were shaped by local needs. The focus on communities' provision of services meant that the government did not dictate personal leisure choices during an era when government programming directives smacked of heavy-handed authoritarian politics and were feared in a volatile post–Second World War society.[96] Further, community recreational pursuits were branded as cure-alls for perceived social, cultural, and political ills. Shirley Tillotson argues that they sought to "correct or prevent moral decay among the weak" and "mould a certain citizen personality," all while encouraging "self-discipline, religious faith, patriotism, and commitment to the heterosexual family."[97] The Centennial Grants Program dovetailed particularly well with the community recreation movement and citizens' post-war needs. Recreation initiatives were frequently spearheaded by community groups and municipal governments in order to reflect local priorities. In addition, recreation services were touted as protecting Canada from dangerous foreign influences that appeared at the border as a result of the post-war immigration boom. Franca Iacovetta notes that leisure programming socialized newcomers to Anglo-Canadian middle-class ideals that shaped them into productive and democratic citizens, and even stemmed incidences of juvenile delinquency among immigrant youth.[98] The result was that leisure facilities responded to increased post-war concerns about the safety of children and how they spent their time.[99]

Social and political commentators believed that providing recreational programming further helped to quell certain Cold War fears. Heightened anxieties about the fate of the baby boom generation culminated in a push to provide safe and supervised recreation activities, and a need to carefully educate, nurture, and construct the country's youngest citizens.[100] These worries thrived during the politically charged Cold War era that produced myriad strategies to deal with what was seen as the "youth problem." These strategies included, as Mary-Louise Adams argues, adult supervised recreational activities that provided positive outlets of expression that were "preventative and corrective" keys to eradicate the youth problem.[101] Joan Sangster has shown that recreation was seen as a partial solution for undercutting delinquency in girls and constructing model citizens.[102] Recreation was therefore touted as an easy and obvious solution to Canada's post-war youth problems.

In Nova Scotia, local recreational centennial projects fit well with larger post-war ideas of protecting the country's youth and providing them with productive, structured, and safe places to spend their leisure time. The Centenary Committee was faced with numerous Centennial Grants Program applications that were structured on this premise. One image frequently invoked by organizers seeking 1967 support for recreation projects was that of youth in peril. For some areas of the province, safe recreational pursuits were more than a simple leisure or infrastructure issue. Instead, many proposals struck at the very heart of serious community issues. Local initiating agencies viewed the Centennial Grants Program as a practical solution to stem social dislocation and to provide their area's youngest citizens with much-needed structured pursuits. Community centres, rinks, and swimming pools were practical projects that ensured that youth were protected from a host of possible, and sometimes very real, harmful and destructive influences.

The town of Mulgrave certainly conjured images of desperation and despair in its Centennial Grants Program application. The town wanted to provide the area's 450 youth with a leisure space that was free from what officials believed were disreputable characters and negative influences. Mayor Willoughby Digdon noted that Mulgrave's youngest citizens completely lacked meaningful recreational and social diversions. The town's faltering fishing industry, the community's primary employer, exacerbated the problem. For many, Digdon wrote, "their only recreation is a bottle." Although he conceded that "admittedly, there are times this can help liven things up a bit," he concluded that "the steady diet is hurting the industry, the town and the people involved." There was thus an urgent need for alternate pursuits for Mulgrave's youth. Even Russian seamen who landed in port, Digdon reported, were dismayed at the town's lack of social and cultural activities.[103] Similarly, Yarmouth's YMCA centennial swimming pool project conjured images of local youth in need of a safe recreational site. Mayor

Frederick J. Emin remarked that the facility was a valuable resource that provided youth, branded as the community's "most precious asset," with "a well-equipped and properly-conducted centre for [their] clean, physical and mental development."[104] The pool promoted recreational democracy by providing all citizens, regardless of their economic, social, or cultural background, with access to the facility, a basis of the YMCA's ideals. However, no other group was expected to gain as much from the pool as the area's youth.[105] As the experiences of Yarmouth and Mulgrave demonstrated, local recreational centennial projects were closely linked to the social, cultural, and economic revitalization of communities. Halifax was no different.

In late 1966, when Halifax cancelled its aquarium project and replaced it with the swimming pool, discussions of the city's 1967 priorities shifted dramatically. Gone was the focus on scientific research, education, tourism, and the creation of a modern city through a major urban renewal initiative. A new discourse focused on active lifestyles and the importance of safe, accessible, and affordable recreational activities. This abrupt deviation to discussions of access to leisure was, in many ways, a necessary consequence of the last-minute project substitution. Until late 1966, the municipal swimming pool had not been considered a possible centennial initiative, and it was never positioned as a rival project to the aquarium. The collapse of the aquarium project, however, forced Halifax to quickly examine its options of where centennial grants could be diverted in order to ensure that funding was not lost. Amazingly, council effortlessly repositioned its urban development priorities and shifted its energies, monies, and rationale towards an entirely new project to retain centennial monies. There was pressure from both politicians and the public to ensure that Centennial Grants Program funding was not forgone. The result was that there was no significant resistance to transferring monies from the aquarium to a municipal pool project.

This became a key moment when talk about providing recreational programs to those living in Halifax's downtown took centre stage. The Halifax Recreation and Playgrounds Commission (Recreation Commission) had toiled for a decade to improve swimming pool services on Halifax's peninsula. The infusion of centennial monies into the pool project focused attention on the importance of recreation activities and the Centennial Grants Program's role in this goal. It was also an indication of citizen demands for better leisure services. Halifax's Recreation Commission, established in 1952, reflected larger North American trends that saw cities take an increased interest in providing recreational activities, programs, and services to citizens. With the pool annointed as Halifax's new local 1967 project, the facility's receipt of additional centennial monies allowed it to literally double in size. The pool's new cachet as a 1967 undertaking threw a spotlight on issues of leisure, health, and accessibility. It was a dramatic discursive shift that included a reimagining of what 1967 meant to citizens and how the city should make best use of its centennial funding.

By the 1960s, Halifax was already home to numerous popular outdoor activity areas that included Point Pleasant Park, the Public Gardens, and the Halifax Commons, all located in the downtown core.[106] The city was heavily invested in all three properties, but none more so than in the Halifax Commons, for which it was responsible for daily operations and upkeep. The site included playgrounds, open green space, sports fields, and an outdoor swimming pool that was popular with families during the summer. The Commons' enduring popularity was undeniable. For two centuries it had served as a centrepiece of Halifax life. Yet, starting in the post-war era, questions were raised, particularly by city administrators, whether the Commons' facilities were sufficient to meet the requirements of the growing city. To address these expanding needs, the city commissioned an assessment of the Commons in the late 1950s to evaluate how it could improve recreational services. Halifax's sweeping post-war urban renewal and modernization efforts made it an ideal time to assess how the site could transform to meet the city's needs. The city hired Abol H. Ziai to make recommendations about how to make best use of the area. In his 1959 report, Ziai evaluated the park's long-term recreational needs and identified areas that required immediate attention. His report focused on the Commons' aquatic facilities, which, he concluded, were in dire need of improvement and did not come anywhere close to meeting the public's increasing demands for more swimming services. "Anyone who has passed by the Common [sic] during fine summer days," he admonished, "could easily notice the long line of children awaiting their turn to go into the pool." Population growth and urban pressures meant that swimming facility needs would continue to grow in the coming decades. To this end, Ziai recommended construction of an outdoor swimming pool on the Commons to accommodate the 1,500 youth who accessed facilities during the height of summer. Ziai argued that this pressure to provide improved recreational facilities was an overall commentary on the city's scarce public leisure space. The realities and challenges of summer life in Nova Scotia further exacerbated the need for improved services. The province's relatively short outdoor swimming season and the frigidness of its beaches compounded the need for a larger public facility.[107]

The city responded quickly. It reserved $600,000 in its 1960 budget for new swimming facilities at a time when the public began to demand improved services. That December, Councillor H.R. Wyman tabled a 1,000-signature petition with city council that called for the construction of a downtown multi-use recreation centre that included an outdoor swimming pool.[108] Requests were made to improve recreational programs for girls from community members. Stephen Cook, a local high school physical education teacher, suggested at a 1961 Recreation Commission meeting that with expanded facilities the city could improve upon its sorely lacking swimming program. Cook argued that, with better programs, Halifax youth would learn valuable lessons such as basic swimming, survival, and safety skills. He also envisioned more opportunities for girls to participate in a wide range of aquatic endeavours. He remarked that a new facility could "provide competitive swimming and ornamental swimming for girls to improve their grace, co-ordination and poise ... there is a complete lack of such a program in Halifax for girls."[109] Walter T. Brooks with the Halifax-Dartmouth & District Labour Council noted that his organization supported new aquatic services. A new swimming pool on the Commons was a "much needed and long overdue part of the recreation facilities" that "the children and citizens of this City are entitled to." The current facilities for youth were "deplorable," and he encouraged immediate action by the city to correct this deficiency.[110] Concerns such as these reflected the problems that many Haligonians had with the state of the city's recreational programs and opportunities.

In early 1962, the Recreation Commission recommended that a second outdoor swimming pool be constructed on the Commons.[111] These plans, however, quickly evolved into visions of a larger project. Almost as soon as the Recreation Commission's plans were tabled, there followed calls to replace this proposed structure with an enclosed, year-round facility. City staff listened and soon recommended construction of a permanent indoor pool in close proximity to the Commons, where there was an overwhelming demand for services. An ideal downtown property had even been identified. A vacant lot at the corner of Cogswell and Gottingen Streets, a mere one block east of the Commons, was deemed the perfect location. By 1965 city council had designated this site as the municipal indoor swimming pool's new home.[112]

Halifax clearly had a desperate need for improved services. A 1966 joint report from the Development Department and the Recreation Commission concluded that an indoor year-round use swimming pool was more beneficial than a second outdoor aquatic facility at the Commons. It studied municipal swimming facilities across the country and noted that their proliferation reflected the increased importance of leisure time for Canadians. Halifax had an obligation to meet these demands. It conducted a survey of annual swims taking place at all Halifax facilities, including the YMCA, YWCA, and the private south end Waegwoltic Club, and found that the city's facilities were "inadequate" and required improvements to meet the expanding needs of the city. "In these days of increased leisure time," the report noted, "the provision of modern facilities seems to be increasingly important. There is little doubt that a new public swimming facility would be used to capacity."[113] This concurred with broader developments as recreation was increasingly falling under the purview of local governments and municipalities. Recreation now occupied a greater portion of citizens' lives, and Canadians required organized leisure programs in order to engage in productive activities. Dramatic demographic, social, and cultural transformations, which included changes to the North American work week, reflected these trends. There was a decrease in work week hours for those engaged in American non-agricultural industries from seventy hours in 1850, to forty hours in 1950. Canadian statistics revealed that many worked thirty-five hours, and that some citizens even worked a thirty-two-hour week.[114] The report noted optimistically that within twenty-five years, the standard Western work week could fall to just one day:

> With acceleration of automation and with rising participation in the labour force, such a reduction could be brought about even earlier. In conditions such as this, recreation can no longer be considered a luxury but is fast becoming a major resource and an activity which is an essential urban industry. Apart from the economic arguments, the need for recreation can be justified on at least two basic presumptions. It is necessary for personal health and development and it is a force for good in the society. The widespread involvement of police and fire forces in developing and maintaining recreation activities for young people is an indication of the belief in

the ability of these actions to forestall delinquency and crime. Adequate relaxation of body and mind is essential for preserving a balanced attitude towards urban life and work. Recreation also contributes to the safety of life in cities. Justification for the cost of certain types of recreation can be easily established in the value of organized activities which keep children in safe environments and help to cut down the social cost of human tragedies.[115]

Those changing conditions resulted in a need for more recreational facilities. In particular, increased incomes, living standards, and affluence were predicted to dramatically affect Western lives and result in demands for state of the art leisure facilities.

For Halifax, there were also pressing socio-economic needs for peninsula residents that had to be considered. Some downtown areas that had high rates of rental accommodations were targeted as a population especially in need of recreational opportunities. Low-income Haligonians with large families, in particular, had an urgent need for accessible and affordable programs and services, as serious socio-economic conditions dramatically affected access:

> It is possible, but probably unattractive, to imagine a situation where people from some sections of the City who are relatively mobile could travel by car out of the area in which they live for several kinds of recreation which they may need. However, it is impossible to justify such an arrangement where low income families are involved. These families are not mobile and their only method of transportation may be the public transit services. Therefore, their recreation needs must be provided within the general vicinity of their homes. The people in the low income categories are those who are most urgently in need not only of housing and employment opportunities, but also of recreation activities located in areas that are accessible to them and are designed to serve their particular needs.[116]

It was clear that all Haligonians had a vested interest in and a right to access recreational facilities. City council stepped up to assume this responsibility, and by 1966 plans for a downtown swimming pool to meet these urgent needs were well underway. The project received a welcome boost that December when it became Halifax's new 1967 Centennial Grants Program initiative.[117] Halifax's new pool was slated to open by the end of the year, thereby meeting the construction and timeline provisions of the Centennial Grants Program.

The project was well received in the city. It was praised for the dramatic impact it would have on recreational services by making programs and services available to many Haligonians. Accessible recreation became a hallmark of local 1967 centennial projects, and the city stressed the importance of this objective. On 6 June 1967, Mayor Allan O'Brien broke ground for the new municipal swimming pool with a silver spade. The mayor remarked that the project was a "unifying factor" within the community that would help to bring much-needed services to peninsula residents.[118] Labour disputes and strikes in Halifax that summer delayed the building's completion, and subsequent supply problems and unfavourable weather conditions pushed construction two months behind schedule.[119] The Centennial Commission granted a time extension until February 1968, when the pool opened to much fanfare.[120] The building, located on Gottingen Street next to the Halifax Citadel, was a striking addition to downtown Halifax. Designed by Merram-Wright architects, the building featured a fifty-metre pool. It quickly became a popular recreational site that offered swimming programs for the public.

Halifax's Centennial Swimming Pool was adorned, as all local 1967 initiatives were, with a plaque that branded the building as a centennial project and featured the centennial symbol.[121] The commemorative inscription noted that the facility was a joint undertaking of the City of Halifax, the Province of Nova Scotia, and the Government of Canada. The plaque served an important purpose. Centennial Grants Liaison Officer A.B. Stoddard noted that it "memorialize[d] works constructed to commemorate the centennial of Confederation in an appropriate and lasting form which will, on the one hand, ensure continuity of appearance from coast to coast, and, on the other, will place a strong visual emphasis on the forward looking spirit of the centennial itself."[122] The plaque reinforced the state's roles in infrastructure development and commemorative initiatives, and literally and figuratively embedded its imprint on centennial projects, reminders that remain on community projects across Canada.

However, Halifax's local centennial projects' histories reveal the realities behind the workings of the Centennial Grants Program. The program was intended to help bolster Canadian identity, leave a tangible mark of the state's presence, and ensure that communities across the country participated in 1967 celebrations. Instead, these lofty ambitions were often eclipsed by meeting fluctuating local demands and needs. The program's operations demonstrate that details of how monies were spent were not as important as ensuring that all available centennial funds were expended. In the end, the federal and provincial governments retained little control over planning and development. To be sure, the power to distribute program funds rested with Nova Scotia's Centenary Committee. Yet this story shows that the province and Ottawa did not interfere with the Centenary Committee's funding decisions and project approvals. Ensuring that Canadian communities had a physical reminder of the federal and provincial governments' role in 1967 infrastructure development and centennial celebrations proved more important than the details of what communities ultimately chose as their individual projects. The role of Halifax City Council in this story reinforces this conclusion. Political disorganization and failure of municipal leadership contributed to the aquarium's demise as a centennial project. Despite a surge of initial support, the aquarium sparked battles between municipal, provincial, and federal politicians over questions of finances and feasibility. The conflicts were exceptionally divisive and drove a wedge between elected officials as the aquarium became a flashpoint for bitter infighting and highlighted the highly fractured state of centennial politics. Moreover, the project represented a significant lost opportunity for Halifax's revitalization.

Halifax's Centennial Grants Program experience also points to an intriguing story of the city's post-war renewal. The aquarium was envisioned as part of larger developments that swept across the city over the course of several decades. From its modern architectural design to its promise of attracting cutting-edge biological research and providing educational opportunities, the facility held great hope for marking the city as an exciting destination. The project's proposal, however, raised questions about initiatives that sought to brand Nova Scotia as a tourism destination. Politicians, the public, and project supporters relied heavily on the aquarium's characterization as a modern attraction that would lure visitors into the city, the province, and the Maritimes in general. The aquarium refuted larger concerns about the province's popular image, a significant issue for some. During a talk to the Sydney Board of Trade in June 1966, Nova Scotia's Deputy Minister of Trade and Industry, K.V. Knight, urged the province to expand economic opportunities. Knight noted that Nova Scotia had "an image of a backward, poor, uneducated area – stuck out in the middle of the Atlantic – dependant almost exclusively on fish and lobster for our existence." The minister noted that this "image gap" hindered economic development opportunities and expansion.[123] The establishment of a modern oceanographic facility in the province's capital would, many believed, go a long way in refuting these characterizations and solidifying the city's progressive and modern image.

It was certainly a deviation from efforts of the tourism industry and the provincial government during previous decades that relied heavily on an entirely different characterization of Nova Scotia. Ian McKay's work recounts attempts to brand the region as an area inhabited by the Folk, where visitors could experience a throwback to a kinder and gentler time. Yet Halifax's aquarium proposal and its discursive positioning disrupt McKay's assertions and reveal potential challenges to his analysis of the province's tourism industry. Although events such as Nova Scotia's 1967 Highland Games and Folk Arts Festival reinforced the idea that tartanism and anti-modernism were alive and well and remained vital components of provincial identity, the history of Halifax's local centennial projects challenges these notions. In particular, discussions of Nova Scotia's modernization and revitalization through urban development expose ruptures in the province's Folk image and indicate that these popular representations were not always dominant. This push to attract tourists through modern projects that cast the province as progressive and forward-thinking point to a Nova Scotia that in the post-war era was grappling to brand itself in ways that did not rely entirely on anti-modern characterizations.

Conversely, the aquarium project can be interpreted as an attempt to reimagine and revise Nova Scotia's Folk identity. The project connected the province to the sea, albeit in a more modern and progressive context. It further fit with other Nova Scotia centennial projects, namely Lunenburg's fisheries museum and nineteenth-century fishing village. As one commentary about that museum noted, the "old-time fishing village will be more than an attraction for the curious. It will perpetuate a way of life which is no more, but which we shall be the poorer if ever it is forgotten ... And because it is to stand side by side with the most modern in fishing equipment and techniques it will help to emphasize the tremendous strides which the industry has made." Halifax's centennial undertaking, it noted, was also "fittingly ... of the sea," and "Canada's birthday will be observed with the construction of facilities which should long remind us that an invaluable part of our heritage as Nova Scotians is the ocean."[124] Alfonso Rojo's assessment of the project reinforced these ideas. He observed that "Halifax is linked to the sea by its geography and history," and that the city was "ready to fill the gap between its oceanographic institutions of high learning and its people whose destiny has forced them to live by the sea. We can even say that every Nova Scotian has some connection with the sea and so we hope that everybody will profit from the projected centennial building."[125] The aquarium, then, embodied Bluenosers' connections to water in a very particular way, and even reinforced particular characterizations of the province.

The aquarium project continues to be discussed. In a September 2011 letter to the *Chronicle-Herald*, Halifax resident Bruce Spears noted that "what Halifax needs in order to attract tourists is something like a large aquarium/marine biology education facility. This is what many truly world-class cities have." He asked Haligonians to "imagine the synergy of a facility that would partner with local universities and organizations such as BIO [Bedford Institute of Oceanography]," positing that "the benefits would not only help students, tourism operators and local business, but more importantly, the environment."[126] A Halifax aquarium, then, remains at the forefront of some minds, even after the project was first seriously considered more than fifty years ago. Its proposal continues to embody the promise of modernization, progress, education, and the lure of the tourist dollar.

In the end, the history of Halifax's local 1967 projects provides a window into the convolutions of post-war municipal politics, urban modernization, and renewal. They also provide a glimpse into the importance of recreation and leisure for citizens, especially youth, a prime concern in post-war Canada. The Centennial Grants Program provided Canadian communities with opportunities to participate in a nation-building project, but the realities of its workings reveal it was more important to meet local infrastructure needs and ensure that monies available through this scheme were spent. While local projects were branded and partly financed by the federal and provincial governments, it was left to individual communities to determine what their areas required. For Halifax, the aquarium represented a bold, albeit badly orchestrated, attempt to revision itself as a modern city. Without a doubt, the lack of municipal leadership contributed to its downfall and the ensuing turmoil over whether Atlantic Canada's largest city would be without a 1967 undertaking. Its replacement with a municipal swimming pool shifted Halifax's vision considerably to provide safe, accessible, and affordable recreational opportunities for citizens. Leo McKay was undoubtedly delighted with the outcome.

Chapter 5

"The Centennial Cure":
The Community Improvement Program

In one form or another science is already reaching into the very heart of the community to transform the lives of each of us. It is essential that the control and development of our environment keeps apace. We have built towns and cities, canals and railroads, highways and other great works of construction at an unprecedented pace. But we have too often in the past made beauty the poor sister of material gain and careless workmanship the price of easy profit. We must lose no more time in making ugliness in our environment as unwelcome as financial losses on our balance sheets.
    Governor General Roland Michener, 1967 Speech from the Throne

In June 1965, Maurice Lamontagne, the federal Secretary of State and minister in charge of centennial affairs, addressed delegates to Canada's first National Community Improvement Program Seminar. The crowd, a cross-section of voluntary association, business, and government representatives, had congregated in Ottawa to launch an environmental awareness program as part of the country's 1967 celebrations. Over the course of the two-day event, participants recommended a series of civic improvement and beautification initiatives that would help produce a "sprightlier, cleaner and lovelier" country and, in turn, a "richer, fuller life" for citizens.[1] Workshops generated suggestions about how to achieve these results. They included recommendations to strengthen provincial legislation to tackle unsightly premises, adopt anti-litter and clean-up campaigns, initiate urban revitalization programs, and preserve historical buildings. These were, according to Lamontagne, significant and timely undertakings. Canada's post-war era had witnessed tremendous growth across many sectors. Massive urban and suburban developments, unprecedented levels of prosperity, a population boom, and commercial expansion had dramatically altered the country's social, economic, and physical landscape.[2] These transformations, however, had come at a very high cost. Poorly planned and unencumbered development proceeded largely unchecked. Industrial pollution devastated natural ecosystems at an alarming rate. The baby boom and waves of post-war immigration stretched the capacity of city life. These changes, the minister argued, harmed the country's environment and citizens' social and cultural welfare. Those residing in increasingly congested urban metropolises were especially afflicted. Many lived "under the dictatorship of machines" surrounded by a "jumbled heap of burly buildings" without access to green spaces. Conditions were anything but ideal. "Here, indeed, is the New Brutalism of the industrialized society," Lamontagne remarked, "here, indeed is the kingdom of the blind and senseless."[3]

Raising Canadians' Consciousness:
The 1960s Environmental Movement

Although the minister painted a stark picture of post-war Canadian life, he was confident that there was an answer to the country's woes. The solution? The Community Improvement Program, a national beautification and revitalization initiative spearheaded by the Centennial Commission. The program was one of Ottawa's most popular and high-profile Programs and Projects of National Significance. Branded as the "Centennial cure" for Canada's dystopia, the program's mandate was to raise awareness about the nation's environmental state, create attractive landscapes, and enhance citizens' quality of life through civic undertakings.[4] Projects included clean-up campaigns, tree and shrub planting, rural enhancement contests, urban renewal grants, legislative reforms, and ecological stewardship.[5] Ottawa underscored the point that while these were key projects for the country's overall well-being, the program also served a more immediate goal. Canadians were expected to tackle visual deficiencies and environmental blights in order to attain a certain aesthetic standard for the centennial year. Projects could be as simple as improving one's own home. Centennial Commissioner John Fisher hoped the year would "be a time when Canadians take pride in Canada," and he encouraged citizens to "cut their lawns and paint their houses for the sake of beautifying the country."[6] Success hinged on the efforts of all Canadians, working individually and collectively towards the goal of a cleaner, tidier, and more environmentally conscious country. Organizers optimistically expected citizens to embrace the Community Improvement Program's goals of eliminating eyesores and ushering in an environmental transformation unprecedented in the country's history.[7] The initiative was branded as potentially the "most truly national" of all 1967 schemes. If successful, it would engage volunteers in communities across the country and leave a legacy of social responsibility for the next generation.[8] The program's emphasis on citizen participation in grassroots projects fit well within Ottawa's 1967 mandate. "It is at the local level," organizers noted, "that the Centennial will develop into a meaningful occasion, when every citizen renews his faith in our nation and his confidence in our future."[9]

Although operational details were largely delegated to the provinces, community organizations, and a legion of volunteers, the Centennial Commission nevertheless enshrined the Community Improvement Program within the Crown corporation's administrative structure. Its designation as an officially sanctioned 1967 initiative guaranteed it a prominent national platform and ensured government support. The scheme was directed by Roderick Clack, a program manager who worked in the Centennial Commission's Planning directorate.[10] Clack arrived in Ottawa in 1965 with a wealth of professional experience and impressive urban planning credentials. An architect from British Columbia, he worked from 1958 to 1965 as a city planner in Victoria, where he designed many of that city's public spaces. He spearheaded numerous revitalization undertakings in that city, including Centennial Square, Centennial Fountain, and Bastion Square, which was later awarded the Massey Medal for Architecture.[11] Clack's job as program manager with the Centennial Commission was to "make Canadians more aware of their environment and to increase interest in improvement and beautification of individuals' homes and of whole communities."[12] During his tenure he worked closely with voluntary organizations, communities, and municipal and provincial governments to ensure that projects were implemented across the country. Under his watch the program became an example of all levels of government working cooperatively to implement beautification projects.

The Community Improvement Program's mandate was intimately connected with notions of environmental responsibility and ecological stewardship. It was also linked to larger shifts taking place in the postwar world. The phenomenal rise of the modern North American environmental movement during the 1960s left an indelible mark as public health concerns escalated over the effects of air and water pollution, natural resource depletion, and chemical use on both citizens and the natural world. This movement was strengthened by the rallying cries of protestors, lobbyists, and scientists who underscored the importance of balancing nature with human activity. The Community Improvement Program reflected and framed the environmental movement, and the relationship proved mutually advantageous. The Centennial Commission effectively used mounting concern about the world's ecological condition to bolster support for and participation in beautification projects. Ottawa was well aware of the movement's powerful appeal and channelled citizen activism into productive undertakings that were usually carried out by the state. Conversely, the environmental movement benefited from the program's platform as a sanctioned centennial scheme that served as a vehicle for Canadians to become part of a larger campaign that advocated ecological responsibility and stewardship.

North American attitudes towards the environment shifted dramatically during the 1960s as the public became increasingly concerned about the effects that human activities had on the planet. This was a striking shift from previous generations when ecological efforts had focused primarily on land management and conservation.[13] This was coupled with a turn away from the widely held belief that pollution was "a private or local matter" and not one that deserved national attention.[14] This perception changed during the 1960s as the devastating effects of industrial growth and Western society's ever-increasing consumption placed visible and unprecedented stress on the natural world.[15] To be sure, environmental activism was not a new concept. Yet the emerging focus on public health hazards caused by pollution, pesticides, radioactivity, plastics, and detergents marked a dramatic shift that placed "human health and welfare front and centre" among the decade's social concerns and spurred a powerful protest lobby.[16] Both middle-class American women and the counterculture movement were central in raising awareness about ecological concerns during the 1960s.[17] Other factors such as the increased use of North America's park systems[18] and the rise of the back-to-the-land movement[19] signalled that ecological issues were coming to the fore. Environmental activism was further bolstered by a wave of other emerging protest movements, many of which shared common concerns about peace, social justice, and equality.[20]

Perhaps no other moment in the modern environmental movement, however, was as influential as the rise of the scientific public intellectual.

In 1962, naturalist and biologist Rachel Carson published *Silent Spring*, a scathing indictment of chemical pesticide use and its devastating effects on humans, animals, and the land. Carson foretold a future where ecosystems had degraded to such an extent that they could no longer sustain wildlife, signalling extinction for many species. She vividly illustrated her point, positing that birds would be the first victims of environmental stressors. The result would be a "silent spring" when no bird songs would be heard.[21] Carson's study reflected what many scientists had long feared – that human activities posed increasingly serious threats to ecosystems and public health. *Silent Spring* sent shockwaves through the North American public, and it became a critical and commercial success. Carson's message left a deep impression, as she made the topic of environmentalism comprehensible through accessible prose – a challenge that had previously plagued scientists who had tried to alert society about the dangers of pollution.[22] As a result of its overwhelming popularity, the book was considered "the first evidence that there was a wide affinity for environmentalism among the American public." Famed biologist Barry Commoner argued that it cemented in citizens' minds the dangers of pesticide use.[23] *Silent Spring* became a rallying point for activists, as hundreds of antipollution groups formed in the wake of its publication.[24] The book further was credited as a major impetus for the 1972 ban on dichlorodiphenyltrichloroethane (DDT) in the United States.

Public intellectuals such as Carson were pivotal for the modern environmental movement, offering professionalism and expertise that legitimized the movement and increased public awareness.[25] Other factors contributed to the rise of environmental consciousness in that era. Pollution and ecological degradation cut across partisan lines and highlighted a problem that affected all sectors of the population, regardless of factors such as class and geographical location. "Not everyone has the time and money necessary to appreciate wilderness, nature-at-a-distance," Robert Paehlke notes, "but everyone eats, drinks, and breathes."[26] These concerns struck a chord. One 1970 survey found that 69 per cent of Canadians considered pollution a "very serious" problem, while another study found public support for government intervention in and responsibility for environmental issues.[27] Canada's federal government responded, albeit slowly, with the creation of the Department of the Environment in 1971 under Prime Minister Pierre Elliott Trudeau.[28] One year earlier, at the behest of President Richard Nixon, the United States established the Environmental Protection

Agency.[29] The celebration of the first Earth Day on 22 April 1970 was the symbolic culmination of a decade's efforts that stressed the importance of ecological matters.[30] Further, the founding of Greenpeace in British Columbia in 1971 signalled the beginnings of a radical and highly organized environmental lobby.[31]

The Community Improvement Program: A Community Effort

It is not surprising that the Centennial Commission harnessed the modern environmental movement's popularity and activism, and channelled it into the Community Improvement Program. Ottawa wagered that the public's new ecological consciousness would translate nicely into an interest in civic enhancement projects that aimed to protect the country's landscapes. It is striking that organizers exploited the concept, power, and language of 1967 to shore up Canadians' participation in the scheme and entice citizens to undertake activities normally carried out by the state. Ottawa was clear about its intentions. "This important program," the Centennial Commission's 1965–6 annual report noted, was "designed to use the Centennial as an incentive to mount a nation-wide drive to improve the appearance of both urban and rural areas."[32] The strategy was successful. Organizers downloaded responsibility for civic improvement projects to provincial and municipal governments, communities, voluntary associations, and individuals that became instrumental in the program. They assumed responsibility and embarked upon myriad beautification projects for the sake of, and in the name of, the centennial. Recruiting citizens en masse to undertake environmentally responsible initiatives further fulfilled one of Ottawa's key mandates to ensure that all Canadians were afforded the opportunity to participate in 1967 activities.[33] These groups also shouldered most fiscal and labour costs, working cooperatively at the local level to execute programming. This relieved Ottawa of a large financial burden normally associated with administering a national 1967 scheme. The $615,766 spent on the Community Improvement Program paled in comparison, for example, to the $47 million budgeted for the Confederation Train and Caravans.[34]

Promoting activities that normally fell under the government's purview proved extremely effective. Many communities, for example, introduced town clean-up campaigns undertaken by citizens that focused on trash collection and tidying downtown centres, tasks usually performed by municipal governments.[35] Glace Bay was a prime example.

In 1966, many were concerned that the town's Centennial Grants Program project, the Cape Breton Miners' Museum, was being built in close proximity to the local dump. To add insult to injury, the community was generally regarded as untidy. The *Cape Breton Post* reported with dismay that the museum "might be Canada's only Centennial project with a dump only a few feet away." The town council (which eventually voted to relocate the landfill) and project organizers implored residents to clean up the area so visitors would feel welcomed to the museum and into the community. Norman Lynk, the museum's campaign manager, remarked that cleaning up the town for 1967 was a responsibility that fell to the entire community.[36] Locally sponsored civic enhancement campaigns such as these proved popular and attracted a large cadre of community volunteers to the program's ranks. Sydney's Centennial Projects Committee, for example, initiated a 1967 garden that revamped the city's downtown and engaged individuals in a significant local initiative.[37] In this way, organizers stressed the importance of environmental enhancement and summoned the spirit of the centennial to encourage Canadians to become involved in grassroots programming.

Organizers emphasized that the Community Improvement Program would be successful only through the combined efforts of provincial and municipal governments, citizens, chambers of commerce, private companies, communities, and voluntary associations. Although logistics were largely downloaded to the local level, this did not mean that the Centennial Commission took a laissez-faire approach. With an initial budget of $85,000, the organization spearheaded promotional initiatives[38] that included producing publications about beautification projects[39] and funding university research on civic improvement.[40] The commission even produced a film, *A Townscape Rediscovered*,[41] about community redevelopment, and worked with the National Film Board on a documentary about civic improvement called *Age of Beauty* (although the project did not make it past preliminary scripting).[42] Documentaries were seen as an effective medium to spread the program's message in a way that also responded to the concerns of some Canadians about promoting environmental responsibility across the country. Delegates at a June 1965 Community Improvement Program Seminar had emphatically noted that there was "not a single film in Canada, made for Canadians devoted completely to anti-litter," and implored Ottawa to rectify this problem.[43]

A plethora of information packages, manuals, and pamphlets produced by Ottawa armed Canadians with practical suggestions to assist them in their beautification quest. Publications that instructed citizens on acceptable visual standards and proper comportment were distributed across the country. They covered topics ranging from urban planning, anti-litter campaigns, and farm beautification, to tree-planting projects. Ottawa relied heavily on provinces and communities to distribute the materials and ensure the Community Improvement Program's message reached as many Canadians as possible.[44] Centennial planners knew, though, that it took more than civic improvement suggestions to guarantee that the country was ready for 1967. To this end, Ottawa produced advice booklets for individuals and groups on everything from proper centennial comportment to acceptable aesthetics. Maintaining a minimum visual standard was important for the Centennial Commission. One booklet titled *Community Facelift* noted that "efficient and attractive communities should be the setting for all our centennial endeavours." It encouraged communities to clean dilapidated areas, brighten up downtown buildings with fresh coats of paint, and adopt "sign control legislation containing appearance standards." City centre signage that cluttered downtown aesthetics was another concern: "Excessive and inconsiderate self-advertisement defeats its own ends when signs compete wildly for attention or overlap. The only result is destruction of the common asset, namely the charm and harmony of the street. The monotony of sign ugliness is self-cancelling. Good sign manners are good for business and make a better looking community."[45]

Businesses were encouraged to promote proper centennial behaviour and act as model corporate citizens. *The Centennial and the Local Businessman*, for example, noted that 1967 was an opportunity for companies to set an example in their communities. They could lead the charge to beautify by painting buildings, removing derelict signage, and cleaning garbage dumps. Businesses also were key in instructing residents how to behave. Owners were encouraged to sponsor classes where citizens could learn how to conduct themselves when dealing with tourists.[46] Nova Scotia's centennial organizers agreed that such instruction was necessary. Communities were advised by provincial organizers to establish special volunteer groups of "official greeters and hospitality officers" that were trained to welcome and assist visitors.[47] For the Centennial Commission and its provincial counterparts, then, Canada not only had to look good, but citizens, community

Figure 5.1: Brochure, *Action 2: Community Face Lift*, © Government of Canada. Reproduced with the permission of Library and Archives Canada (2016). Source: Library and Archives Canada, Centennial Commission Fonds, AMICUS no. 24752774, cover page

Figure 5.2: Brochure, *Action 6: Centennial Clean Up*, © Government of Canada. Reproduced with the permission of Library and Archives Canada (2016). Source: Library and Archives Canada, Centennial Commission Fonds, AMICUS no. 24752774, cover page

organizations, and businesses required instruction on proper etiquette. Comportment was central to the program and the centennial's overall success.

Beautification efforts were bolstered through Community Improvement Program seminars that brought together organizers and stakeholders from across the country. The seminars were some of Ottawa's most significant civic improvement initiatives. The three annual gatherings held between 1965 and 1967 were catalysts in shaping the Community Improvement Program's mandate. Participants advised on beautification endeavours, developed policy, and worked to coordinate provincial, municipal, and community efforts.[48] In June 1965, an estimated 125 delegates gathered in Ottawa for the inaugural seminar. Maurice Lamontagne opened the event and spoke about the central role that civic enhancement and beautification efforts were expected to play during the centennial. Activities that revitalized Canada's environment, the minister remarked, gave citizens an opportunity to make a meaningful contribution to the 1967 celebrations. Delegates took this mandate to heart as they worked over the course of the seminar to determine programming priorities. Policy workshops tackled strategies to deal with national environmental issues such as air and water pollution, forest fire prevention, urban and rural landscaping, derelict road signs and properties, and wildlife and ecosystem preservation. The "Rural Story" workshop, for instance, recommended that provincial governments implement uniform unsightly premises legislation to help tackle visually unpleasant properties. This would ensure that the provinces had ample powers to deal with eyesores such as car cemeteries, manure lagoons, litter, dumps, pollution, and dilapidated structures.[49] In addition, it was recommended that provinces create protected areas for flora and fauna to offset rapid urban developments that harmed wildlife. "Clean-Up" workshop delegates remarked that citizens had to be armed with the proper tools to fight urban and rural blight. To this end, they proposed that curb-side garbage collections be coordinated and that litter boxes be installed across the country. Montreal and Ottawa had had great success with their garbage collection schemes, and other parts of Canada were encouraged to adopt similar measures. "People are more inclined to prevent or clean up litter," the workshop's report concluded, "if conditions are created to make this easier."[50] Many of the workshops' recommendations were subsequently adopted as civic improvement projects by provincial and municipal governments and voluntary associations across the country.

The Centennial Commission hosted a second seminar in Ottawa during the spring of 1966. This one-day gathering was well attended with 267 delegates that again reflected strong stakeholder representation from government, communities, and the private sector.[51] While the 1965 seminar had focused on strategies to improve Canada's environment, the 1966 proceedings highlighted ways to generate widespread citizen participation in civic improvement. Centennial Commissioner John Fisher stressed that the key was a community grassroots movement. "It is the homeowner, the businessman, the industry and the associations at the local level," Fisher remarked, "that must plan and co-ordinate the job, handle the paintbrush and plant the tree."[52] To this end, Ottawa looked to provinces, voluntary associations, and individuals to shoulder the bulk of planning Community Improvement Program activities.

Nova Scotia enthusiastically accepted the Centennial Commissioner's challenge. In July 1965, Premier Robert L. Stanfield established the Interdepartmental Committee on Beautification to oversee a host of community improvement initiatives across the province. Chaired by Trade and Industry Minister W.S.K. Jones, this group included representatives from the Nova Scotia Tourist Bureau, the Nova Scotia Information Service, the Attorney General's Office, and the Departments of Agriculture, Lands and Forests, and Highways.[53] Its mandate was to maintain the province's natural beauty through cooperative government efforts, provide leadership for community projects, and support local initiatives.[54] The committee knew that long-term investments in civic improvement would pay dividends to the tourism industry.[55] A clean, tidy, and beautiful province was, after all, an inviting destination. This group reviewed letters written by visitors to the province to determine which matters most deserved immediate attention, and prioritized its activities based on this feedback. Common complaints from tourists included excessive litter, highly visible junkyards, rundown structures, and unattractive landscaping. To tackle these problems, the group assigned tasks to various government departments. The Attorney General's Office revised the *Unsightly Premises Act* to provide stiffer fines for derelict properties. Additionally, it strengthened penalties for automobile graveyards under the *Salvage Yards Licensing Act*.[56] The Lands and Forests ministry coordinated tree planting and park programs, while the Department of Highways rolled out a public relations campaign to deter littering. Public Works beautified government buildings, while Trade and Industry promoted historic sites across the province.⁵⁷ Not only did these initiatives address the litany of grievances, but they also aimed to "instill a sense of pride" in Nova Scotians.⁵⁸

These efforts produced welcome results across the province. In Cape Breton, the Department of Lands and Forests tackled landscapes that had been ravaged by decades of unimpeded industrial activity. The Cape Breton Regional Planning Commission, with the ministry's assistance, introduced a successful tree-planting program. The commission's director, W.B. Thomson, remarked in 1966 that even though it was in only its second year, the project had already produced dramatic visual improvements to some of the island's most environmentally derelict sites. Newly transplanted greenery at coal-mining waste dumps, for example, made "bleak" sections of Cape Breton more aesthetically pleasing. Trees and shrubbery, Thomson noted, hid these neglected landscapes from public view. The program transformed other public spaces. With the assistance of children, trees were planted at numerous schools throughout Cape Breton. This initiative, Thompson argued, educated students on the importance of conservation, stewardship, and environmental responsibility.⁵⁹ The Centennial Commission was delighted with these efforts, characterizing them as practical and aesthetically pleasing that also offered "artful camouflage" for an otherwise desolate and inhospitable landscape, and transformed eyesores into a "delightful oasis in the concrete desert."⁶⁰

Nova Scotia's Interdepartmental Committee on Beautification also devised programs that responded to concerns raised during the National Community Improvement Program seminars. Delegates at the 1966 seminar were alarmed about the state of Canada's villages and towns, and reported that many had suffered at the hands of rapid post-war expansion. Those affected communities were described as "dying of neglect, by-passed by railroads and super-highways," with "building and re-development ... largely concentrated in rapidly proliferating urban complexes."⁶¹ This observation resonated with Nova Scotia's Department of Municipal Affairs, which proposed a solution. The ministry's director of community planning, Reginald Lang, recommended that local architects be commissioned to help restore historically significant buildings.⁶² What developed from this proposal was "Downtown Paint-Up,"⁶³ an urban beautification initiative, based on Great Britain's Norwich Plan, which had been introduced by the U.K. Civic Trust in 1957 to revitalize community centres. It was launched in Norwich, on Britain's southwestern shore, where the municipal council and the Civic Trust undertook a reconstruction and improvement project. An architect, a group of urban planners, and local businesses worked together to revitalize, redecorate, and aesthetically improve Magdalen Street, a central downtown thoroughfare. Properties were painted in a coordinated colour scheme, new bus shelters were constructed, dilapidated buildings were torn down, and new signage and light standards were installed along the street.[64] As a result of this successful revitalization, similar "face-lift" initiatives were implemented across Great Britain that "cost virtually no public money but did a lot for morale."[65]

The Norwich Plan was adopted in Canada in 1961 when business owners in Oakville, Ontario, came together to rejuvenate their city and attract shoppers to the downtown.[66] The program was eventually adopted in over fifty communities across the country and was branded as a simple scheme that could make a huge difference for neighbourhoods.[67] "All that is required to implement the Norwich Plan," a promotional pamphlet noted, "is that the Street or area be examined by an experienced eye and an organized plan set up to bring out the points of beauty, to cover the ugly blemishes or to remove them entirely." The scheme was not a "purely aesthetic idea of beauty for beauty's sake, rather it is recognition of the well-known merchandising fact that people like to shop where the surroundings are pleasant." The program proved so popular across Canada that a film about its adoption in Niagara Falls was produced.[68] The Norwich Plan also built on general urban beautification and clean-up schemes that already had been undertaken in several communities during the early years of centennial planning, and that had become very popular. Cities like Victoria, British Columbia, and St. Thomas, Ontario, were early adopters of beautification efforts that paved the way for more targeted urban programming through initiatives like the Norwich Plan.[69]

Nova Scotia's Downtown Paint-Up program adopted the Norwich Plan's urban renewal mandate, which fit well with the province's revitalization efforts. Launched in the spring of 1967, Downtown Paint-Up introduced a wide range of beautification initiatives that included cleaning up urban shopping and business centres, producing visually coherent and attractive cityscapes, and enhancing the overall appearances of towns and villages. It did so through coordinated paint schemes that welcomed residents and visitors to an aesthetically appealing town centre. Organizers argued that Nova Scotia's communities often suffered from a mishmash of clashing designs and colours. Sadly, as the program's promotional literature reminded citizens, this hodgepodge produced an unattractive downtown. "When it's every man for himself,"

miracle on main street

This project concerns your village street, the main street in your town, the shopping street nearest your home. Every commercial street has its own character, it is the centre of daily activity, the shop window of the community. But many buildings on these streets are drab, unpainted, uninteresting, undistinguished, they look untidy. The mass of unrelated storefronts, signs, and building facades, all add up to a depressing effect.

Look at the main streets in your community and become aware of their potential, their chance of coming into their own and the means by which they can be brought to life in their own individual way.

le miracle de la rue principale

Le projet intéresse la rue principale qui traverse votre village et votre ville, la rue commerciale la plus rapprochée de votre demeure. Chaque rue commerciale a son caractère propre: c'est le centre de l'activité quotidienne, l'endroit où les gens font du lèche-vitrine. Mais bon nombre de bâtiments qui s'alignent le long de ces rues sont décolorés, monotones, sans aucun caractère, d'aspect médiocre et dépenaillé. La masse hétéroclite des devantures de magasins et des enseignes constituent une véritable cacophonie visuelle.

Examinez les principales rues de votre localité et essayez de voir les possibilités d'amélioration qui s'offrent; essayez de déterminer les moyens à prendre pour leur donner un caractère vraiment distinctif.

Figure 5.3: Brochure, *Action 2: Community Face Lift*. © Government of Canada. Reproduced with the permission of Library and Archives Canada (2016). Source: Library and Archives Canada, Centennial Commission Fonds, AMICUS no. 24752774, "Miracle on Main Street"

one brochure noted, "a crazy-quilt pattern is often produced. Building character and architectural design get lost. Seldom is the result a harmonious and unified street scene."[70]

The scheme alleviated eyesores and created inviting and serene downtown districts. To fulfil its mandate, Downtown Paint-Up organizers assembled teams from the Nova Scotia Association of Architects that coordinated architecture, paint, and design plans tailored specifically for each participating community.[71] The initiative was funded through a $10,000 provincial grant announced in March 1967 by G.I. Smith, Nova Scotia's acting Minister of Trade and Industry.[72] The Department of Municipal Affairs paid two-thirds of the costs up to a maximum of $750, while the sponsoring municipality covered the remainder.[73] At the program's official launch, Smith remarked that downtown centres had to foster a sense of urban beauty that complemented the province's natural surroundings.[74] Nova Scotia's civic improvement and renewal plans included reclaiming derelict sites by converting "anti-human places" into "people places." Downtown Paint-Up helped to achieve these beautification goals. After all, Smith argued, a town's buildings and streetscapes were indicative of its overall image.[75] Promotional literature promised that citizens and communities would reap the program's rewards. For local businesses, an attractive urban centre translated into a more hospitable place to work, shop, and spend leisure time. Renewal bolstered local pride, encouraged cooperation, restored civic vibrancy, and created a beautiful downtown that left a lasting and positive impression on tourists.[76] Thousands were expected to visit Nova Scotia in 1967, and Downtown Paint-Up fit nicely with efforts of the Interdepartmental Committee on Beautification to ensure that the province was prepared to greet tourists.

With such an obvious appeal, Downtown Paint-Up proved to be exceptionally popular, with more than fifty Nova Scotia communities participating in the program.[77] Wolfville, in the province's picturesque Annapolis Valley, was the program's pilot project area. The town initiated a coordinated painting scheme that was completed in July 1967 to coincide with the official opening of the local centennial park. It installed light standards, removed dangerous overhead wires, and built tree and shrub planters along the streets. Mayor Murdock MacLeod praised these revitalization efforts that complemented the area's residential properties, attracted new businesses, and encouraged visitors to spend more time downtown.[78] Some communities struck their own Norwich Plan committees. Sydney's local board of trade coordinated civic improvement projects along Charlotte Street, the city's shopping and business centre. Board president and local businessman Harvey Webber noted that this initiative modernized the downtown, and that improvements were expected to have a positive economic impact on the area. He reminded residents that "community cleanliness is everyone's business," and that Canadians had a responsibility to participate in civic improvement projects.[79]

Downtown Paint-Up garnered national accolades and was singled out by the Centennial Commission as an example of the positive impact that civic improvement projects had on communities. Roderick Clack praised it as one of Canada's most imaginative beautification schemes. He noted, in particular, that it filled a serious gap in Nova Scotia's programming, which had previously focused largely on rural initiatives.[80] It was also an example of "excellent co-operation" and partnership between Ottawa, Halifax, and the Nova Scotia Architects Association that epitomized the federal government's vision for collaborative 1967 undertakings.[81] Clack lauded the province for its leadership in assuming a good portion of the scheme's finances, which lessened Ottawa's obligations.[82] In addition, public administration professionals acknowledged the initiative's importance. "Civic pride is restored, community cooperation increased and tourists get the impression of a progressive community and province," the *Civic Administration* journal noted, observing that "the life of older buildings is extended, shopping made pleasant and the tourist trade stimulated."[83] Downtown Paint-Up's supporters argued that the program provided communities with opportunities to reinvent their appearance and revitalize local economies.

While provincial government initiatives such as Downtown Paint-Up focused on urban beautification, Nova Scotia's voluntary associations spearheaded rural projects. Keeping with the mandate of the Community Improvement Program to create attractive and tidied landscapes, several organizations challenged citizens to revitalize their properties for centennial year. The Village and Town Beautification Contest was one such program. Sponsored by the Nova Scotia Division of the Community Planning Association of Canada, the contest was open to those who lived in incorporated communities. Contestants submitted "before" and "after" colour photographs of their homes to a jury that awarded cash prizes for "painting, tidiness, condition of lawns, shrubbery, trees, driveways, fences, floral decorations and the general improved appearance of the property and building."[84] Similarly, the Women's Institute of Nova Scotia (WINS) and the Nova Scotia Federation of Agriculture (NSFA) jointly launched a Rural Beautification Program that encouraged citizens to spruce up their properties. The program was based on the Federated Women's Institutes of Canada's centennial project, "Making Canada Lovelier." Adopted across the country, the program's mandate was to encourage citizens to make civic improvements to their properties that welcomed tourists to "a better and brighter Canada."[85] The program fit well with other beatification initiatives adopted by the Federated Women's Institutes of Canada. The federation also introduced a program that placed picnic tables in parks across the country, including the International Peace Garden in Boissevain, Manitoba.[86] "Making Canada Lovelier," along with similar activities carried out by 4-H Clubs, promoted the advantages of tidier landscapes, especially in rural areas. The program was introduced in Nova Scotia in 1965 and was supported by $25,000 in grants from the province's Department of Trade and Industry.[87] When the department's minister, W.S.K. Jones, announced program funding, he stressed that visitors should experience "a neat landscape, tidy farm homes and buildings and litter-free highways" that complemented the region's natural beauty.[88]

In addition to these programs, WINS and NSFA designated 1–7 May 1967 as Rural Beautification Week. Events included the Rural Beautification Contest, which challenged property owners to clean up yards, demolish derelict buildings, paint houses, and plant shrubbery.[89] Unlike the Village and Town Beautification Contest, this initiative targeted residents who lived in non-chartered areas. Entrants competed in categories for most impressive transformations to farm houses, buildings, and century farms. There was also a division for projects initiated by youth.[90] A commercial category encouraged businesses to clean up restaurants, street signs, and accommodations. Organizers argued that these enhancements made "good economic sense," helped companies "take greater pride in their premises," and ensured that the province was ready to greet the million tourists expected to visit the province in 1967.[91] The Rural Beautification Contest was lauded as another community improvement success for the province. By August 1967, eighty-six Nova Scotia communities had taken part,[92] with over 250 entries from seventeen counties.[93] The century farms category, for family properties over 100 years old, alone garnered 140 submissions.[94] WINS and NSFA even sponsored seminars to encourage participation.[95] For its part, the provincial government waived municipal tax assessment increases normally commensurate with the higher property value for land improvements, as an incentive to encourage participation.[96]

While such contests proved popular, local initiatives also roused widespread interest in civic improvement throughout Nova Scotia. Indeed, citizens and voluntary associations were cast as the key to the Community Improvement Program's success. Not only did this downloaded responsibility fulfil the Centennial Commission's mandate for nationwide engagement, it laid the groundwork for the program's post-centennial continuance. Speaking at a conference in Sydney, Roderick Clack reminded delegates that the program's long-term success rested solely with their efforts. He warned, however, that although various levels of government were obvious funding sources, their continued monetary support for civic enhancements was not guaranteed. Rather, those working at the local level were responsible to ensure that projects were not only initiated but that they were sustainable post-1967. Local businesses had a particular leadership role to play to ensure a solid foundation for ongoing civic responsibility.[97] Clack argued that this was particularly relevant to places such as Cape Breton, where there was significant "evidence of decay." He singled out women's groups and boards of trade as invaluable sources of program support and remarked that it was their work that would secure the scheme's long-term viability.[98] Centennial Commission organizers could not stress enough that it was local efforts that made the Community Improvement Program a success.

Indeed, Nova Scotia's community grassroots initiatives lured an army of volunteers en masse to the program's ranks. Helping them along the way was Lorne V. Hutt, the province's centennial planning coordinator, whose job was to make certain that all Nova Scotians were afforded the opportunity to participate in 1967 activities.[99] By Hutt's account, citizens took to projects in droves. In August 1967 he reported to Clack that no fewer than seventy-eight communities had launched beautification programs, the most popular of which were town clean-ups. In his view, the province's revitalized environment was a source of pride for Nova Scotians who now felt that they lived in a region "noted for its inherent tidiness." Bluenosers beautified their communities through a variety of different projects. Hutt singled out one unnamed "semi-depressed mining community" (referring in all likelihood to either Glace Bay or Springhill), whose youth had "paraded through the streets ... armed with brooms, mops, pails of water" in a valiant effort to clean up the downtown. Their endeavours were complemented by the town's local centennial group that planted flowers and shrubs throughout the community to "uplift and rekindle community pride."[100]

These citizens were not alone in their efforts. North Sydney's town council instructed its engineer to estimate the cost of buying metal trash cans to help clean up streets and deter littering. Local police were requested to watch for debris falling from vehicles headed towards the dump to ensure that waste was not spread throughout the area.[101] In March 1967, Spryfield's local board of trade embarked on a campaign, spearheaded by the group's chair and future provincial premier John M. Buchannan, to fight "visual poverty" and clean up the community.[102] In Digby, Mrs Charlie Best, co-chair of Nova Scotia's Rural Beautification Committee, urged citizens to "keep the precious heritage of the first permanent Canadian settlers [of] our beautiful province clean, pure and shiny." Best equated beautification and revitalization projects with a much-needed sense of order. The *Digby Courier* reported that "litter and garbage on our beaches and highways spell disorder. Therefore any person littering our highways should be subjected to a citizen's arrest."[103] There is no evidence to suggest, however, that vigilante litter squads patrolled Nova Scotia's streets and highways.

Halifax also initiated a clean-up campaign. City councillors suggested various ways to involve residents in beautification and tidy the city, which was described by Councillor Hedley Ivany as "unsanitary." Ivany proposed undertakings designed to enhance the city's aesthetics, including a clean-up of the iconic Grand Parade Square. Renewed attractions, he argued, would entice visitors and residents downtown.[104] Ivany noted that if every Haligonian planted one flower seed, the result would produce over 100,000 blooms for 1967 that would improve the city's aesthetics.[105] Councillor Don LeBlanc called upon city council to spearhead tidying programs and even suggested that labour contracts be waived to allow union workers to assist with these efforts.[106] Beautification was promoted in other ways. One Halifax newspaper published a checklist to help property owners improve their land that included a questionnaire to help assess cleanliness, aesthetics, and landscaping. The Halifax Board of Trade offered services and advice to homeowners about how to improve their properties.[107]

Nova Scotia Centennial News Briefs, a monthly publication about the province's 1967 activities, was another invaluable source for suggestions on how to create attractive urban centres, conceal dumps, remove derelict and dilapidated signage, and strategically plant greenery.[108] A designated provincial clean-up in May 1967 encouraged Nova Scotians to "spare no effort" in beautifying communities to make them "as attractive to visitors as possible."[109] These efforts to tidy the province and

168　　　　　　　The Centennial Cure

camouflage environmental blights demonstrate that a wider environmental ethos had not yet been fully formed. Community Improvement Program efforts came at a transitional stage where government and community organizers were concerned more about aesthetics than tackling the root causes of environmental problems. Nova Scotia's community improvement efforts reflected this philosophy, while nevertheless offering citizens copious grassroots activities.

Recruiting a Legion of Volunteers: Economic, Military, and Environmental Discourses

As Nova Scotia's experiences revealed, the Community Improvement Program's success depended heavily on local volunteer efforts. Yet organizers did not rely on the assumption that Canadians would simply offer up their services to better the country's environment. Rather, stakeholders used numerous discourses that encouraged individuals and corporations to volunteer their time and efforts. A series of carefully crafted economic, militaristic, and environmental discourses were employed to frame the program's larger aims and encourage Canadians' involvement in civic improvement. They drew heavily from citizenship rhetoric that cast participants in a variety of different roles. Economic discourses made participation in Community Improvement Program activities more attractive, especially for governments, industries, and corporations. Beautification projects were likened to doing "good business" and were presented as key tools for fiscal growth at the community, provincial, and national levels. Organizers argued that tidy and picturesque landscapes branded the country as a lovely and modern vacation destination that fuelled local economies and stimulated Canada's burgeoning tourism industry. Visitors who were impressed with their surroundings, Ottawa insisted, would spend their time and money discovering the country. Just as important, a clean landscape could lure them back after the excitement of centennial and Expo 67 had faded away. To prepare for this onslaught of international and domestic visitors, citizens and businesses were asked to review landscapes with a critical eye and take appropriate action to put the country's best foot forward. "The requirement is to persuade Canadians to see their surroundings as visitors view them," the Centennial Commission noted, "and then persuade Canadians to make these surroundings so attractive that visitors will be impressed."[110] The Rural Beautification Program and Downtown Paint-Up mandates addressed these concerns. Nova Scotia recognized that the financial spinoffs from a beautiful environment could prove particularly lucrative. The Community Improvement Program held significant potential to grow the tourism industry, which was becoming increasingly central to Nova Scotia's livelihood. A tidied, orderly, attractive, and welcoming environment that included revitalized urban shopping and downtown centres boosted local economies by enticing travellers – and even residents – to explore the province.

Nova Scotia had good reason to anticipate a tourist boom. Upwards of one million international and domestic visitors were predicted to travel to the province in 1967. Many were expected to travel eastwards to Atlantic Canada after visiting Expo 67.[111] Organizers predicted that countrywide centennial activities, festivals, and attractions would increase travel that year, especially during the summer months, and would be a boon for the entire country. There was lingering concern, though, that Expo 67 would prove to be a double-edged sword for those outside Quebec. With such a focus on attracting people to Montreal, some worried that that city's events would harm the rest of Canada's tourist industry. This necessitated an increased commitment to Community Improvement Program activities in outlying provinces to persuade visitors to travel outside the Montreal area. For Nova Scotia, this increased pressure to initiate beautification projects. Halifax Councillor Hedley Ivany spoke on the eve of Expo's opening in April 1967, and he addressed concerns that Montreal's mega-event would shift citizens' attention westwards, away from Halifax.[112] Now was the time, he remarked, for Haligonians to ensure that the city was as prepared as it could be to welcome travellers.

The Community Improvement Program was integral to the Nova Scotia government's larger tourism development strategy. Yet the program raised questions about how the province sold itself to visitors. Paradoxically, the scheme introduced images of the province that contrasted with those popular ideas that cultural promoters had relied upon during the first half of the twentieth century to promote tourism. Beginning in the 1930s, Nova Scotia had branded itself as an anti-modern destination. Visitors were encouraged to turn their tourist gaze towards the region's Folk, who were portrayed as figures frozen in a simpler, quainter, and unproblematic time. These personas were presented as embodying the essence of Nova Scotia's cultural identity, and they were used as a popular trope that became the basis for a flourishing tourism industry.[113] Nova Scotia's anti-modern image, however, clashed with many of the Community Improvement Program's discourses. Civic enhancement and beautification contrasted starkly with the popular Folk image and disrupted the province's anti-modern characterizations. Downtown Paint-Up branded the province as a modern destination. Indeed, the "enhancement of Nova Scotia's progressive image" was touted in promotional literature as one of the scheme's many benefits.[114] While in some ways Community Improvement Program initiatives can be read as restorative efforts that transformed communities by harking back to anti-modern times, they overwhelmingly focused on presenting the province as progressive and modern. Ironically, tidied landscapes, new transportation facilities, better amenities, and exciting attractions all facilitated visitors' experiences with the anti-modern Folk.[115] The Community Improvement Program challenged the traditional ways in which the province was presented to, and consumed by, tourists and pointed to larger changes that were taking place in Canada. Cleaning up landscapes and preparing them for tourists pointed to new standards and expectations that were implemented to attract visitors. Expectations of what cities and towns looked like were elevated. In this way, Nova Scotia was being integrated into a national aesthetic framework that established a set of standards of tourists' expectations.

While civic enhancement schemes cast Nova Scotia as a progressive and modern destination, they aimed, first and foremost, to impress tourists and entice them to spend time exploring the province. Not surprisingly, some communities already recognized the potential economic spinoffs of beautification efforts. In early 1964, Inverness, on Cape Breton's western shore, undertook a three-year clean-up campaign. This project was spearheaded by the Home and School Council of Inverness North, which believed that civic improvements promoted tourism, provided much-needed employment for the area's youth, increased business activity, and encouraged economic diversification. Residents were asked to undertake initiatives that included tree and flower planting, painting projects, and removing derelict buildings.[116] Such efforts, organizers argued, stimulated the local economy and prepared the county for the influx of tourists expected in 1967.

Businesses that participated in the Community Improvement Program, though, were expected to negotiate between fostering genuine community civic activism and blatantly profiting from increased visitor traffic. To this end, centennial organizers deployed a careful discourse that warned companies about certain dangers. Business owners were advised to ensure that their premises were welcoming and orderly, and that they reflected an enthusiasm for 1967. At the same time, they were instructed not to exploit the spirit of the centennial for profits. A "Made in Canada" promotional campaign, one booklet advised, provided an opportunity for businesses to showcase domestic products and foster local pride. Nevertheless, there was a fine line between national pride and self-promotion. A Made-in-Canada campaign should not be too ostentatious. "The Centennial, of course, is not the time for evident commercialism," one publication noted, "but at the same time this important event provides an opportunity for business to put its best foot forward and show interest and enthusiasm for things Canadian."[117] Some Nova Scotia businesses ignored this advice and jumped on the beautification bandwagon. The Halifax Seed Company launched a flower-planting campaign. Promotional materials asked people to "join the crusade against ugly" and cast individuals as "Anti-Ugly Crusaders." Their motto? "Down with Ugly! Up with Tulips!" Included with a purchase of tulips from the store were an "anti-ugly trowel" and a "beautiful Ugly Button" that proclaimed "I Hate Ugly."[118]

The Centennial Commission also used economic discourses to entice businesses to subsidize Community Improvement Program projects. Companies, for example, were encouraged to sponsor shopping district renovations. One promotional handout pictured a well-lit retail area that featured a description intended to strike fear into the heart of businesses and consumers alike. Potential dangers, it pointed out, lurked in unsafe downtown areas because of poorly lit streets and cracked sidewalks, which posed serious threats to good Canadian shoppers. Dangers only worsened when night fell and inadequately illuminated features became more perilous. Evening shopping was "quite a challenge" as consumers "grope[d] their way from store to store, after moving through long dark canyons of unyielding pavements, crossings and buildings." This experience was contrasted with shopping centres whose numbers had increased dramatically during the post-war era. Modern malls made "night time shopping, or just plain walking, a safe and pleasant experience for the very young, the young and the old."[119] Another handout depicting "Main Street, Typicalville, Canada" noted that "proper outdoor lighting" eliminated and reduced "personal attacks, acts of vandalism, accidents and even just plain getting lost."[120] Businesses were encouraged to sponsor lighting projects that improved access to retail areas and ensured shoppers' safety. These discussions were tied to ideas about post-war consumption. Making downtowns more inviting enriched Canadians'

CENTENNIAL COMMISSION COMMUNITY IMPROVEMENT PROGRAM

centennial clean-up

The immediate task is to make a gigantic improvement in the appearance of the Canadian scene. Every community—urban and rural—should look its sparkling best for Centennial guests and for the residents of these places themselves. There is no excuse for litter, anywhere. I suggest volunteer workers knock on every door in Canada to seek the co-operation of every Canadian in Community clean-up.

JOHN FISHER.

Clean-up and beautification share the Centennial spotlight because the everyday appearance of our communities is the backdrop for centennial events.

A clean, tidy and attractive appearance influences the attitude of residents, visitors and prospective business toward the community. To achieve this, vigorous and continuous clean-up, anti-litter, and beautification efforts must involve action by all citizens. To be the "Cleanest Community in Canada" is a worthwhile and rewarding goal for the Centennial and every year.

"Centennial Clean-up" aims to arouse the sense of individual responsibility and pride in clean attractive surroundings for Canadians.

The litter problem results from everyday thoughtless actions by millions of individuals. It is paper wrappers strewn on the side-walk or dropped on the street, discarded material on a vacant lot or left in a park, an untidy playground, derelict cars on the countryside, the refuse scattered along the highway, from automobiles, or debris seen around commercial or industrial property. Litter is costly, litter can be a fire hazard, litter may be a health menace, litter is everybody's problem.

Cleaning up existing litter is the important first step, leading to the continuing educational task of litter prevention. This involves a change in the habits and attitudes of people.

Every litter bit hurts your community, yet constant exposure to litter breeds indifference and acceptance of the "litter habit." In fact, when people develop the trick of not really seeing it they don't develop the "tidy habit."

Be observant, see your community through the eyes of a discriminating visitor. Don't be an apologist, take action. Use the check list to think Community Clean-up and Beautification.

how aware are you?

YES NO
☐ ☐ 1. Are you aware of the litter in your community?
☐ ☐ 2. Is your community litter conscious?
☐ ☐ 3. Do school children participate in clean-up and beautification?
☐ ☐ 4. Does a Service Club sponsor Youth clean-up activities?
☐ ☐ 5. Do you read or hear about anti-litter through the mass media?
☐ ☐ 6. Are there enough litter containers on the streets?
☐ ☐ 7. Are the streets around playgrounds or schools litter free?
☐ ☐ 8. Does the municipality sponsor an annual clean-up campaign?
☐ ☐ 9. Do you want your community to look clean, tidy and attractive?
☐ ☐ 10. Would you volunteer your time to work with others to help make yours the Cleanest Community in Canada?

Figure 5.4: Brochure, *Action 6: Centennial Clean Up*, © Government of Canada. Reproduced with the permission of Library and Archives Canada (2016). Source: Library and Archives Canada, Centennial Commission Fonds, AMICUS no. 24752774, "How Aware Are You"

shopping experiences and stimulated economic growth. In addition, Nova Scotia's Provincial Centennial Office promoted illumination as a worthwhile project and suggested that downtowns could be aesthetically improved through strategic lighting. That office urged communities to "light up what we have cleaned up."[121]

While economic discourses encouraged communities and businesses to clean up the landscape, other tactics enticed participation in civic improvement. Perhaps the most striking was citizenship rhetoric that asserted that the general public was responsible for beautifying the country. Canadians were cast in boosters' language as "citizen soldiers" who were expected to fulfil their patriotic duty by waging war against visual disharmony, ugliness, and disorder. A carefully crafted militaristic language encouraged Canadians to declare a war against ugliness in an effort to reclaim a more liveable environment. These citizen soldiers were the country's front line of defence against urban and rural blight, untidiness, and the new brutalism. The country required a vanguard of volunteers who were implored to take up arms – in this case brooms, garbage bags, and paintbrushes – in this epic battle against environmental blight. Organizers argued that Canadians had a patriotic duty to enlist in the Community Improvement Program and to ensure that the country was beautified. The scheme, they insisted, shored up positive feelings of national unity as individuals from coast to coast came together in a collective struggle.

Martial language framed the program's promotional literature. Pamphlets, press releases, and speeches invoked images of soldiers, wars, and calls to arms. Nowhere was this more obvious than in the Centennial Commission's Community Improvement Program circulars. One 1966 newsletter asked Canadians to become "citizen soldiers" and "worker soldiers" who defended the country from environmental blight. This literature was defined by exceptionally disciplined and masculine language. Yet evidence suggests that programming was not necessarily taken up in gendered ways. Surprisingly, the emphasis on collective, community work overrode initiatives that targeted particular groups. Rather, promoters stressed the program's potential to transcend differences and make real change in the name of nationalistic goals.

Individuals and communities were solicited to join the fight and launch a "massive offensive" against "man-made ugliness," and participants were begged to "attack this enemy of ugliness bravely." Ottawa saw this promotional material as some of its most important front-line weapons to instruct Canadians on beautification. "Canada's Centennial

Commission will provide intelligence and ammunition to local groups," one newsletter noted, "and it is at this level – on the actual battleground – where the war will be won." Ottawa was clear that there was a large battle to be fought. Rapid post-war development and industrialization had done little to preserve the country's natural environment. Canada's good citizen soldiers were asked to initiate activities that offset eyesores such as vacant lots, garbage dumps, and car cemeteries. Workers were requested to hide, rather than clean up, these messes. Greenery and fencing could be used in clever ways to "disguise" environmental blights that could be easily "hidden from the world." Canadians were also advised to work with city planners to design urban green space and remove wiring from city skylines.[122] Arming citizen soldiers with proper instruction, organizers argued, guaranteed that the battle against environmental degradation would be won in time for the centennial year.

Success of the Community Improvement Program depended largely on local volunteer efforts from the country's citizen soldiers. The epic battle against environmental degradation, the Centennial Commission asserted, would be won only through the collective work of all Canadians in every community:

> This massive offensive on ugliness cannot be truly successful unless ... committees recruit battalions of volunteer workers to knock on every door in Canada and to seek the co-operation of every Canadian. This means the door of every home, store, office, factory and farmstead in the land. And it is probable the worker-soldiers will have to call at a door many more times to produce the kind of mass participation the project demands ... With tact and diplomacy and enthusiasm and subtle forcefulness, this key worker will approach the residents or merchants or farmers to encourage Centennial Community improvement activity and to make helpful suggestions about the sort of work which might be carried out ... This can be the most important campaign in which Canadians were ever engaged ... Canada has declared a war on ugliness – Canada asks you to get out there and fight![123]

The newsletter continued,

> It is at the community level, of course, that the actual fight for a more beautiful, attractive and enjoyable Canada is taking place. The enormous program of research and planning at Federal and Provincial levels is ineffective until it is brought to the individual who will do the actual work. It

is the Community Improvement Committee of the local Centennial organization which can provide the required initiative. Without it, our citizen soldier is fighting the war on ugliness alone; his vital contribution to our campaign – its very keystone – is in jeopardy. If there is not yet a strong Centennial Community Improvement group in your community, take immediate action to ensure that one is formed. Do it now, today – we are desperately short of time.[124]

This militaristic language was invoked to recruit volunteers to the program's ranks. During a 1966 address to a local board of trade, Frank Wallace, the Centennial Commission's regional officer for Nova Scotia, encouraged citizens, communities, and businesses to undertake activities to ensure that the country could win the battle against environmental damage.[125] Similarly, in an October 1967 speech to the National Community Improvement Program Seminar, Centennial Commissioner John Fisher stressed that all Canadians could assume the citizen soldier persona. Their contributions, no matter how small or large, would make for a significant centennial legacy by improving the country's aesthetics. "Our citizen 'soldier,'" Fisher proclaimed, "is the man on the street – your street, my street, every Canadian street."[126]

For some, the Community Improvement Program's broad appeal and its altruistic aims were so captivating that they had the power to transcend gender, ethnic, regional, and class differences. The result was that the program was seen as one of the more truly national, inclusive, and patriotic 1967 initiatives. Halifax Councillor Hedley Ivany remarked that civic improvement gave "all classes of the community" the opportunity to "enlist actively." He noted that "good citizenship is good business" and that beautification should be taken up by "every person concerned about his home, his community, his country, his business."[127] Canadians had an obligation to fight environmental blight, which Ivany described as the "menace to the well-being of our communities."[128] The country's landscapes were presented as a battlefield where all Canadians could engage the ugliness enemy. "The downtown areas of our larger cities," one publication noted, "often look as if they'd been subjected to massive bombing attacks."[129] The notion of the citizen solider going to war was a constant theme. Without their collective and patriotic efforts, organizers argued, the program's full potential would never be realized.

Not surprisingly, environmental discourses were deployed to encourage Canadians to participate in the Community Improvement Program.

Yet the emphasis on ecological stewardship stood in stark contrast to the military language that attempted to rouse citizen interest in civic improvement. Martial language relied on the discourses of past experiences and on the imagery of military conflicts. Meanwhile, the program's environmental discourses drew on notions of responsibility for the country's future. Language emphasized the urgent need to stem the destruction of the natural landscape and to make certain that later generations would be able to enjoy the land. Ultimately, the program's boosters emphasized that beautification that improved the country's "outdoor living room" contributed to the greater good of society, enhanced Canadians' lives, and preserved the environment for future generations.

Beautification projects also held the potential, organizers argued, to fundamentally improve Canadians' social and cultural welfare by creating a higher standard of living that elevated citizens' well-being and overall health. Organizers recognized that it was important to promote individual responsibility and awareness for the country's natural heritage. Instilling these notions in the general public would have positive long-term results that would reverberate through to future generations. Creating green spaces, protecting parks, and tidying communities, then, were important investments in Canadians' social and cultural welfare. A clean neighbourhood was, apparently, a happy neighbourhood. "What is required is an awakening in personal pride," delegates to the 1965 National Community Improvement Program Seminar noted, "and a deepening of personal responsibility for our environment – urban or rural, owned by the individual, or by the municipality or by the Crown."[130]

One of the most extraordinary themes that framed this discourse of improving citizen welfare was that bettering the environment countered the new brutalism of Canada's industrialized society. It is striking that these discussions were often instigated by senior government and Centennial Commission officials in public forums. It is remarkable, and somewhat astonishing, that government representatives employed anti-capitalist language that openly critiqued the adverse effects of post-war expansion. The consequences of human activity on the natural world and the impact on Canadians' welfare, many politicians argued, could no longer be ignored. Improved landscapes were expected to offset those deleterious effects of development and attack what Lamontagne referred to as the country's new brutalism. Everything from suburban growth, to industrial and commercial expansion, to national park desecration came under scrutiny. In her keynote address at the 1966 National Community Improvement Program Seminar, newly appointed federal Secretary of State Judy LaMarsh remarked that sweeping changes had to be made across all sectors of Canadian society in order to confront this new brutalism. Her speech was a searing indictment of capitalism. She stated that "public opinion must ... be aroused to the need for rehabilitation, the need for eradication of blight, with what is called the brutalism of the machine, of what is called progress, which is often an euphemism used by profiteers to make money." She continued, "Much of the ugliness in this country is due to brutalism, [and] much of it is also due to sheer apathy and indifference." No landscape was immune. The post-war era had produced an aesthetically unpleasant environment, where ugly urban developments, dirty streets, rural eyesores, and the country's neglected national parks had disfigured the country from coast to coast. Citizens had a duty to tackle these blemishes and leave the environment in a much better state. The best way to accomplish this, LaMarsh stated, was for Canadians to become active participants in the Community Improvement Program.[131]

Beautification and civic enhancement initiatives were expected to offset those adverse effects of post-war growth and, it was hoped, provide citizens with the opportunity to think about future development. Far too often, the Centennial Commission noted, individuals were distracted by the "pressure of progress" that diverted citizens' attention from reflecting on the effect that their actions had on the landscape.[132] State officials championed a wide range of programming to counter the new brutalism, and there was no shortage of suggestions from Ottawa about how to tackle the problem. During a speech to the Canadian Society of Landscape Architects and Town Planners, Peter Aykroyd, the Centennial Commission's director of public relations and information, stated there was an urgent need to "salvage" what few city green spaces existed and create new parks and environmental sanctuaries. Many Canadians were "suffocating in asphalt, brick and concrete," he noted, despite the country's abundance of land. Aykroyd implored the group to do what it could to preserve a "tiny green patch for the respite of ... harassed citizenry."[133] Such projects offset the new brutalism and helped restore balance between humans and nature, especially in heavily congested urban areas.

The state of Canadian cities was another focus for Community Improvement Program boosters. Maurice Lamontagne, for example, campaigned to preserve historically significant architectural sites. Cities, he argued, required "airing, face-lifting and replanning to eliminate what is transitory and gross and to conserve and construct what is historical and good." Attention had to be paid to aesthetic surroundings and citizens had to work "for the rebirth and renewal of our urban areas as dignified habitations of man."[134] Centennial Commissioner John Fisher agreed that post-war pressures had brought unwelcome developments to bear on Canadian society: "The whirlwind growth of our society, brought on by technological change, tends to prevent us from pausing to admire the beauty around us. The point is often reached when this beauty is allowed to tarnish and deteriorate. Machines today provide us with extra comforts, well-being and leisure, but additional hours of leisure are not necessarily spent on creating beauty or in preserving the heritage bequeathed to us by our ancestors."[135] In a country as affluent as Canada, there was no reason to allow the environment's continued defilement. Although the country was "superlatively endowed with natural beauty," Fisher noted, citizens were desecrating the landscape at a "frighteningly increasing rate." Steps had to be taken to reverse this trend and ensure that Canada's second century was much more ecologically responsible than its first.[136]

A key concern for officials like Lamontagne, LaMarsh, Aykroyd, and Fisher, then, was how to convince Canadians that they should be more self-aware and make a concerted effort to produce a more beautified country in an effort to combat the country's post-war excesses. Their public pronouncements about the need to rein in the impacts of capitalism are significant. It was unusual to hear such language from state officials. At the same time, it raises questions whether these statements were made to pander to the public's growing interest in the environmental movement but stopped short of inciting any real change. In any case, this anti-capitalist language was frequently invoked by Community Improvement Program boosters, was a cornerstone of promotional literature, and became one of the program's hallmarks.

The Centennial Commission argued that civic enhancement improved citizens' social and cultural welfare and, ultimately, created a more liveable society.[137] These topics were used to rally Canadians to the Community Improvement Program's cause and dovetailed with larger transformations taking place across the country. "Now that the days of well-being, security, and leisure are here," one promotional booklet noted, "to beautify is as vital as it once was to survive."[138] For many, the prosperous post-war world had already arrived. Increased disposable income, the emergence of leisure and recreation as recognized citizenship rights, and changes to labour laws had dramatically altered middle-class life.[139] During the 1965 National Community Improvement Program Seminar, Maurice Lamontagne remarked that "in the not too distant future, because of enlightened social policies, because of modern economies and because of science and automation, we will feel the soothing folds of the affluent society, with our creature comforts cared for and our leisure time greatly expanded."[140] The country's landscapes were expected to mirror these larger societal advancements and live up to these new expectations of the modern world. With new postwar entitlements and expectations, citizens had a right to access and enjoy beautified landscapes. It was everyone's centennial responsibility, then, to ensure that the environment was suitable for Canada's new leisured society.

Community Improvement Program promoters recognized that these changes provided an opportunity to endorse particular activities. Ottawa targeted local businesses, for instance, to sponsor projects that allowed families to spend more leisure time together. Businesses were also expected to lead in ecological preservation and were considered "naturals" to sponsor parks and conservation areas.[141] To this end, the Centennial Commission produced a series of handouts that featured glossy pictures of generic landscapes that were accompanied by descriptions of possible community undertakings.[142] One publication suggested that companies fund outdoor lighting for recreational facilities. It noted that "valuable and healthy hours of outdoor activity are lost [during darkness] at a time when families have the hours to play in. Father, and sometimes mother, are out to work through the daylight hours, and children contained by schoolroom activities. It makes a lot of sense to open up recreation areas to them at night, by the application of outdoor lighting."[143] Another handout, featuring a picture of an outdoor skating rink, extolled the virtues of external lighting. It noted that recreation areas during the winter months were "completely deserted, for the simple reason that it's too dark to play."[144] Yet another glossy pictured a ski hill lift, posited that a poorly lit lift area was "hazardous, especially for women and children," and suggested improved outdoor lighting to increase enjoyment.[145] These projects, organizers argued, helped Canadians maximize their leisure time productively.

The Community Improvement Program was concerned primarily with defects in the country's landscape. However, the program's spirit also was invoked to address concerns about crime. These anxieties spoke less about ecological worries and more about how the program could effectively control behaviour. Several Centennial Commission publications suggested that companies sponsor lighting projects to guarantee public security. Illumination initiatives were ideal 1967 projects for community gardens and green spaces, as well as for the supposedly sinister streets. One handout played on fears about potential dangers lurking in dark places at night. It featured a picture of a lit up park and it asked the pressing question, "How many parks in your community allow families to enjoy an evening stroll without having to endure a fear of the dark, and all that it entails?"[146]

Other Centennial Commission publications advised that civic enhancements could be used as effective methods to highlight symbols of the state's power. One handout pictured an old brick administrative building with a caption that noted such structures represented "security, and control, and justice" during daylight hours. It advised local businesses to install lighting fixtures throughout their communities as a way to highlight these embodiments of state power. Improved lighting ensured that there was no loss of this "symbol of authority when the sun goes down" and everything "seems all wrong."[147] Correlations between state, security, and civic improvement activities were unusual. However, anxieties about the night were nothing new in Western society.[148] The Centennial Commission played upon these worries to shore up support for projects in ways that spoke more to concerns about dangerous individuals and tempering fears about darkness than about pursuing environmentally responsible projects.

Similarly, some Nova Scotians conjured the Community Improvement Program's spirit to garner support for eliminating other perceived threats. In April 1967, Halifax County's Planning Board was petitioned by fifty citizens to remove purportedly derelict "shacks" and their residents located along the Bedford Highway. The group characterized the land as a notable eyesore along one of the province's scenic tourist drives and requested that the municipality remove the offending buildings. The petitioners cited neighbourhood safety concerns and referred to a case where a man allegedly exposed himself to local schoolchildren. Echoing a common prejudice of the time, the group hoped that the buildings would be removed before there was another "incident by any homosexual" and demanded that the board make this "a centennial project instead of a disaster for our children."[149] This spoke more to concerns about crime than it did about the Community Improvement Program's larger, benevolent aims. This illustrated the ways in which concerned citizens opportunistically used the scheme to achieve goals not necessarily connected to the program's mandate.

The program was also cast as a vehicle that improved Canadians' social welfare. Organizers were keenly aware that the population's physical environment directly affected its well-being. They charged that citizens remained oblivious to the "visual disharmony" and "ugliness" that surrounded them. It was a situation that could be remedied only when individuals became aware of the state of their lived environment.[150] Halifax community improvement supporters recognized that civic projects enhanced living standards. In an address to Halifax's Kiwanis Club, Councillor Hedley Ivany likened the Community Improvement Program's mandate to one of biblical proportions. "I make no excuse for appearing as an evangelist coming with a gospel – a message, not of repent but of beautification," he told the crowd, suggesting that citizens tackle projects such as painting electrical poles, cleaning streets, and building playgrounds.[151] Using the popular "outdoor living room" analogy, the councillor challenged Haligonians to become more attuned to their surroundings. Ivany worried that citizens had become so used to "dullness and drabness" that beautification possibilities were clouded and they were unable to fathom improved living conditions.[152]

For some communities, these discourses mirrored larger debates about post-war efforts to modernize and revitalize downtown centres. This was particularly important to Halifax during the 1960s when urban renewal discussions dominated city business. In April 1967, Ivany singled out Africville, the African-Canadian community in the city's north end, as an ideal area for redevelopment that would improve residents' standards of living. "It looks dismal in Africville now," he remarked, "but what a challenge to move into this area and create a new atmosphere." He argued that the community was the perfect site for a new recreational area that included public swimming facilities.[153] By this time, the majority of Africville residents had been subjected to a violent and systematic relocation. Ivany's statement was, to say the least, ironic. After years of Africville residents requesting that basic municipal services be provided to their community, it was only after citizens were brutally displaced that Halifax City Council sought to develop the area.[154]

Others used the Community Improvement Program's national platform to discuss larger issues of Canada's living standards. Calls to improve citizens' social and cultural welfare were key components of the program. However, these discussions overwhelmingly appealed to middle-class concerns about landscape aesthetics, cleaning up shopping districts, and enhancing the national, provincial, and local economies. Very few spoke about the need to address the country's class and socio-economic disparities. Indeed, those who addressed these issues stood out as solitary voices. The relative absence of those who used the Community Improvement Program's platform to elevate living standards across the board for all citizens was striking. Nevertheless, the handful of those who addressed these disparities made significant arguments about using the program as a platform for a larger social justice agenda. Ian MacLennan, vice-president of the Canada Mortgage and Housing Corporation (CMHC), recognized that the program could draw attention to systemic discrimination throughout the country. Addressing delegates at the 1967 National Community Improvement Program Seminar in Ottawa, he warned that despite widespread post-war prosperity, little had been done to alleviate the material differences between the lower and upper classes of Canadian society. Instead, disparities between groups were becoming more apparent. MacLennan cautioned that technological and professional skills were the keys to individuals' economic prosperity and would continue to play a key role in society. Those without these abilities and education would find themselves at the lower end of the economic ladder and would be "segregated in increasing densities in sub-standard housing and living areas." MacLennan stated that "what we can and must do is offer hope that better times are ahead for those who live in the slums and poor housing conditions ... and because we are now a mature country we can no longer be tolerant of buildings born, shack-like, during a pioneering era."[155] He cautioned that the country had to ensure that all Canadians benefited from this new affluence.

Other seminar participants spoke about the environment's role in Canadians' lives. Craig Mooney, a psychologist with the Mental Health Division of the federal Department of National Health and Welfare, argued that unhealthy surroundings resulted in serious negative psychological effects:

> People can tolerate many irritations and frustrations provided their personal lives have order and meaning. When, however, environmental afflictions become so numerous or severe as to prevent them from achieving order or meaning in their daily lives, they become subject to feelings of

desperation. This sense of desperation becomes greater when people perceive that those who are in a position to remedy invidious conditions are unapproachable or, if approachable, are unable, incapable, or uninterested in doing anything. Their desperation becomes dangerous if they suspect that those in command of human affairs are actually indifferent to the states and fates of individual men.[156]

Clyde Batten, a Centennial Commission senior public relations officer, recognized that citizens had a responsibility to fellow Canadians that extended far beyond the scope of simply celebrating 1967 through commemorative activities. "We cannot let the incalculable richness of our resources," he told the Nova Scotia Innkeepers Guild annual meeting in 1965, "blind us to the fact that there yet remain in Canada many who are hungry, naked and sick." Despite widespread prosperity and a thriving economy, not all citizens reaped these benefits. Many lived below the subsistence level, and "much agony and anguish" persisted. These issues required "the sympathy and compassion of millions of Canadians," and he noted that "no amount of legislation in the world can cure the problems. Government can only set a stage."[157]

Although the Community Improvement Program emphasized improved living standards, it clearly had its limits. Despite discussions about the need to eliminate poverty and combat welfare issues, there were few civic enhancement projects that made genuine efforts to address these larger systemic matters. In a post-war world that for many brought increased and guaranteed wages, leisure time, and prosperity, those at the very bottom of the socio-economic scale did not benefit from the program. Organizers perhaps believed that general beautification efforts and civic improvements would elevate all of the country's citizens, including society's most vulnerable. Some likely thought that changes to middle-class lifestyles would have a trickledown effect that prompted the poor into instituting similar changes. The Community Improvement Program was not focused on uplifting the poor. Rather, it was more concerned with enhancing middle-class lifestyles and imposing certain aesthetic standards on the country. What made this program unusual, though, was that it was the government that dictated and promoted this way of life. The government set a standard for how Canadians were expected to live their lives, and its paternalistic approach was clear from the beginning. Those who did not live up to this ideal were cautioned about their (in)actions by the Centennial Commission and its legion of citizen soldier workers.

Commentators such as MacLennan, Mooney, and Batten emphasized that the centennial year generally and the Community Improvement Program specifically should aim to improve the lives of *all* Canadians. Yet they were isolated voices in the cacophony of calls that focused on making environmental improvements that strengthened the economy and increased tourism activities through tidied landscapes. In similar ways, the U.S. environmental movement in the 1960s has been critiqued for diverting attention from larger socio-economic issues and, specifically, those issues affecting African-Americans. Finis Dunaway argues that many environmental organizations and much of the media attention during that decade targeted the middle class and ignored large segments of the country's population. Some initiatives further entrenched socio-economic inequalities. Dunaway contends that "new policies did help clean up the nation's air and water, but they also exacerbated environmental inequalities by increasing the levels of pollution in minority neighbourhoods, the spaces so often ignored by mainstream environmentalists and hidden from view by media coverage of the environmental crisis."[158] Andrew Hurley's work on post-war pollution in Gary, Indiana, illustrates how issues of social welfare, race, class, and industrial capitalism collided when competing environmental issues were at stake.[159] Similarly, Robert Gottlieb's examination of uranium mining development on Indigenous reservation land in the southwest United States reveals how this activity resulted in hazardous working and living conditions for particular sectors of American society.[160]

Critics of the Community Improvement Program expressed similar concerns and questioned whether the scheme's ambitious goals would ever produce its much promised results. Detractors doubted that the program would have the national impact its organizers expected. The *Cape Breton Highlander* likened the "lofty" undertaking to "the fabled search for 'pie in the sky when you die.'" Editor John Campbell asked whether it was even possible to foster enough grassroots support for the program. He noted the "monumental task of wiping the ugliness from the face of the nation" and argued that while the program had many supporters, they tended to pay mostly "lip service" to the scheme's goals. He was concerned that there was already an overall unwillingness for authorities to uphold Nova Scotia's "anti-ugliness" laws and questioned whether the program made any difference.[161] Further, despite those calls to improve the lives of all citizens, several experts who attended the October "Action '67" conference were accused of being out of touch with the average Canadian. Some even came under fire for using elitist language that perpetuated class divisions. Robert Phillips, a local historian, made "an impassioned plea for planning experts to speak to Mr Average Citizen in a language he can understand." Phillips reminded attendees that "I don't live in an 'urban environment.' I live on a street with cracking pavement and littered with bits of paper which the kids have thrown. I want to know what is being done about the wires slapping the trees on my streets and the Coca-Cola signs on the corner."[162]

Even though the Community Improvement Program was based on governments and local organizations banding together to promote acceptable aesthetic standards, there is little evidence that citizens resented these very public interventions and critiques about their lifestyles. Detractors, such as those who appeared in the *Cape Breton Highlander*, appeared to be exceptional in their protests. Instead, the program benefited from wide-spread participation in many of its activities. If there was dissent or backlash, these voices were likely silenced in the face of overwhelming support for this program. Indeed, the Community Improvement Program was one of the most successful centennial initiatives. One 1967 assessment concluded that it was "one of the most exciting" schemes that accomplished a "good deal of success."[163] Judy LaMarsh remarked that it had "developed a substantial grass roots interest" and showed signs of "growing support" across the country. The program seemed destined to carry on, and recommendations were made for its continuance post-1967. Yet, in the end, little concrete action was taken to ensure its survival in any meaningful, long-term way. This was not for a lack of initial interest. Many were concerned that after the Centennial Commission concluded its work the collective efforts to organize 1967 programs would quickly be forgotten.[164] A 1966 study for the Department of the Secretary of State that examined the long-term viability of centennial programs advocated that the scheme be continued. The program's cooperation at multiple levels was seen as "breaking new ground and achieving a good deal of success, indicating much future potential – at a minimum of expense."[165]

The federal government certainly saw the potential. It struck a committee, headed by Ian MacLennan, which recommended that the program continue under the auspices of the CMHC and the Community Planning Association of Canada.[166] This was a logical suggestion. CMHC had been heavily involved in civic improvement. It spearheaded a "Beautifying Towns" project and played an active role in the 1966 national seminar.[167] MacLennan's committee recommended a

$500,000 budget for the first three to five years of operations in order to fund provincial offices, promotional material, film production, and consultancy work.[168] The emphasis on local participation remained a major component of the program.[169] The proposal struck a chord with Action '67 delegates who passed a unanimous resolution that the program continue post-centennial year.[170] By December 1967, however, letters were sent to Community Improvement Program coordinators informing them that the program would not be continued.[171]

In the end, the Community Improvement Program created an intriguing paradox and, at times, disseminated contradictory messaging. The goal of stemming seemingly unrestrained expansion and preserving the environment contrasted greatly with those public messages of modernity and progress on display at Montreal's Expo 67. The program promoted many projects designed specifically to counter the new brutalism of modern life. The push to preserve Canada's outdoor living room and the focus on activities that engaged citizens in grassroots activities were tailored for community engagement in environmental action. L.B. Kuffert notes that much of this centennial programming was a pushback against the pressures of modernity that were "intended to counter the mechanization and standardization of work and life outside work. Complaints about mechanization and standardization had been around for decades, but acknowledging the pervasive nature of technology and bemoaning continental pressures had become more common." Expo 67 celebrated Canada's technological advances and the country's push to define itself as a modern country.[172] The event was a display of modernity at every turn. In everything from technologies used in displays to architectural feats accomplished on the site, Expo 67 was branded as a public exhibition of what constituted the "modern."[173] The Community Improvement Program's emphasis on stemming the effects of the new brutalism caused by modernity, technology, and capitalism were, in many ways, the antithesis of those public images and discourses celebrated in Montreal. It was a contrast that was impossible to ignore.

At the same time, though, the Community Improvement Program underscored the larger themes of development and modernity that were embodied in Expo and centennial programming. Initiatives such as Downtown Paint-Up portrayed Nova Scotia as a modern province through the presentation of tidy and contemporary downtown areas. When Harvey Webber spoke about Sydney's efforts to revitalize and modernize its shopping district inspired by the success of the Norwich

Plan, he addressed the many advantages that improving the downtown held for the area. He stated that the community's efforts allowed tourists to "see us as we look, not as we are."[174] His statement is telling. For some, then, beautification and community improvement were not intended to uncover a real Nova Scotia lurking underneath the new brutalism. Rather, Webber's comments indicate that many worked to create a surface image that appealed to tourists just as the Folk myth had done. By creating a welcoming, modern, and aesthetically pleasing facade, Community Improvement Program activities also attempted to construct an artificial Nova Scotia that obscured the realities of the province during the 1960s. Such efforts are all the more contrasted when considering the harsh realities that faced many Nova Scotia communities during this time due to the harsh effects of deindustrialization in areas such as Glace Bay.

Ultimately, the Community Improvement Program successfully engaged Canadians, businesses, voluntary organizations, and governments in a wide range of civic improvement and beautification activities. Programming materials employed a discourse that tried to convince people to participate in an environmental awareness campaign and persuade them that their contributions were worthwhile. The program asked citizens to "examine their surroundings with a critical eye" and take steps to improve their lives. Although it was an excellent vehicle for ensuring grassroots participation in 1967 activities, it worked towards myriad other ends. The Centennial Commission harnessed the power and the popularity of the 1960s environmental movement to secure widespread interest in the program. Directing attention away from traditional modes of political activism, Ottawa used the Community Improvement Program to channel citizens' energies into practical and productive initiatives to perform activities normally carried out by the state. In this way, the program tempered protest in other arenas.[175] The scheme's language highlighted in Lamontagne's 1965 speech to the national seminar further points to an intriguing undercurrent in Canadian politics. Lashing out against the country's new brutalism and attacking the ravages of rapid post-war industrialization, there emerged a compelling, unapologetically superficial, and surprising, anti-capitalist discourse promoted by the Canadian government and the Centennial Commission. This stood in stark contrast to many other centennial initiatives spearheaded by the federal government.

The Centennial Commission declared that the Community Improvement Program was a resounding success. Citizens, communities, and municipal and provincial governments jumped at the opportunity to participate in this state-sponsored scheme. Its 1966 progress report remarked that that "the mark of our progress as a nation will be judged in 1967 by the achievement of our communities."[176] In the end, the program represented a broader attempt to improve citizens' lives and boost the country's economy through ecologically conscious activities. The Community Improvement Program also sought to beautify the country in order to produce controlled, manicured, and curated spaces for tourists. In this way, some of its initiatives were different from the broader environmental movement of the 1960s that focused its efforts on preserving nature and curtailing pollution created by industry. Nevertheless, the Community Improvement Program was clearly positioned within the broader context of the environmental movement by its boosters. Riding the popularity of the 1960s environmental movement, the program made inroads in improving the country's aesthetics and landscape and engaged Canadians in a plethora of community activities.

Conclusion

Canada's 1967 Centennial Commemorative Legacy

The 1967 centennial was a transformational moment for Canada. Following years of preparation and planning, the country was thrown into a flurry of celebratory events that included commemorative activities and the construction of thousands of local infrastructure projects that transformed communities across the country. These initiatives addressed Maurice Lamontagne's concerns about Canada's "cultural poverty," and they emerged as poignant symbols of the role that the state played in the anniversary celebrations. At the National Centennial Conference's meeting in Quebec City in April 1967, Prime Minister Lester B. Pearson remarked that community centennial projects were significant "material achievements" that represented "tangible evidence of our success in pursuing the Canadian dream." However, as important as these were, he noted that the centennial's most significant legacy was immaterial and not easily discernible. "Let us remember that the better part of any nation is not tangible," Pearson stated, but rather "it is that part which lives in the hearts of the people. So it is for us to ensure that the national purposes we pursue ... are founded upon human principles that have universal and permanent value. Then we can be as certain as any people that our nation will endure because it will deserve to endure."[1]

Despite the importance that many attached to this intangible legacy, the centennial left in its wake significant material reminders of the year's events. While Montreal's Expo 67 was the crown jewel of the anniversary celebrations, the impact of local programming cannot be overlooked. Community projects transformed the country's landscape through the construction of badly needed infrastructure. The government's commitment to and investment in these initiatives represented an important shift in policy. During the first half of the twentieth century, cultural activities were supported largely by educational organizations and private philanthropists.[2] However, the federal government's commitment to modernization and development during the post-war era resulted in its intervention in various sectors of Canadian life, including the cultural arena. The country's centennial celebrations were no exception. Ottawa's investment of millions of dollars in an extensive 1967 commemorative policy represented "the high-water mark of government support for culture"[3] that allowed the celebrations to emerge as a defining moment of the twentieth century.

While centennial projects were part of larger efforts to improve Canada's cultural life, Nova Scotia's celebratory initiatives took on additional significance that symbolized a key moment in the province's post-war transition. Centennial Grants Program undertakings were conceived as integral components of the region's modernization that marked a new era of economic, social, and cultural development for many communities. In one way or another, these initiatives fundamentally reimagined public space and epitomized post-war renewal efforts. The Cape Breton Miners' Museum exemplified industrial Cape Breton's transformation from an economy based on extractive resources and industrial production, to one that was increasingly tied to the province's growing tourism industry. Halifax's aquarium was imagined as a key component of the city's modernization and urban renewal efforts. Its replacement with the Centennial Swimming Pool signalled the importance of serving the recreational and leisure needs of the growing city and expanding citizenship rights during this era. Programs and Projects of National Significance also marked crucial changes that took place in post-war Nova Scotia. The Community Improvement Program aimed to create a more liveable Canadian society through environmentally responsible projects that countered what Maurice Lamontagne referred to as the "new brutalism" of modernity. Activities initiated under this program presented the province as a progressive, tidy, and aesthetically pleasing destination that was ready to welcome tourists. The 1967 Highland Games and Folk Festival demonstrated the shifting nature of Nova Scotia's provincial identity. Through this event, the provincial government realized the potential of large-scale cultural initiatives to attract visitors to the region and expand the province's tourism industry.

Several key themes emerge from an investigation into Nova Scotia's experience during Canada's 1967 centennial celebrations. Communities were largely successful in setting their own commemorative agendas. Projects both responded to and prioritized initiatives based on local needs in ways that regional development policies could not. Although Nova Scotia's Centenary Committee and the National Centennial Commission exercised significant control over 1967 resources, a close examination of 1967 programming reveals how communities and citizens were active participants in the memorialization process. These local actors played key roles in the celebrations, as they negotiated with the state and its many apparatuses in hopes of attracting government support for commemorations. The resulting 1967 projects largely responded to and were driven by local mandates and priorities. This memorialization process was framed by a recurrent and urgent narrative that underscored the importance of capitalizing on lucrative centennial funding formulas. Organizers were keenly aware that state support for their commemorative projects was a once-in-a-lifetime economic development opportunity. Not surprisingly, 1967 initiatives emerged as contested terrains where local planners clashed over priorities and how best to take advantage of monies. This system created fierce competition as communities vied for the chance to take advantage of centennial grants that were presented as significant regional economic development mechanisms that took on particular significance in Nova Scotia. They led to economic development across the province that was positioned as important regional growth.

The history of Nova Scotia's centennial projects also reveals how particular citizens became very influential during this commemorative process. Nina Cohen's relentless championing of the Miners' Museum illustrates the power of individual activists within this framework. Concomitantly, many local initiatives demonstrate that, surprisingly, patronage did not play a central role in funding decisions. Despite a long and storied history of patronage throughout the twentieth century,[4] 1967 activities appeared to have escaped the long reach of backdoor politics, at least in Centenary Committee decisions. The provincial government eschewed political interference when doling out monies for the Centennial Grants Program. Premier Robert L. Stanfield appointed a politically diverse Centenary Committee and was quick to defend accusations of cronyism when they were levelled against the group. The Nova Scotia government, much like its counterparts in other provinces, was likely driven by an official pronouncement from Ottawa that all Canadians had to be afforded the opportunity to partake in the 1967 celebrations. With significant federal government monies at stake, it is unlikely that Stanfield or other Canadian politicians wanted to risk allegations of patronage. While this did not necessarily preclude patronage from working on other levels within the system, the Centenary Committee appears to have functioned – at least on the surface – at arm's length from political interference.

Centennial projects were major cultural infrastructure initiatives that were an integral part of larger post-war modernization strategies. For many Nova Scotia communities, they became significant regional economic and community development tools. Nina Cohen positioned the Miners' Museum as a significant step in revitalizing industrial Cape Breton's struggling economy. Harvey Webber argued that Community Improvement Program projects were important civic programs that lured locals and tourists to downtown shopping districts. Beautification efforts, he suggested, cast communities as modern and progressive destinations that helped visitors to see the area in a different light.[5] K.V. Knight, Nova Scotia's Deputy Minister of Trade and Industry, proposed that such undertakings countered the province's image as "a backward, poor, uneducated area – stuck out in the middle of the Atlantic – dependent almost exclusively on fish and lobster for our existence."[6] The province's 1967 commemorative initiatives, then, were closely associated with post-war modernization, urban renewal, and regional economic development.

These development efforts infused significant amounts of money across Nova Scotia, with the federal government providing $750,720 and the provincial government giving $750,719 under the Centennial Grants Program. Another $2,120,586 was provided by municipal governments, organizations, and other local sources that were initiating agencies for local projects. Together, the amount spent through Nova Scotia's Centennial Grants Program totalled $3,622,025.[7] These projects parallel the "province-building" impetus that was integral to British Columbia's anniversary celebrations. Nova Scotia did not organize its own major provincial commemorative anniversary events during the post-war period similar to celebrations in other provinces. Rather, those infrastructure initiatives that took place under the guise of the national 1967 centennial were flexible enough to serve as a significant vehicle for province-building in Nova Scotia. The flexibility of national programming allowed the province to accomplish provincial infrastructure-building and cultural capital goals via a national celebration instead.

Further, many of these centennial projects were associated with a burgeoning tourism industry and pointed to a growing interest in the country's history. Robyn Gillam argues that 1967 "was a bonanza for museums, especially the small, local variety,"[8] and that the celebrations became a pivotal moment for museological activities. Many local museums across Nova Scotia, including the Cape Breton Miners' Museum, were constructed with the help of government centennial funds. The state was now firmly committed to sponsoring historical and archival activities across the country. Although the Massey Commission's 1951 recommendations made it abundantly clear that the federal government had a key role to play in the country's cultural activities, the experience of the centennial ensured its responsibility in and commitment to this sector.

Nova Scotia's centennial projects also demonstrate the fluctuating nature of provincial identity. During the post-war era, the Folk continued to have a powerful grip on the province's image. While they have been characterized by some scholars as primarily anti-modern, quaint, and pastoral, others contend that a more nuanced reading is required. In particular, Alan Gordon's work on Iona's Highland Village Museum, a site that commemorates and presents a story of Cape Breton's Scottish diasporic community, "reveals a tension between a romanticized folk and a progressive people." He argues that the Scottish experience captured at this museum uncovers the fact that "these were not the quaint folk of McKay's 1950s tartanism but a progressive people building on the labour of successive generations and improving themselves materially over time."[9] This aligns with Greg Marquis's assertion that many Nova Scotians cast themselves as part of a modern, progressive, and urban society, challenging those anti-modern, quaint, and pastoral images of the Folk.[10] This characterization faced significant challenges as a more nuanced and multicultural understanding of the province's history emerged in the 1960s. Yet while the Folk paradigm was challenged during this era, strong cultural connections remained for diasporic Scots who imagined and constructed a particular idea about Scotland as their "homeland." As Paul Basu argues, "Scotland is at once notional and a material reality, an imagined place as much as a geographical territory, a symbol, even a sacred one, that may yet to be seen, touched, photographed, drive across, walked upon."[11] Halifax's 1967 Highland Games and Folk Festival attempted to replicate a Scottish "homeland" in Nova Scotia during the centennial. This provincial celebration also captured the tension between powerful Folk images and the assertion that Nova Scotia was a modern and progressive province. The event privileged Scottish identity in Nova Scotia. However, the multicultural

Folk Festival pointed to a growing appreciation and acceptance of non-Celtic identities. It reminded attendees that the province was not as tartanized as popular characterizations led many to believe.

Nova Scotia's Highland Games and Folk Festival represented a significant moment of transition for the province. Jerry Bannister and Roger Marsters argue that "antimodernism may have been the dominant framework for understanding the politics of heritage a generation ago, but it no longer fits Atlantic Canada." Rather, by the mid-1970s, modernism and cultural diversity emerged as central themes in tourism marketing in the "*post*-folk era." This was the product of a "Trudeau-era multiculturalist ethos, [where] the province's tourism promotion attempted to appeal to broader and more diverse populations by stressing Nova Scotia's ethnic and cultural diversity."[12] Nova Scotia's experience with its centennial projects reveals, however, that this shift dates back to a decade earlier with the 1967 Highland Games and Folk Festival, where the forces of the Folk and ethnic diversity publicly collided during this state-sponsored provincial festival.

Ultimately, Canada's 1967 centennial celebrations left an important national legacy. Programming introduced massive capital projects and cemented the state's role and responsibility in fostering cultural activity across the country. For Nova Scotia, centennial undertakings were significant commemorative and regional economic development initiatives. While the 1967 celebrations did not necessarily make Nova Scotians – nor other Canadians – more nationalistic, they were nevertheless successful in leaving a lasting cultural legacy that left citizens more optimistic about life in the province and the region's future. Centennial projects emerged as significant modernization strategies that fundamentally altered Nova Scotia's cultural landscapes. In the process, these projects buoyed citizens' hope for a bright future as economic opportunities expanded and new infrastructure projects offered communities the chance to reimagine and renew public spaces. In this way, the 1967 anniversary celebrations unquestionably were a resounding success for Nova Scotia.

Almost fifty years after the 1967 centennial celebrations, the country started to turn its attention earnestly towards the 150th anniversary of Canadian Confederation. In September 2012, the House of Commons Standing Committee on Canadian Heritage submitted its report, *Canada's 150th Anniversary in 2017*, which offered recommendations about how the country should mark the year. Speaking at the committee's hearings, James Moore, Minister of Canadian Heritage and

Official Languages, stated that the upcoming anniversary "should be an occasion for reflecting on what we have achieved as a relatively young country, and it should be an opportunity to promote a strong sense of pride and belonging for all Canadians."[13] While the event is viewed by some as an opportunity to promote a strong and united sense of Canadian national identity, others see it as a chance to further the cultural capital agenda that was introduced in 1967. Several witnesses who appeared before the Standing Committee argued that the 150th anniversary should be a time to renew Ottawa's commitment to repairing and revitalizing the country's centennial cultural capital infrastructure projects, many of which, fifty years on, are in desperate need of repair. However, it ultimately did not commit federal government resources for commemorative initiatives anywhere on the scale of those that were procured in 1967. Rather, proposals were comparatively sparse. Museum exhibit development was encouraged, as were travelling exhibits, both of which aim to bring Canada's history to citizens across the country.

Despite these initial austere pronouncements, the federal government has since committed significant funds for both national and community events to mark the sesquicentennial. In 2016, Canadian Heritage Minister Mélanie Joly announced $17.5 million for Canada's 150th celebrations, including $10 million for community projects administered through Community Foundations of Canada.[14] The Province of Nova Scotia has followed suit with its launch of the 150 Forward Fund announced on 1 July 2016. That fund set aside $4 million for non-profit societies and cooperatives, to "provide opportunities for Nova Scotians to create, promote and participate in local and regional events and programs that will build a sense of pride in Nova Scotia" that "demonstrate Nova Scotia's vibrant past and promising future." Projects are expected to "demonstrate a plan for bringing local and/or regional community together; engaging youth and/or celebrating diversity and inclusion."[15] The fund endeavours to support a wide range of community initiatives reminiscent of centennial activities, yet it remains to be seen what projects will be approved for funding.

A significant part of Canada's 1967 material legacy, therefore, remains in the balance. Local centennial projects still display the distinctive commemorative plaques. Yet many of these structures are sorely in need of monies for renovations, rehabilitation, and repairs if they are to continue to operate and be maintained as public institutions. In its agreement with the provinces and local initiating agencies, the federal government insisted as a prerequisite for funding that Centennial Grants

Program undertakings prove that they were able to operate without government funding. Since 1967, however, many museums, community centres, libraries, and other projects have come to rely heavily on such monies for their operations and maintenance. Recent debates in Halifax over whether to renovate or demolish and rebuild the city's Centennial Swimming Pool, which relies heavily on municipal funds, illustrate concern expressed across the country for many of 1967's cultural capital infrastructure initiatives. Although that pool has recently been fitted with several environmentally friendly renovations, including the addition of solar panels, deliberations about what to do with the facility, and many others like it, will continue. The seemingly abundant fiscal resources of Canada's federal and provincial governments in the 1960s allowed for the spending of millions of dollars on cultural capital projects and activities across the country. Yet the current state of fiscal conservatism and economic crises that prevails in Canada, and much of the Western world, means that spending on the levels of the 1967 centennial celebrations is a luxury that governments can no longer afford. With many local projects in desperate need of attention and a lack of public resources to maintain these undertakings, the material legacy of Canada's 1967 projects is uncertain. Yet, despite these infrastructure challenges, these centennial initiatives left a significant legacy that reshaped the country's cultural landscape. Nova Scotia's projects transformed the province and epitomized a new era of government involvement in the country's cultural life. While the province's initiatives responded to Maurice Lamontagne's appeal to stem Canada's "cultural poverty," 1967 projects and activities also reflected those larger economic, social, and political post-war transformations that swept across the region during the 1960s.

Notes

Introduction

1 "Students Must Fight Canada's Cultural Poverty and Help Mould Canada's National Identity," *Canadian High News* 25, no. 5 (January 1965), 20.
2 Ibid.
3 Nova Scotia Archives and Records Management (NSARM), Attorney General Department, RG 10, series E: Miscellaneous, vol. 114: Canada's Centennial-Press Releases II, National Centennial Commission bulletin, no. 2, November 1965.
4 See, for example, National Centennial Commission, *Canada 67: The Best of Centennial in Pictures* (Ottawa: Centennial Commission, 1968); and *Birthday of a Nation: The Story of Canada's Centennial* (Time International of Canada, 1968).
5 Pierre Berton, *1967: The Last Good Year* (Toronto: Doubleday Canada, 1997), 41.
6 J.M. Bumsted, "The Birthday Party," *The Beaver* 76, no. 2 (April/May 1996): 4–15.
7 J.L. Granatstein, *Canada 1957–1967: The Years of Uncertainty and Innovation* (Toronto: McClelland and Stewart, 1986), 304.
8 Peter H. Aykroyd, *The Anniversary Compulsion: Canada's Centennial Celebrations. A Model Mega-Anniversary* (Toronto: Dundurn, 1992), xii, 82.
9 Helen Davies, *The Politics of Participation: Learning from Canada's Centennial Year* (Toronto: MASS LBP, 2010), 28, 31, 148.
10 Misao Dean, "The Centennial Voyageur Pageant as Historical Re-enactment," *Journal of Canadian Studies* 40, no. 3 (Fall 2006): 43–67.
11 PearlAnn Reichwein, "Expedition Yukon 1967: Centennial and the Politics of Mountaineering in Kluane," *Canadian Historical Review* 92, no. 3 (September 2011): 481–514.

12 Mia Reimers, "'BC at Its Most Sparkling, Colourful Best': Post-war Province Building through Centennial Celebrations" (PhD diss., University of Victoria, 2007), 2–3.
13 Forrest Pass, "Pacific Dominion: British Columbia and the Making of Canadian Nationalism, 1858–1958" (PhD diss., University of Western Ontario, 2008), 4, 443.
14 Frances Swyripa, "Celebrating Together, Celebrating Apart: Albertans and their Golden Jubilee," in *Alberta Formed – Alberta Transformed*, ed. Michael Payne, Donald Wetherall, and Catherine Cavanaugh, 589–610 (Calgary: University of Calgary Press, 2006).
15 See, for example, *Expo 67: The Memorial Album of the First Category Universal and International Exhibition Held in Montreal from the Twenty-Seventh of April to the Twenty-Ninth of October Nineteen Hundred and Sixty-Seven* (Toronto: T. Nelson, 1968); Robert Fulford, *This Was Expo* (Toronto: McClelland and Stewart, 1968); Robert Fulford, *Remember Expo: A Pictorial Record* (Toronto: McClelland and Stewart, 1968); and Raymond Grenier, *Inside Expo 67*, trans. Patrick Gossage (Montreal: Les Éditions de l'Homme, 1965).
16 *The Canadian Pavilion, Expo 67*, directed by Marc Beaudet (National Film Board, 1967); and *Impressions of Expo*, directed by William Brind (National Film Board, 1967).
17 Daniel Francis, "One Brief Shining Moment: The World's Fair That Put Canada (Fleetingly) on the Map," *Literary Review of Canada* 20, no. 6 (July/August 2012): 5–6.
18 Geoff Pevere and Greig Dymond, *Mondo Canuck: A Canadian Pop Culture Odyssey* (Scarborough, ON: Prentice Hall Canada, 1996), 50. This sense of nostalgia is also captured in the documentary, *Expo 67: Back to the Future ...*, directed by Mark Starowicz (Canadian Broadcasting Corporation, 2004).
19 John Lownsbrough, *The Best Place to Be: Expo 67 and Its Time* (Toronto: Allan Lane, 2012), 2.
20 Aurora Wallace, "Girl Watching at Expo 67," in *Expo 67: Not Just a Souvenir*, ed. Rhona Richman Kenneally and Johanne Sloan (Toronto: University of Toronto Press, 2010), 109–22; and Emily Kirkman, "Fashioning Identity: The Hostesses of Expo 67" (Master's thesis, Concordia University, 2011), 27–34, 37–8.
21 Anna Graham, "Stories in the Sediment: DDD Use at Expo 67" (Master's thesis, Queen's University, 2012); and Tamzin Melinda El-Fityani, "Pesticide Use at Expo 67: Can We Find the Evidence 40 Years Later?" (Master's thesis, Queen's University, 2010).

22 Allison Whitney, "Labyrinth: Cinema, Myth and Nation at Expo 67" (Master's thesis, McGill University, 1999).
23 Alain Marcoux, "Expo 67 vitrine de l'expressionisme formel en architecture: investigations sur son contenu, son contexte, et son impact" (PhD diss., Université du Québec à Montréal, 2007); and Edward Jae Hamilton, "Ceci n'est pas un parc: Reconsidering the Island Site of Expo 67" (Master's thesis, University of Waterloo, 2011).
24 André Jansson, "Encapsulations: The Production of a Future Gaze at Montreal's Expo 67," *Space and Culture* 10, no. 4 (November 2007): 418–36.
25 Isabelle Massicotte, "The Architecture of Expo 67: National Identities and the Signs of Time" (Master's thesis, Carleton University, 2003), 1, 4.
26 Rhona Richman Kenneally and Johanne Sloan, eds., *Expo 67: Not Just a Souvenir* (Toronto: University of Toronto Press, 2010), 7–10.
27 Sonja Macdonald, "Expo 67, Canada's National Heterotopia: A Study of the Transformative Role of International Exhibitions in Modern Society" (Master's thesis, Carleton University, 2003), 1.
28 Gary Miedema, *For Canada's Sake: Public Religion, Centennial Celebrations and the Re-making of Canada in the 1960s* (Montreal and Kingston: McGill-Queen's University Press, 2005).
29 Pauline Curien, "L'identité nationale exposeé: représentations du Québec à l'Exposition universelle de Montréal 1967 (Expo 67)" (PhD diss., Laval University, 2003).
30 Michel Hellman, "Art, identité et Expo 67: l'expression du nationalisme dans les oeuvres des artistes québécois du Pavillon de La Jeunesse à l'Exposition universelle de Montréal" (Master's thesis, McGill University, 2005).
31 Myra Rutherdale and Jim Miller, "'It's our country': First Nations' Participation in the Indian Pavilion at Expo 67," *Journal of the Canadian Historical Association* 17, no. 2 (2006): 148–73; Sherry Brydon, "The Indians of Canada Pavilion at Expo 67," *American Indian Art Magazine* 22, no. 3 (1997): 54–63; and Richard Gordon Kicksee, "Scaled Down to Size: Contested Liberal Commonsense and the Negotiation of Indian Participation in the Canadian Centennial Celebrations and Expo 67, 1963–1967" (Master's thesis, Queen's University, 1996).
32 Karen Dubinsky, Catherine Krull, Susan Lord, Sean Mills, and Scott Rutherford, eds., *New World Coming: The Sixties and the Shaping of Global Consciousness* (Toronto: Between the Lines, 2009), 2–4.
33 Sean Mills, *The Empire Within: Postcolonial Thought and Political Activism in Sixties Montreal* (Montreal and Kingston: McGill-Queen's University Press, 2010), 19.

34 Andrew Marwick, *The Sixties: Cultural Revolution in Britain, France, Italy, and the United States, c. 1958–1974* (New York: Oxford University Press, 1998), 7.
35 Van Gosse, *Rethinking the New Left: An Interpretive History* (New York: Palgrave Macmillan, 2005), ix. See also David Farber, ed., *The Sixties: From Memory to History* (Chapel Hill: University of North Carolina Press, 1994).
36 Bryan D. Palmer, *Canada's 1960s: The Ironies of Identity in a Rebellious Era* (Toronto: University of Toronto Press, 2009), 23–4.
37 Ibid., 4–5.
38 Joan Sangster, "Radical Ruptures: Feminism, Labor, and the Left in the Long Sixties in Canada," *American Review of Canadian Studies* 40, no. 1 (March 2010): 2, 9–11.
39 Philip Jenkins, *Decade of Nightmares: The End of the Sixties and the Making of Eighties America* (New York: Oxford University Press, 2006), 4.
40 Todd Gitlin, *The Sixties: Years of Hope and Days of Rage* (Toronto: Bantam Books, 1987), 2–3.
41 For a discussion of rapid post-war changes, see, for example, Magda Fahrni and Robert Rutherdale, eds., *Creating Postwar Canada: Community, Diversity, and Dissent 1945–1975* (Vancouver: UBC Press, 2008); Alvin Finkel, *Our Lives: Canada after 1945* (Toronto: James Lorimer, 1997); and Doug Owram, *Born at the Right Time: A History of the Baby-Boom Generation* (Toronto: University of Toronto Press, 1996).
42 Daniel Macfarlane, "To the Heart of the Continent: Canada and the Negotiation of the St Lawrence Seaway and Power Project" (PhD diss., University of Ottawa, 2010); and Claire Puccia Parham, *The St Lawrence Seaway and Power Project: An Oral History of the Greatest Construction Show on Earth* (New York: Syracuse University Press, 2009).
43 David W. Monaghan, *Canada's "New Main Street": The Trans-Canada Highway as Idea and Reality, 1912–1956* (Ottawa: Canada Science and Technology Museum, 2002). On the construction of the Trans-Canada Highway, see also Daniel Francis, *A Road for Canada: The Illustrated History of the Trans-Canada Highway* (Vancouver: Stanton Atkins & Dosil Publishers, 2006).
44 Danielle Robinson, "Modernism at a Crossroad: The Spadina Expressway Controversy in Toronto, Ontario, ca. 1960–1971," *Canadian Historical Review* 92, no. 2 (June 2011): 295–322.
45 Paul Litt, *The Muses, the Masses and the Massey Commission* (Toronto: University of Toronto Press, 1992).
46 Margaret Conrad, "The 1950s: The Decade of Development," in *The Atlantic Provinces in Confederation*, ed. E.R. Forbes and D.A. Muise (Toronto: University of Toronto Press, 1993), 382–3.

47 Edward MacDonald, *If You're Stronghearted: Prince Edward Island in the Twentieth Century* (Charlottetown: Prince Edward Island Museum and Heritage Foundation, 2000), 227.
48 Corey Slumkoski, *Inventing Atlantic Canada: Regionalism and the Maritime Reaction to Newfoundland's Entry into Canadian Confederation* (Toronto: University of Toronto Press, 2011).
49 James L. Kenny and Andrew G. Secord, "Engineering Modernity: Hydroelectric Development in New Brunswick, 1945–1970," *Acadiensis* 39, no. 1 (Winter/Spring 2010): 3–26.
50 Jason L. Churchill, "Pragmatic Federalism: The Politics behind the 1969 Churchill Falls Contract," *Newfoundland Studies* 15, no. 2 (1999): 215–46. See also Jerry Bannister, "A River Runs through It: Churchill Falls and the End of Newfoundland History," *Acadiensis* 41, no. 1 (Winter/Spring 2012): 211–25; James P. Feehan, "Smallwood, Churchill Falls, and the Power Corridor through Quebec," *Acadiensis* 40, no. 2 (Summer/Autumn 2011): 112–27; and Philip Smith, *Brinco: The Story of Churchill Falls* (Toronto: McClelland and Stewart, 1975).
51 Lisa Pasolli, "Bureaucratizing the Atlantic Revolution: The 'Saskatchewan Mafia' in the New Brunswick Civil Service, 1960–1970," *Acadiensis* 38, no. 1 (Winter/Spring 2009): 126–50.
52 Greg Marquis, "'A Reluctant Concession to Modernity': Alcohol and Modernization in the Maritimes, 1945–1980," *Acadiensis* 32, no. 2 (Spring 2003): 31–59.
53 Tina Loo, "Africville and the Dynamics of State Power in Postwar Canada," *Acadiensis* 39, no. 2 (Summer/Autumn 2010): 23–47; Jennifer J. Nelson, *Razing Africville: A Geography of Racism* (Toronto: University of Toronto Press, 2008); and *Remember Africville*, directed by Shelagh Mackenzie (National Film Board, 1991).
54 See Maritime History Archive, "'No Great Future': Government Sponsored Resettlement in Newfoundland and Labrador since Confederation," http://www.mun.ca/mha/resettlement/rs_intro.php; Gerald Sider, *Between History and Tomorrow: Making and Breaking Everyday Life in Rural Newfoundland* (Peterborough, ON: Broadview, 2003), 280–90; Kevin Major, *As Near to Heaven by Sea: A History of Newfoundland and Labrador* (Toronto: Penguin Books, 2001), 418–22; Sean T. Cadigan, *Newfoundland and Labrador: A History* (Toronto: University of Toronto Press, 2009), 246–52; and Linda White, "Resettlement," *Newfoundland Quarterly* 99, no. 4 (2007): 4–8.
55 Alan MacEachern, *Natural Selections: National Parks in Atlantic Canada, 1935–1970* (Montreal and Kingston: McGill-Queen's University Press, 2001).

56 James Overton, *Making a World of Difference: Essays on Tourism, Culture and Development in Newfoundland* (St John's, NL: Institute of Social and Economic Research, 1996), 171–90.
57 Edward MacDonald, "A Landscape ... with Figures: Tourism and Environment on Prince Edward Island," *Acadiensis* 40, no. 1 (Winter/Spring 2011): 71, 80.
58 Meaghan Beaton and Del Muise, "The Canso Causeway, Tartan Tourism, Industrial Development and the Promise of Progress for Cape Breton," *Acadiensis* 38, no. 2 (Summer/Fall, 2008): 39–69; and Beaton, "The Canso Causeway: Regionalism, Reconstruction, Representations, and Results" (Master's thesis, Saint Mary's University, 2001).
59 Ian McKay, *The Quest of the Folk: Antimodernism and Cultural Selection in Twentieth-Century Nova Scotia* (Montreal and Kingston: McGill-Queen's University Press, 1994). *The Quest of the Folk* is the culmination of the author's previous work, including McKay, "Among the Fisherfolk: J.F.B. Livesay and the Invention of Peggy's Cove," *Journal of Canadian Studies* 23, nos 1 & 2 (Spring/Summer 1988): 23–45; McKay, "Helen Creighton and the Politics of Anti-modernism," in *Myth and Milieu: Atlantic Literature and Culture, 1918–1939*, ed. Gwendolyn Davies, 1–16 (Fredericton, NB: Acadiensis, 1993); McKay, "Tartanism Triumphant: The Construction of Scottishness in Nova Scotia, 1933–1945," *Acadiensis* 21, no. 2 (Spring 1992): 5–47; McKay, "History and the Tourist Gaze: The Politics of Commemoration in Nova Scotia, 1935–1964," *Acadiensis* 22, no. 2 (Spring 1993): 102–38. See also Ian McKay and Robin Bates, *In the Province of History: The Making of the Public Past in Twentieth-Century Nova Scotia* (Montreal and Kingston: McGill-Queen's University Press, 2010).
60 Monica MacDonald, "Railway Tourism in the 'Land of Evangeline,' 1882–1946," *Acadiensis* 35, no. 1 (Autumn 2005): 180. See also Barbara LeBlanc, *Postcards from Acadie: Grand-Pré, Evangeline & the Acadian Identity* (Kentville, NS: Gaspereau, 2003); and Roger Marsters, "'The Battle of Grand Pré': The Historic Sites and Monuments Board of Canada and the Commemoration of Acadian History," *Acadiensis* 36, no. 1 (Autumn 2006): 29–50.
61 Greg Marquis, "Commentary: *The Quest of the Folk*," *Acadiensis* 35, no. 1 (Autumn 2005): 145–7.
62 Herb Wyile, *Anne of Tim Hortons: Globalization and the Reshaping of Atlantic Canada Literature* (Waterloo, ON: Wilfrid Laurier Press, 2011), 22–3.
63 Bruce Muirhead, "Ottawa, the Provinces, and the Evolution of Canadian Trade Policy since 1963," in *Framing Canadian Federalism: Historical Essays in Honour of John T. Saywell*, ed. Dimitry Anastakis and P.E. Bryden (Toronto: University of Toronto Press, 2009), 215; and Robert Young,

"Open Federalism and Canadian Municipalities," in *Open Federalism: Interpretations, Significance*, ed. Keith Banting, Roger Gibbins, Peter Leslie, Alain Noel, Richard Simeon, and Robert Young (Kingston: Institute of Intergovernmental Relations, 2006), 10.
64 Joe Ruggeri, *Canadian Federalism at the Cross-Roads* (Fredericton: Policy Studies Centre, University of New Brunswick, 2006), 8–9.
65 Muirhead, "Ottawa, the Provinces, and the Evolution of Canadian Trade Policy"; and Jennifer Smith, *Federalism* (Vancouver: UBC Press, 2004), 22; and Dimitry Anastakis, "Cars, Conflict, and Cooperation: The Federalism of the Canadian Auto Industry," in Anastakis and Bryden, *Framing Canadian Federalism*, 185–210.
66 Herman Bakvis and Grace Skogstad, "Canadian Federalism: Performance, Effectiveness, and Legitimacy," in *Canadian Federalism: Performance, Effectiveness, and Legitimacy*, ed. Herman Bakvis and Grace Skogstad (Don Mills, ON: Oxford University Press, 2002), 8.
67 See, for example, T. Stephen Henderson, "'A New Federal Vision': Nova Scotia and the Rowell-Sirois Report, 1938–1948" in Anastakis and Bryden, *Framing Canadian Federalism*, 51–74.
68 See, for example, James Struthers, *No Fault of Their Own: Unemployment and the Canadian Welfare State, 1914–1941* (Toronto: University of Toronto Press, 1983); and James Struthers, *The Limits of Affluence: Welfare in Ontario, 1920–1970* (Toronto: Government of Ontario, published by University of Toronto Press, 1994).
69 P.E. Bryden, *Planners and Politicians: Liberal Politics and Social Policy, 1957–1968* (Montreal and Kingston: McGill-Queen's University Press, 1997), xvi.
70 W.S. MacNutt, "The Atlantic Revolution: A Commentary on the Atlantic Premiers' Conference at Halifax, on May 8th, 1957," *Atlantic Advocate* no. 9 (June 1957): 11–13.
71 E.R. Forbes, *The Maritime Rights Movement, 1919–1927: A Study in Canadian Regionalism* (Montreal and Kingston: McGill-Queen's University Press, 1979).
72 Margaret Conrad, "The 'Atlantic Revolution' of the 1950s," in *Beyond Anger and Longing: Community and Development in Atlantic Canada*, ed. Berkeley Fleming, (Sackville, NS, and Fredericton: Centre for Canadian Studies and Acadiensis, 1988), 55–96.
73 Margaret R. Conrad and James K. Hiller, *Atlantic Canada: A Concise History* (Don Mills, ON: Oxford University Press, 2006), 191.
74 Conrad, "The 1950s," 419.
75 Donald J. Savoie, "Regional Development: A Policy for All Seasons and Regions," in *New Trends in Canadian Federalism*, ed. François Rocher and

Miriam Smith (Peterborough, ON: Broadview, 2003), 353. See also Donald J. Savoie, *Visiting Grandchildren: Economic Development in the Maritimes* (Toronto: University of Toronto Press, 2006).

76 Donald J. Savoie, *Regional Economic Development: Canada's Search for Solutions*, 2nd ed. (Toronto: University of Toronto Press, 1992), 14.
77 Ibid., 26; and Savoie, *Visiting Grandchildren*, 81–2.
78 P.E. Bryden, "The Obligations of Federalism: Ontario and the Origins of Equalization," in Anastakis and Bryden, *Framing Canadian Federalism*, 76. Section 36 of Canada's Constitution Act 1982, c. 11 (U.K.), Schedule B, "Equalization and Regional Disparities," enshrined the responsibility for alleviating regional disparities with the federal government.
79 James Bickerton, *Nova Scotia, Ottawa, and the Politics of Regional Development* (Toronto: University of Toronto Press, 1990), chaps 5 and 6.
80 Della Stanley, "The 1960s: The Illusions and Realities of Progress," in Forbes and Muise, *Atlantic Provinces in Confederation*, 421.
81 Paul Connerton, *How Societies Remember* (Cambridge: Cambridge University Press, 1989), 3–4, 70.
82 Brian Osborne, "Landscapes, Memory, Monuments and Commemoration: Putting Identify in its Place," in *Canadian Ethnic Studies* 33, no. 3 (Fall 2001): 39–77.
83 John Bodnar, *Remaking America: Public Memory, Commemoration, and Patriotism in the Twentieth Century* (Princeton: Princeton University Press, 1992), 228, 243.
84 Jonathan F. Vance, *Death So Noble: Memory, Meaning, and the First World War* (Vancouver: UBC Press, 1997), 3, 7, 261–2, 267.
85 Benedict Anderson, *Imagined Communities: Reflections on the Origins and Spread of Nationalism*, 3rd ed. (London: Verso, 2006), 5–6.
86 Lyn Spillman, *Nation and Commemoration: Creating National Identities in the United States and Australia* (Cambridge: Cambridge University Press, 1997), 1, 14–15, 34–7.
87 Sasha Mullally and Edward MacDonald, "On National Heritage, Grand Narratives, and 'Making History Fun': Founders' Hall, Prince Edward Island and the Story of Canada," *International Journal of Heritage Studies* 13, no. 3 (May 2007): 288, 291, 292.
88 Matthew Hayday, "Fireworks, Folk-Dancing, and Fostering a National Identity: The Politics of Canada Day," *Canadian Historical Review* 91, no. 2 (June 2010): 292.
89 H.V. Nelles, *The Art of Nation Building: Pageantry and Spectacle at Quebec's Tercentenary* (Toronto: University of Toronto Press, 1999), 12, 13.

90 John R. Gillis, "Memory and Identity: The History of a Relationship," in *Commemorations: The Politics of National Identity*, ed. John R. Gillis (Princeton: Princeton University Press, 1994), 4–5.
91 Ronald Rudin, *Founding Fathers: The Celebration of Champlain and Laval in the Streets of Quebec, 1878–1908* (Toronto: University of Toronto Press, 2003).
92 Ron Rudin, *Remembering and Forgetting in Acadie: A Historian's Journey through Public Memory* (Toronto: University of Toronto Press, 2009).
93 Alan Gordon, *Making Public Pasts: The Contested Terrain of Montreal's Public Memories, 1891–1930* (Montreal and Kingston: McGill-Queen's University Press, 2001), 16–17.
94 Ian Radforth, *Royal Spectacle: The 1860 Visit of the Prince of Wales to Canada and the United States* (Toronto: University of Toronto Press, 2004), 7.
95 Keith Walden, *Becoming Modern in Toronto: The Industrial Exhibition and the Shaping of Late Victorian Culture* (Toronto: University of Toronto Press, 1997), xvi.
96 Robert Cupido, "'Sixty Years of Canadian Progress': The Diamond Jubilee and the Politics of Commemoration," in *Canadian Identity: Region, Country, Nation: Selected Proceedings of the 24th Annual Conference of the Association for Canadian Studies, Held at Memorial University of Newfoundland, June 6–8, 1997*, ed. Caroline Andrew, Will Straw, and J.-Yvon Thériault (Montreal: Association for Canadian Studies, 1998), 20–3. See also Cupido, "Appropriating the Past: Pageants, Politics, and the Diamond Jubilee of Canada," *Journal of the Canadian Historical Association* vol. 9, no. 1 (1998): 155–86; and Cupido, "The Medium, the Message and the Modern: The Jubilee Broadcast of 1927," *International Journal of Canadian Studies* 26 (Fall 2002): 101–23.

Chapter One

1 "City Ushers in Centennial Year with Flame and Flag," *Chronicle-Herald*, 2 January 1967.
2 "Bells, Speeches Launch Centennial Celebrations," *Chronicle-Herald*, 2 January 1967.
3 "City Ushers in Centennial Year with Flame and Flag."
4 "Noise-Making, Fire-Lighting Usher in 1967," *Chronicle-Herald*, 2 January 1967.
5 "Torchlight Parade Is Salute to Centennial," *Chronicle-Herald*, 2 January 1967.
6 "Church Service for Opening of Centennial Year," *Chronicle-Herald*, 31 December 1967.

7 "Bonfire Greets Centennial Year," *Cape Breton Post*, 2 January 1967.
8 "Colorful Affair: 1500 Attend Civic Levee," *Cape Breton Post*, 3 January 1967.
9 "Cities Area Levees Set," *Chronicle-Herald*, 31 December 1966; and "Levees Today for Halifax, Dartmouth," *Chronicle-Herald*, 2 January 1967.
10 See Miedema, *For Canada's Sake*, 66–7, on Ottawa's ceremonies.
11 National Centennial Commission, *Centennial Commission Annual Report 1965–1966* (Ottawa: National Centennial Commission, 1966), 5.
12 National Centennial Commission, *Canada 67: The Best of Centennial in Pictures* (Ottawa: Centennial Commission, 1968), n.p.
13 Equivalent to $1,416,483,516 in 2016 when adjusted for inflation. Bank of Canada, Inflation Calculator, http://www.bankofcanada.ca/rates/related/inflation-calculator/.
14 For a list of projects funded through the Centennial Commission, see National Centennial Commission, *Second Annual Report of the Centennial Commission for the Fiscal Year 1963–1964* (Ottawa: National Centennial Commission, 1964), 9–13; and National Centennial Commission, *Centennial Commission Annual Report 1965–1966*, 5–45.
15 For a discussion of Voyageur Canoe Pageant, see Dean, "Centennial Voyageur Pageant," 43–67.
16 "To Echo across the Land," *Cape Breton Post*, 4 January 1967; and "Train Heads West," *Cape Breton Post*, 2 January 1967.
17 "The Centennial as Welcomed across Canada," *Chronicle-Herald*, 3 January 1967; "Confederation Train on Way West," *Globe and Mail*, 2 January 1967; and "Train Heads West," *Cape Breton Post*.
18 Peter H. Aykroyd, *The Anniversary Compulsion: Canada's Centennial Celebrations. A Model Mega-Anniversary* (Toronto: Dundurn, 1992), 124–6.
19 National Centennial Commission, *Canada 67*, 183.
20 Helen Davies summarizes the Centennial Commission's administrative history in *Politics of Participation*, 34–56. See also Miedema, *For Canada's Sake*, 68–70; and L.B. Kuffert, *A Great Duty: Canadian Responses to Modern Life and Mass Culture, 1939–1967* (Montreal and Kingston: McGill-Queen's University Press, 2003), 219, 225–9.
21 Canadian Centenary Council, quoted in Davies, *Politics of Participation*, 35.
22 Ibid., 36. For a detailed bureaucratic history of the organization, see Anne Hanna, *The Canadian Centenary Council, 1959–1967* (Ottawa: Canadian Centenary Council, 1968).
23 National Centennial Commission, *Centennial Commission Annual Report 1965–1966*, 46.
24 Davies, *Politics of Participation*, 36.

25 Aykroyd, *Anniversary Compulsion*, 41; and Davies, *Politics of Participation*, 37–8.
26 Aykroyd, *Anniversary Compulsion*, 42.
27 Davies, *Politics of Participation*, 36.
28 Canada, *House of Commons Debates* (18 September 1961), p. 8465 (Right Hon. J.G. Diefenbaker).
29 Library and Archives Canada (LAC), Centennial Commission fonds, RG 69, vol. 6, file 1-3-4-1, "Memorandum to Cabinet," 23 July 1963.
30 Ibid.
31 Canada, *Royal Commission on Bilingualism and Biculturalism: Preliminary Report* (Ottawa: Queen's Printer, 1965), "Appendix I," 151–2. On the Royal Commission on Bilingualism and Biculturalism, see Matthew Hayday, *Bilingual Today, United Tomorrow: Official Languages in Education and Canadian Federalism* (Montreal and Kingston: McGill-Queen's University Press, 2005), 28–45.
32 LAC, RG 69, vol. 6, file 1-3-4-1, "Memorandum to Cabinet," 23 July 1963.
33 National Centennial Commission, *The Centennial Handbook: A Handbook of Information on the 1967 Centennial Organizations, Their Constitutions, Their Aims and Objectives* (Ottawa: Queen's Printer and Controller of Stationery, 1964), 27.
34 Ibid., 13; and LAC, RG 69, vol. 6, file 1-3-4-1, "Memorandum to Cabinet," 23 July 1963.
35 Canada, *House of Commons Debates* (18 September 1961), p. 8465 (Right Hon. J.G. Diefenbaker).
36 Canada, *House of Commons Debates* (18 September 1961), p. 8469 (Lester B. Pearson, MP).
37 Ibid.
38 Canada, *House of Commons Debates* (18 September 1961), p. 8482 (Right Hon. J.G. Diefenbaker); and *An Act Respecting the Observance of the Centennial of Confederation in Canada*, RSC 1960–61, c 60 (*Centennial Act*).
39 *Centennial Act*, s 9(1).
40 Ibid., ss 10–11, 14.
41 Ibid., ss 3–8.
42 National Centennial Commission, *Second Annual Report of the Centennial Commission*, 6.
43 *Centennial Act*, ss 17–27; and National Centennial Commission, *Second Annual Report of the Centennial Commission*, 6.
44 *Centennial Act*, s 17; and Davies, *Politics of Participation*, 37.
45 LAC, Lester B. Pearson fonds, MG 26 N 3, vol. 1, Lesage to Diefenbaker, 10 October 1961. See LAC, MG 26 N 3, vol. 1: Centennials and Anniversaries,

Jean Lesage to John G. Diefenbaker, 4 October 1961; Diefenbaker to Lesage, 13 January 1962; Lesage to Diefenbaker, 30 January 1962; Lesage to Lester B. Pearson, 2 May 1963; Lesage to Pearson, 18 June 1963; and Pearson to Lesage, 7 June 1963.

46 See LAC, MG 26 N 3, vol. 1, Lesage to Pearson, 2 May 1963; Lesage to Pearson, 18 June 1963; and Pearson to Lesage, 7 June 1963.
47 *An Act to Amend the National Centennial Act*, Bill C-107 (1963).
48 Davies, *Politics of Participation*, 37–42; and Aykroyd, *Anniversary Compulsion*, 41–53.
49 Davies, *Politics of Participation*, 39; and Aykroyd, *Anniversary Compulsion*, 49–50. On Fisher, see Bill McNeil, *John Fisher: "Mr. Canada"* (Markham, ON: Fitzhenry and Whiteside, 1983); "The Tory Mr Canada Carries On for the Liberals," *Toronto Telegram*, 26 May 1965; and Judy LaMarsh, *Memoirs of a Bird in a Gilded Cage* (Toronto: McClelland and Stewart, 1969), 176–84.
50 National Centennial Commission, *Third Annual Report of the Centennial Commission for the Fiscal Year 1964–1965* (Ottawa: Queen's Printer, 1965), 28–9.
51 National Centennial Commission, *Second Annual Report of the Centennial Commission*, 13; and National Centennial Commission, *Centennial Commission Annual Report 1965–1966*, 42.
52 This program's origins are disputed. Forrest Pass claims that L.J. Wallace, British Columbia's 1958 provincial centennial celebration committee chairman, claimed "his own persistence led to [the Centennial Commission's] adoption of the per capita grants system" that was used in that province's celebrations. See Pass, "Pacific Dominion," 442. Meanwhile, Aykroyd claims that it was the Privy Council Office's John Hodgson who proposed the funding model for the 1967 celebrations. See Aykroyd, *Anniversary Compulsion*, 77.
53 Nova Scotia Archives and Records Management (NSARM), Attorney General Department, RG 10, series E: Miscellaneous, vol. 129: Canada's Centennial: Youth Travel Program, "Proceedings of Third Meeting of the National Committee on the Centennial," Annex "A," memorandum, 6 October 1961. Available government funds were determined by a per capita scheme based on the province's or territory's population on 1 June 1963. See LAC, RG 69, vol. 983, file: National Centennial Fund (Nova Scotia): Administrative Accounts, "Agreement between National Centennial Administration and the Government of the Province of Nova Scotia for Centennial Projects," 21 October 1963. Section 1(b) noted that for, funding purposes, Nova Scotia's population was 756,000.
54 LAC, RG 69, vol. 407, news release, 25 November 1964.

55 National Centennial Commission, *Third Annual Report of the Centennial Commission*, 28–9.
56 LAC, RG 69, vol. 5, file 1-3-2-1, Privy Council, P.C. 1963-1255, 21 August 1963.
57 National Centennial Commission, *Second Annual Report of the Centennial Commission*, 12.
58 Equivalent to $10,708,615 in 2016 when adjusted for inflation. Bank of Canada, Inflation Calculator.
59 NSARM, RG 10, series E, vol. 167: Centennial grants. Approved. Correspondence, financial statements etc. Halifax, A.B. Stoddard to A.W. Churchill, 7 August 1967.
60 National Centennial Commission, *Second Annual Report of the Centennial Commission*, 6.
61 LAC, RG 69, vol. 10, file 1-3-35-1, "Memorandum to Cabinet," 9 August 1965.
62 Aykroyd, *Anniversary Compulsion*, appendix J, 198–9.
63 LAC, RG 69, vol. 10, file 1-3-35-1, "Memorandum to Cabinet," 9 August 1965.
64 NSARM, RG 10, series E, vol. 111: Centennial. News Releases #1, "Bulletin No. 18: A Real Adventure in Learning," 7 October 1966.
65 NSARM, RG 10, series E, vol. 129, "Working Paper Prepared by the Centennial Commission for the Second Federal-Provincial Conference on Youth Travel," 4 November 1964.
66 Ibid.
67 "Inviting the National Breeze," *Cape Breton Post*, 20 August 1965.
68 "Bringing Life and Soul to Our Birthday Party," *Globe and Mail*, 15 December 1964.
69 Aykroyd, *Anniversary Compulsion*, 127.
70 National Centennial Commission, *Progress Report on Projects of National Significance for the Celebration of Canada's Centennial of Confederation* (Ottawa: National Centennial Commission, 1966), 61.
71 "Canada Should Seek Unity in Diversity: Judy LaMarsh," *Chronicle-Telegraph*, 25 April 1967.
72 NSARM, RG 10, series E, vol. 138: Canada's Centennial, National Committee meetings, notes and correspondence, 6 May 1959 to 21 September 1961, "Inaugural Meeting of the Provisional National Committee on Canada's Centennial," 8 February 1960.
73 NSARM, C.B. Fergusson Papers, MG 1, vol. 1479: Confederation Centenary Celebration Committee, Confederation Centenary Celebration Committee minutes, 28 May 1963; and "Centennial: 'Something for All.'"

74 The Centenary Committee was established through the *Confederation Centenary Celebration Act*, RSNS c 2, 1963. The bill was introduced on 15 February 1961 by R.A. Donahoe and received royal assent on 13 March 1961.
75 "Name Planners for Centennial," *Mail-Star* (Halifax), 20 March 1963; and "Speakers Warn Committee about Dissipation of Centennial Funds," *Chronicle-Herald*, 29 May 1963.
76 Isobel MacAulay's last name was occasionally spelled "MacAuley" or "McAulay."
77 MacLean hailed from Eureka, Nova Scotia. Her name was occasionally spelled "McLean."
78 C. Bruce Fergusson, *Alderman Abbie Lane of Halifax* (Windsor: Lancelot, 1976), 22; and "Abbie Lane Passes Away in Halifax," *Chronicle-Herald*, 20 December 1965.
79 "No, Not That Abbie Lane: This One's in Politics," *Windsor Star*, 21 May 1965; and "Ubiquitous Is the Word for Abbie," *Maclean's*, 15 February 1953.
80 Lilla Stirling, *In the Vanguard: Nova Scotia Women Mid-Twentieth Century* (Windsor: Lancelot, 1976), 36; and Fergusson, *Alderman Abbie Lane of Halifax*, 22–36. See also Judith Fingard and Janet Guildford, "Introduction," in *Mothers of the Municipality: Women, Work, and Social Policy in Post-1945 Halifax*, ed. Judith Fingard and Janet Guildford, 3–4 (Toronto: University of Toronto Press, 2005).
81 NSARM, Miscellaneous Manuscript Collection, MG 100, vol. 141, file #36, "Obituary: Charles Bruce Fergusson"; "Dr C. Bruce Fergusson, Former Archivist, Dies," *Mail-Star* (Halifax), 21 September 1978; and editorial, "Dedicated Historian," *Chronicle-Herald*, 22 September 1978.
82 "Dr R.S. Longley, of Acadia, Dies," *Mail-Star* (Halifax), 9 January 1967.
83 NSARM, MG 1, vol. 1479, Confederation Centenary Celebration Committee minutes, 11 June 1965.
84 NSARM, MG 1, vol. 1479, Confederation Centenary Celebration Committee minutes, 31 January 1964.
85 On 15 April 1966, Wyman became chair following Lane's death, at the age of sixty-seven, as a result of a heart attack. See "Abbie Lane Passes Away in Halifax," *Chronicle-Herald*.
86 In 1979 Donahoe was appointed to the Senate by Prime Minister Joe Clark, where he served until 1984. See "Murray, Donahoe to Join Senate," *Chronicle-Herald*, 14 September 1979.
87 NSARM, MG 1, vol. 1479, Confederation Centenary Celebration Committee minutes, 28 May 1963. Some communities needed little encouragement to submit proposals. At this meeting the group had already

received two proposals: a miners' museum in Glace Bay and adult education centres to be established across the province.
88 NSARM, MG 1, vol. 1479, Confederation Centenary Celebration Committee minutes, 28 May 1963; and "Speakers Warn Committee about Dissipation of Centennial Funds," *Chronicle-Herald*. Letters sent to municipalities encouraged them to establish local centennial committees by 30 September 1963. See NSARM, RG 10, series E, vol. 139: Canada's Centennial, National Committee meetings, notes and correspondence, 7 October 1963 to 11 December 1963, "Verbatim Proceedings of the Fourth Meeting of the National Committee Held in Conjunction with the National Conference on Canada's Centennial," 14 October 1963.
89 "Speakers Warn Committee about Dissipation of Centennial Funds," *Chronicle-Herald*.
90 Editorial, "Defective Planning," *Chronicle-Herald*, 3 June 1963.
91 NSARM, RG 10, series E, vol. 139, "Verbatim Proceedings," 14 October 1963; NSARM, RG 10, series E, vol. 140: Canada's Centennial, National Committee meetings, notes and correspondence, 24–7 January 1964, "Report of the National Centennial Conference: National Centennial Conference Minutes," 16 December 1963.
92 NSARM, MG 1, vol. 1479, Confederation Centenary Celebration Committee minutes, 31 January 1964.
93 Ibid.
94 LAC, RG 69, vol. 353, file 130-2, "Report by Director of Special Projects on Visit to New Brunswick and Nova Scotia," March 1964.
95 NSARM, RG 10, series E, vol. 235: Canadian Centennial Commission, Nova Scotia, "Nova Scotia Confederation Centenary Celebrations Committee Plan of Action for 1965," n.d.
96 NSARM, MG 1, vol. 1479, Confederation Centenary Celebration Committee minutes, 13 November 1964.
97 LAC, RG 69, vol. 983, file: National Centennial Fund (Nova Scotia)—Administrative Accounts, "Agreement between National Centennial Administration and the Government of the Province of Nova Scotia for Centennial Projects," 21 October 1963; and NSARM, RG 10, series E, vol. 246, "Nova Scotia Federal-Provincial Centennial Grants Program," n.d.
98 "26 Municipal Projects Approved for Grants," *Chronicle-Herald*, 14 November 1964; and "Give Reason," *Amherst Daily News & Sentinel*, 18 November 1964.
99 NSARM, RG 10, series E, vol. 235, Confederation Centenary Celebration Committee minutes, 24 September 1965.

100 NSARM, Office of the Premier fonds, RG 100, vol. 6, file 12-8: Centenary, 1967, Robert L. Stanfield to Peter Nicholson, 22 June 1965.
101 NSARM, RG 10, series E, vol. 273: Agreement between National Centennial Administration and Province of Nova Scotia for Centennial Projects, folder II, R.A. Donahoe to T.G. Adams, 21 June 1965; and NSARM, RG 10, series E, vol. 235, Confederation Centenary Celebration Committee minutes, 24 September 1965.
102 NSARM, RG 10, series E, vol. 273, Donahoe to Adams, 21 June 1965. Similarly, Annapolis's Ken Green expressed concerns about the Centenary Committee's impartiality. He complained to Stanfield that his town's proposal was rejected for unknown reasons, noting that nearby Bridgetown and Milton had received funding to the exclusion of Annapolis. He wrote that the decision "has left a bad taste with some of our people, many of whom are strong fellows of our party." Stanfield rejected the accusation of partiality, stating that the Centenary Committee was "quite representative and I am sure tries to be fair." See NSARM, RG 100, vol. 6, file 12-8, Green to Stanfield, 14 July 1965; and NSARM, RG 100, vol. 6, file 12-8, Stanfield to Green, 16 July 1965.
103 Editorial, "The Centenary City," *Truro Daily News*, 17 February 1965.
104 LAC, RG 69, vol. 52, file 2-3-2-1, J.M. Murphy to John Fisher, 14 April 1965.
105 LAC, RG 69, vol. 52, file 2-3-2-1, memorandum, Jack Golding to Fisher, 25 May 1965; and LAC, RG 69, vol. 52, file 2-3-2-1, Fisher to Murphy, 26 May 1965.
106 See NSARM, RG 10, series E, vol. 116: Nova Scotia Confederation Centenary Celebration Committee Notes from meetings (Internal), "Report Given at Nova Scotia Union of Municipalities 60th Anniversary," 23 August 1965.
107 NSARM, MG 1, vol. 1479, Confederation Centenary Celebration Committee minutes, 24 September 1965; and NSARM, RG 10, series E, vol. 233: Progress reports. Nova Scotia Centennial Projects, newspaper clippings, news release, 27 July 1965.
108 NSARM, RG 10, series E, vol. 233, news release, 27 July 1965; and "Confederation Projects in by September," *Chronicle-Herald*, 14 July 1965.
109 Editorial, "Six Weeks More," *Chronicle-Herald*, 22 July 1965.
110 NSARM, RG 10, series E, vol. 153: Centennial grants. Approved. Correspondence, financial statements etc. Annapolis Royal, A.P. Hanson to Adams, 3 December 1965. See also NSARM, RG 10, series E, vol. 153: "Centennial Grants Program-Project Application Statement," various dates, 19, 21 January, 24 February 1966; "Federal-Provincial Centennial

Grants Application," various dates, 26 August, 5, 27 September 1967; NSARM, RG 10, series E, vol. 153, Adams to Stoddard, 26 August 1967; Hanson to Adams, 2 March 1966; and telegram, J.M. Weldon to Hanson, 25 February 1966.

111 NSARM, RG 10, series E, vol. 115, "Minister's Report on Centennial Activities in Nova Scotia for Presentation to National Centennial Conference," 29 November 1965.
112 NSARM, RG 10, series E, vol. 231, "Progress Reports. Nova Scotia Centennial Projects," "Centennial Grants Program: Review of Progress in 1965," 31 December 1965.
113 NSARM, RG 10, series E, vol. 235, Confederation Centenary Celebration Committee minutes, 23 August 1967.
114 NSARM, RG 10, series E, vol. 161, "Centennial grants. Approved. Correspondence, financial statements etc. Clare," Stoddard to Weldon, 19 May 1967; NSARM, RG 10, series E, vol. 161, Le Club Richelieu to Centenary Committee, 15 April 1967; NSARM, RG 10, series E, vol. 161, Stoddard to Julius Comeau, 19 May 1967; NSARM, RG 10, series E, vol. 161, telegram, Weldon to Stoddard, 27 June 1967; and NSARM, RG 10, series E, vol. 235, Confederation Centenary Celebration Committee minutes, 23 August 1967.
115 NSARM, RG 10, series E, vol. 189: Centennial grants. Approved. Correspondence, financial statements etc. Sir Charles Tupper Medical Building, "Report on Centennial Projects in Nova Scotia," n.d.
116 Aykroyd, *Anniversary Compulsion*, appendix D, 181.
117 National Centennial Commission, *Centennial Commission Annual Report 1965–1966*, 38.
118 Aykroyd, *Anniversary Compulsion*, 73.
119 Ibid., 5–6.
120 Berton, *1967*, 38.
121 Aykroyd, *Anniversary Compulsion*, 75–9.
122 Cupido, "'Sixty Years of Canadian Progress,'" 19–33.
123 Robert Hartje, *Bicentennial USA: Pathways to Celebration* (Nashville: American Association for State and Local History, 1983), quoted in Davies, *Politics of Participation*, 141.
124 As Shirley Tillotson argues in *The Public at Play: Gender and the Politics of Recreation in Post-War Ontario* (Toronto: University of Toronto Press, 2000), conceptions of "citizen participation" varied widely during the post-war period and were not necessarily inclusive or reflective of Canadian society.
125 Spillman, *Nation and Commemoration*.
126 Ibid., 96.

Chapter Two

1 "Spectacular Finish to Highland Games," *Chronicle-Herald*, 28 August 1967; and "Brilliant Display as Centennial Show Ends," *Mail-Star* (Halifax), 26 August 1967.
2 "'Old' Scotland Twirls for 'New,'" *Mail-Star* (Halifax), 26 August 1967.
3 While officially titled "Nova Scotia Centennial Spectacular, Folk Arts Festival and Highland Games," organizers and the media referred to this event in a variety of ways, including the "Centennial Spectacular" and the "Highland Games and Folk Arts Festival." For consistency, I refer to it as the "Highland Games and Folk Festival."
4 LAC, RG 69, vol. 776, Fisher to Donahoe, 8 March 1965.
5 *Centennial Act*.
6 LAC, RG 69, vol. 776, Fisher to Donahoe, 8 March 1965.
7 Marjorie Major, "History of the Nova Scotia Tartan," *Nova Scotia Historical Quarterly* 2, no. 2 (June 1972): 191–214; and McKay, *Quest of the Folk*, 206–12.
8 McKay, *Quest of the Folk*; McKay, "Tartanism Triumphant," 5–47; McKay, "History and the Tourist Gaze," 102–38; and McKay and Bates, *In the Province of History*, chap. 5.
9 On Macdonald, see T. Stephen Henderson, *Angus L. Macdonald: A Provincial Liberal* (Toronto: University of Toronto Press, 2007).
10 Ibid., 204; and McKay, "Tartanism Triumphant."
11 Beaton and Muise, "Canso Causeway," 39–69.
12 McKay, "Tartanism Triumphant," 6.
13 Ibid., 16. See also Marjory Harper and Michael Vance, "Myth, Migration and the Making of Memory: An Introduction," in *Myth, Migration and the Making of Memory: Scotia and Nova Scotia, c. 1700–1990*, ed. Marjory Harper and Michael Vance (Halifax: Fernwood Publishing, 1999), 18 and 31.
14 McKay and Bates, *In the Province of History*, 256.
15 Ibid., 310, 311.
16 McKay, *Quest of the Folk*, 33–7, 210–12; McKay, "Tartanism Triumphant," 5–47; McKay, "History and the Tourist Gaze," 107–8; and McKay and Bates, 253–316.
17 Harper and Vance, "Myth, Migration, and the Making of Memory," 33–7.
18 NSARM, C. Bruce Fergusson fonds, MG 1, vol. 1479, Confederation Centenary Celebration Committee minutes, 28 May 1965; and NSARM, MG 1, vol. 1479, "Secretary's Report," 27 May 1965.
19 LAC, RG 69, vol. 776, Robbins Elliott to C. Bruce Fergusson, 3 June 1965.

20 LAC, RG 69, vol. 776, memorandum, Elliott to Fisher and Georges Gauthier, 18 June 1965.
21 LAC, RG 69, vol. 776, Robbins Elliott to C. Bruce Fergusson, 3 June 1965.
22 LAC, RG 69, vol. 776, Fisher to Donahoe, 22 September 1965.
23 LAC, RG 69, vol. 776, Fergusson to Fisher, 7 June 1965.
24 NSARM, MG 1, vol. 1479, memorandum, 11 June 1965.
25 NSARM, Department of the Attorney General fonds, RG 10, series E: Miscellaneous, vol. 116: Nova Scotia Confederation Centenary Celebration Committee Notes from meetings (Internal), "Minister's Report on Centennial Activities in Nova Scotia for Presentation to National Centennial Conference," 25 November 1965.
26 NSARM, RG 10, series E, vol. 279: Nova Scotia Spectacular. 1967, Fergusson to Donahoe, 10 December 1965.
27 NSARM, MG 1, vol. 1479, Confederation Centenary Celebration Committee minutes, 28 January 1966.
28 LAC, RG 69, vol. 813, news release, 29 October 1965.
29 NSARM, MG 1, vol. 1479, Confederation Centenary Celebration Committee minutes, 28 January 1966.
30 LAC, RG 69, vol. 8, file 1-3-28-sub. 3, Elliott to Frank Wallace, 3 February 1966.
31 NSARM, RG 10, series E, vol. 279, "Outline of Proposal to Special Committee Set Up by the Nova Scotia Confederation Centenary Celebration Committee to Investigate a Spectacular Celebration Sponsored by the Province of Nova Scotia for 1967 Centennial," 8 February 1966.
32 Ibid.
33 NSARM, RG 10, series E, vol. 116, "A Special Meeting to Consider a Provincial Centennial Programme," 1 March 1966.
34 NSARM, RG 10, series E, vol. 235: Canadian Centennial Commission Nova Scotia, Confederation Centenary Celebration Committee minutes, 22 April 1966.
35 NSARM, RG 10, series E, vol. 115: Canadian Centennial. News releases. Nova Scotia Centennial Projects, "A Proposal for a Highland Games and Folk Festival in Halifax, Nova Scotia, to Be the Province of Nova Scotia Spectacular in Celebration of the Centennial of Confederation in Canada," June 1966.
36 Ibid.
37 Ibid.
38 Ibid.
39 Ibid.

40 Ibid.
41 Stuart Henderson, "'While There Is Still Time ...': J. Murray Gibbon and the Spectacle of Difference in Three CPR Folk Festivals, 1928–1931," *Journal of Canadian Studies* 39, no. 1 (2005): 156.
42 National Centennial Commission, *Sixth Annual and Final Report*, 10–11.
43 LAC, Centennial Commission fonds, RG 69, vol. 6, file 1-3-4-1, "Memorandum to Cabinet," 23 July 1963.
44 Anthony Shay, *Choreographing Identities: Folk Dance, Ethnicity and Festival in the United States and Canada* (Jefferson, NC: McFarland, 2006), 22, 37–8, 157.
45 Philip V. Bohlman, *The Study of Folk Music in the Modern World* (Bloomington: Indiana University Press, 1988), 66.
46 Gordana Lazarevich, "The Role of the Canadian Pacific Railway in Promoting Canadian Culture," in *A Celebration of Canada's Arts, 1930–1970*, ed. Glen Carruthers and Gordana Lazarevich (Toronto: Canadian Scholars' Press, 1996), 6.
47 Henderson, "'While There Is Still Time,'" 154–7.
48 Eva Mackey, *House of Difference: Cultural Politics and National Identity in Canada* (Toronto: University of Toronto Press, 2002), 79.
49 Daniel Francis, *The Imaginary Indian: Images of the Indian in Canadian Culture* (Vancouver: Arsenal Pulp, 1992), 102–3.
50 Shay, *Choreographing Identities*, 31–2, 131.
51 NSARM, RG 10, series E, vol. 235: Canadian Centennial Commission. Nova Scotia, Confederation Centenary Celebration Committee minutes, 6 June 1966.
52 NSARM, Office of the Premier fonds, RG 100, vol. 19, file 12-8, E.R. Gourley to Robert L. Stanfield, 13 June 1966.
53 NSARM, RG 10, series E, vol. 279, Donahoe to Gourley, 21 June 1966.
54 NSARM, MG 1, vol. 1479, "A Meeting of a Special Committee," 24 May 1966; and LAC, RG 69, vol. 252, file 4-17-72-1, Donahoe to Fisher, 15 July 1966.
55 NSARM, RG 10, series E, vol. 279, Fisher to Donahoe, 22 July 1966; and NSARM, RG 10, series E, vol. 279, Wallace to Dan Woodbury, 6 July 1966. Others intervened on the province's behalf to lobby for federal funding approval, including Frank Wallace, Lester Page, and Hugh O. Mills, a high-profile Haligonian and National Centennial director. See LAC, RG 69, vol. 24, file 1-10-13, H.O. Mills to Claude Gauthier, July 1967; LAC, RG 69, vol. 799, Wallace to J.H. Golding, 6 October 1966; and NSARM, RG 10, series E, vol. 116, "Report to the Confederation Centenary Celebration Committee," 4 October 1966.

56 LAC, RG 69, vol. 10, file 1-3-35-1, memorandum, Elliott to Executive Council, 18 July 1966.
57 NSARM, RG 10, series E, vol. 235, minutes, Confederation Centenary Celebration Committee, 13 December 1966; NSARM, MG 1, vol. 1479, "Secretary's Report," 13 December 1966; and NSARM, RG 10, series E, vol. 279, Memorandum of Agreement, 8 February 1967.
58 NSARM, MG 1, vol. 1479, "Secretary's Report," 13 December 1966; and NSARM, RG 10, series E, vol. 279, Donahoe to Leo Chisholm, 14 December 1966.
59 NSARM, RG 10, series E, vol. 279, A.J. Gorman to Donahoe, 27 June 1966.
60 NSARM, MG 1, vol. 1479, "Sub-Committee Meeting," 20 January 1967.
61 NSARM, RG 10, series E, vol. 279, H.R. Wyman to Gourley, 31 January 1967; NSARM, RG 10, series E, vol. 279 and Donahoe to Gourley, 1 February 1967. NSARM, RG 10, series E, vol. 279, Gourley to Donahoe, 6 February 1967; and NSARM, MG 1, vol. 1479, "Sub-Committee Meeting," 8 February 1967.
62 NSARM, MG 1, vol. 1479, "Sub-Committee Meeting," 14 February 1967; NSARM, RG 10, series E, vol. 279, "Terms of Reference for the Director of the Nova Scotia Centennial Folk Festival and Highland Games," 15 March 1967; and NSARM, RG 10, series E, vol. 279, 16 March 1967. See "Heron Named N.S. Co-ordinator," *Chronicle-Herald*, 17 February 1967; and NSARM, RG 10, series E, vol. 279, news release, 8 March 1967.
63 NSARM, RG 10, series E, vol. 279, "First Report to the Centennial Commission," 16 March 1967.
64 NSARM, C.B. Fergusson fonds, MG 1, vol. 1480, handwritten notes, March 1967.
65 NSARM, RG 10, series E, vol. 279, "First Report to the Centennial Commission," 16 March 1967.
66 NSARM, RG 10, series E, vol. 279, "Second Report to the Centennial Commission of Nova Scotia," 17 May 1967.
67 NSARM, RG 10, series E, vol. 279, news release, 20 March 1967.
68 LAC, RG 69, vol. 537, Bruce Cochran to Clyde Batten, 24 August 1967; and LAC, RG 69, vol. 24, file 1-10-13, telegram, Mills to Claude Gauthier, July 1966.
69 NSARM, RG 10, series E, vol. 279, news release, 29 May 1967.
70 LAC, RG 69, vol. 537, Cochran to Batten, 24 August 1967.
71 NSARM, RG 10, series E, vol. 268: Correspondence and memos concerning Patrick Heron, "Meeting Held in the Office of the Regional Officer Centennial Commission," 21 August 1967.

72 NSARM, MG 1, vol. 1479, Confederation Centenary Celebration Committee minutes, 23 August 1967.
73 Advertisements, *Chronicle-Herald*, 22 August 1967.
74 "Highland Festival Opens," *Chronicle-Herald*, 23 August 1967; and "Over 700 Athletes Are Slated for Dominion Highland Games," *Dartmouth Free Press*, 17 August 1967.
75 "Halifax's Highland Games Largest Staged in Nation," *Mail-Star* (Halifax), 22 August 1967; and "Scotland's Top Athletes Take Part in Games," *Mail-Star* (Halifax), 23 August 1967.
76 "N.S. Highland Festival off to a 'Booming' Start," *Chronicle-Herald*, 24 August 1967.
77 NSARM, vertical file 53, no. 5, program, Nova Scotia Centennial Spectacular, Folk Arts Festival and Highland Games, 1967.
78 LAC, RG 69, vol. 796, Patrick Heron to Wallace, 30 June 1967.
79 NSARM, RG 10, series E, vol. 279, Heron to Sir Fitzroy MacLean, 1 March 1967.
80 See NSARM, RG 10, series E, vol. 279, news release, 11 April 1967; LAC, RG 69, vol. 252, file 4-17-72-1: National Project: A Folk Festival and Highland Games, news release, 9 August 1967; and editorial, "Major Attraction," *Mail-Star* (Halifax), 14 August 1967.
81 "N.S. Highland Festival off to a 'Booming' Start," *Chronicle-Herald*
82 Ibid.
83 "A Person from Scotland," *Chronicle-Herald*, 24 August 1967.
84 "Spectacular Finish to Highland Games," *Chronicle-Herald*.
85 MacNeill's name was frequently misspelled as "Shamus MacNeil," and "Seumas MacNeil."
86 NSARM, RG 10, series E, vol. 279, "First Report to the Centennial Commission," 16 March 1967.
87 NSARM, RG 10, series E, vol. 116, "Third Report to the Centennial Commission of Nova Scotia," 18 July 1967.
88 "Games Site Mass of Sounds, Color, Movement," *Chronicle-Herald*, 26 August 1967.
89 "N.S. Open Marks Shattered in Highland Games Action," *Chronicle-Herald*, 28 August 1967; and "A Record-Smashing Day at the Highland Games," *Mail-Star* (Halifax), 26 August 1967.
90 "Scotland's Top Athletes Take Part in the Games," *Mail-Star* (Halifax).
91 "A Swinging Scot," *Chronicle-Herald*, 26 August 967; "Highland Star," *Mail-Star* (Halifax), 24 August 1967; and "World's Best," *Mail-Star* (Halifax), 23 August 1967.

92 "Nova Scotia's Centennial Tribute," *Progress-Enterprise* (Lunenburg), 4 October 1967.
93 "Games Site Mass of Sounds, Color, Movement," *Chronicle-Herald*.
94 "Pipe Band Arrives from Old Country," *Mail-Star* (Halifax), 21 August 1967. "Bearskin or Busby," *Mail-Star* (Halifax), 22 August 1967, featured a child trying on the uniform of a member of the Muirhead Band. "In Its First Appearance," *Chronicle-Herald*, 23 August 1967; "Pipers Parade," *Mail-Star* (Halifax), 23 August 1967; and "Welcome to the Scots," *Mail-Star* (Halifax), 21 August 1967.
95 NSARM, RG 10, series E, vol. 116, "Third Report to the Centennial Commission of Nova Scotia," 18 July 1967.
96 Piobaireachd, also commonly referred to as Ceòl Mór, is a specific genre of traditional bagpipe music.
97 Strathspeys is a type of Scottish music that is traditionally sung but has been adapted for bagpiping.
98 "Shadow of Skirl," *Mail-Star* (Halifax), 24 August 1967.
99 "On Such a Hot Day," *Chronicle-Herald*, 26 August 1967; "Duet Piping Champs," *Mail-Star* (Halifax), 24 August 1967.
100 Seann triubhas is a form of highland dance.
101 "Games Site Mass of Sound, Color, Movement," *Chronicle-Herald*.
102 "If You Step on a Sword You're Out," *Chronicle-Herald*, 24 August 1967; "Booming Tee Off," *Chronicle-Herald*, 24 August 1967; "Wins for the West," *Mail-Star* (Halifax), 24 August 1967; "The Fling and the Kilt," *Chronicle-Herald*, 26 August 1967; and "It's a Long Way," *Chronicle-Herald*, 26 August 1967.
103 "The Fling and the Kilt," *Chronicle-Herald*.
104 NSARM, vertical file 53, no. 5, program, Nova Scotia Centennial Spectacular, Folk Arts Festival and Highland Games, 1967; and LAC, RG 69, vol. 252, file 4-17-72-1, news release, 3 August 1967.
105 NSARM, RG 10, series E, vol. 282: Performing Arts, "Report on Folk Art Festivals, by Claude Bede, Co-ordinator to Donald Wetmore, President, Nova Scotia Folk Arts Council," n.d. See also NSARM, RG 10, series E, vol. 116, "Third Report to the Centennial Commission of Nova Scotia," 18 July 1967; and "Folk Festival, Highland Games Largest on Continent," *Chronicle-Herald*, 23 August 1967.
106 NSARM, RG 10, series E, vol. 282, "Report on Folk Art Festivals," n.d.
107 Ibid.
108 NSARM, RG 10, series E, vol. 282, "Report of the Antigonish-Guysborough Folk Arts Festival," n.d.

109 NSARM, RG 10, series E, vol. 282, "Report on Folk Art Festivals," n.d.
110 Advertisement, *Chronicle-Herald*, 23 August 1967; and advertisement, *Chronicle-Herald*, 23 August 1967.
111 Advertisements, *Chronicle-Herald*, 23 August 1967; and *Mail-Star* (Halifax), 24 August 1967
112 "Crowd of 5,000 Watch Folk Arts Festival Show," *Mail-Star* (Halifax), 25 August 1967.
113 "Folk Festival, Highland Games Largest on Continent," *Chronicle-Herald*; "Ethnic Groups Present Folk Artistry Pageant," *Chronicle-Herald*, 25 August 1967.
114 Untitled photo caption, *Chronicle-Herald*, 26 August 1967; "Polish 'Clan' Performs," *Chronicle-Herald*, 25 August 1967; and "Some of the Action," *Mail-Star* (Halifax), 25 August 1967.
115 "Ethnic Groups Present Folk Artistry Pageant," *Chronicle-Herald*.
116 Untitled photo caption, *Chronicle-Herald*, 25 August 1967.
117 Ibid.; and "Ethnic Groups Present Folk Artistry Pageant," *Chronicle-Herald*; and "Arts Festival Opens July 8," *Cape Breton Post*, 3 July 1967.
118 "Nova Scotia's Centennial Tribute," *Progress-Enterprise* (Lunenburg).
119 LaMarsh, *Memoirs of a Bird in a Gilded Cage*, 178.
120 Ibid., 222.
121 "Crowd of 5,000 Watch Folk Arts Festival Show," *Mail-Star* (Halifax).
122 Eugene P. Holden, "Wonderful Event," *Chronicle-Herald*, 30 August 1967.
123 "Nova Scotia's Centennial Tribute," *Progress-Enterprise* (Lunenburg).
124 "Centennial Theme," *Chronicle-Herald*, 24 August 1967.
125 "Salutary Lesson," *Chronicle-Herald*, 28 August 1967.
126 "Brilliant Display as Centennial Show Ends," *Mail-Star* (Halifax). Skirling means "to play a song on bagpipes," or refers specifically to the high-pitched sound that is made by the instrument.
127 "Spectacular Finish to Highland Games," *Chronicle-Herald*.
128 "'Old' Scotland Twirls for 'New,'" *Mail-Star* (Halifax).
129 "Spectacular Finish to Highland Games," *Chronicle-Herald*.
130 "'Old' Scotland Twirls for 'New,'" *Mail-Star* (Halifax).
131 "Spectacular Finish to Highland Games," *Chronicle-Herald*.
132 "Brilliant Display as Centennial Show Ends," *Mail-Star* (Halifax).
133 "Shadow of Skirl," *Mail-Star* (Halifax).
134 "On Such a Hot Day," *Chronicle-Herald*.
135 NSARM, RG 10, series E, vol. 268, D.A. Stallard, J.A. MacIsaac, J.R. Stewart, and R.F. MacBeth to Fergusson, 31 August 1967.
136 "Poor Example," *Chronicle-Herald*, 6 September 1967.
137 "Games Site Mass of Sounds, Color, Movement," *Chronicle-Herald*.

138 NSARM, RG 10, series E, vol. 235, Confederation Centenary Celebration Committee minutes, 23 August 1967.
139 NSARM, RG 10, series E, vol. 279, Donahoe to Heron, 5 September 1967; and NSARM, RG 10, series E, vol. 279, Mrs Patrick Heron to Donahoe, 9 September 1967.
140 NSARM, RG 10, series E, vol. 267: Centennial Grant Programme. Financial Statements, Eileen Cameron Henry to Donahoe, 6 September 1967.
141 NSARM, RG 10, series E, vol. 268, Henry to Donahoe, 17 September 1967.
142 NSARM, RG 10, series E, vol. 268, Peter Richard to Wyman, 5 October 1967. See also NSARM, RG 10, series E, vol. 268, Wyman to Henry, 13 November 1967.
143 NSARM, RG 10, series E, vol. 262: Correspondence of A.B. Stoddard on the Canadian Centennial, 18 April 1967 to 15 December 1967, A.B. Stoddard to Page, 6 December 1967; NSARM, RG 10, series E, vol. 268, Allan MacDougall to Gerald J. Doucet, 28 September 1967; NSARM, RG 10, series E, vol. 268, Gerald J. Doucet to Donahoe, 4 October 1967; NSARM, RG 10, series E, vol. 269: Project of as Lasting Nature in Nova Scotia. Financial statements, Graham D. Walker to Page, 13 February 1968; and NSARM, RG 10, series E, vol. 268, Wyman to Heron, 21 June 1968.
144 NSARM, MG 1, vol. 1480, report, n.d.
145 NSARM, RG 10, series E, vol. 235, Confederation Centenary Celebration Committee minutes, 14 February 1968.
146 "Games Site Mass of Sounds, Color, Movement," *Chronicle-Herald*.
147 "Spectacular Finish to Highland Games," *Chronicle-Herald*.
148 Paul Basu, *Highland Homecomings: Genealogy and Heritage Tourism in the Scottish Diaspora* (New York: Routledge, 2007), 82–4.
149 Harold Woodman, *A Pictorial History of the Apple Blossom Festival* (Hantsport, NS: Lancelot, 1992) and *An Act to Incorporate the Annapolis Valley Apple Blossom Festival*, RSNS 1935, c 107, as am.
150 Simon Falconer, *Royal Nova Scotia International Tattoo* (Fredericton, NB: Goose Lane Editions, 2010), 59.
151 Ibid., 24.

Chapter Three

1 "Miners' Museum Officially Opened: LaMarsh Says C.B. Centennial Project Unique," *Cape Breton Post*, 1 August 1967.
2 Ibid.
3 Paul MacEwan, *Miners and Steelworkers: Labour in Cape Breton* (Toronto: Samuel Stevens Hakkert, 1976); David Frank, "The Cape Breton Coal

Industry and the Rise and Fall of the British Empire Steel Corporation," *Acadiensis* 7, no. 1 (Autumn 1977): 6; and Frank, *J.B. McLachlan: A Biography* (Toronto: James Lorimer, 1999), 93.

4 Colin Howell, "The 1900s: Industry, Urbanization, and Reform," in *The Atlantic Provinces in Confederation*, ed. E.R. Forbes and D.A. Muise (Toronto: University of Toronto Press, 1993), 172.

5 Frank, *J.B. McLachlan*, 46–7.

6 Ian McKay, "Strikes in the Maritimes, 1901–1914," in *Labour and Working-Class History in Atlantic Canada: A Reader*, ed. David Frank and Gregory S. Kealey (St John's, NL: Institute of Social and Economic Research, 1995), 194.

7 Frank, *J.B. McLachlan*, 46–7. On Maritime industrialization during this period, see T.W. Acheson, "The National Policy and the Industrialization of the Maritimes, 1880–1910," *Acadiensis* 1, no. 2 (Spring 1972): 3–28.

8 Frank, "Cape Breton Coal Industry," 6.

9 Frank, *J.B. McLachlan*, 92–3.

10 *Canadian Mining Journal*, quoted in Frank, *J.B. McLachlan*, 93.

11 Frank, *J.B. McLachlan*, 93.

12 MacEwan, *Miners and Steelworkers*, 7.

13 David Frank, "Tradition and Culture in the Cape Breton Mining Community in the Early Twentieth Century," in *Cape Breton at 200: Historical Essays in Honour of the Island's Bicentennial, 1785–1985*, ed. Ken Donovan (Sydney, NS: University College of Cape Breton Press, 1985), 203.

14 Ian McKay "Strikes in the Maritimes," 192, 197–9.

15 MacEwan, *Miners and Steelworkers*, 23, 39.

16 Joan Bishop, "Sydney Steel: Public Ownership and the Welfare State, 1967 to 1975," in *The Island: New Perspectives on Cape Breton History, 1713–1990*, ed. Kenneth Donovan (Sydney and Fredericton: University College of Cape Breton Press and Acadiensis, 1990), 165; and Frank, *J.B. McLachlan*, 97–109.

17 David Frank, "The 1920s: Class and Region, Resistance and Accommodation," in Forbes and Muise, *Atlantic Provinces in Confederation*, 245.

18 David Frank, "Class Conflict in the Coal Industry in Cape Breton 1922," in *Essays in Working Class History*, ed. Gregory S. Kealey and Peter Warrian, 161–84 (Toronto: McClelland and Stewart, 1976).

19 Frank, *J.B. McLachlan*, 355, 380–4. 11 June is recognized as William Davis Miners' Memorial Day, an annual day of remembrance observed in many Nova Scotia mining communities. In 2008 the Nova Scotia Legislature passed the *William Davis Miners' Memorial Day Act*, RSNS, c 47, acts of 2008, 2nd session, 60th General Assembly, 57 Elizabeth II, 2008. On Davis

Day, see Christina M. Lamey, "Davis Day through the Years: A Cape Breton Coal Mining Tradition," *Nova Scotia Historical Review* 16, no. 2 (1996): 23–33.
20 Richard MacKinnon, "Protest Song and Verse in Cape Breton Island," *Ethnologies* 30, no. 2 (2008): 33–71; and Dawn Fraser, *Echoes from Labour's War: Industrial Cape Breton in the 1920s* (Toronto: New Hogtown, 1976).
21 Bickerton, *Nova Scotia, Ottawa, and the Politics of Regional Development*, 44.
22 Frank, *J.B. McLachlan*, 201–2.
23 Frank, "Cape Breton Coal Industry," 6, 9–10, 25–6, 33; and Frank, *J.B. McLachlan*, 202.
24 Frank, *J.B. McLachlan*, 397–434.
25 Michael Earle, "'Down with Hitler and Silby Barrett': The Cape Breton Miners' Slowdown Strike of 1941," in *Workers and the State in Twentieth-Century Nova Scotia*, ed. Michael Earle (Fredericton, NB: Published for the Gorsebrook Research Institute of Atlantic Canada Studies by Acadiensis, 1989), 116.
26 MacEwan, *Miners and Steelworkers*, 286; and Michael D. Stevenson, "Conscripting Coal: The Regulation of the Coal Labour Force in Nova Scotia during the Second World War," *Acadiensis* 29, no. 2 (Spring 2000): 58–88.
27 E.R. Forbes, "Consolidating Disparity: The Maritimes and the Industrialization of Canada during the Second World War," *Acadiensis* 15, no. 2 (Spring 1987): 23.
28 Canada, *Report of the Royal Commission on Coal, 1946* (Ottawa: King's Printer, 1947), 582–5, 590, 594–9.
29 Canada, *Royal Commission on Canada's Economic Prospects* (Ottawa: Queen's Printer, 1958); MacEwan, *Miners and Steelworkers*, 309; Conrad, "'Atlantic Revolution' of the 1950s," 78–9; and Beaton and Muise, "Canso Causeway," 65–6.
30 Conrad, "'Atlantic Revolution' of the 1950s," 59.
31 Bickerton, *Nova Scotia, Ottawa, and the Politics of Regional Development*, 105–6.
32 Canada, *Royal Commission on Coal, 1960* (Ottawa: Queen's Printer, 1960), quoted in MacEwan, *Miners and Steelworkers*, 309.
33 Economics and Research Division, Nova Scotia Department of Labour, *The Nova Scotia Labour Force: Industry, Occupation, Earnings, Employment* (Halifax: Nova Scotia Department of Labour, 1965), table 1, "Number and Percentage of Population in the Labour Force by Sex with Occupation Division, for Nova Scotia, 1911–1961," 1.
34 Canada, *Royal Commission on Coal, 1960*, 46–8.
35 Beaton and Muise, "Canso Causeway," 66–7.

36 J.R. Donald, *The Cape Breton Coal Problem* (Ottawa: Queen's Printer, 1966), vii.
37 Ibid., 1–5.
38 Ibid., 21–2.
39 Ibid., 1–4.
40 Ibid., 1, 23, 24, 34.
41 Ibid., 9, 12, 19, 34, 35.
42 Norman Pearson and Canadian-British Engineering Consultants, *Town of Glace Bay, Nova Scotia, Urban Renewal Study* (Halifax: n.p., 1966), foreword, 1.
43 For a discussion of company homes in Cape Breton, see Richard MacKinnon, "Making a House a Home: Company Housing in Cape Breton Island," *Material History Review* 47 (Spring 1998): 46–56.
44 Ibid., foreword, 2–5, 9.
45 C. Bruce Fergusson served as Nova Scotia's provincial member on the Historic Sites and Monuments Board of Canada from 1955 to 1969. On this organization's history, see C.J. Taylor, *Negotiating the Past: The Making of Canada's National Historic Parks and Sites* (Montreal and Kingston: McGill-Queen's University Press, 1990).
46 NSARM, C.B. Fergusson fonds, MG 1, vol. 1847, folder 8: Proposal for a Miners' Museum in Glace Bay, 1959–1967, N. Layton Fergusson to Alvin Hamilton, 18 August 1959; and NSARM, MG 1, vol. 1847, folder 8, C. Bruce Fergusson to J.D. Hebert, 24 September 1959.
47 NSARM, MG 1, vol. 1847, folder 8, Hebert to C. Bruce Fergusson, 12 February 1960.
48 NSARM, MG 1, vol. 1847, folder 8, C. Bruce Fergusson to Hebert, 23 February 1960; and C. Bruce Fergusson to Hebert, 25 February 1960.
49 NSARM, MG 1, vol. 1847, folder 8, Hebert to C. Bruce Fergusson, 18 March 1960.
50 LAC, Nina Cohen fonds, MG 30 C 152, vol. 3: Correspondence: Nina Cohen, Woman of the Century, 1867–1967 for the Province of Nova Scotia Awarded by the National Council of Jewish Women 1967.
51 "Diary of a Vagabond," *New Glasgow News*, 15 January 1968.
52 On gender, class, and coal mining, see Steven Penfold, "'Have you no manhood in you?': Gender and Class in the Cape Breton Coal Towns, 1920–1926," *Acadiensis* 23, no. 2 (Spring 1994): 21–44.
53 Terry MacLean, *Louisbourg Heritage: From Ruins to Reconstruction* (Sydney, NS: University College of Cape Breton Press, 1995).
54 Nina Cohen, interview by Gary Lipshutz, place unknown, 1982, T-2058, Beaton Institute.

55 On Katharine McLennan, see A.J.B. Johnston, "Into the Great War: Katharine McLennan Goes Overseas, 1915–1919," in Donovan, *Island: New Perspectives*, 129–44.
56 NSARM, MG 1, vol. 1847, folder 8, "First Meeting of Miner's Museum," 3 January 1963.
57 Donald Wright, *The Professionalization of History in English Canada* (Toronto: University of Toronto Press, 2005), 169–70. See also Carl Berger, *The Writing of Canadian History: Aspects of English-Canadian Historical Writing since 1900* (Toronto: University of Toronto Press, 1986), 259–62.
58 Christy Vodden and Ian Dyck, *A World Inside: A 150-Year History of the Canadian Museum of Civilization* (Gatineau, QC: Canadian Museum of Civilization, 2006), 62.
59 Robyn Gillam, *Hall of Mirrors: Museums and the Canadian Public* (Banff: Banff Centre, 2001), 75, 79, 86.
60 "Touching the Heart of the Plan," *Cape Breton Post*, 5 January 1963 (emphasis in original).
61 NSARM, MG 1, vol. 1847, folder 8, "First Meeting of Miner's Museum," 3 January 1963; and "Museum Plans Discussed Many Ideas Fine Support for Project," *Cape Breton Post*, 4 January 1963.
62 NSARM, MG 1, vol. 1847, folder 8, "First Meeting of Miner's Museum," 3 January 1963.
63 NSARM, MG 1, vol. 1847, folder 8, Cohen to C. Bruce Fergusson, 5 March 1963.
64 "Mrs Nina Cohen Recalls Events Leading to Construction of the Miners' Museum," *Cape Breton Post*, 3 July 1982.
65 "Speakers Warn Committee about Disposition of Centennial Funds," *Chronicle-Herald*, 29 May 1963; and NSARM, MG 1, vol. 1847, Confederation Centenary Celebration Committee minutes, 28 May 1963.
66 NSARM, MG 1, vol. 1847, Confederation Centenary Celebration Committee minutes, 28 May 1963.
67 *An Act to Incorporate the Cape Breton Miners Foundation*, RSNS 1964, c 63.
68 NSARM, Office of the Premier fonds, RG 100, vol. 6, file 12-8, untitled report, D. Shadbolt, August 1964.
69 LAC, Centennial Commission fonds, RG 69, vol. 983, file: National Centennial Fund (Nova Scotia): Administrative Accounts, "Agreement between National Centennial Administration and the Government of the Province of Nova Scotia for Centennial Projects," 21 October 1963; and NSARM, RG 10, series E, vol. 246: Project reports and progress, 1967–68, "Nova Scotia Federal-Provincial Centennial Grants Program," n.d.

70 NSARM, RG 100, vol. 6, file 12-8, Nina Cohen to Robert L. Stanfield, 8 May 1965.
71 NSARM, RG 100, vol. 6, file 12-8, Cohen to Stanfield, 28 August 1964.
72 Ibid.
73 NSARM, RG 100, vol. 6, file 12-8, Stanfield to Cohen, 21 September 1964.
74 See NSARM, RG 10, series E, vol. 274: Cape Breton Miner's Museum: Glace Bay Centennial Project, memorandum, D.A. MacDonald to Leo McIntyre, 29 October 1964; NSARM, RG 10, series E, vol. 274, McIntyre to MacDonald, 2 November 1964; and *An Act to Enable the Town of Glace Bay to Make a Contribution toward the Cost of Cape Breton Miners' Museum*, SNS 1965, c 85.
75 "5-Year Tax Exemption for Museum," *Cape Breton Post*, 11 January 1966.
76 NSARM, MG 1, vol. 1479, Confederation Centenary Celebration Committee minutes, 13 November 1964.
77 "$250,000 Campaign Objective," *Cape Breton Post*, 31 December 1964; and "Campaign Opens," *Cape Breton Post*, 25 January 1965.
78 For a picture of fundraising headquarters, see Roger Guimond, "A Mining Museum for Nova Scotia!" *Mining in Canada* 38, no. 5 (May 1965): 8.
79 "A Personal Message to the Citizens of Cape Breton," *Cape Breton Post*, 1 February 1965; and "Message Issued by Chair," *Cape Breton Post*, 22 February 1965.
80 NSARM, RG 10, series E, vol. 166: Centennial grants. Approved. Correspondence, financial statements etc. Glace Bay, file II, unaddressed letter, n.d.
81 Vance, *Death So Noble*, 219, 258–63.
82 "Rumors Dog Museum: Launch Publicity Campaign," *Cape Breton Highlander*, 24 February 1965.
83 NSARM, RG 10, series E, vol. 114: Canadian Centennial press releases II, Lynk to Layton Fergusson, 23 February 1965.
84 NSARM, Attorney General Department, RG 10, series E: Miscellaneous, vol. 165: Centennial grants. Approved. Correspondence, financial statements etc., Glace Bay, file I: Glace Bay Approved, press release, 3 March 1965; "No Deadline Yet Established for Miners' Museum Campaign," *Chronicle-Herald*, 4 March 1965; and "Donahoe Scuttles Rumors of Museum Drive Deadline," *Cape Breton Highlander*, 10 March 1965.
85 "Big Boost to Museum Fund," *Chronicle-Herald*, 22 July 1965.
86 "Museum Drive at $152,000: Near Objective," *Cape Breton Post*, 20 August 1965.
87 "Province Approves Miners' Museum," *Chronicle-Herald*, 26 August 1965.
88 NSARM, RG 10, series E, vol. 166, Donahoe to Cohen, 25 August 1965.

89 NSARM, RG 10, series E, vol. 165, file I, "Federal Provincial Centennial Grants Application Form for Project N.S. 23," various dates: 31 August 1965, 3 September 1965, 7 December 1965. See also NSARM, RG 10, series E, vol. 165, file I, Hanson to Cohen, 13 December 1965; and "Approve Museum Grants," *Chronicle-Herald*, 17 December 1965.
90 "Museum Site Is Donated," *Cape Breton Post*, 27 December 1965.
91 NSARM, RG 10, series E, vol. 165, file I, H.S. Haslam to Cohen, 8 October 1965; NSARM, RG 10, series E, vol. 165, file I, Cohen to Haslam, 11 August 1965; and "Coal Available at Ocean Deeps," *Cape Breton Post*, 7 December 1966.
92 "Veteran Miner to Turn Sod at Museum Site," *Chronicle-Herald*, 11 May 1966; NSAMR, RG 10, series E, vol. 114, Centennial Commission bulletin no. 12, 24 June 1966.
93 NSARM, RG 10, series E, vol. 115: Canadian Centennial press releases Nova Scotia Centennial Projects, press release, 26 May 1966.
94 "Museum Project Generates New Heat – Urquhart Irked – Rejection Blamed on Aldermen," *Cape Breton Post*, 19 November 1964; "Museum Project Blasted by Council – Feud Sizzles – Somebody Led down Garden Path: Mayor," *Cape Breton Post*, 20 November 1964; and "Crabby Corner," *Cape Breton Post*, 19 December 1964.
95 "Lukewarm Reception," *Cape Breton Post*, 21 November 1964.
96 "Cape Breton Miners' Museum," *Cape Breton Post*, 25 November 1964.
97 "Won't Endorse Museum Project," *Chronicle-Herald*, 18 February 1965; "Museum Project Reaction Cool," *Cape Breton Post*, 13 February 1965; and "Statement by Council," *Cape Breton Post*, 17 February 1965.
98 "Centennial Grants," *Antigonish Casket*, 26 November 1964.
99 "Lest We Forget," *Cape Breton Post*, 27 November 1964.
100 "Collective Effort for Museum Urged," *Cape Breton Post*, 5 January 1965.
101 "People's Forum," *Cape Breton Post*, 24 November 1964.
102 "Centennial Project: Out with the Stupid Clap Trap," *Cape Breton Highlander*, 24 February 1965.
103 "United Appeal is Commended – By UMW Head," *Cape Breton Post*, 12 March 1965.
104 "Union Leader Endorses C.B. Miners' Museum," *Cape Breton Post*, 16 July 1965.
105 NSARM, RG 10, series E, vol. 120: Nova Scotia Centennial News Briefs (L.V. Hutt), Nova Scotia Centennial News Brief, no. 6, April 1966; and NSARM, RG 10, series E, vol. 235, Canadian Centenary Council bulletin, Sept. 1965, vol. III, no. 5.
106 "Museum Taking Shape," *Chronicle-Herald*, 21 April 1966

107 NSARM, RG 10, series E, vol. 165, file I, Cohen to *Chronicle-Herald*, unpublished, 5 May 1966.
108 NSARM, RG 10, series E, vol. 165, file I, Cohen to Hanson, 26 May 1966.
109 NSARM, RG 10, series E, vol. 165, file I, Hanson to Cohen, 9 June 1966; and NSARM RG 10, series E, vol. 165, file I, Donahoe to Cohen, 20 June 1966.
110 MacKinnon, "Protest Song and Verse in Cape Breton," 34. On the Men of the Deeps, see Allister MacGillivray, *Diamonds in the Rough: 25 Years with the Men of the* Deeps (Sydney: Men of the Deeps Music, 1991); MacGillivray, *The Men of the Deeps: The Continuing Saga* (New Waterford, NS: Men of the Deeps Music, 2000); and John C. O'Donnell, *"And Now the Fields Are Green": A Collection of Coal Mining Songs in Canada* (Sydney, NS: University College of Cape Breton Press, 1992). MacKinnon notes that while there was no miners' choir tradition in Cape Breton (and little in Canada, for that matter), Britain had a history of such groups. On miners' choir tradition in industrial British communities, see Gareth Williams, *Valleys of Song: Music and Society in Wales, 1840–1919* (Cardiff: University of Wales Press, 1998).
111 NSARM, Atlantic Pavilion of Expo 1967 fonds, RG 43, vol. 2, press release, 31 July 1967.
112 John C. O'Donnell, *The Men of the Deeps Melody Collection* (Waterloo, ON: Waterloo Music, 1975), preface.
113 "Famed Folklorist Assists Society in Search for Miners Songs & Stories," *Cape Breton Highlander*, 9 March 1966.
114 NSARM, Helen Creighton fonds, MG 1, vol. 2811, file 106, Cohen to Helen Creighton, 2 May 1967. In May 1967, Cohen suggested that she and Creighton produce a "Cape Breton Miners Folk Book," which would include "the miners superstitions and other tales." The possibility of working with renowned Canadian folklorist Edith Fowke, who had approached Cohen about working together, was raised but summarily dismissed by Cohen, who told Creighton "we do not need Edith Fowke." See NSARM, MG 1, vol. 2811, file 106, Cohen to Creighton, 2 May 1967; and NSARM, MG 1, vol. 2811, file 106, Cohen to Creighton, 5 December 1966. See also McKay, *Quest of the Folk*, 145–50, on the often strained professional relationship between Creighton and Fowke.
115 "Men of the Deeps: An Impressive Debut," *Cape Breton Post*, 3 November 1966; and NSARM, RG 43, vol. 2, press release, 31 July 1967.
116 LAC, RG 69, vol. 319, file 7-3-2-1, Cohen to Allan MacEachen, 16 May 1967.

117 NSARM, RG 10, series E, vol. 166, MacDonald to Borden (A.B.) Stoddard, 8 November 1967; LAC, RG 69, vol. 52, file 2-3-3-10, Stoddard to Weldon, 11 September 1967; NSARM, RG 10, series E, vol. 235, Confederation Centenary Celebration Committee minutes, 23 August 1967; NSARM, RG 10, series E, vol. 189: Centennial grants. Approved. Correspondence, financial statements etc. Sir Charles Tupper Medical Building, file I, "Report on Centennial Projects in Nova Scotia," A.B. Stoddard, n.d.; and NSARM, RG 10, series E, vol. 245: Canada's Centennial. General correspondence. April 1965–October 1967, Stoddard to C.F. Prevey, 18 September 1967.
118 LAC, RG 69, vol. 8, file 1-3-28, subfile 3, Cohen to Frank Wallace, 26 May 1966.
119 LAC, RG 69, vol. 8, file 1-3-28, subfile 3, Cohen to John Fisher, 26 May 1966.
120 LAC, RG 69, vol. 319, file 7-3-2-1, memorandum, Peter Aykroyd to Fisher, 7 July 1966.
121 LAC, RG 69, vol. 319, file 7-3-2-1, Marcel Dubuc to Cochran, 28 July 1966.
122 LAC, RG 69, vol. 319, file 7-3-2-1, Cochran to Aykroyd, 20 July 1966.
123 LAC, RG 69, vol. 319, file 7-3-2-1, Dubuc to Cochran, 28 July 1966.
124 "Impressive Floats Feature Big Parade," *Cape Breton Post*, 1 August 1967.
125 LAC, RG 69, vol. 774, Wallace to Bill Neville, 30 May 1967.
126 "MacKeen Says Miners' Museum World Project," *Chronicle-Herald*, 1 August 1967.
127 "Miners' Museum Officially Opened," *Cape Breton Post*.
128 "MacKeen Says Miners' Museum World Project," *Chronicle-Herald*.
129 "Tourists Flocking to the Miners' Museum," *Cape Breton Post*, 26 August 1967.
130 McKay, *Quest of the Folk*; McKay, "History and the Tourist Gaze"; and McKay, "Tartanism Triumphant."
131 "Nova Scotia Looks Ahead to Million-Visitor Year," *Financial Post*, 6 July 1967.
132 NSARM, RG 100, vol. 6, file 12-8, untitled report, D. Shadbolt, August 1964.
133 See Shirley Tillotson, "Time, Swimming Pools, and Citizenship: The Emergence of Leisure Rights in Mid-Twentieth-Century Canada," in *Contesting Canadian Citizenship: Historical Readings*, ed. Robert Adamoski, Dorothy E. Chunn and Robert Menzies, 199–221 (Peterborough, ON: Broadview, 2002); Tillotson, *Public at Play*; and Dimitry Anastakis, *Car Nation: An Illustrated History of Canada's Transformation behind the Wheel* (Toronto: James Lorimer, 2008), 55–70.

134 "Abbie Lane Supports Cape Breton Centennial Project," *Chronicle-Herald*, 25 May 1965.
135 "Ask Council for Donation: Miners' Museum," *Cape Breton Post*, 5 February 1965.
136 Wyile, *Anne of Tim Hortons*, 55–7.
137 On thanatourism and the 1992 Westray disaster, see Peter Thompson, "Tourism and the Extractive Gaze on Leo MacKay's Foord St" (paper for the Association of Canadian Studies, Dublin, Ireland, 11 May 2012).
138 Guimond, "Mining Museum for Nova Scotia!" 10–11.
139 "Glace Bay Centennial Project Is Tribute to World's Coal Miners," *Ship & Shore News*, September 1967.
140 Edwin Payn, "Miners' Museum," *Atlantic Advocate* 56, no. 3 (November 1965): 49.
141 Guimond, "Mining Museum for Nova Scotia!" 8 and 9.
142 "People's Forum," *Cape Breton Post*.
143 Elizabeth J. Hiscott, "A Lasting Monument," *Atlantic Advocate* 57, no. 12 (August 1967): 19.
144 "25,000 Visit Miners' Museum: Since July," *Cape Breton Post*, 11 October 1967.
145 "Nina's Big Day," *Cape Breton Post*, 2 August 1967.
146 NSARM, MG 1, vol. 2811, file 106, Cohen to Creighton, 23 June 1968.
147 LAC, MG 30 C 152, vol. 3, untitled address, n.d.
148 Cohen, interview by Lipshutz.
149 Ibid.
150 "Mrs Nina Cohen Recalls Events Leading to Construction of the Miners' Museum," *Cape Breton Post*, 3 July 1982.
151 "Fire Destroys Miners' Museum," *Cape Breton Post*, 20 August 1980; "'We'll build again' Says Museum Chairman," *Cape Breton Post*, 21 August 1980; and "Minister Tours Fire Ruins; Rebuilding Plans under Way," *Cape Breton Post*, 23 August 1980.
152 "Miners' Museum Re-opens," *Cape Breton Post*, 5 July 1982; and Edwin Payn, "Where Miners Are Remembered," *Atlantic Advocate* 73, no. 4 (December 1982), 11.
153 "Miners' Museum Re-opens," *Cape Breton Post*; and "Museum Fund Boosted by Federal Grant," *Chronicle-Herald*, 16 June 1981.
154 "Museum Fund Boosted by Federal Grant," *Chronicle-Herald*.
155 "Miners' Museum Re-opens," *Cape Breton Post*.
156 Payn, "Where Miners Are Remembered," 11.
157 Palmer, *Canada's 1960s*, 211–41.
158 Cohen, interview by Lipshutz.

159 Robert Summerby-Murray, "Regenerating Cultural Identity through Industrial Heritage Tourism: Visitor Attitudes, Entertainment, and the Search for Authenticity at Mills, Mines, and Museums of Maritime Canada," *London Journal of Canadian Studies* 30 (2015): 64–89.
160 Ibid.

Chapter Four

1 "A Bunch of Fish," *Mail-Star* (Halifax), 19 January 1966.
2 Nelson, *Razing Africville*, 57. On urban planning and economic development in Halifax during the 1950s, see Beverly A. Sandalack and Andrei Nicolai, *Urban Structure – Halifax: An Urban Design Approach* (Halifax: Tuns, 1998), 9.
3 Judith Fingard, Janet Guildford, and David Sutherland, *Halifax: The First 250 Years* (Halifax: Formac Publishing, 1999), 160–78. See also Fingard and Guildford, *Mothers of the Municipality*.
4 David M. Cameron and Peter Aucoin, "Halifax," in *City Politics in Canada*, ed. Warren Magnusson and Andrew Sancton (Toronto: University of Toronto Press, 1983), 169.
5 Atlantic Provinces Economic Council, *Atlantic Canada Today*, quoted in Stanley, "The 1960s: The Illusions and Realities of Progress," 445; and Nova Scotia Development, Economics and Statistics Division, *Halifax County Profile* (Halifax: Nova Scotia Development, Economics and Statistics Division, 1974), appendix, table 1, "Growth of Population in Nova Scotia and Halifax County," 65.
6 Fingard, Guildford, and Sutherland, *Halifax*, 165–9; Conrad and Hiller, *Atlantic Canada*, 192–4, 197–8; Stanley, "The 1960s," 421–2; and Cameron and Aucoin, "Halifax," 171–2.
7 Stanley, "The 1960s," 446–7.
8 Paul A. Erickson, *Halifax's North End: An Anthropologist Looks at the City* (Hantsport, NS: Lancelot, 1986), 81. On the Uniacke Square development, see Krys Verrall, "Art and Urban Renewal: MOMA's New City Exhibition and Halifax's Uniacke Square," in *The Sixties: Passion, Politics, and Style*, ed. Dimitry Anastakis, 145–66 (Montreal and Kingston: McGill-Queen's University Press, 2008).
9 Fingard, Guildford, and Sutherland, *Halifax*, 165–9; Conrad and Hiller, *Atlantic Canada*, 421–2.
10 Bickerton, *Nova Scotia, Ottawa*, 162–3, 179–82.
11 Ibid., 146–8, 234–7. On Dartmouth's Volvo plant, see Dimitry Anastakis, "Building a 'New Nova Scotia': State Intervention, the Auto Industry and

the Case of Volvo in Halifax, 1963–1998," *Acadiensis* 34, no. 1 (Autumn 2004): 3–30. On Clairtone Sound Corporation, see Nina Munk and Rachel Gotlieb, *The Art of Clairtone: The Making of a Design Icon, 1958–1971* (Toronto: McClelland and Stewart, 2008); Roy E. George, *The Life and Times of Industrial Estates Limited* (Halifax: Henson College, Dalhousie University, 1974); and Garth Hopkins, *Clairtone: The Rise and Fall of a Business Empire* (Toronto: McClelland & Stewart, 1978).

12 Robert Vaison and Peter Aucoin, "Class Voting in Recent Halifax Mayoralty Elections," in *Politics and Government of Urban Canada: Selected Readings*, 3rd ed., ed. L.D. Feldman and M.D. Goldrick (Toronto: Methuen, 1976), 202.

13 Fingard, Guildford, and Sutherland, *Halifax*, 169; and Marquis, "Reluctant Concession to Modernity.'"

14 Fingard, Guildford, and Sutherland, *Halifax*, 161.

15 Ibid., 169–77; and Heritage Trust of Nova Scotia, *Founded upon a Rock* (Halifax: Heritage Trust of Nova Scotia, 1967), about the impact of urban renewal on heritage buildings.

16 Gordon Stephenson, *A Redevelopment Study of Halifax, Nova Scotia: 1957* (Toronto: University of Toronto Press, 1957) viii.

17 Ibid., 27; Fingard, Guildford, and Sutherland, *Halifax*, 169–74, and Nelson, *Razing Africville*, 57–8.

18 Nelson, *Razing Africville*, 5, 23, 57; and Conrad and Hiller, *Atlantic Canada*, 204. On Africville, see also Loo, "Africville and the Dynamics of State Power in Postwar Canada."

19 Africville Genealogical Society, eds., *The Spirit of Africville* (Halifax: Formac Publishing, 1992), 56–8.

20 "Will Inordinate Delay Kill Aquarium?" *Mail-Star* (Halifax), 3 December 1965.

21 NSARM, Attorney General Department, RG 10, series E: Miscellaneous, vol. 132: Canada's Centennial – projects refused, R.J. McCleave to R.A. Donahoe, 26 April 1961.

22 "Aquarium Excellent Centennial Project," *Mail-Star* (Halifax), 1 October 1965.

23 Halifax Regional Municipality Archives (HRMA), Halifax City Council Submissions, RG 102-1B, "A Public Aquarium for the County of Halifax: A Proposal to Commemorate the Centenary of Confederation," 12 November 1964.

24 HRMA, Halifax City Council Records, RG 102-1, Halifax City Council minutes, 30 July 1964.

25 HRMA, RG 102-1, "Report – Centennial Committee," 27 August 1964.

26 Ibid.

27 HRMA, RG 102-1, "Report – Centennial Committee," 27 August 1964.
28 NSARM, C.B. Fergusson fonds, MG 1, vol. 1479, Confederation Centenary Celebration Committee, Confederation Centenary Celebration Committee minutes, 25 September 1964; and NSARM, MG 1, vol. 1479, Confederation Centenary Celebration Committee minutes, 13 November 1964. Under the Centennial Grants Program, Halifax County was eligible for $473,670 in funding, with $100,000 allocated for Dartmouth's museum and library project. See NSARM, RG 10, series E, vol. 235: Canadian Centennial Commission Nova Scotia, "Centennial Grants Program: Nova Scotia," n.d.; HRMA, RG 102-1, Halifax City Council minutes, 12 November 1964.
29 LAC, RG 69, vol. 52, file 2-3-2-1, Kitz to Robichaud, 21 August 1964; LAC, RG 69, vol. 52, file 2-3-2-1, Robichaud to Fisher; and LAC, Centennial Commission fonds, RG 69, vol. 52, file 2-3-2-1: Local projects – Nova Scotia – Municipal – General, Robichaud to John Fisher, 1 October 1964.
30 LAC, RG 69, vol. 52, file 2-3-2-1, Fisher to Robichaud, 9 October 1964.
31 HRMA, RG 102-1, Halifax City Council minutes, 17 June 1965.
32 Letter to *Mail-Star* (Halifax), 10 June 1966. See also Alfonso Rojo, "The Halifax Centennial Aquarium," *PROBE* 1, no. 2 (March 1966): 9–10.
33 "Aquarium Costs Soar Near Million," *Chronicle-Herald*, 23 September 1966.
34 "Aquarium: A Provincial Asset," *Chronicle-Herald*, 3 June 1966.
35 HRMA, RG 102-1, Halifax City Council minutes, 12 August 1965. In December 1965 Halifax contracted Aza Avramovitch Associates Ltd to design the aquarium at a cost of $35,000. See HRMA, RG 102-1, Halifax City Council minutes, 16 December 1965; and HRMA, RG 102-1B, "Staff Report – Centennial Aquarium – Appointment of Architects," 12 August 1965.
36 NSARM, Aza Avramovitch fonds, Accession 2001-036001-004, file 1, bibliographic notes.
37 Letter to *Mail-Star* (Halifax), 21 July 1966.
38 NSARM, Accession 2001-036001-004, file 1, bibliographic notes. On centennial projects and architecture, see Colin Ripley, "Emptiness and Landscape: National Identity in Canada's Centennial Projects," *Journal of the Society for the Study of Architecture in Canada* 30, no. 1 (2005): 37–45.
39 NSARM, Accession 2001-036001-004, file 3, Aquarium project, 1966; and NSARM, RG 10, series E, vols 205–9, architectural drawings, n.d.
40 "Aquarium: A Provincial Asset," *Chronicle-Herald*; and "Proposed Aquarium," *Mail-Star* (Halifax), 15 March 1966.
41 "Experts Claim $400,000 Too Low for Aquarium: Could Do Fairly Good Job," *Mail-Star* (Halifax), 14 October 1965.
42 "'Get Moving Halifax': Centennial," *Chronicle-Herald*, 30 November 1965.

43 "Will Inordinate Delay Kill Aquarium?," *Mail-Star* (Halifax).
44 NSARM, RG 10, series E, vol. 272: Agreement between National Centennial Administration and Provincial of Nova Scotia for Centennial Projects, notes, 23 December 1965.
45 "Aquarium Site Causing Delay," *Mail-Star* (Halifax), 30 November 1965.
46 HRMA, RG 102-1, Halifax City Council minutes, 30 December 1965; and NSARM, RG 10, series E, vol. 241: Correspondence, clippings and miscellaneous material related to cancelled project, Halifax aquarium, Board of Directors for Centennial Aquarium minutes, 5 January 1966.
47 Nova Scotia Museum of Natural History, "About the Museum," https://naturalhistory.novascotia.ca/about-museum.
48 HRMA, RG 102-1, Halifax City Council minutes, "Staff Report Re: Letter from the Premier of Nova Scotia: Location of Halifax Centennial Aquarium," 13 January 1966; and HRMA, RG 102-1, Halifax City Council minutes, R.L. Stanfield to Vaughan, 6 January 1966.
49 "Aquarium Site Selected," *Mail-Star* (Halifax), 14 January 1966.
50 Ibid.
51 HRMA, RG 102-1, Halifax City Council minutes, 13 January 1966; NSARM, RG 10, series E, vol. 241, "Federal-Provincial Centennial Grants Application Form," various dates, 14, 21 January, 5 May 1966; LAC, RG 10, vol. 52, file 2-3-3-2: Local projects – Nova Scotia – Rural Municipalities – Generally, Order-in-Council, P.C. 1967-7/782, 5 May 1966; LAC, RG 69, vol. 52, file 2-3-2-4: Local Projects – City of Halifax (Nova Scotia), Order-in-Council, P.C. 1967-10/216, 9 February 1967; and LAC, RG 69, vol. 981, file: Centennial Commission – Publicity Material – Nova Scotia, press release, 3 June 1966.
52 NSARM, RG 10, series E, vol. 241, Board of Directors for Centennial Aquarium minutes, 5 January 1966.
53 "Oppose Site for Aquarium," *Mail-Star* (Halifax), 20 January 1966.
54 HRMA, RG 102-1, Halifax City Council minutes, 17 February 1966; and "Aquarium Plans Get Green Light," *Mail-Star* (Halifax), 25 May 1966.
55 LAC, RG 69, vol. 981, press release, 3 June 1966.
56 "Aquarium Still on Drawing Board," *Mail-Star* (Halifax), 16 May 1966.
57 NSARM, RG 10, series E, vol. 115: Canadian Centennial – Press releases – Nova Scotia Centennial Projects, "Minister's Report on Centennial Activities in Nova Scotia for Presentation to National Centennial Conference," 29 November 1965; and "Aquarium Still on Drawing Board," *Mail-Star* (Halifax).
58 NSARM, RG 10, series E, vol. 241, Vaughan to A.P. Hanson, 24 May 1966.
59 NSARM, RG 10, series E, vol. 241, Donahoe to Vaughan, 31 May 1966.

60 HRMA, RG 102-1, Halifax City Council minutes, 26 May 1966.
61 "Proposes New Shock Treatment," *Mail-Star* (Halifax), 30 May 1966; "Aldermen Agree to Hold Line on Aquarium costs," *Mail-Star* (Halifax), 27 May 1966; and HRMA, City Manager's Office Correspondence, RG 102-4A, vol. 12-A.276: Aquarium. 1965–1966, Hedley Ivany to Halifax City aldermen, 30 May 1966.
62 HRMA, City Manager's Office Correspondence, RG 102-4A, vol. 12-A.276: Aquarium. 1965–1966, Hedley Ivany to Halifax City aldermen, 30 May 1966.
63 "Aquarium: A Provincial Asset," *Chronicle-Herald*; editorial, "Further Aid," *Chronicle-Herald*, 4 June 1966; and "Reminder of Our Heritage," *Chronicle-Herald*, 16 June 1966.
64 "Aquarium in B.C. Blessed, Plagued by Success," *Chronicle-Herald*, 10 June 1966.
65 HRMA, RG 102-1, Halifax City Council minutes, 16 June 1966.
66 LAC, RG 69, vol. 52, file 2-3-2-4, Vaughan to Robichaud, 3 June 1966.
67 "Further Aid," *Chronicle-Herald*; and "Ottawa Would Consider Larger Grant," *Chronicle-Herald*, 3 June 1966.
68 "Further Aid," *Chronicle-Herald*.
69 "More Federal Aid Possible for Aquarium," *Chronicle-Herald*, 14 July 1966; and editorial, "Greater Federal Aid for Aquarium," *Mail-Star* (Halifax), 18 July 1966.
70 Ibid.
71 LAC, MG 26 N 4, vol. 6, Vaughan to Lester B. Pearson, 14 July 1966.
72 LAC, MG 26 N 4, vol. 6, Vaughan to Robichaud, 22 September 1966; and "Aquarium Costs Soar Near Million," *Chronicle-Herald*.
73 "Council Names Committee for Last Ditch Effort," *Mail-Star* (Halifax), 30 September 1966; and NSARM, RG 10, series E, vol. 167: Centennial grants approved – correspondence, financial statements etc. Halifax, Allan O'Brien to Hanson, 6 December 1966.
74 "Council Names Committee for Last Ditch Effort," *Mail-Star* (Halifax); and HRMA, RG 102-1, Halifax City Council minutes, 16 June 1966.
75 "Aquarium Costs Soar Near Million," *Chronicle-Herald*.
76 "Council Names Committee for Last Ditch Effort," *Mail-Star* (Halifax).
77 Editorial, "City Must Go Ahead with Aquarium," *Mail-Star* (Halifax), 24 September 1966.
78 NSARM, RG 10, series E, vol. 235, Confederation Centenary Celebration Committee minutes, 5 October 1966.
79 NSARM, RG 10, series E, vol. 272, "A Proposal for a Public Aquarium in Halifax, N.S.," as appended to letter from Ivany to Donahoe, 10 November 1966.

80 Advertisements, *Chronicle-Herald*, 13, 14 October 1966.
81 Vaison and Aucoin, "Class Voting," 202–3.
82 Advertisements, *Chronicle-Herald*, 10, 14, 17 October 1966.
83 "Halifax's Changing Skyline," *Financial Post*, 1 October 1966.
84 "It's Front Page News across the Nation: Evidence of Progress," *Chronicle-Herald*, 12 October 1966.
85 Vaison and Aucoin, "Class Voting," 205; "O'Brien Elected Mayor," *Chronicle-Herald*, 20 October 1966; and "O'Brien Promises Civic Speedup after Big Win," *Mail-Star* (Halifax), 20 October 1966.
86 HRMA, RG 102-1, Halifax City Council minutes, 1 December 1966.
87 NSARM, RG 10, series E, vol. 167, O'Brien to Hanson, 9 December 1966.
88 NSARM, RG 10, series E, vol. 167, Hanson to O'Brien, 9 December 1966; NSARM, RG 10, series E, vol. 235, Confederation Centenary Celebration Committee minutes, 13 December 1966; NSARM, RG 10, series E, vol. 167, Hanson to J.M. Weldon, 22 December 1966; NSARM, RG 10, series E, vol. 167, Weldon to Hanson, 15 February 1967; NSARM, RG 10, series E, vol. 167, Hanson to O'Brien, 16 February 1967; and NSARM, RG 10, series E, vol. 167, "Federal-Provincial Centennial Grants Program Project Application Statement," 20, 21 December 1966, 15 February 1967. An Order in Council to this effect was passed by the Privy Council on 9 February 1967, revoking the previous Order in Council approving the aquarium project, and approving, in its place, the swimming pool project. See LAC, RG 69, vol. 381, Order in Council, P.C. 1967-10/216, 9 February 1967.
89 HRMA, RG 102-1, Halifax City Council minutes, 12 December 1966.
90 "Aquarium and Shift of City Field off List," *Chronicle-Herald*, 2 December 1966.
91 NSARM, RG 10, series E, vol. 189: Centennial grants. Approved. Correspondence, financial statements etc. Sir Charles Tupper Medical Building, "Report on Centennial Projects in Nova Scotia," n.d.
92 Tillotson, "Time, Swimming Pools, and Citizenship," 199–206, 209–17; and Tillotson, *Public at Play*, 6–8, 13, 70–6. Tillotson argues that Canada's "leisure law" derived from "social science research and labour activism, as well as from the electoral calculations of politicians and from responses to market forces."
93 Caroline Andrew, Jean Harvey, and Don Dawson, "Evolution of Local State Activity: Reaction Policy in Toronto," *Leisure Studies* 13 (1994): 1, 11. On post-war leisure initiatives, see Mark Searle and Russell Brayley, *Leisure Services in Canada: An Introduction*, 2nd ed. (State College, PA: Venture Publishing, 2000), 19–22.

94 Canadian Youth Commission, *Youth and Recreation: New Plans for New Times* (Toronto: Ryerson, 1946), vi.
95 Canadian Council of Resource Ministers, *The Administration of Outdoor Recreation in Canada* (Montreal: Canadian Council of Resource Ministers, 1968), 1.
96 Tillotson, "Time, Swimming Pools, and Citizenship" 199, 200, 207, 212.
97 Tillotson, *Public at Play*, 7, 14–15, 17, 37. On other aspects of leisure rights, see Michael Dawson, "Leisure, Consumption, and the Public Sphere: Postwar Debates over Shopping Regulations in Vancouver and Victoria during the Cold War," in *Creating Postwar Canada: Community, Diversity, and Dissent, 1945–75*, ed. Magda Fahrni and Robert Rutherdale, 193–216 (Vancouver: UBC Press, 2008).
98 Franca Iacovetta, *Gatekeepers: Reshaping Immigrant Lives in Cold War Canada* (Toronto: Between the Lines, 2006), 174–88, 192–200; and Iacovetta, "Making 'New Canadians': Social Workers, Women, and the Reshaping of Immigrant Families," in *A Nation of Immigrants: Women, Workers, and Communities in Canadian History, 1840s–1960s*, ed. Franca Iacovetta, Paula Draper, and Robert Ventresca, 482–513 (Toronto: University of Toronto Press, 1998).
99 Steve Penfold, "'Selling by the Carload': The Early Years of Fast Food in Canada," in Fahrni and Rutherdale, *Creating Postwar Canada*, 178–82.
100 Neil Sutherland, *Growing Up: Childhood in English Canada from the Great War to the Age of Television* (Toronto: University of Toronto Press, 1997), 222–3.
101 Mary Louise Adams, *The Trouble with Normal: Postwar Youth and the Making of Heterosexuality* (Toronto: University of Toronto Press, 1997), 3–4, 41, 74–7. See also Adams, "Constructing Normal Citizens: Sex Advice for Postwar Teens," in *Contesting Canadian Citizenship: Historical Readings*, ed. Robert Adamoski, Dorothy E. Chunn, and Robert Menzies, 273–92 (Peterborough, ON: Broadview, 2002); and Cynthia Comacchio, "Lost in Modernity: 'Maladjustment' and the 'Modern Youth Problem,' English Canada, 1920–50," in *Lost Kids: Vulnerable Children and Youth in Twentieth-Century Canada and the United States*, ed. Mona Gleason, Tamara Myers, Leslie Paris, and Veronica Strong-Boag, 53–71 (Vancouver: UBC Press, 2010).
102 Joan Sangster, *Girl Trouble: Female Delinquency in English Canada* (Toronto: Between the Lines, 2002), 57.
103 NSARM, RG 10, series E, vol. 132, Willoughby Digdon to Donahoe, 11 January 1966.
104 "A Blueprint for Tomorrow toward Greater Progress," *Vanguard* (Yarmouth), 8 May 1968.
105 NSARM, RG 10, series E, vol. 188: Centennial grants approved – correspondence, financial statements etc. Yarmouth, brochure, n.d.

106 On the Public Gardens and Point Pleasant Park, see Bruce Armstrong and John Davis, *Sanctuary: Halifax's Parks and Public Gardens* (Halifax: Nimbus Publishing Limited, 1996); and Janet Kitz and Gary Castle, *Point Pleasant: An Illustrated History* (Halifax: Pleasant Point Publishing, 1999).

107 HRMA, Halifax Recreation and Playgrounds Commission Minutes, RG 102-37B, file 6: Halifax Recreation and Playgrounds Commission Minutes, February 1956–October 1959, "Report Prepared by Abol H. Ziai for the Recreation and Playgrounds Commission Meeting," 28 July 1959.

108 HRMA, RG 102-1, Halifax City Council minutes, 15 December 1960.

109 HRMA, RG 102-37B, file 7: Recreation and Playgrounds Commission minutes, 1960–1963, "Halifax Recreation and Playgrounds Commission meeting," 30 January 1961.

110 HRMA, RG 102-1, Halifax City Council minutes, 20 June 1962.

111 HRMA, Development Department Records, RG 102-41, file B.2: Development Committee – Submissions and Staff Report – January 1964, "City of Halifax – Progress Report on Some of the Major Projects Undertaken by the City," 5 December 1963.

112 HRMA, RG 102-1, "Report – Recreation Commission Re: Site for Municipal Indoor Swimming Pool," 30 September 1965.

113 HRMA, Halifax Town Planning and Board Submissions, RG 102-40B, file 6: Submissions to Town Planning Board, 1966, "Recreation Facilities – Report 1 – Swimming Pool – City of Halifax, Nova Scotia," January 1966.

114 HRMA, RG 102-40B, file 6, "Development Plan Series – Report 3 – Recreation – City of Halifax, Nova Scotia," January, 1966.

115 Ibid.

116 Ibid.

117 HRMA, RG 102-1, Halifax City Council minutes, 12 December 1966.

118 "Mayor Uses Silver Spade for Pool," *Mail-Star* (Halifax), 8 June 1967.

119 NSARM, RG 10, series E, vol. 167, "Federal-Provincial Grants Program Progress Report," 1 February 1968.

120 NSARM, RG 10, series E, vol. 167, S.A. Ward to A.B. Stoddard, 25 September 1967; and LAC, RG 69, vol. 52, file 2-3-2-4, Stoddard to Gilles Bergeron, 31 October 1967.

121 The symbol was designed by Gilles Coutu of Montreal, who received $2,500 for the winning design. A news release about the symbol noted that it was "readily identifiable" and could "easily be drawn by children, and lends itself to colour variations." See NSARM, RG 10, series E, vol. 230: Miscellaneous correspondence re: Canada's Centennial, press release, 19 January 1965.

122 NSARM, RG 10, series E, vol. 167, Stoddard to A.W. Churchill, 7 August 1967.
123 "Nova Scotia Must Change Images as 'Backward Area,' Board Told," *Chronicle-Herald*, 2 June 1966.
124 "Reminder of Our Heritage," *Chronicle-Herald*, 16 June 1966.
125 Rojo, "Halifax Centennial Aquarium," 9.
126 Bruce Spears, letter to *Chronicle-Herald*, 14 September 2011.

Chapter Five

1 LAC, Deputy Minister's Office Registry Files, RG 22, vol. 304, file 84-3-55: Community Improvement, "Report on the Discussion, Suggestions and Recommendations of the Community Improvement and Rural Beautification Seminar," 2–3 June 1965; LAC, Centennial Commission fonds, RG 69, vol. 661, file: Community Improvement & Beautification, 1963–1965, press release, n.d.; "Lamontagne Hopes to End 'Dictatorship of Machines,'" *Ottawa Citizen*, 3 June 1965; and "Clean Up for '67, Minister Urges," *Globe and Mail*, 3 June 1965.
2 Fahrni and Rutherdale, "Introduction," 3–4; Adam Rome, "'Give Earth a Chance': The Environmental Movement and the Sixties," *Journal of American History* 90, no. 2 (September 2003): 526, 528–9, 531; and Robert C. Paehlke, *Environmentalism and the Future of Progressive Politics* (New Haven, CT: Yale University Press, 1989), 219.
3 LAC, RG 22, vol. 304, file 84-3-55, "Report on the Discussion, Suggestions and Recommendations of the Community Improvement and Rural Beautification Seminar."
4 National Centennial Commission, *Progress Report on Projects of National Significance*, 61; LAC, RG 22, vol. 304, file 84-3-55, "Report on the Discussion, Suggestions and Recommendations of the Community Improvement and Rural Beautification Seminar"; LAC, RG 69, vol. 661, press release, n.d.; and Aykroyd, *Anniversary Compulsion*, 127.
5 NSARM, Attorney General Department, RG 10, series E: Miscellaneous, vol. 130: Canada's Centennial-Community Improvement and Rural Beautification, Georges E. Gauthier to R.A. Donahoe, 31 December 1965.
6 "John Fisher Outlines Centennial Projects," *Chronicle-Herald*, 30 November 1965; and LAC, Hugh Macdonell Wallis fonds, MG 31 D 21, vol. 12, newsletter, "Community Improvement – Action," n.d.
7 National Centennial Commission, *Progress Report on Projects of National Significance*, 61; and NSARM, RG 10, series E, vol. 111: Canadian

Centennial Press Releases #1, press release, 5 April 1966; and LAC, RG 69, vol. 660, file: Community Improvement and Beautification /66-30 Apr/66, press release, 5 April 1966.
8 "It's Time to Wage War on Ugliness: Ivany," *Mail-Star* (Halifax), 25 April 1967.
9 NSARM, RG 10, series E, vol. 235: Canadian Centennial Commission, "Nova Scotia, Nova Scotia Centennial News Brief," no. 9, November 1965.
10 National Centennial Commission, *Second Annual Report of the Centennial Commission*, 6.
11 University of Victoria, The Emergence of Architectural Modernism in Victoria, http://uvac.uvic.ca/Architecture_Exhibits/.
12 Aykroyd, *Anniversary Compulsion*, 128.
13 Michael Egan, "Shamans of the Spring: Environmentalism and the New Jeremiad," in *New World Coming: The Sixties and the Shaping of Global Consciousness*, ed. Karen Dubinsky, Catherine Krull, Susan Lord, Sean Mills, and Scott Rutherford (Toronto: Between the Lines, 2009), 297. See also Jennifer Read, "'Let us heed the voice of youth': Laundry Detergents, Phosphates and the Emergence of the Environmental Movement in Ontario," *Journal of the Canadian Historical Association* 7, no. 1 (1996): 228.
14 R. Brian Woodrow, "Resources and Environmental Policy-Making at the National Level: The Search for Focus," in *Resources and the Environment: Policy Perspectives for Canada*, ed. O.P. Dwivedi (Toronto: McClelland and Stewart, 1980), 25; and Read, "'Let us heed the voice of youth,'" 231–2, 242.
15 Rome, "Give Earth a Chance," 526, 528–9, 531; and Samuel P. Hays, "From Conservation to Environment: Environmental Politics in the United States since World War II," in *Environmental History: Critical Issues in Comparative Perspective*, ed. Kendall E. Bailes (Boston: University Press of America, 1985), 216–17, 222. On the history of the environmental movement in the United States, see Robert Gottlieb, *Forcing the Spring: The Transformation of the American Environmental Movement* (Washington: Island Press, 1993); and Adam Rome, *The Bulldozer in the Countryside: Suburban Sprawl and the Rise of American Environmentalism* (Cambridge: Cambridge University Press, 2001).
16 Egan, "Shamans of the Spring," 297.
17 Rome, "Give Earth a Chance," 534–52.
18 MacEachern, *Natural Selections*, 19.
19 Sharon Weaver, "First Encounters: 1970s Back-to-the-Land Cape Breton, NS and Denman, Hornby and Lasqueti Islands, BC," *Oral History Forum d'histoire orale* 30 (2010): 1–30.
20 Egan, "Shamans of the Spring," 301.

21 Rachel Carson, *Silent Spring* (New York: Houghton Mifflin, 1962).
22 Egan, "Shamans of the Spring," 299–300.
23 Ibid., 298; and Paehlke, 34–6. On Barry Commoner see Michael Egan, *Barry Commoner and the Science of Survival: The Remaking of American Environmentalism* (Cambridge: MIT Press, 2007).
24 Egan, "Shamans of the Spring," 298.
25 Ibid.
26 Paehlke, *Environmentalism and the Future of Progressive Politics*, 1, 21.
27 M. Paul Brown, "Organizational Design as Policy Instrument: Environment Canada in the Canadian Bureaucracy," in *Canadian Environmental Policy: Ecosystems, Politics, and Process*, ed. Robert Boardman (Toronto: Oxford University Press, 1992), 26, as cited in Peter Aucoin, "Portfolio Structures and Policy Coordination," in *Public Policy in Canada*, ed. G. Bruce Doern and Peter Aucoin, 213–38 (Toronto: Macmillan of Canada, 1979); and Donald Savoie, *The Politics of Public Spending in Canada* (Toronto: University of Toronto Press, 1990), 64.
28 Alan F.J. Artibise and Gilbert A. Stetler, "Conservation Planning and Urban Planning: The Canadian Commission of Conservation in Historical Perspective," in *Consuming Canada: Readings in Environmental History*, ed. Char Gaffield and Pam Gaffield (Toronto: Copp Clark, Toronto, 1995), 163.
29 Hal K. Rothman, *The Greening of a Nation? Environmentalism in the United States since 1945* (Fort Worth, TX: Harcourt Brace College Publishers, 1998), 117–21.
30 On Earth Day, see Finis Dunaway, "Gas Masks, Pogo, and the Ecological Indian: Earth Day and the Visual Politics of American Environmentalism," *American Quarterly* 60, no. 1 (March 2008): 1, 67–99; Rome, "Give Earth a Chance," 549–51; Rothman, *Greening of a Nation?*, 121–5; Adam Rome, "The Genius of Earth Day," *Environmental History* 15, no. 2 (April 2010): 194–205; and Gottlieb, *Forcing the Spring*, 105–14.
31 Frank Zelko, "Making Greenpeace: The Development of Direct Action Environmentalism in British Columbia," *BC Studies* 142/143 (Summer/Autumn 2004): 197–239.
32 National Centennial Commission, *Centennial Commission Annual Report 1965–1966*, 18.
33 National Centennial Commission, *Sixth Annual and Final Report*, 10.
34 Aykroyd, *Anniversary Compulsion*, 198.
35 James Overton, "Dirt and Danger, Development and Decency in Newfoundland," in Overton, *Making a World of Difference: Essays on Tourism, Culture and Development in Newfoundland*, 81–98 (St John's, NL: Institute of Social and Economic Research, 1996).

36 "Removal of Dump Requested," *Cape Breton* Post, 24 August 1966; and "Clean-up for Centennial Is Requested," *Cape Breton Post*, 4 May 1966.
37 Beaton Institute (BI), Sydney Centennial Commission, MG 14.120, file 2, Teresa MacNeil to M.R. Campbell, 13 July 1966.
38 LAC, RG 22, vol. 304, file 84-3-55, "Memorandum to Executive Council on National Community Improvement and Beautification Program," 6 September 1966; and LAC, RG 22, vol. 304, file 84-3-55, Order-in-Council, PC 1965-9/2255, 2 December 1965.
39 *Centennial Commission Annual Report 1965–1966*, 18.
40 LAC, RG 69, vol. 239, file 4–15–1: National project-Community Improvement-generally, memorandum, Ian MacLennan, 10 August 1967.
41 LAC, RG 69, vol. 408, brochure, n.d.
42 LAC, RG 22, vol. 304, file 84-3-55, "Memorandum to Executive Committee: A Documentary Film on Community Improvement," 19 September 1966.
43 LAC, RG 22, vol. 304, file 84-3-55, "Report on the Discussions, Suggestions and Recommendations of the Community Improvement and Rural Beautification Seminar."
44 NSARM, RG 10, series E, vol. 130, Gauthier to Donahoe, 31 December 1965.
45 LAC, RG 69, vol. 597, booklet, "Community Facelift" (Ottawa: Centennial Commission, 1966).
46 NSARM, RG 10, series E, vol. 270: Booklets, pamphlets and brochures related to Canada's Centennial Celebrations, brochure, "The Centennial and the Local Businessman," n.d.
47 NSARM, RG 10, series E, vol. 120: Nova Scotia Centennial News Briefs, "Nova Scotia Centennial News Brief," vol. 9, November 1965. On the professionalization of hospitality in British Columbia during the post-war era, see Michael Dawson, *Selling British Columbia: Tourism and Consumer Culture, 1890–1970* (Vancouver: UBC Press, 2004), 202–10.
48 LAC, RG 22, vol. 304, file 84-3-55, memorandum, Gauthier to Executive Committee, n.d.
49 LAC, RG 22, vol. 304, file 84-3-55, "Report on the Discussion, Suggestions and Recommendations of the Community Improvement and Rural Beautification Seminar"; and LAC, RG 69, vol. 661, press release, n.d.
50 LAC, RG 22, vol. 304, file 84-3-55, "Report on the Discussion, Suggestions and Recommendations of the Community Improvement and Rural Beautification Seminar."
51 LAC, RG 22, vol. 304, file 84-3-55, memorandum to Executive Council, 6 September 1966.
52 LAC, RG 69, vol. 660, press release, 5 April 1966.

53 NSAMR, RG 10, series E, vol. 130, "Interdepartmental Beautification Committee," 14 July 1965.
54 NSARM, RG 10, series E, vol. 130, press release, 16 July 1965,
55 "To Make Province More Attractive," *Liverpool Advance*, 20 May 1965.
56 *Unsightly Premises Act*, RSNS 1967, c 231, s 2; LAC, RG 69, vol. 520, Graham Walker to Roderick Clack, 30 November 1965; and LAC, RG 69, vol. 598, "Minutes of the Fourth Meeting of the Sub-Committee on Community Improvement and Beautification," 15 February 1966.
57 NSARM, RG 10, series E, vol. 130, "Interdepartmental Beautification Committee," 14 July 1965.
58 NSARM, RG 10, series E, vol. 130, press release, 16 July 1965.
59 NSARM, RG 10, series E, vol. 137: Canadian Centennial Committee Appointments National and Provincial, file 44(17), W.B. Thomson to Fergusson, 14 January 1966.
60 LAC, MG 31 D 21, vol. 12, *Community Improvement: Action Newsletter*, n.d.
61 LAC, Canadian Centenary Council fonds, MG 28 I 70, vol. 21, file 6, National Centennial Commission, "A Working Paper on Community Improvement and Rural Beautification," n.d.
62 NSARM, Office of the Premier, RG 100, vol. 19, file 12-8, minutes, Inter-Departmental Committee on Beautification, 9 November 1966.
63 "Paint-Up" was also spelled "Paintup" in some official materials. For consistency I use "Paint-Up."
64 Eleanor Smith Morris, *British Town Planning and Urban Design: Principles and Policies* (Harlow, UK: Addison Wesley Longman, 1997), 166.
65 Lionel Esher, *A Broken Wave: The Rebuilding of England, 1940–1980* (London: Allen Land, 1981), 73.
66 Norwich Union, *The Norwich Plan for Downtown Restoration* (Toronto: Norwich Union, n.d.), n.p.
67 LAC, RG 69, vol. 597, Paul Morton, "A Working Paper on Community Improvement and Rural Beatification," 12.
68 Norwich Union, *Norwich Plan for Downtown Restoration*, n.p.
69 LAC, RG 69, Vol. 597, "Steering Committee Meeting, Improvement and Beautification Program," 6–7 October 1965, 14.
70 LAC, RG 69, vol. 778, brochure, "Downtown Paintup," n.d.
71 "N.S. Providing $10,000 for Beautification Programs," *Chronicle-Herald*, 31 March 1967; and LAC, RG 69, vol. 519, Clack to Robbins Elliott, 17 April 1967.
72 NSARM, RG 10, series E, vol. 120, press release, 30 March 1967; and "N.S. Providing $10,000 for Beautification Programs."

73 LAC, RG 69, vol. 778, report, [Lorne Hutt] to [Roderick Clack], [August 1967].
74 NSARM, RG 10, series E, vol. 120, press release, 30 March 1967.
75 "'Downtown Paintup' Publicly Launched," *Chronicle-Herald*, 18 May 1967; NSARM, RG 100, vol. 19, file 12-8, minutes, Inter-Departmental Committee on Beautification, 9 November 1966.
76 LAC, RG 69, vol. 778, brochure, "Downtown Paintup," n.d.
77 LAC, RG 69, vol. 778, Hutt to Roderick, 10 August 1967.
78 "Pilot Project to Be at Wolfville," *Chronicle-Herald*, 18 May 1967.
79 "Trade Board Head Urges Clean Up," *Cape Breton Post*, 19 May 1967.
80 "'Downtown Paintup' Publicly Launched," *Chronicle-Herald*; NSARM, RG 100, vol. 19, file 12-8, minutes, Inter-Departmental Committee on Beautification, 9 November 1966; and LAC, RG 69, vol. 517, report, Roderick Clack, 11 September 1967.
81 LAC, RG 69, vol. 239, file 4-15-1-3-1, memorandum, Clack to D.C. Evans, 19 May 1967.
82 "Action Is Necessary," *Cape Breton Post*, 16 May 1967.
83 Frank Morgan, "$250 Buys Town a Facelift Plan," *Civic Administration*, September 1967, 45.
84 NSARM, RG 10, series E, vol. 120, Nova Scotia Centennial News Briefs, vol. 3, no. 4, March 1967; and "Village and Town Beautification Contest," *Progress-Enterprise* (Lunenburg), 29 March 1967. On the ascribed meaning of modern lawns, see Andrew J. Weigert, "Lawn of Weeds: The American Lawn as Status Struggling with Life," in *Self, Interaction, and Natural Environment: Refocusing our Eyesight*, 111–29 (Albany: State University of New York Press, 1997), where he argues that "modern lawnscapes sustain identity and status. They display community aesthetics and signal a sense of self-enhancement" (122).
85 LAC, Federated Women's Institutes of Canada fonds, MG 28 I 316, vol. 2, "Annual Board Meeting – Report: Agriculture and Canadian Industries," 19–21 April 1966; and LAC, MG 28 I 316, vol. 8, annual report, Federated Women's Institutes of Canada, 19–21 April 1963.
86 Morton, "Working Paper on Community Improvement and Rural Beatification," 24–5.
87 NSARM, RG 10, series E, vol. 130, file 44(14), press release, 11 May 1965; and NSARM, RG 10, series E, vol. 130, file 44(14), press release, 4 June 1965.
88 NSARM, RG 10, series E, vol. 130, file 44(14), press release, 11 May 1965.
89 "To Enhance Beauty of Province," *Mail-Star* (Halifax) (supplement), 28 April 1967. "Rural Beauty ... A Citizen's Duty," *Bridgewater Monitor*,

26 April 1967, showed crudely drawn before-and-after pictures of a home transformed through beautification efforts. See also NSARM, vertical file 486, #19, brochure, "Nova Scotia Rural Beautification Centennial project," n.d.; and NSARM, vertical file 482, #22, "Nova Scotia Rural Beautification Centennial Project 1966, Sponsored by Women's Institutes of Nova Scotia and Nova Scotia Federation of Agriculture," n.d.
90 "Plan Now to Beautify during Rural Beautification Week: May 1 to May 7," *Mail-Star* (Halifax) (supplement), 28 April 1967.
91 "To Enhance Beauty of Province," *Mail-Star* (Halifax); and "Observe Rural Beautification Week," *Vanguard* (Yarmouth), 26 April 1967. This included up to seventy-five points for new shrubs and trees, sixty points for building repairs, forty points for painting or whitewashing, and twenty-five points for a flagpole with a flag.
92 "86 N.S. Communities Have Entered Rural Beautification Contest," *Truro Weekly News*, 24 August 1967.
93 NSARM, Women's Institute of Nova Scotia fonds, MG 20, vol. 953, folder 40, *Throughout the Years – The Women's Institute Story – A History of W.I.N.S., 1913–1979* [Halifax: n.p., December 1979], 35.
94 "86 N.S. Communities Have Entered Rural Beautification Contest," *Truro Weekly News*.
95 NSARM, MG 20, vol. 953, folder 40, *Throughout the Years*, 35.
96 LAC, RG 22, vol. 304, file 84-3-55, "Report on the Discussions, Suggestions and Recommendations of the Community Improvement and Rural Beautification Seminar."
97 LAC, MG 28 I 70, vol. 21, file 6, National Centennial Commission, "Working Paper on Community Improvement and Rural Beautification," n.d.
98 "Action Is Necessary," *Cape Breton Post*.
99 NSARM, RG 10, series E, vol. 116: Nova Scotia Confederation Centenary Celebration Committee notes from meetings (Internal), Lorne V. Hutt to Confederation Centenary Celebration Committee, 28 January 1966, appendix C.
100 LAC, RG 69, vol. 239, file 4-15-1-23, Hutt to Clack, 7 August 1967.
101 "Clean-Up Campaign Suggested," *Cape Breton Post*, 4 February 1967; and "Clean-Up Program Is Urged," *Cape Breton Post*, 24 May 1967.
102 "Spryfield Starts Fight against Ugliness," *Mail-Star* (Halifax), 25 March 1967.
103 "Mrs Comeau Chairman Rural Beautification Committee," *Digby Courier*, 20 April 1967.
104 "Clean Walls, Says Ivany," *Mail-Star* (Halifax), 11 March 1967.

105 "Civic Beautification Is Good Business," *Mail-Star* (Halifax), 29 April 1967.
106 "'Clean the Streets' Plea by LeBlanc," *Chronicle-Herald*, 31 March 1967.
107 "125 Sites Selected for Beautification," *Commercial News* (Halifax), May 1967.
108 NSARM, RG 10, series E, vol. 120, "Nova Scotia Centennial News Brief," vol. 9, November 1965.
109 "Clean-Up Week May 1st to 6th," *Bridgewater Bulletin*, 29 March 1967.
110 National Centennial Commission, *Progress Report on Projects of National Significance*, 61.
111 NSARM, RG 10, series E, vol. 130, file 44(14), press release, 11 May 1965.
112 "It's Time to Wage War on Ugliness: Ivany," *Mail-Star* (Halifax).
113 McKay, *Quest of the Folk*; McKay, "Tartanism Triumphant"; McKay, "History and the Tourist Gaze"; and McKay and Bates, *In the Province of History*.
114 LAC, RG 69, vol. 778, brochure, "Downtown Paintup," n.d.
115 McKay, "Among the Fisherfolk"; and Beaton and Muise, "Canso Causeway."
116 "Inverness Beautiful," *Victoria-Inverness Bulletin*, 29 April 1964.
117 NSARM, RG 10, series E, vol. 270, brochure, "The Centennial and the Local Businessman," n.d.
118 Advertisement, "Join the Crusade against Ugly," *Chronicle-Herald*, 1 October 1966.
119 LAC, RG 69, vol. 773, handout, n.d.
120 Ibid.
121 NSARM, RG 10, series E, vol. 120, "Nova Scotia Centennial News Brief," vol. 3, no. 4, August 1967.
122 LAC, MG 31 D 21, vol. 12, newsletter, "Community Improvement: Action Newsletter," n.d.
123 Ibid.
124 Ibid.
125 LAC, RG 69, vol. 774, address, Frank L. Wallace to Board of Trade, 7 November 1966.
126 LAC, MG 31 D 21, vol. 10, address, John Fisher to Community Improvement Seminar, 22 April 1966.
127 "Civic Beautification Is Good Business," *Mail-Star* (Halifax).
128 Ibid.; and "It's Time to Wage War on Ugliness: Ivany," *Mail-Star* (Halifax).
129 LAC, MG 28 I 70, vol. 21, file 6, National Centennial Commission, "Working Paper on Community Improvement and Rural Beautification," n.d.
130 LAC, RG 22, vol. 304, file 84-3-55, "Report on the Discussions, Suggestions and Recommendations of the Community Improvement and Rural Beautification Seminar."

131 LAC, MG 31 D 21, vol. 12, speech, Judy LaMarsh to Community Improvement Program, Seminar '66, 22 April 1966.
132 LAC, RG 22, vol. 304, file 84-3-55, pamphlet, "Community Improvement Program: Action Seminar 66," 22 April 1966.
133 LAC, RG 69, vol. 25, file 1-13-1-1, speech, Peter H. Aykroyd to Annual Conference of the Canadian Society of Landscape Architects and Town Planners, 19 October 1963.
134 LAC, RG 22, vol. 304, file 84-3-55, address, Maurice Lamontagne to Community Improvement Seminar, 2 June 1965.
135 LAC, RG 69, vol. 597, "Report on Seminar on Community Improvement and Rural Beautification," July 1965.
136 LAC, MG 31 D 21, vol. 12, newsletter, "Community Improvement: Action Newsletter," n.d.
137 National Centennial Commission, *Progress Report on Projects of National Significance*, 61; and LAC, RG 69, vol. 774, newsletter, "Call to Action," n.d.
138 LAC, RG 69, vol. 597, booklet, "Beautifying Towns" (Ottawa: Centennial Commission, 1966).
139 Tillotson, "Time, Swimming Pools, and Citizenship."
140 LAC, RG 22, vol. 304, file 84-3-55, address, Maurice Lamontagne to Community Improvement Seminar, 2 June 1965.
141 NSARM, RG 10, series E, vol. 270, brochure, "The Centennial and the Local Businessman," n.d.
142 LAC, RG 69, vol. 773, Wallace to Ferris Abbass, 29 September 1966.
143 LAC, RG 69, vol. 773, handout, n.d.
144 Ibid.
145 Ibid.
146 Ibid.
147 Ibid.
148 Peter C. Baldwin, *In the Watches of the Night: Life in the Nocturnal City, 1820–1930* (Chicago: University of Chicago Press, 2012), 138–54.
149 LAC, RG 69, vol. 778, letter and petition to County Planning Board, Municipality of County of Halifax, 6 April 1967.
150 LAC, RG 69, vol. 774, newsletter, "Call to Action," n.d.
151 "It's Time to Wage War on Ugliness: Ivany," *Mail-Star* (Halifax).
152 "Civic Beautification Is Good Business"; and LAC, RG 69, vol. 774, newsletter, "Call to Action," n.d.
153 "It's Time to Wage War on Ugliness: Ivany," *Mail-Star* (Halifax).
154 Nelson, *Razing Africville*; and Loo, "Africville and the Dynamics of State Power in Postwar Canada."
155 LAC, RG 69, vol. 521, "Notes for Mr Ian MacLennan at the Community Improvement Program Seminar," 20 October 1967.

156 LAC, RG 69, vol. 521, address, Dr Craig Mooney to Community Improvement Action '67, 20 October 1967.
157 "Centennial: A Super Challenge," *Mail-Star* (Halifax), 13 November 1965.
158 Dunaway, "Gas Masks, Pogo, and the Ecological Indian," 90–4.
159 Andrew Hurley, *Environmental Inequalities: Class, Race, and Industrial Pollution in Gary, Indiana, 1945–1980* (Chapel Hill: University of North Carolina Press, 1995). See also Gottlieb, *Forcing the Spring*, 235–69.
160 Gottlieb, *Forcing the Spring*, 250–3.
161 Editorial, "Opinions Expressed Here Are Not Necessarily …," *Cape Breton Highlander*, 27 April 1966.
162 "Planning Experts Urged to Speak Plainly," *Ottawa Citizen*, 23 October 1967.
163 LAC, RG 69, vol. 239, file 4-15-1: National project – Community Improvement – generally, memorandum, Ian MacLennan, 10 August 1967.
164 LAC, RG 22, vol. 304, file 84-3-55, "Report on the Discussions, Suggestions and Recommendations of the Community Improvement and Rural Beautification Seminar."
165 LAC, RG 69, vol. 239, file 4-15-1, memorandum, Ian MacLennan, 10 August 1967.
166 LAC, RG 22, vol. 299, file 84-3-1, memorandum to Executive Committee on the Disposition and Future Exploitation of Centennial Programs, 24 August 1967; and LAC, RG 69, vol. 239, file 4-15-1, Judy LaMarsh to Federal Cabinet, 21 September 1967.
167 LAC, RG 22, vol. 304, file 84-3-55, "Memorandum to Executive Council on National Community Improvement and Beautification Program," 6 September 1966.
168 LAC, RG 22, vol. 299, file 84-3-1, memorandum to Executive Committee on the Disposition and Future Exploitation of Centennial Programs, Appendix A, 24 August 1967.
169 "Planning Experts Urged to Speak Plainly," *Ottawa Citizen*.
170 LAC, RG 69, vol. 239, file 4-15-1, Judy LaMarsh to Federal Cabinet, 21 September 1967.
171 LAC, RG 69, vol. 239, file 4-15-1: National Project – Community Improvement – Generally, letter to David Gagnon, 27 December 1967.
172 Kuffert, *Great Duty*, 228.
173 Kenneally and Sloan, *Expo 67*.
174 "Trade Board Head Urges Clean Up," *Cape Breton Post*.
175 On 1960s protest, see Palmer, *Canada's 1960s*.
176 National Centennial Commission, *Progress Report on Projects of National Significance*, 61.

Conclusion

1. LAC, Lester B. Pearson fonds, MG 26 N 9, vol. 43, notes for the Prime Minister's Speech to the National Centennial Conference Dinner, 30 April 1967.
2. Maria Tippett, "Organizing the Culture of a Region: Institutions and the Arts in Atlantic Canada, 1867–1957," in *The Sea and Culture of Atlantic Canada: A Multidisciplinary Sampler*, ed. Larry McCann and Carrie MacMillan, 107–26 (Sackville, NS: Centre for Canadian Studies, 1992), 109; and Tippett, *Making Culture: English-Canadian Institutions and the Arts before the Massey Commission* (Toronto: University of Toronto Press, 1990).
3. Jonathan F. Vance, *A History of Canadian Culture* (Don Mills, ON: Oxford University Press, 2009), 378.
4. On the history of patronage in Nova Scotia, see T. Stephen Henderson, "Nova Scotia's Liberal Patronage System in the 1930s," *Journal of the Royal Nova Scotia Historical Society* 11 (2009): 89–109; J. Murray Beck, *The Politics of Nova Scotia*, vol. 2, *1896–1988* (Tantallon: Four East Publications, 1988); Peter Clancy, James Bickerton, Rodney Haddow, and Ian Stewart, *The Savage Years: The Perils of Reinventing Government in Nova Scotia* (Halifax: Formac Publishing, 2000); and Jeffrey Simpson, *Spoils of Power: The Politics of Patronage* (Don Mills, ON: Collins, 1988).
5. "Trade Board Head Urges Clean Up," *Cape Breton Post*.
6. "Nova Scotia Must Change Images as 'Backward Area,' Board Told," *Chronicle-Herald*, 2 June 1966.
7. Aykroyd, *Anniversary Compulsion*, appendix C, 180.
8. Gillam, *Hall of Mirrors*, 72.
9. Alan Gordon, "The Highland Heart in Nova Scotia: Place and Memory at the Highland Village Museum," in *Placing Memory and Remembering Place in Canada*, ed. James Opp and John C. Walsh (Vancouver: UBC Press, 2010), 113–14, 120–1.
10. Greg Marquis, "Commentary."
11. Basu, *Highland Homecomings*, 1.
12. Jerry Bannister and Roger Marsters, "The Politics of the Past: Memory and Politics in Atlantic Canada since 2000," in *Shaping an Agenda for Atlantic Canada*, ed. John G. Reid and Donald J. Savoie (Halifax: Fernwood, 2011), 113–15, 117.
13. Canada, House of Commons, *Report of the Standing Committee on Canadian Heritage: Canada's 150th Anniversary in 2017*, September 2012, 41st Parliament, 1st Session (Ottawa: Public Works and Government Services Canada, 2012), 1.

14 CBC News, "Canada 150: Federal Government Funding Microgrants, Musical Celebration" 14 March 2016.
15 Province of Nova Scotia, "150 Forward Fund," http://novascotia.ca/programs/150-forward-fund/.

Bibliography

Primary Sources

Archival Repositories and Collections

Abbie Lane, MG 1, vol. 539, Nova Scotia Archives and Records Management, Halifax
Atlantic Pavilion of Expo 1967, RG 43, Nova Scotia Archives and Records Management, Halifax
Attorney General Department, RG 10, Nova Scotia Archives and Records Management, Halifax
Aza Avramovitch, Accession 2001-036001-004, Nova Scotia Archives and Records Management, Halifax
Beaton Institute (BI), Sydney
C.B. Fergusson, MG 1, vols. 1479, 1480, and 1847, Nova Scotia Archives and Records Management, Halifax
Canadian Centenary Council, MG 28 I 70, Library and Archives Canada, Ottawa
Centennial Commission, RG 69, Library and Archives Canada, Ottawa
City Manager's Office Correspondence, RG 102-4A, Halifax Regional Municipality Archives, Halifax
Deputy Minister's Office Registry Files, RG 22, Library and Archives Canada, Ottawa
Development Department Records, RG 102–41, Halifax Regional Municipality Archives, Halifax
Federated Women's Institutes of Canada, MG 28 I 316, Library and Archives Canada, Ottawa
Halifax City Council Records, RG 102–1, Halifax Regional Municipality Archives, Halifax

Halifax City Council Submissions, RG 102–1B, Halifax Regional Municipality Archives, Halifax
Halifax Recreation and Playgrounds Commission Minutes, RG 102–37B, Halifax Regional Municipality Archives, Halifax
Halifax Regional Municipality Archives (HRMA), Halifax
Halifax Town Planning and Board Submissions, RG 102-40B, Halifax Regional Municipality Archives, Halifax
Helen Creighton, MG1, vol. 2811, Nova Scotia Archives and Records Management, Halifax
Hugh Macdonell Wallis, MG 31 D 21, Library and Archives Canada, Ottawa
Lester B. Pearson, MG 26 N 3-9, Library and Archives Canada, Ottawa
Library and Archives Canada (LAC), Ottawa
Miscellaneous Manuscript Collection, MG 100, Nova Scotia Archives and Records Management, Halifax
Nina Cohen, MG 30 C 152, Library and Archives Canada, Ottawa
Nova Scotia Archives and Records Management (NSARM), Halifax
Office of the Premier, RG 100, Nova Scotia Archives and Records Management, Halifax
Sydney Centennial Commission, MG 14.120, Beaton Institute, Sydney
Women's Institute of Nova Scotia, MG 20, Nova Scotia Archives and Records Management, Halifax

Film

The Canadian Pavilion, Expo '67. Directed by Marc Beaudet. National Film Board, 1967.
Expo 67: Back to the Future ... Directed by Mark Starowicz. Canadian Broadcasting Corporation, 2004.
Helicopter Canada. Directed by Eugene Boyko. National Film Board, 1966.
Impressions of Expo. Directed by William Brind. National Film Board, 1967.
Remember Africville. Directed by Shelagh Mackenzie. National Film Board, 1991.

Government Documents and Royal Commissions

Canada. *Debates of the Senate*.
Canada. *House of Commons Debates*.
Canada. House of Commons. *Report of the Standing Committee on Canadian Heritage: Canada's 150th Anniversary in 2017*. September 2012, 41st Parliament, 1st Session. Ottawa: Public Works and Government Services Canada, 2012.

Canada. *Report of the Royal Commission on Coal,* 1946. Ottawa: King's Printer, 1947.
Canada. *Royal Commission on Bilingualism and Biculturalism: Preliminary Report.* Ottawa: Queen's Printer, 1965.
Canada. *Royal Commission on Canada's Economic Prospects.* Ottawa: Queen's Printer, 1958.
Canada. *Royal Commission on Coal, 1960.* Ottawa: Queen's Printer, 1960.
Donald, J.R. *The Cape Breton Coal Problem.* Ottawa: Queen's Printer, 1966.

Legislation

An Act to Enable the Town of Glace Bay to Make a Contribution toward the Cost of Cape Breton Miners' Museum, SNS 1965, c 85.
An Act to Incorporate the Annapolis Valley Apple Blossom Festival, RSNS 1935 c 107.
An Act to Incorporate the Cape Breton Miners' Foundation, RSNS 1964, c 63.
An Act Respecting the Observance of the Centennial of Confederation in Canada, RSC 1960–61, c 60, as am. by 1963, c 36.
Confederation Centenary Celebration Act, RSNS 1963, c 2.
Constitution Act 1982, c 11 (UK), Schedule B.
Unsightly Premises Act, RSNS 1967, c 231.
William Davis Miners' Memorial Day Act, RSNS 2008, c 47.

Newspapers

Amherst Daily News & Sentinel
Antigonish Casket
Bridgewater Bulletin
Bridgewater Monitor
Canadian High News
Cape Breton Highlander
Cape Breton Post
Charlottetown Patriot
Chronicle-Herald
Chronicle-Telegraph
Commercial News (Halifax)
Dartmouth Free Press
Digby Courier
Financial Post
Globe and Mail

Liverpool Advance
Mail-Star (Halifax)
New Glasgow News
Ottawa Citizen
Progress-Enterprise (Lunenburg)
Ship & Shore News
Star Weekly
Toronto Telegram
Truro Daily News
Truro Weekly News
Vanguard (Yarmouth)
Victoria-Inverness Bulletin
Windsor Star

Periodicals

Atlantic Advocate
The Beaver
Civic Administration
Maclean's
Mining in Canada
PROBE

Websites

Bank of Canada. Inflation Calculator. http://www.bankofcanada.ca/rates/related/inflation-calculator/.
Maritime History Archive. "'No Great Future': Government Sponsored Resettlement in Newfoundland and Labrador since Confederation." http://www.mun.ca/mha/resettlement/rs_intro.php.
Nova Scotia Museum of Natural History. "About the Museum." https://naturalhistory.novascotia.ca/about-museum.
University of Victoria. The Emergence of Architectural Modernism in Victoria. http://uvac.uvic.ca/Architecture_Exhibits/.

Secondary Sources

Books, Articles, and Book Chapters

Acheson, T.W. "The National Policy and the Industrialization of the Maritimes, 1880–1910." *Acadiensis* 1, no. 2 (Spring 1972): 3–28.

Bibliography

Adams, Mary Louise. "Constructing Normal Citizens: Sex Advice for Postwar Teens." In *Contesting Canadian Citizenship: Historical Readings*, edited by Robert Adamoski, Dorothy E. Chunn, and Robert Menzies, 273–92. Peterborough, ON: Broadview, 2002.

– *The Trouble with Normal: Postwar Youth and the Making of Heterosexuality*. Toronto: University of Toronto Press, 1997.

Africville Genealogical Society, ed. *The Spirit of Africville*. Halifax: Formac Publishing, 1992.

Anastakis, Dimitry. "Building a 'New Nova Scotia': State Intervention, the Auto Industry and the Case of Volvo in Halifax, 1963–1998." *Acadiensis* 34, no. 1 (Autumn 2004): 3–30.

– *Car Nation: An Illustrated History of Canada's Transformation behind the Wheel*. Toronto: James Lorimer, 2008.

– "Cars, Conflict, and Cooperation: The Federalism of the Canadian Auto Industry." In *Framing Canadian Federalism: Historical Essays in Honour of John T. Saywell*, edited by Dimitry Anastakis and P.E. Bryden, 185–210. Toronto: University of Toronto Press, 2009.

Anderson, Benedict. *Imagined Communities: Reflections on the Origins and Spread of Nationalism*. 3rd ed. London: Verso, 2006.

Andrew, Caroline, Jean Harvey, and Don Dawson. "Evolution of Local State Activity: Reaction Policy in Toronto." *Leisure Studies* 13 (1994): 1–16.

Armstrong, Bruce, and John Davis. *Sanctuary: Halifax's Parks and Public Gardens*. Halifax: Nimbus Publishing, 1996.

Artibise, Alan F.J., and Gilbert A. Stetler. "Conservation Planning and Urban Planning: The Canadian Commission of Conservation in Historical Perspective." In *Consuming Canada: Readings in Environmental History*, edited by Char Gaffield and Pam Gaffield, 152–69. Toronto: Copp Clark, Toronto, 1995.

Aucoin, Peter. "Portfolio Structures and Policy Coordination." In *Public Policy in Canada*, edited by G. Bruce Doern and Peter Aucoin, 213–38. Toronto: Macmillan of Canada, 1979.

Aykroyd, Peter H. *The Anniversary Compulsion: Canada's Centennial Celebrations. A Model Mega-Anniversary*. Toronto: Dundurn, 1992.

Bakvis, Herman. *Regional Ministers: Power and Influence in the Canadian Cabinet*. Toronto: University of Toronto Press, 1991.

Bakvis, Herman, and Grace Skogstad. "Canadian Federalism: Performance, Effectiveness, and Legitimacy." In *Canadian Federalism: Performance, Effectiveness, and Legitimacy*, edited by Herman Bakvis and Grace Skogstad, 3–23. Don Mills, ON: Oxford University Press, 2002.

Baldwin, Peter C. *In the Watches of the Night: Life in the Nocturnal City, 1820–1930*. Chicago: University of Chicago Press, 2012.

Bannister, Jerry. "A River Runs through It: Churchill Falls and the End of Newfoundland History." *Acadiensis* 41, no. 1 (Winter/Spring 2012): 211–25.

Bannister, Jerry, and Roger Marsters. "The Politics of the Past: Memory and Politics in Atlantic Canada since 2000." In *Shaping an Agenda for Atlantic Canada*, edited by John G. Reid and Donald J. Savoie, 111–31. Halifax: Fernwood, 2011.

Basu, Paul. *Highland Homecomings: Genealogy and Heritage Tourism in the Scottish Diaspora*. New York: Routledge, 2007.

Beaton, Meaghan, and Del Muise. "The Canso Causeway, Tartan Tourism, Industrial Development and the Promise of Progress for Cape Breton." *Acadiensis* 38, no. 2 (Summer/Fall 2008): 39–69.

Beck, J. Murray. *The Politics of Nova Scotia*, vol. 2, *1896–1988*. Tantallon: Four East Publications, 1988.

Berger, Carl. *The Writing of Canadian History: Aspects of English-Canadian Historical Writing since 1900*. Toronto: University of Toronto Press, 1986.

Berton, Pierre. *1967: The Last Good Year*. Toronto: Doubleday Canada, 1997.

Bickerton, James P. *Nova Scotia, Ottawa, and the Politics of Regional Development*. Toronto: University of Toronto Press, 1990.

Bishop, Joan. "Sydney Steel: Public Ownership and the Welfare State, 1967 to 1975." In *The Island: New Perspectives on Cape Breton History, 1713–1990*, edited by Kenneth Donovan, 165–86. Sydney and Fredericton: University College of Cape Breton Press and Acadiensis, 1990.

Bodnar, John. *Remaking America: Public Memory, Commemoration, and Patriotism in the Twentieth Century*. Princeton: Princeton University Press, 1992.

Bohlman, Philip V. *The Study of Folk Music in the Modern World*. Bloomington: Indiana University Press, 1988.

Brodie, Janine. *The Political Economy of Canadian Regionalism*. Toronto: University of Toronto Press, 1990.

Bryden, P.E. "The Obligations of Federalism: Ontario and the Origins of Equalization." In *Framing Canadian Federalism: Historical Essays in Honour of John T. Saywell*, edited by Dimitry Anastakis and P.E. Bryden, 75–94. Toronto: University of Toronto Press, 2009.

– *Planners and Politicians: Liberal Politics and Social Policy, 1957–1968*. Montreal and Kingston: McGill-Queen's University Press, 1997.

Brydon, Sherry. "The Indians of Canada Pavilion at Expo 67." *American Indian Art Magazine* 22, no. 3 (1997): 54–63.

Buckner, P.A. "'Limited Identities' Revisited: Regionalism and Nationalism in Canadian History." *Acadiensis* 30, no. 1 (Autumn 2000): 4–15.

Bumsted, J.M. "The Birthday Party." *The Beaver* 76, no. 2 (April/May 1996): 4–15.

Cadigan, Sean T. *Newfoundland and Labrador: A History*. Toronto: University of Toronto Press, 2009.

Cameron, David M., and Peter Aucoin. "Halifax." In *City Politics in Canada*, edited by Warren Magnusson and Andrew Sancton, 213–38. Toronto: University of Toronto Press, 1983.
Canadian Council of Resource Ministers. *The Administration of Outdoor Recreation in Canada*. Montreal: Canadian Council of Resource Ministers, 1968.
Canadian Youth Commission. *Youth and Recreation: New Plans for New Times*. Toronto: Ryerson, 1946.
Carson, Rachel. *Silent Spring*. New York: Houghton Mifflin, 1962.
Churchill, Jason L. "Pragmatic Federalism: The Politics behind the 1969 Churchill Falls Contract." *Newfoundland Studies* 15, no. 2 (1999): 215–46.
Clancy, Peter, James Bickerton, Rodney Haddow, and Ian Stewart. *The Savage Years: The Perils of Reinventing Government in Nova Scotia*. Halifax: Formac Publishing, 2000.
Clarke, P.D. "L'Acadie perdue; Or, Maritime History's Other." *Acadiensis* 30, no. 1 (Autumn 2000): 73–91.
Comacchio, Cynthia. "Lost in Modernity: 'Maladjustment' and the 'Modern Youth Problem,' English Canada, 1920–50." In *Lost Kids: Vulnerable Children and Youth in Twentieth-Century Canada and the United States*, edited by Mona Gleason, Tamara Myers, Leslie Paris, and Veronica Strong-Boag, 53–71. Vancouver: UBC Press, 2010.
Connerton, Paul. *How Societies Remember*. Cambridge: Cambridge University Press, 1989.
Conrad, Margaret. "Apple Blossom Time in the Annapolis Valley, 1880–1957." *Acadiensis* 9, no. 2 (Spring 1980): 14–39.
– "The 'Atlantic Revolution' of the 1950s." In *Beyond Anger and Longing: Community and Development in Atlantic Canada*, edited by Berkeley Fleming, 55–96. Sackville, NS, and Fredericton: Centre for Canadian Studies and Acadiensis, 1988.
– "The 1950s: The Decade of Development." In *The Atlantic Provinces in Confederation*, edited by E.R. Forbes and D.A. Muise, 382–420. Toronto: University of Toronto Press, 1993.
Conrad, Margaret, and James K. Hiller. *Atlantic Canada: A Concise History*. Don Mills, ON: Oxford University Press, 2006.
– *Atlantic Canada: A Region in the Making*. Don Mills, ON: Oxford University Press, 2001.
Cupido, Robert. "Appropriating the Past: Pageants, Politics, and the Diamond Jubilee of Canada." *Journal of the Canadian Historical Association* 9, no. 1 (1998): 155–86.
– "The Medium, the Message and the Modern: The Jubilee Broadcast of 1927." *International Journal of Canadian Studies* 26 (Fall 2002): 101–23.

- "'Sixty Years of Canadian Progress': The Diamond Jubilee and the Politics of Commemoration." In *Canadian Identity: Region, Country, Nation: Selected Proceedings of the 24th Annual Conference of the Association for Canadian Studies, Held at Memorial University of Newfoundland, June 6–8, 1997*, edited by C. Andrews, W. Straw, and J. Yvon Thériault, 19–33. Montreal: Association of Canadian Studies, 1997.
Davies, Helen. *The Politics of Participation: Learning from Canada's Centennial Year*. Toronto: MASS LBP, 2010.
Dawson, Michael. "Leisure, Consumption, and the Public Sphere: Postwar Debates over Shopping Regulations in Vancouver and Victoria during the Cold War." In *Creating Postwar Canada: Community, Diversity, and Dissent, 1945–75*, edited by Magda Fahrni and Robert Rutherdale, 193–216. Vancouver: UBC Press, 2008.
- *Selling British Columbia: Tourism and Consumer Culture, 1890–1970*. Vancouver: UBC Press, 2004.
Dean, Misao. "The Centennial Voyageur Pageant as Historical Re-enactment." *Journal of Canadian Studies* 40, no. 3 (Fall 2006): 43–67.
Dubinsky, Karen, Catherine Krull, Susan Lord, Sean Mills, and Scott Rutherford, eds. *New World Coming: The Sixties and the Shaping of Global Consciousness*. Toronto: Between the Lines, 2009.
Dunaway, Finis. "Gas Masks, Pogo, and the Ecological Indian: Earth Day and the Visual Politics of American Environmentalism." *American Quarterly* 60, no. 1 (March 2008): 67–99.
Earle, Michael. "'Down with Hitler and Silby Barrett': The Cape Breton Miners' Slowdown Strike of 1941." In *Workers and the State in Twentieth-Century Nova Scotia*, edited by Michael Earle, 109–43. Fredericton: Published for the Gorsebrook Research Institute of Atlantic Canada Studies by Acadiensis, 1989.
Economics and Research Division, Nova Scotia Department of Labour. *The Nova Scotia Labour Force: Industry, Occupation, Earnings, Employment*. Halifax: Nova Scotia Department of Labour, 1965.
Egan, Michael. *Barry Commoner and the Science of Survival: The Remaking of American Environmentalism*. Cambridge, MA: MIT Press, 2007.
- "Shamans of the Spring: Environmentalism and the New Jeremiad." In *New World Coming: The Sixties and the Shaping of Global Consciousness*, edited by Karen Dubinsky, Catherine Krull, Susan Lord, Sean Mills, and Scott Rutherford, 296–303. Toronto: Between the Lines, 2009.
Erickson, Paul A. *Halifax's North End: An Anthropologist Looks at the City*. Hantsport, NS: Lancelot, 1986.
Esher, Lionel. *A Broken Wave: The Rebuilding of England, 1940–1980*. London: Allen Land, 1981.

Expo 67: The Memorial Album of the First Category Universal and International Exhibition Held in Montreal from the Twenty-Seventh of April to the Twenty-Ninth of October Nineteen Hundred and Sixty-Seven. Toronto: T. Nelson, 1968.

Fahrni, Magda, and Robert Rutherdale. "Introduction." In *Creating Postwar Canada: Community, Diversity and Dissent, 1945–1975*, edited by Magda Fahrni and Robert Rutherdale, 1–20. Vancouver: UBC Press, 2008.

Falconer, Simon. *Royal Nova Scotia International Tattoo*. Fredericton, NB: Goose Lane Editions, 2010.

Farber, David, ed. *The Sixties: From Memory to History*. Chapel Hill: University of North Carolina Press, 1994.

Feehan, James P. "Smallwood, Churchill Falls, and the Power Corridor through Quebec." *Acadiensis* 40, no. 2 (Summer/Autumn 2011): 112–27.

Fergusson, C. Bruce. *Alderman Abbie Lane of Halifax*. Windsor, ON: Lancelot, 1976.

Fingard, Judith, and Janet Guildford, eds. *Mothers of the Municipality: Women, Work, and Social Policy in Post-1945 Halifax*. Toronto: University of Toronto Press, 2005.

Fingard, Judith, Janet Guildford, and David Sutherland. *Halifax: The First 250 Years*. Halifax: Formac Publishing, 1999.

Finkel, Alvin. *Our Lives: Canada after 1945*. Toronto: James Lorimer, 1997.

Forbes, E.R. "Consolidating Disparity: The Maritimes and the Industrialization of Canada during the Second World War." *Acadiensis* 15, no. 2 (Spring 1986): 3–27.

– *The Maritime Rights Movement, 1919–1927: A Study in Canadian Regionalism*. Montreal and Kingston: McGill-Queen's University Press, 1979.

Francis, Daniel. *The Imaginary Indian: Images of the Indian in Canadian Culture*. Vancouver: Arsenal Pulp, 1992.

– "One Brief Shining Moment: The World's Fair That Put Canada (Fleetingly) on the Map." *Literary Review of Canada* 20, no. 6 (July/August 2012): 5–6.

– *A Road for Canada: The Illustrated History of the Trans-Canada Highway*. Vancouver: Stanton Atkins & Dosil Publishers, 2006.

Frank, David. "The Cape Breton Coal Industry and the Rise and Fall of the British Empire Steel Corporation." *Acadiensis* 7, no. 1 (Autumn 1977): 3–34.

– "Class Conflict in the Coal Industry in Cape Breton 1922." In *Essays in Working Class History*, edited by Gregory S. Kealey and Peter Warrian, 161–84. Toronto: McClelland and Stewart, 1976.

– *J.B. McLachlan: A Biography*. Toronto: James Lorimer, 1999.

– "The 1920s: Class and Region, Resistance and Accommodation." In *The Atlantic Provinces in Confederation*, edited by E.R. Forbes and D.A. Muise, 233–71. Toronto: University of Toronto Press, 1993.

– "Tradition and Culture in the Cape Breton Mining Community in the Early Twentieth Century." In *Cape Breton at 200: Historical Essays in Honour of the*

Island's Bicentennial, 1785–1985, edited by Ken Donovan, 203–18. Sydney, NS: University College of Cape Breton Press, 1985.

Fraser, Dawn. *Echoes from Labour's War: Industrial Cape Breton in the 1920s*. Toronto: New Hogtown, 1976.

Fulford, Robert. *Remember Expo: A Pictorial Record*. Toronto: McClelland and Stewart, 1968.

– *This Was Expo*. Toronto: McClelland and Stewart, 1968.

George, Roy E. *The Life and Times of Industrial Estates Limited*. Halifax: Henson College, Dalhousie University, 1974.

Gillam, Robyn. *Hall of Mirrors: Museums and the Canadian Public*. Banff: Banff Centre, 2001.

Gillis, John R. "Memory and Identity: The History of a Relationship." In *Commemorations: The Politics of National Identity*, edited by John R. Gillis, 3–24. Princeton: Princeton University Press, 1994.

Gitlin, Todd. *The Sixties: Years of Hope and Days of Rage*. Toronto: Bantam Books, 1987.

Gleason, Mona, Tamara Myers, Leslie Paris, and Veronica Strong-Boag, eds. *Lost Kids: Vulnerable Children and Youth in Twentieth-Century Canada and the United States*. Vancouver: UBC Press, 2010.

Gordon, Alan. "The Highland Heart in Nova Scotia: Place and Memory at the Highland Village Museum." In *Placing Memory and Remembering Place in Canada*, edited by James Opp and John C. Walsh, 107–29. Vancouver: UBC Press, 2010.

– *Making Public Pasts: The Contested Terrain of Montreal's Public Memories, 1891–1930*. Montreal and Kingston: McGill-Queen's University Press, 2001.

Gosse, Van. *Rethinking the New Left: An Interpretive History*. New York: Palgrave Macmillan, 2005.

Gottlieb, Robert. *Forcing the Spring: The Transformation of the American Environmental Movement*. Washington: Island Press, 1993.

Granatstein, J.L. *Canada 1957–1967: The Years of Uncertainty and Innovation*. Toronto: McClelland and Stewart, 1986.

Grenier, Raymond. *Inside Expo 67*, translated by Patrick Gossage. Montreal: Les Éditions de l'Homme, 1965.

Guimond, Roger. "A Mining Museum for Nova Scotia!" *Mining in Canada* 38, no. 5 (May 1965): 8–11.

Hanna, Anne. *The Canadian Centenary Council, 1959–1967*. Ottawa: Canadian Centenary Council, 1968.

Harper, Marjory, and Michael Vance. "Myth, Migration and the Making of Memory: An Introduction." In *Myth, Migration and the Making of Memory: Scotia and Nova Scotia, c. 1700–1990*, edited by Marjory Harper and Michael Vance, 14–48. Halifax: Fernwood Publishing, 1999.

Hartje, Robert. *Bicentennial USA: Pathways to Celebration*. Nashville: American Association for State and Local History, 1983.

Hayday, Matthew. *Bilingual Today, United Tomorrow: Official Languages in Education and Canadian Federalism*. Montreal and Kingston: McGill-Queen's University Press, 2005.

– "Fireworks, Folk-Dancing, and Fostering a National Identity: The Politics of Canada Day." *Canadian Historical Review* 91, no. 2 (June 2010): 287–314.

Hays, Samuel P. "From Conservation to Environment: Environmental Politics in the United States since World War II." In *Environmental History: Critical Issues in Comparative Perspective*, edited by Kendall E. Bailes, 198–241. Boston: University Press of America, 1985.

Henderson, T. Stephen. *Angus L. Macdonald: A Provincial Liberal*. Toronto: University of Toronto Press, 2007.

– "'A New Federal Vision': Nova Scotia and the Rowell-Sirois Report, 1938–1948." In *Framing Canadian Federalism: Historical Essays in Honour of John T. Saywell*, edited by Dimitry Anastakis and P.E. Bryden, 51–74. Toronto: University of Toronto Press, 2009.

– "Nova Scotia's Liberal Patronage System in the 1930s." *Journal of the Royal Nova Scotia Historical Society* 11 (2009): 89–109.

Henderson, Stuart. *Making the Scene: Yorkville and Hip Toronto in the 1960s*. Toronto: University of Toronto Press, 2011.

– "'While There is Still Time ...': J. Murray Gibbon and the Spectacle of Difference in Three CPR Folk Festivals, 1928–1931." *Journal of Canadian Studies* 39, no. 1 (2005): 139–74.

Heron, Craig. *Booze: A Distilled History*. Toronto: Between the Lines, 2003.

Heritage Trust of Nova Scotia. *Founded upon a Rock*. Halifax: Heritage Trust of Nova Scotia, 1967.

Hiller, James K. "Is Atlantic Canadian History Possible?" *Acadiensis* 30, no. 1 (Autumn 2000): 16–22.

Hiscott, Elizabeth J. "A Lasting Monument." *Atlantic Advocate* 57, no. 12 (August 1967): 19.

Hopkins, Garth. *Clairtone: The Rise and Fall of a Business Empire*. Toronto: McClelland & Stewart, 1978.

Howell, Colin. "The 1900s: Industry, Urbanization, and Reform." In *The Atlantic Provinces in Confederation*, edited by E.R. Forbes and D.A. Muise, 155–91. Toronto: University of Toronto Press, 1993.

Hurley, Andrew. *Environmental Inequalities: Class, Race, and Industrial Pollution in Gary, Indiana, 1945–1980*. Chapel Hill: University of North Carolina Press, 1995.

Iacovetta, Franca. *Gatekeepers: Reshaping Immigrant Lives in Cold War Canada*. Toronto: Between the Lines, 2006.

- "Making 'New Canadians': Social Workers, Women, and the Reshaping of Immigrant Families." In *A Nation of Immigrants: Women, Workers, and Communities in Canadian History, 1840s–1960s*, edited by Franca Iacovetta, Paula Draper, and Robert Ventresca, 482–513. Toronto: University of Toronto Press, 1998.
Jansson, André. "Encapsulations: The Production of a Future Gaze at Montreal's Expo 67." *Space and Culture* 10, no. 4 (November 2007): 418–36.
Jenkins, Philip. *Decade of Nightmares: The End of the Sixties and the Making of Eighties America*. New York: Oxford University Press, 2006.
Johnston, A.J.B. "Into the Great War: Katharine McLennan Goes Overseas, 1915–1919." In *The Island: New Perspectives on Cape Breton's History 1713–1990*, edited by Kenneth Donovan, 129–44. Fredericton, NB, and Sydney, NS: Acadiensis and University College of Cape Breton Press, 1990.
Kenneally, Rhona Richman, and Johanne Sloan, eds. *Expo 67: Not Just a Souvenir*. Toronto: University of Toronto Press, 2010.
Kenny, James L., and Andrew G. Secord. "Engineering Modernity: Hydroelectric Development in New Brunswick, 1945–1970." *Acadiensis* 39, no. 1 (Winter/Spring 2010): 3–26.
Kitz, Janet, and Gary Castle. *Point Pleasant: An Illustrated History*. Halifax: Pleasant Point Publishing, 1999.
Kuffert, L.B. *A Great Duty: Canadian Responses to Modern Life and Mass Culture, 1939–1967*. Montreal and Kingston: McGill-Queen's University Press, 2003.
LaMarsh, Judy. *Memoirs of a Bird in a Gilded Cage*. Toronto: McClelland and Stewart, 1969.
Lamey, Christina M. "Davis Day through the Years: A Cape Breton Coal Mining Tradition." *Nova Scotia Historical Review* 16, no. 2 (1996): 23–33.
Lazarevich, Gordana. "The Role of the Canadian Pacific Railway in Promoting Canadian Culture." In *A Celebration of Canada's Arts, 1930–1970*, edited by Glen Carruthers and Gordana Lazarevich, 3–13. Toronto: Canadian Scholars' Press, 1996.
LeBlanc, Barbara. *Postcards from Acadie: Grand-Pré, Evangeline & the Acadian Identity*. Kentville, NS: Gaspereau, 2003.
Lexier, Roberta. "Do You Remember the Sixties?: The Scholarship of Resistance and Rebellion." *Labour/Le Travail* 66 (Fall 2010): 183–93.
Litt, Paul. *The Muses, the Masses and the Massey Commission*. Toronto: University of Toronto Press, 1992.
Loo, Tina. "Africville and the Dynamics of State Power in Postwar Canada." *Acadiensis* 39, no. 2 (Summer/Autumn 2010): 23–47.
Lownsbrough, John. *The Best Place to Be: Expo 67 and Its Time*. Toronto: Allan Lane, 2012.

MacDonald, Edward. *If You're Stronghearted: Prince Edward Island in the Twentieth Century*. Charlottetown: Prince Edward Island Museum and Heritage Foundation, 2000.
- "A Landscape ... with Figures: Tourism and Environment on Prince Edward Island." *Acadiensis* 40, no. 1 (Winter/Spring 2011): 70–85.

MacDonald, Monica. "Railway Tourism in the 'Land of Evangeline,' 1882–1946." *Acadiensis* 35, no. 1 (Autumn 2005): 158–80.

MacEachern, Alan. *Natural Selections: National Parks in Atlantic Canada 1935–1970*. Montreal and Kingston: McGill-Queen's University Press, 2001.

MacEwan, Paul. *Miners and Steelworkers: Labour in Cape Breton*. Toronto: Samuel Stevens Hakkert, 1976.

MacGillivray, Allister. *Diamonds in the Rough: 25 Years with the Men of the Deeps*. Sydney, NS: Men of the Deeps Music, 1991.
- *The Men of the Deeps: The Continuing Saga*. New Waterford, NS: Men of the Deeps Music, 2000.

Mackey, Eva. *House of Difference: Cultural Politics and National Identity in Canada*. Toronto: University of Toronto Press, 2002.

MacKinnon, Richard. "Making a House a Home: Company Housing in Cape Breton Island." *Material History Review* 47 (Spring 1998): 46–56.
- "Protest Song and Verse in Cape Breton Island." *Ethnologies* 30, no. 2 (2008): 33–71.

MacLean, Terry. *Louisbourg Heritage: From Ruins to Reconstruction*. Sydney, NS: University College of Cape Breton Press, 1995.

MacLeod, Malcolm. "Another Look at *The Atlantic Provinces in Confederation*." *Acadiensis* 23, no. 2 (Spring 1994): 191–7.

McNeil, Bill. *John Fisher: "Mr Canada."* Markham, ON: Fitzhenry and Whiteside, 1983.

MacNutt, W.S. "The Atlantic Revolution: A Commentary on the Atlantic Premiers' Conference at Halifax, on May 8th, 1957," *Atlantic Advocate* no. 9 (June 1957): 11–13.

Major, Kevin. *As Near to Heaven by Sea: A History of Newfoundland and Labrador*. Toronto: Penguin Books, 2001.

Major, Marjorie. "History of the Nova Scotia Tartan." *Nova Scotia Historical Quarterly* 2, no. 2 (June 1972): 191–214.

Marquis, Greg. "Commentary: *The Quest of the Folk*." *Acadiensis* 35, no. 1 (Autumn 2005): 144–7.
- "Confederation's Casualties: The 'Maritimer' as a Problem in 1960s Toronto." *Acadiensis* 39, no. 1 (Winter/Spring 2010): 83–107.
- "'A Reluctant Concession to Modernity': Alcohol and Modernization in the Maritimes, 1945–1980." *Acadiensis* 32, no. 2 (Spring 2003): 31–59.

Marsters, Roger. "'The Battle of Grand Pré': The Historic Sites and Monuments Board of Canada and the Commemoration of Acadian History." *Acadiensis* 36, no. 1 (Autumn 2006): 29–50.

Marwick, Andrew. *The Sixties: Cultural Revolution in Britain, France, Italy, and the United States, c. 1958–1974*. New York: Oxford University Press, 1998.

McKay, Ian. "Among the Fisherfolk: J.F.B. Livesay and the Invention of Peggy's Cove." *Journal of Canadian Studies* 23, nos 1 and 2 (1998): 23–45.

– "Helen Creighton and the Politics of Anti-Modernism." In *Myth and Milieu: Atlantic Literature and Culture, 1918–1939*, edited by Gwendolyn Davies, 1–16. Fredericton, NB: Acadiensis, 1993.

– "History and the Tourist Gaze: Politics and Commemoration in Nova Scotia, 1935–1964." *Acadiensis* 22, no. 2 (Spring 1993): 102–38.

– *The Quest of the Folk: Antimodernism and Cultural Selection in Twentieth-Century Nova Scotia*. Montreal and Kingston: McGill-Queen's University Press, 1994.

– "Strikes in the Maritimes, 1901–1914." In *Labour and Working-Class History in Atlantic Canada: A Reader*, edited by David Frank and Gregory S. Kealey, 190–232. St John's, NL: Institute of Social and Economic Research, 1995.

– "Tartanism Triumphant: The Construction of Scottishness in Nova Scotia, 1933–1945." *Acadiensis* 21, no. 2 (Spring 1992): 5–47.

McKay, Ian, and Robin Bates. *In the Province of History: The Making of the Public Past in Twentieth-Century Nova Scotia*. Montreal and Kingston: McGill-Queen's University Press, 2010.

Miedema, Gary. *For Canada's Sake: Public Religion, Centennial Celebrations and the Re-making of Canada in the 1960s*. Montreal and Kingston: McGill-Queen's University Press, 2005.

Mills, Sean. *The Empire Within: Postcolonial Thought and Political Activism in Sixties Montreal*. Montreal and Kingston: McGill-Queen's University Press, 2010.

Monaghan, David W. *Canada's "New Main Street": The Trans-Canada Highway as Idea and Reality, 1912–1956*. Ottawa: Canada Science and Technology Museum, 2002.

Morgan, Frank. "$250 Buys Town a Facelift Plan." *Civic Administration*, September 1967, 45.

Morris, Eleanor Smith. *British Town Planning and Urban Design: Principles and Policies*. Harlow, UK: Addison Wesley Longman, 1997.

Muirhead, Bruce. "Ottawa, the Provinces, and the Evolution of Canadian Trade Policy since 1963." In *Framing Canadian Federalism: Historical Essays in Honour of John T. Saywell*, edited by Dimitry Anastakis and P.E. Bryden, 211–30. Toronto: University of Toronto Press, 2009.

Mullally, Sasha, and Edward MacDonald. "On National Heritage, Grand Narratives, and 'Making History Fun': Founders' Hall, Prince Edward Island and the Story of Canada." *International Journal of Heritage Studies* 13, no. 3 (May 2007): 288–94.
Munk, Nina, and Rachel Gotlieb. *The Art of Clairtone: The Making of a Design Icon, 1958–1971*. Toronto: McClelland and Stewart, 2008.
National Centennial Commission. *Canada 67: The Best of Centennial in Pictures*. Ottawa: Centennial Commission, 1968.
– *Centennial Commission Annual Report 1965–1966*. Ottawa: Centennial Commission, 1966.
– *The Centennial Handbook: A Handbook of Information on the 1967 Centennial Organizations, Their Constitutions, Their Aims and Objectives*. Ottawa: Queen's Printer and Controller of Stationery, 1964.
– *Progress Report on Projects of National Significance for the Celebration of Canada's Centennial of Confederation*. Ottawa: National Centennial Commission, 1966.
– *Second Annual Report of the Centennial Commission for the Fiscal Year 1963–1964*. Ottawa: National Centennial Commission, 1964.
– *Sixth Annual and Final Report of the Centennial Commission for the Fiscal Year 1967–1968*. Ottawa: National Centennial Commission, 1968.
– *Third Annual Report of the Centennial Commission for the Fiscal Year 1964–1965*. Ottawa: Queen's Printer, 1965.
Nelles, H.V. *The Art of Nation Building: Pageantry and Spectacle at Quebec's Tercentenary*. Toronto: University of Toronto Press, 1999.
Nelson, Jennifer J. *Razing Africville: A Geography of Racism*. Toronto: University of Toronto Press, 2008.
Norwich Union. *The Norwich Plan for Downtown Restoration*. Toronto: Norwich Union, n.d.
Nova Scotia Development, Economics and Statistics Division. *Halifax County Profile*. Halifax: Nova Scotia Development, Economics and Statistics Division, 1974.
O'Donnell, John C. *"And Now the Fields Are Green": A Collection of Coal Mining Songs in Canada*. Sydney, NS: University College of Cape Breton Press, 1992.
– *The Men of the Deeps Melody Collection*. Waterloo, ON: Waterloo Music, 1975.
Opp, James, and John C. Walsh. *Placing Memory and Remembering Place in Canada*. Vancouver: UBC Press, 2010.
Osborne, Brian. "Landscapes, Memory, Monuments and Commemoration: Putting Identity in Its Place." *Canadian Ethnic Studies* 33, no. 3 (Fall 2001): 39–77.
Overton, James. "Dirt and Danger, Development and Decency in Newfoundland." In Overton, *Making a World of Difference: Essays on Tourism, Culture*

and Development in Newfoundland, 81–98. St John's, NL: Institute of Social and Economic Research, 1996.
– *Making a World of Difference: Essays on Tourism, Culture and Development in Newfoundland*. St John's, NL: Institute of Social and Economic Research, 1996.
Owram, Doug. *Born at the Right Time: A History of the Baby-Boom Generation.* Toronto: University of Toronto Press, 1996.
– *The Government Generation: Canadian Intellectuals and the State 1900–1945.* Toronto: University of Toronto Press, 1986.
Paehlke, Robert C. *Environmentalism and the Future of Progressive Politics.* New Haven, CT: Yale University Press, 1989.
Pal, Leslie A. *Interests of State: The Politics of Language, Multiculturalism, and Feminism in Canada*. Montreal and Kingston: McGill-Queen's University Press, 1993.
Palaeologu, M. Athena, ed. *The Sixties in Canada: A Turbulent and Creative Decade*. Montreal: Black Rose Books, 2009.
Palmer, Bryan D. *Canada's 1960s: The Ironies of Identity in a Rebellious Era.* Toronto: University of Toronto Press, 2009.
Parham, Claire Puccia. *The St Lawrence Seaway and Power Project: An Oral History of the Greatest Construction Show on Earth*. New York: Syracuse University Press, 2009.
Pasolli, Lisa. "Bureaucratizing the Atlantic Revolution: The 'Saskatchewan Mafia' in the New Brunswick Civil Service, 1960–1970." *Acadiensis* 38, no. 1 (Winter/Spring 2009): 126–50.
Payn, Edwin. "Miners' Museum." *Atlantic Advocate* 56, no. 3 (November 1965): 49–52.
– "Where Miners Are Remembered." *Atlantic Advocate* 73, no. 4 (December 1982): 10–12.
Pearson, Norman, and Canadian-British Engineering Consultants. *Town of Glace Bay, Nova Scotia, Urban Renewal Study*. Halifax: n.p., 1966.
Penfold, Steven. "'Have you no manhood in you?': Gender and Class in the Cape Breton Coal Towns, 1920–1926." *Acadiensis* 23, no. 2 (Spring 1994): 21–44.
– "'Selling by the Carload': The Early Years of Fast Food in Canada." In *Creating Postwar Canada: Community, Diversity, and Dissent, 1945–75*, edited by Magda Fahrni and Robert Rutherdale, 162–89. Vancouver: UBC Press, 2008.
Pevere, Geoff, and Greig Dymond. *Mondo Canuck: A Canadian Pop Culture Odyssey*. Scarborough, ON: Prentice Hall Canada, 1996.

Radforth, Ian. *Royal Spectacle: The 1860 Visit of the Prince of Wales to Canada and the United States*. Toronto: University of Toronto Press, 2004.

Read, Jennifer. "'Let us heed the voice of youth': Laundry Detergents, Phosphates and the Emergence of the Environmental Movement in Ontario." *Journal of the Canadian Historical Association* 7, no. 1 (1996): 227–50.

Reichwein, PearlAnn. "Expedition Yukon 1967: Centennial and the Politics of Mountaineering in Kluane." *Canadian Historical Review* 92, no. 3 (September 2011): 481–514.

Ripley, Colin. "Emptiness and Landscape: National Identity in Canada's Centennial Projects." *Journal of the Society for the Study of Architecture in Canada* 30, no. 1 (2005): 37–45.

Ripley, Donald F. *Bagman: A Life in Nova Scotia Politics*. Toronto: Key Porter Books, 1993.

Robinson, Danielle. "Modernism at a Crossroad: The Spadina Expressway Controversy in Toronto, Ontario, ca. 1960–1971." *Canadian Historical Review* 92, no. 2 (June 2011): 295–322.

Rome, Adam. *The Bulldozer in the Countryside: Suburban Sprawl and the Rise of American Environmentalism*. Cambridge: Cambridge University Press, 2001.

– "The Genius of Earth Day." *Environmental History* 15, no. 2 (April 2010): 194–205.

– "'Give Earth a Chance': The Environmental Movement and the Sixties." *Journal of American History* 90, no. 2 (September 2003): 525–54.

Rothman, Hal K. *The Greening of a Nation? Environmentalism in the United States since 1945*. Fort Worth, TX: Harcourt Brace College Publishers, 1998.

Rudin, Ronald, *Founding Fathers: The Celebration of Champlain and Laval in the Streets of Quebec, 1878–1908*. Toronto: University of Toronto Press, 2003.

– *Remembering and Forgetting in Acadie: A Historian's Journey through Public Memory*. Toronto: University of Toronto Press, 2009.

Ruggeri, Joe. *Canadian Federalism at the Cross-Roads*. Fredericton: Policy Studies Centre, University of New Brunswick, 2006.

Rutherdale, Myra, and Jim Miller. "'It's our country': First Nations' Participation in the Indian Pavilion at Expo 67." *Journal of the Canadian Historical Association* 17, no. 2 (2006): 148–73.

Sandalack, Beverly A., and Andrei Nicolai. *Urban Structure – Halifax: An Urban Design Approach*. Halifax: Tuns, 1998.

Sangster, Joan. *Girl Trouble: Female Delinquency in English Canada*. Toronto: Between the Lines, 2002.

– "Radical Ruptures: Feminism, Labor, and the Left in the Long Sixties in Canada." *American Review of Canadian Studies* 40, no. 1 (March 2010): 1–21.

Savoie, Donald J. "All Things Canadian Are Now Regional." *Journal of Canadian Studies* 35, no. 1 (Spring 2000): 203–17.
- *The Politics of Public Spending in Canada*. Toronto: University of Toronto Press, 1990.
- *Regional Economic Development: Canada's Search for Solutions*. 2nd ed. Toronto: University of Toronto Press, 1992.
- "Regional Development: A Policy for All Seasons and Regions." In *New Trends in Canadian Federalism*, edited by François Rocher and Miriam Smith, 353–74. Peterborough, ON: Broadview, 2003.
- *Visiting Grandchildren: Economic Development in the Maritimes*. Toronto: University of Toronto Press, 2006.

Searle, Mark, and Russell Brayley. *Leisure Services in Canada: An Introduction*. 2nd ed. State College, PA: Venture Publishing, 2000.

Shay, Anthony. *Choreographing Identities: Folk Dance, Ethnicity and Festival in the United States and Canada*. Jefferson, NC: McFarland, 2006.

Sider, Gerald. *Between History and Tomorrow: Making and Breaking Everyday Life in Rural Newfoundland*. Peterborough, ON: Broadview, 2003.

Simpson, Jeffrey. *Spoils of Power: The Politics of Patronage*. Don Mills, ON: Collins, 1988.

Slumkoski, Corey. *Inventing Atlantic Canada: Regionalism and the Maritime Reaction to Newfoundland's Entry into Canadian Confederation*. Toronto: University of Toronto Press, 2011.

Smith, Jennifer. *Federalism*. Vancouver: UBC Press, 2004.

Smith, Philip. *Brinco: The Story of Churchill Falls*. Toronto: McClelland and Stewart, 1975.

Spillman, Lyn. *Nation and Commemoration: Creating National Identities in the United States and Australia*. Cambridge: Cambridge University Press, 1997.

Stanley, Della. "The 1960s: The Illusions and Realities of Progress." In *The Atlantic Provinces in Confederation*, edited by E.R. Forbes and D.A. Muise, 421–59. Toronto and Fredericton: University of Toronto Press and Acadiensis, 1993.

Stephenson, Gordon. *A Redevelopment Study of Halifax, Nova Scotia – 1957*. Toronto: University of Toronto Press, 1957.

Stevenson, Michael D. "Conscripting Coal: The Regulation of the Coal Labour Force in Nova Scotia during the Second World War." *Acadiensis* 29, no. 2 (Spring 2000): 58–88.

Stirling, Lilla. *In the Vanguard: Nova Scotia Women Mid-Twentieth Century*. Windsor, ON: Lancelot, 1976.

Struthers, James. *The Limits of Affluence: Welfare in Ontario, 1920–1970*. Toronto: Government of Ontario, published by University of Toronto Press, 1994.

- *No Fault of Their Own: Unemployment and the Canadian Welfare State 1914–1941*. Toronto: University of Toronto Press, 1983.
Summerby-Murray, Robert. "Regenerating Cultural Identity through Industrial Heritage Tourism: Visitor Attitudes, Entertainment, and the Search for Authenticity at Mills, Mines, and Museums of Maritime Canada." *London Journal of Canadian Studies* 30 (2015): 64–89.
Sutherland, Neil. *Growing Up: Childhood in English Canada from the Great War to the Age of Television*. Toronto: University of Toronto Press, 1997.
Swyripa, Frances. "Celebrating Together, Celebrating Apart: Albertans and Their Golden Jubilee." In *Alberta Formed – Alberta Transformed*, edited by Michael Payne, Donald Wetherall, and Catherine Cavanaugh, 589–610. Calgary: University of Calgary Press, 2006.
Taylor, C.J. *Negotiating the Past: The Making of Canada's National Historic Parks and Sites*. Montreal and Kingston: McGill-Queen's University Press, 1990.
Tillotson, Shirley. *The Public at Play: Gender and the Politics of Recreation in Post-War Ontario*. Toronto: University of Toronto Press, 2000.
- "Time, Swimming Pools, and Citizenship: The Emergence of Leisure Rights in Mid-Twentieth-Century Canada." In *Contesting Canadian Citizenship: Historical Readings*, edited by Robert Adamoski, Dorothy E. Chunn, and Robert Menzies, 199–221. Peterborough, ON: Broadview, 2002.
Time. *Birthday of a Nation: The Story of Canada's Centennial*. Toronto: Time International of Canada, 1968.
Tippett, Maria. *Making Culture: English-Canadian Institutions and the Arts before the Massey Commission*. Toronto: University of Toronto Press, 1990.
- "Organizing the Culture of a Region: Institutions and the Arts in Atlantic Canada, 1867–1957." In *The Sea and Culture of Atlantic Canada: A Multidisciplinary Sampler*, edited by Larry McCann and Carrie MacMillan, 107–26. Sackville, NS: Centre for Canadian Studies, 1992.
Tye, Diane. *Baking as Biography: A Life Story in Recipes*. Montreal and Kingston: McGill-Queen's University Press, 2010.
Vaison, Robert, and Peter Aucoin. "Class Voting in Recent Halifax Mayoralty Elections." In *Politics and Government of Urban Canada: Selected Readings*, 3rd ed., edited by L.D. Feldman and M.D. Goldrick, 200–19. Toronto: Methuen, 1976.
Vance, Jonathan F. *Death So Noble: Memory, Meaning, and the First World War*. Vancouver: UBC Press, 1997.
- *A History of Canadian Culture*. Don Mills, ON: Oxford University Press, 2009.
Verrall, Krys. "Art and Urban Renewal: MOMA's New City Exhibition and Halifax's Uniacke Square." In *The Sixties: Passion, Politics, and Style*, edited

by Dimitry Anastakis, 145–66. Montreal and Kingston: McGill-Queen's University Press, 2008.

Vodden, Christy, and Ian Dyck. *A World Inside: A 150-Year History of the Canadian Museum of Civilization*. Gatineau, QC: Canadian Museum of Civilization, 2006.

Walden, Keith. *Becoming Modern in Toronto: The Industrial Exhibition and the Shaping of Late Victorian Culture*. Toronto: University of Toronto Press, 1997.

Weaver, Sharon. "First Encounters: 1970s Back-to-the-Land Cape Breton, NS and Denman, Hornby and Lasqueti Islands, BC." *Oral History Forum d'histoire orale* 30 (2010): 1–30.

Weigert, Andrew J. *Self, Interaction, and Natural Environment: Refocusing Our Eyesight*. Albany: State University of New York Press, 1997.

White, Linda. "Resettlement." *Newfoundland Quarterly* 99, no. 4 (2007): 4–8.

Williams, Gareth. *Valleys of Song: Music and Society in Wales, 1840–1919*. Cardiff: University of Wales Press, 1998.

Woodman, Harold. *A Pictorial History of the Apple Blossom Festival*. Hantsport, NS: Lancelot, 1992.

Woodrow, R. Brian. "Resources and Environmental Policy-Making at the National Level: The Search for Focus." In *Resources and the Environment: Policy Perspectives for Canada*, edited by O.P. Dwivedi, 23–48. Toronto: McClelland and Stewart, 1980.

Wright, Donald. *The Professionalization of History in English Canada*. Toronto: University of Toronto Press, 2005.

Wyile, Herb. *Anne of Tim Hortons: Globalization and the Reshaping of Atlantic Canada Literature*. Waterloo, ON: Wilfrid Laurier University Press, 2011.

Young, Robert. "Open Federalism and Canadian Municipalities," in *Open Federalism: Interpretations, Significance*, edited by Keith G. Banting, Roger Gibbins, Peter Leslie, Alain Noel, Richard Simeon, and Robert Young, 7–24. Kingston: Institute of Intergovernmental Relations, 2006.

Zelko, Frank. "Making Greenpeace: The Development of Direct Action Environmentalism in British Columbia." *BC Studies* 142/143 (Summer/Autumn 2004): 197–239.

Unpublished Papers and Theses

Beaton, Meaghan. "The Canso Causeway: Regionalism, Reconstruction, Representations, and Results." Master's thesis, Saint Mary's University, 2001.

Curien, Pauline. "L'identité nationale exposeé: représentations du Québec à l'Exposition universelle de Montréal 1967 (Expo 67)." PhD diss., Laval University, 2003.

Davies, Helen. "The Politics of Participation: A Study of Canada's Centennial Celebrations." PhD diss., University of Winnipeg, 1999.
El-Fityani, Tamzin Melinda. "Pesticide Use at Expo 67: Can We Find the Evidence 40 Years Later?" Master's thesis, Queen's University, 2010.
Graham, Anna. "Stories in the Sediment: DDD Use at Expo 67." Master's thesis, Queen's University, 2012.
Hamilton, Edward Jae. "Ceci n'est pas un parc: Reconsidering the Island Site of Expo 67." Master's thesis, University of Waterloo, 2011.
Hamilton, Melanie. "Centennial Celebrations in Toronto-Area Schools." Master's thesis, University of Toronto, 2009.
Hellman, Michel. "Art, identité et Expo 67: l'expression du nationalisme dans les oeuvres des artistes québécois du Pavillon de La Jeunesse à l'Exposition universelle de Montréal." Master's thesis, McGill University, 2005.
Kicksee, Richard Gordon. "Scaled Down to Size: Contested Liberal Commonsense and the Negotiation of Indian Participation in the Canadian Centennial Celebrations and Expo 67, 1963–1967." Master's thesis, Queen's University, 1996.
Kirkman, Emily. "Fashioning Identity: The Hostesses of Expo 67." Master's thesis, Concordia University, 2011.
Macdonald, Sonja. "Expo 67, Canada's National Heterotopia: A Study of the Transformative Role of International Exhibitions in Modern Society." Master's thesis, Carleton University, 2003.
Macfarlane, Daniel. "To the Heart of the Continent: Canada and the Negotiation of the St Lawrence Seaway and Power Project." PhD diss., University of Ottawa, 2010.
Marcoux, Alain. "Expo 67 vitrine de l'expressionisme formel en architecture: investigations sur son contenu, son contexte, et son impact." PhD diss., Université du Québec à Montréal, 2007.
Massicotte, Isabelle. "The Architecture of Expo 67: National Identities and the Signs of Time." Master's thesis, Carleton University, 2003.
Pass, Forrest. "Pacific Dominion: British Columbia and the Making of Canadian Nationalism, 1858–1958." PhD diss., University of Western Ontario, 2008.
Reimers, Mia. "'BC at Its Most Sparkling, Colourful Best': Post-war Province Building through Centennial Celebrations." PhD diss., University of Victoria, 2007.
Thompson, Peter. "Tourism and the Extractive Gaze on Leo MacKay's Foord St." Conference paper, Association of Canadian Studies in Ireland, 11 May 2012.
Whitney, Allison. "Labyrinth: Cinema, Myth and Nation at Expo 67." Master's thesis, McGill University, 1999.

Index

Acadia University, 39
Adams, T.G., 43–4, 46
aesthetics, 21, 155, 167–8, 175, 182, 188
Africville, 13, 121, 181
Age of Beauty (film), 154
Agricultural and Rural Development Agency (ARDA), 16
Alberta, infrastructure development in, 8
Alexander Graham Bell Museum, 91, 108
Anderson, Benedict, 18
Anderson, Bill, 68
Angus L. Macdonald Bridge, 119–20
Annapolis: Apple Blossom Festival in, 79; District Community Centre, 46; Downtown Paint-Up in, 163; folk festivals in, 69; infrastructure development in, 43–6
Antigonish: folk festivals in, 69; and Halifax Folk Festival, 71; and Highland Games, 61–2, 74, 79; infrastructure development in, 45
Antigonish Casket, 100
Antigonish Highland Society, 61–2
Apple Blossom Festival, 79

aquarium. *See* Halifax Aquarium
Armdale Chorus, 73
Association of Scottish Societies of Nova Scotia, 60
Athletic Association of Canada, 67
Atlantic Canada Pavilion at Expo 67, 39, 95
Atlantic Development Board (ADB), 16, 120
Atlantic Provinces Economic Council, 86
Avramovitch, Aza, 125, 127–8, 130–2, 233n35
Aykroyd, Peter, 7, 28, 42, 48, 104, 177–8, 208n52
Aza Avramovitch Associates Ltd, 125, 233n35

Bannister, Jerry, 194
Basu, Paul, 77, 193
Bates, Robin, 53
Batten, Clyde, 183
beautification projects: and Community Improvement Program, 150, 154–5, 159–61, 163, 167–70, 173, 175–6, 181, 187; and Halifax Aquarium, 121; Rural

Beautification Program, 26, 165, 167, 168
Bede, Claude, 69–70
Berton, Pierre, 7, 48
Bickerton, James, 16
bilingualism and biculturalism, 26, 29
Bishop, Keith C., 39
Bodnar, John, 17
Bohlman, Philip, 60
Bond, James, 55
Boyd, Carl, 130
British Columbia: beautification projects in, 161; centennial celebrations in, 8, 51, 192; environmentalism movement in, 153; lumber trade in, 90; urban planning in, 150
Brooks, Walter T., 141
Bruce Cochran Associates Ltd, 63, 103
Bryden, Penny, 15–16
Buchannan, John M., 167
budget. *See* funding
Bumsted, J.M., 7
Burchell, David, 94

Canada Day, 18
Canada Mortgage and Housing Corporation (CMHC), 88, 182, 185
Canada Pavilion at Expo 67, 9
Canada Youth Commission, 137
Canadian Armed Forces Tattoo, 79–80
Canadian Association for Adult Education, 27
Canadian Broadcasting Corporation (CBC), 33, 39, 54, 93
Canadian Centenary Council, 28, 33, 39, 94

Canadian Citizenship Council, 27
Canadian Historical Association, 39
Canadian Jewish Congress War Orphan Placement Service, 90
Canadian Labour Congress, 101
Canadian Mental Health Association, 39
Canadian Mining Journal, 83
Canadian Pacific Railway (CPR), 60
Canso, 80, 103
Canso Causeway, 14, 46, 52
Cape Breton Miners' Foundation, 94, 100, 106–7
Cape Breton Miners' Museum, 81–117; and Centenary Committee, 43, 46–7; and coal-mining legacy, 82–9; as commemorative project, 5, 20, 89–104; and Community Improvement Program, 154; design of, 125; funding for, 90, 96, 103–4, 191–2, 193; and identity of region, 82, 104–17, 190
Cape Breton Tourist Association, 90, 101
capitalism, 14, 177–8, 184, 186
Carson, Rachel, 152
Cartier, Jacques, 32
Celtic Colours International Festival, 80
Centenary Celebration Act, 37, 42
Centenary Committee (Nova Scotia): and Cape Breton Miners' Museum, 94, 97, 99, 102, 109, 114–15; and Centennial Commission, 25, 27; and funding decisions, 191–2; and Halifax Aquarium, 123, 126, 134–5, 138, 145; and Highland Games and Folk Festival, 54–7, 60–3, 75–6, 78–9; planning role of, 20, 37–49

Centenary Council, 28, 33, 39, 94
Centennial Commission: and
  Cape Breton Miners' Museum,
  94–5, 98, 104, 115; and Centenary
  Committee, 38, 40, 42, 44, 47–8;
  and Community Improvement
  Program, 149–51, 153–5, 159–60,
  164, 166, 168, 171, 174–80, 183,
  185–7; Final Report, 3; and Halifax
  Aquarium, 119, 124, 127, 130, 135,
  144; and Highland Games and
  Folk Festival, 51, 54, 56, 60, 63–4,
  71; legacy of, 189–96; planning
  role of, 4, 7, 20–1, 24–37
Centennial Grants Program: and
  Cape Breton Miners' Museum,
  90–1, 94–7, 99, 113–16; and
  Centenary Committee, 41–7; and
  Centennial Commission, 33, 34;
  and Halifax Aquarium, 119, 122,
  124, 130, 136–8, 143–4, 147; and
  Halifax Centennial Swimming
  Pool, 143–4, 147; projects funded
  by, 20–1, 191–2; role of, 4, 6. *See
  also specific projects*
Centennial Handbook, The, 30
*Centennial of Canadian Confederation
  Act*, 33
Centennial Swimming Pool. *See
  Halifax Centennial Swimming
  Pool*
Charlottetown: and Confederation,
  29, 122; Fathers of Confederation
  Buildings, 30; Founders' Hall, 18
Choquette, Robert, 33
Chronicle-Herald: on Cape Breton
  Miners' Museum, 102; on
  Centenary Committee, 45; on
  funding decisions, 41; on Halifax
  Aquarium, 125, 131–3, 147;
  on Highland Games and Folk
  Festival, 64, 68, 71, 74–5
Churchill Falls hydroelectric power
  station (Labrador), 13
citizen participation, 25, 34, 40, 150,
  159, 213n124
citizenship: and Community
  Improvement Program, 21, 36,
  168, 173, 175; and identity, 78;
  leisure as right of, 5
civic improvement. *See Community
  Improvement Program*
civil rights movement, 10
Clack, Roderick, 36, 150, 164, 166
Clairtone Sound Corporation, 120
Clare Centennial Recreation Park,
  46–7
Clark, Joe, 210n86
coal industry, 14, 81–94, 97–115. *See
  also Cape Breton Miners' Museum*
Cochran, Bruce, 63, 64, 103–4
Cohen, Harry, 90, 101, 112
Cohen, Nina, 20, 89–117, 191–2,
  228n114
Colchester County's Centenary
  Celebration Committee, 44
Comeau, Julius, 39
commemorative activities. *See
  Cape Breton Miners' Museum;
  Centenary Committee; Centennial
  Commission*
Commoner, Barry, 152
Community Improvement Program,
  148–88; and Centennial Commission, 26, 36; and commemorative
  activities, 20; and environmental
  movement, 149–53; goals of, 150,
  190; legacy of, 192; planning and
  organization of, 5, 21, 153–68; volunteers for, 20, 150, 166, 168–88

Confederation Caravans and Train, 26, 27, 35, 153
Confederation Centenary Celebration Committee (Nova Scotia). *See* Centenary Committee
Confederation Memorial Program, 34
Connerton, Paul, 17
Conrad, Margaret, 12–13, 15–16
Cook, Stephen, 141
Coutu, Gilles, 238n121
Creighton, Helen, 102, 103, 112, 116, 228n114
crime, 143, 179–80
cultural capital: and Centenary Committee, 45; and Centennial Commission, 34; and commemoration, 17; as goal of centennial celebrations, 195, 196; and infrastructure development, 3–6, 8, 11–12, 20, 192, 195
cultural identity: and Community Improvement Program, 169; and Highland Games and Folk Festival, 51, 53, 57, 59–60, 69, 72, 76, 78–9; and infrastructure development, 21; and modernism, 194; and tartanization, 6, 14, 52–3, 56, 77–8, 80, 146, 193; transformations in, 5–6, 10–12, 196
cultural poverty, 3–4, 6, 17, 21, 189, 196
cultural welfare, 149, 176, 178, 182
Curien, Pauline, 9
Currie, Lauchlin "Lauchie" D., 94, 103, 115

Dalhousie University, 51, 122, 124
dance, 20, 57–9, 61, 65–6, 68, 73–4
Davies, Helen, 7, 27

Dean, Misao, 7–8
Dell Hill Dancers, 73
Department of Environment (Canada), 152
Department of Regional Economic Expansion (DREE), 16, 120
Diamond Jubilee celebrations (1927), 19
Dictionary of Canadian Biography, 26
Diefenbaker, John, 28, 30–3, 37
Digby, 24, 46, 167
Digdon, Willoughby, 138
Donahoe, Richard A.: and Cape Breton Miners' Museum, 98, 102, 105; and Centenary Committee, 40–1, 44, 62, 210n86; and Halifax Aquarium, 122, 127, 128, 130–1; and Highland Games and Folk Festival, 52, 55, 61
Donald, J.R., 87–8, 110
Downtown Paint-Up Program, 160–1, 163–4, 168, 170, 186
dualism, 29
Dubuc, Marcel, 104
Dymond, Greig, 9

Earth Day, 153
economic development: and Cape Breton Miners' Museum, 88, 115, 192; and Centenary Committee, 47; and Community Improvement Program, 184; and Highland Games and Folk Festival, 80; and industrialization, 13–14; and modernization, 12; and public policy, 15, 190
Elliott, Robbins, 35, 54
Emin, Frederick J., 139
environmental movement, 21, 149–53, 178, 184, 187–8

Environmental Protection Agency (US), 152–3
equalization programs, 16
Expo 67, 5, 8–9, 10, 34, 39, 51, 63, 77, 95, 103, 123, 168, 169, 186, 189

Fathers of Confederation Buildings (Charlottetown), 30
federalism, 6–7, 15–16
Federal-Provincial Centennial Grants Program. *See* Centennial Grants Program
Federated Women's Institutes of Canada, 165
feminist movement, 10, 11
Fergusson, C. Bruce: and Cape Breton Miners' Museum, 89, 91, 94; and Centenary Committee, 39, 41; and Highland Games and Folk Festival, 54–5, 64; and Historic Sites and Monuments Board of Canada, 224n45
Festival Canada, 26
Festival of the Strait, 60
Festival of the Tartans, 60
Fisher, John: and Cape Breton Miners' Museum, 104–5, 115; and Centenary Committee, 44, 48; and Centennial Commission, 33; and Community Improvement Program, 149, 159, 175, 178; and Halifax Aquarium, 124; and Highland Games and Folk Festival, 50–2, 53, 54–6, 62, 73, 76
fisheries, 124, 132
Fleur de Lis Trail, 108
Foley, Terry, 126
Folk Arts Council, 59
Folk Festival. *See* Highland Games and Folk Festival

Fortress of Louisbourg, 30, 86, 91, 92, 108
Founders' Hall (Charlottetown), 18
Fowke, Edith, 228n114
Francis, Daniel, 8, 61
Frank, David, 83–4
French Canadians, 25–6, 32
Frost, Lou, 93
Fund for Rural Economic Development (FRED), 16
funding: for Cape Breton Miners' Museum, 90, 93, 96, 103–4, 113, 191–2, 193; and Centenary Committee, 37, 40, 43; and Centennial Commission, 25–6, 30, 32, 34, 37; for Community Improvement Program, 153–4, 186; for Halifax Aquarium, 119, 124, 126, 128, 130–2; for Halifax Centennial Swimming Pool, 135, 139, 141; for Highland Games and Folk Festival, 55–6, 61–2, 64; subsidies, 87. *See also* Centennial Grants Program

Garbory, Evelyn, 59, 72
Gauthier, Georges, 33
geography, 29–30, 36, 38, 146
Gibbon, J. Murray, 60
Gillam, Robyn, 192
Gillis, John, 18
Gitlin, Todd, 11
Glace Bay: and Cape Breton Miners' Museum, 5, 81, 83, 87–94, 97, 100, 102–5, 108, 111–12, 114; and Centenary Committee, 39; and Community Improvement Program, 153, 166, 187; and Highland Games and Folk Festival, 74

Gordon, Alan, 19
Gordon, Harold, 92
Gorman, A.J., 39, 62
Gosse, Van, 10
Gourley, E.R., 61–2
Graham, Alasdair, 54
Granatstein, Jack, 7
Green, Ken, 212n102
Greenpeace, 153
Grey, Henry, 68

Halifax Aquarium, 5, 20, 21, 45, 118–36, 139, 145, 146–7, 190; and modernization efforts, 119–21, 123, 125, 126, 127, 131, 145–6, 147, 190; planning for, 5, 21, 122–36
Halifax Centennial Aquarium Board, 124–5, 126, 130, 131, 133, 134
Halifax Centennial Swimming Pool, 135–47, 190, 196; legacy of, 290; leisure and public recreation role of, 136–47; planning for, 5, 20, 21, 118, 119, 122–36
Halifax City Council, 39, 45, 118, 119, 121, 123, 124, 125, 126, 127, 129, 131, 133, 134, 135, 141, 142, 143, 145, 167
Halifax Commons, 57, 125, 129, 130, 135, 140, 141, 142
Halifax County Planning Board, 180
Halifax International Airport, 120
Halifax Symphony, 56
Hamilton, Alvin, 89
Hayday, Matthew, 18
Hebert, J.D., 89–90
Henderson, Stuart, 59, 60
Henderson, T. Stephen, 52
Henry, Eileen Cameron, 75–6
Heron, Patrick, 62–7, 75–6, 79

highland dancers, 65–6, 68, 73–4
Highland Games and Folk Festival, 50–80; and commemorative activities, 19–20; event timeline, 65–9; legacy of, 194; music of, 69–80; planning for, 5, 53–64
Hiller, James, 15
Hiscott, Elizabeth, 111
Historic Sites and Monuments Board of Canada (HSMBC), 89–90, 224n45
Hobsbawm, Eric, 10
Hodgson, John, 208n52
Hutt, Lorne V., 55, 64, 130, 166

identity: and Cape Breton Miners' Museum, 82, 104–17, 190; and Centenary Committee, 37; and Centennial Commission, 29–30, 33, 35; and citizenship, 78; and commemoration, 18; community vs., 6; and Expo 67, 9–10, 26; and Halifax Aquarium, 119; and Highland Games and Folk Festival, 61, 65, 72, 77–8; national, 7, 9, 11, 17–19, 25, 49, 60, 72, 144, 195; politics of, 10; Scottish, 51–3, 56, 58, 64–5, 70–8, 193; and tartanization, 6, 52–3, 56, 77–8, 80, 146, 193. *See also* cultural identity
Indians of Canada Pavilion, 9
Indigenous peoples, 7–10, 53, 56, 61, 71, 184
Industrial Estates Limited (IEL), 120
industrialization: in Cape Breton, 81–3, 85–90, 98, 105–6, 109–11, 114, 117; and Community Improvement Program, 159, 163, 165, 168, 188, 192; and economic

development, 13–14; in Halifax, 125, 138, 145–6; and Highland Games and Folk Festival, 53, 62
infrastructure development: and Centenary Committee, 44–6; and cultural capital, 3–6, 8, 11–12; and Halifax Aquarium, 122; and Halifax Centennial Swimming Pool, 144–5; legacy of, 194, 195; in post-war period, 13
Inverness, 69, 83, 132, 170
Irish communities, 53
Ivany, Hedley, 130–2, 133, 167, 169, 175, 181

Jenkins, Philip, 11
Joly, Mélanie, 195

Kenneally, Rhona Richman, 9
Kennedy, John F., 11
Keynesian economics, 15
Kidd, John, 27
Kitz, L.A., 123–4
Kiwanis Boys Pipe Band, 73–4

LaMarsh, Judy: and Cape Breton Miners' Museum, 81, 105, 110, 112; and Centennial Commission, 26, 37; and Community Improvement Program, 177–8, 185; and Highland Games and Folk Festival, 71
Lamontagne, Maurice: and Centennial Commission, 29–30; and Community Improvement Program, 148–9, 158, 176, 177, 178, 179, 187; on cultural poverty, 3–4, 21, 190; on Youth Travel program, 36

Lane, Abigail "Abbie," 38–9, 40, 42–4, 109, 116
Lang, Reginald, 160
Layton, J.H., 39
LeRoux, Leopold, 99
Lesage, Jean, 32
living standards, 21, 136, 143, 181–2
Longfellow, Henry Wadsworth, 14
Longley, Ronald Stewart, 39
Lownsbrough, John, 9
lumber industry, 90
Lunenburg Fisheries Museum, 47, 146
Lunenburg Folk Festival, 80
Lynk, John R., 39
Lynk, Norman, 97–8, 109, 154

MacAulay, Isobel, 38–9, 55, 57–8, 60–1, 62, 63
Macdonald, Angus L., 40, 52, 94
MacDonald, A.X., 99
MacDonald, Dan A., 39, 94
MacDonald, Donald, 101
MacDonald, Edward, 13
MacDonald, Monica, 14
Macdonald, Sonja, 9
MacEachen, Allan J., 54, 73, 103, 132
MacKeen, Alice, 103
MacKeen, Henry P., 23, 65, 66, 103, 105–6
MacKenzie, Daisy, 67, 76
MacKenzie, James L., 67, 68
Mackey, Eva, 60
MacLean, Ellen, 38–9
MacLean, Hugh Fitzroy, 66, 73, 77
MacLennan, Ian, 182, 184, 185
MacLeod, Bert, 62, 93
MacLeod, C.I.C., 62
MacNeill, Seamus, 74, 75, 77

Mactaquac hydroelectric dam (New Brunswick), 13
Made-in-Canada campaign, 171
Maritime Rights Movement, 15
Marquis, Greg, 14, 193
Marsters, Roger, 194
Marwick, Andrew, 10
Massey Commission. *See* Royal Commission on National Development in the Arts, Letters, and Sciences
McCleave, Robert J., 122
McKay, Ian: on coal industry, 84; on folk identity, 6, 103, 108, 109, 146, 193; on Scottish identity in Nova Scotia, 52–3, 77, 193; on tartanization, 6, 14
McKay, Leo, 118, 147
McLennan, Katharine, 92, 94
McQuay, Cindy, 68
Men of the Deeps, 102, 105, 106, 115, 116
Messer, Don, 54
Michener, Roland, 112
Miedema, Gary, 9
Mi'kmaw, 56, 71
Mills, Hugh O., 63–4
Mills, Sean, 10
Miners' Museum. *See* Cape Breton Miners' Museum
mines and mining. *See* coal industry
modernity, 14, 49, 186, 190
modernization initiatives: and centennial celebrations, 5, 6; and Halifax Aquarium, 119, 131, 147; and Halifax Centennial Swimming Pool, 140, 147; implementation of, 12–14, 21; legacy of, 190

Montreal: aquarium in, 131; and Community Improvement Program, 158, 169, 186; Expo 67 in, 5, 8–9, 10, 34, 39, 51, 63, 77, 95, 103, 123, 168, 169, 186, 189; tourism in, 123
Mooney, Craig, 182, 184
Moore, James, 194
Muirhead Pipe Band, 50, 64, 65–6, 68, 74
Mulgrave, 138–9
Munro, J.S., 24
Murphy, John M., 39, 44
Myers, Bruce, 64

National Centennial Commission. *See* Centennial Commission
National Community Improvement Program Seminar, 148, 160, 175–7, 179, 182
National Conference on Canada's Centennial, 32
National Film Board, 8, 154
nationalism, 8, 9, 72
National Museum, 92, 112
nation-building project, 18, 60, 147
Nelles, H.V., 18
Nelson, Jennifer J., 121
Newfoundland: coal industry in, 83; social and economic reforms in, 13; tourism in, 108
New Left, 10
Newman, Murray, 126
New Waterford: and Cape Breton Miners' Museum, 101–2; coal industry in, 83–4
Nicholson, Peter, 44
Nixon, Richard, 11, 152
North Sydney, 24, 108, 167

Norwich Plan, 160, 161, 163, 186–7
Nova Scotia Archives, 127
Nova Scotia Association of Architects, 163, 164
Nova Scotia Bureau of Information, 63
Nova Scotia Folk Arts Council, 59, 69, 70, 72
Nova Scotia Historical Society, 39
Nova Scotia Home for Coloured Children, 125
Nova Scotia Information Services, 64, 159
Nova Scotia Innkeepers Guild, 183
Nova Scotia Institute of Science, 122
Nova Scotia Provincial Exhibition, 79
Nova Scotia Research Foundation, 122, 124
Nova Scotia Technical College, 95, 125
Nova Scotia Tourist Bureau, 159
Nyanza Micmac Children's Choir, 71

O'Brien, Allan, 23
Ocean Deeps Colliery, 81, 105, 107

Padmore, D.G., 39
Paehlke, Robert, 152
Page, Lester, 55, 58, 63–4, 70
Palmer, Bryan, 10
Parker, J. Austen, 39
Pass, Forrest, 8, 208n52
patronage, 4, 38, 40, 191
Pearson, Lester B.: and Cape Breton Miners' Museum, 88–9, 103; and Centenary Committee, 38; centennial celebrations presided over by, 24; and Centennial Commission, 31–3; on centennial projects, 189; election of, 15; and Halifax Aquarium, 133
Pearson, Norman, 88–9, 112, 115
Pevere, Geoff, 9
Phillips, Robert, 185
Preston Spiritualaires, 73
Prince Edward Island: modernization in, 13; tourism industry in, 13, 18
Programs and Projects of National Significance, 4, 5, 21, 35, 149, 190
publicity, 64–5, 104, 113
Pullen, H.F., 39

Quarry Point, 81, 99–100, 105–6
Quebec: aquarium in, 123; and Cape Breton Miners' Museum, 112; and Centenary Committee, 71–2; and Centennial Commission, 32–3, 37; commemorative activities in, 18; and Community Improvement Program, 169; and Halifax Aquarium, 123; and Highland Games and Folk Festival, 66; identity in, 9; separatist movement in, 25–6

Radforth, Ian, 19
Rand, Ivan, 86–7, 91
Recreation Commission (Halifax), 135, 139, 141–2
Reichwein, PearlAnn, 8
Reimers, Mia, 8
Robichaud, Hédard, 124, 132–3
Rojo, Alfonso, 125, 146
Rowe, Arthur, 68
Rowell-Sirois Commission, 14, 15

Royal Canadian Legions, 24
Royal Canadian Navy, 39
Royal Commission on Bilingualism and Biculturalism, 29
Royal Commission on Canada's Economic Prospects, 85
Royal Commission on Coal, 85–6, 91
Royal Commission on Dominion-Provincial Relations, 15
Royal Commission on National Development in the Arts, Letters, and Sciences, 12, 92, 193
Royal Nova Scotia International Tattoo, 79–80
Rudin, Ron, 18
Rural Beautification Program, 26, 165, 167, 168

Sainte Anne's College, 46, 67
Saint Mary's University, 124, 125
Sangster, Joan, 11, 138
Savoie, Donald, 16
Scottish Country Dancers, 71
Scottish identity, 51–3, 56, 58, 64–5, 70–8, 193
Scottish Sanctioning Board, 67
Shadbolt, Douglas, 95, 106, 108–9, 114
Shay, Anthony, 61
Silent Spring, 152
Sinclair, James, 133
Sloan, Johanne, 9
Smallwood, Joseph R., 13
Smith, G.I., 65, 163
social welfare programs, 12–13
Spadina Expressway (Toronto), 12
Spillman, Lyn, 49
Stan Rogers Festival, 80
Stanfield, Robert L., 23, 38, 40–2, 44, 95, 96, 105, 120, 159, 191

Stellarton: and Cape Breton Miners' Museum, 83, 102; and Clairtone Sound Corporation, 120; and Halifax Aquarium, 120
Stephenson, Gordon, 121
St Francis Xavier University, 102
St Lawrence Seaway, 12
Students for Democratic Society, 11
subsidies, 87
Summerby-Murray, Robert, 116
swimming pools, 5–6, 34, 47, 118, 129, 135–6, 138–43. *See also* Halifax Centennial Swimming Pool
Sydney: and Cape Breton Miners' Museum, 83, 87, 97, 99, 100, 101, 103, 109; and centennial celebrations, 24; and Centennial Commission, 24; and coal and steel industries, 83, 84, 85, 87, 113; and Community Improvement Program, 145, 154, 163–4, 166, 186; and Highland Games and Folk Festival, 69, 71
Sydney Academy, 24, 92–3
Sydney Mines, 39, 83, 100, 101
Sydney Steel, 84–5, 113

tartanization, 6, 52–3, 56, 77–8, 80, 146, 193. *See also* Scottish identity
Thomson, W.B., 160
Tillotson, Shirley, 137, 213n124, 236n92
Toronto: Highland Games and Folk Festival participants, 68, 71; infrastructure projects in, 12; International Exhibition, 19
tourism: and Cape Breton Miners' Museum, 86–7, 89, 91, 92, 107–9, 115, 117; and Community Improvement Program, 159,

168–9; and economic development, 13, 190, 192; and Halifax Aquarium, 123, 133, 139, 146; and Highland Games and Folk Festival, 52–3, 57, 62, 79–80
Townscape Rediscovered, A (film), 154
Trade Fair and Naval Review, 51
Trans-Canada Highway, 12
Trudeau, Pierre Elliott, 25, 152, 194

United States: bicentennial celebrations in, 48; coal industry in, 83–4; environmental movement in, 152–3
University of British Columbia, 132
University of Toronto, 121
urban revitalization programs, 148. *See also* Community Improvement Program; infrastructure development
Urquhart, Russell, 24, 199

Vance, Jonathan, 17, 98
Vance, Michael, 53
Vancouver: aquarium in, 123, 126, 130–3; and Highland Games and Folk Festival, 68, 73–4
Vanier, Georges, 26
Vanier, Pauline, 26
Vaughan, Charles, 118, 129, 130–1, 132–4
volunteers, 20, 150, 166, 168–88
Voyageur Canoe Pageant, 5, 7–8, 26, 35

Walden, Keith, 19
Wallace, Frank L., 55–61, 63, 129, 175
Wallace, L.J., 208n52
Wanderers Grounds, 57, 65, 67, 73
Webber, Harvey, 101, 111, 164, 186–7, 192
Weldon, John, 33
Wetmore, Donald, 59, 72
William Davis Miners' Memorial Day, 222n19
Wright, Donald, 92
Wyile, Herb, 14, 109
Wyman, H.R., 40, 141

Yarmouth: and Centenary Committee, 45–6; and YMCA Swimming Pool, 138–9
youth: Canada Youth Commission, 137; and Cape Breton Miners' Museum, 96, 111; and Centennial Commission, 26, 29–30, 35–6; and Community Improvement Program, 165–6; and Halifax Centennial Swimming Pool, 136, 138–41, 147; and Highland Games and Folk Festival, 68
Youth Travel program, 26, 30, 35–6
Yukon Alpine Centennial Expedition, 8

Zatzman, Joseph, 24
Ziai, Abol H., 140

www.ingramcontent.com/pod-product-compliance
Lightning Source LLC
Chambersburg PA
CBHW030307080526
44584CB00012B/479